Routledge Philosophy GuideBook to

Wittgenstein and the *Tractatus*

Ludwig Wittgenstein is the most influential philosopher of the twentieth century. The *Tractatus Logico Philosophicus* is arguably his most widely read work yet remains one of the most cryptic and controversial philosophy books ever written. With its profound insights into the nature of language, reality and representation it has inspired not only philosophers but also writers and musicians.

Wittgenstein and the Tractatus introduces and assesses:

- Wittgenstein's life and the background to the *Tractatus*
- the ideas and text of the *Tractatus*
- the continuing importance of Wittgenstein's work to philosophy today.

A much-needed guide to a widely studied text, *The Routledge Philosophy GuideBook to Wittgenstein and the* Tractatus is essential reading for all students of Wittgenstein, philosophy of language and metaphysics.

Michael Morris is Professor of Philosophy at the University of Sussex.

Routledge Philosophy GuideBook to

Wittgenstein and the *Tractatus Logico-Philosophicus*

Michael
Morris

Routledge
Taylor & Francis Group

LONDON AND NEW YORK

First published 2008
by Routledge
2 Park Square, Milton Park, Abingdon, Oxon, OX14 4RN

Simultaneously published in the USA and Canada
by Routledge
711 Third Ave, New York, NY 10017

Routledge is an imprint of the Taylor & Francis Group, an informa business

Typeset in Series Design Selected Aldus and Scala by
Taylor & Francis Books

British Library Cataloguing in Publication Data
A catalogue record for this book is available from the British Library

Library of Congress Cataloging in Publication Data
A catalog record for this book has been requested

ISBN13: 978-0-415-35721-0 (hbk)
ISBN13: 978-0-415-35722-7 (pbk)
ISBN13: 978-0-203-00309-1 (ebk)

CONTENTS

PREFACE

This book derives ultimately from some lecture handouts which I produced when I first taught the *Tractatus* in an undergraduate course. My friend Julian Dodd and I had the idea of putting these handouts together with some things he was interested in — about the notion of truth, and about recent interpretations of the *Tractatus* — to form a book. With this in mind, we worked together on a paper on the apparent paradox of the *Tractatus* (Morris and Dodd 2008), whose main points appear in the final chapter of this book.

In the end, however, other philosophical commitments took Julian away from this project, and that paper was the only thing we wrote together. That means that everything in this book, apart from those parts of the final chapter which derive from our joint paper, is solely my responsibility. I am, however, extremely grateful to Julian for his encouragement in the writing of this book, as well as for his part in producing that joint paper.

Large thanks are also due to a number of people for things they have said in conversation, by means of which they have helped me more than they, perhaps, ever realized. Among these I would like to mention the following people in particular: Leo Cheung, Richard Gaskin, Andreas Georgallides, Warren Goldfarb, Colin Johnston, Marie McGinn, Adrian Moore, Michael Potter, Thomas Ricketts, Tanja Staehler, Roger White, and José Zalabardo. Peter Sullivan read the penultimate draft of the whole book, and made a large number of very helpful comments and suggestions which saved me from several errors and led me to understand the *Tractatus* better: I am enormously grateful to him. Finally, I would like to thank Gemma Dunn at Routledge, for her tolerance and help in seeing the project through.

INTRODUCTION

1 THE WORK AND ITS HISTORY

Wittgenstein's *Tractatus Logico-Philosophicus* is one of the great philosophical works of the twentieth century. For the range of its concerns and the depth of its thought its closest companions are two unfinished works: Heidegger's *Being and Time*, and Wittgenstein's own *Philosophical Investigations*. But even in this company the *Tractatus* looks eccentric. It is very short, and written in a style which is at least epigrammatic. The character of the work is a reflection of the nature of the man who wrote it, and of his cast of mind when he wrote it.

Ludwig Wittgenstein was born in Austria in 1889, into one of the wealthiest families in Europe. His upbringing was one of enormous privilege, but also deeply cultured, and it brought with it an intensity of expectation which was not easy to live with (two of his brothers committed suicide while Wittgenstein was still a boy). After school, he began to study engineering, first in Berlin and then in Manchester. While in Manchester he developed an interest in mathematics, and then in the foundations of mathematics. He read two ground-breaking works in the foundations of mathematics, which had then only recently been published: Bertrand Russell's early work, *The Principles of Mathematics*, and Gottlob Frege's more-or-less contemporary *Grundgesetze der Arithmetik* (*Basic Laws of Arithmetic*), which attempts to show that arithmetic rests on nothing more than logic. In 1911 he visited Frege in Jena, who recommended that he study under Russell in Cambridge.

By this time Russell's views had developed and changed. He had just published, with Alfred North Whitehead, the monumental *Principia Mathematica*, which develops the general view of Frege's *Grundgesetze* in enormous detail and with great technical sophistication — much of which was needed to circumvent a contradiction which Russell had found in Frege's system. Russell was at this time the great figure in contemporary logic, but, by his own account, worn out from his work on *Principia*. Wittgenstein attached himself to him, and was something of a pest, pursuing Russell back to his room, and badgering him with questions, even while Russell was dressing. But he was not just a nuisance: he learned extraordinarily fast, and before long Russell felt that Wittgenstein would be the person to carry on the technical logical work which he felt that he himself was no longer up to.

By 1913 Wittgenstein was shaping the views on logic which would later become the backbone of the *Tractatus*. The first record of these views is the *Notes on Logic* of that year: this work (now published as an appendix to the later *Notebooks*) is an important resource for those trying to understand the *Tractatus*. By the end of 1913, however, Wittgenstein felt that he could no longer do the work he was capable of while staying in Cambridge, so he decided to go and live alone in Norway and work there. In the spring of 1914 he was visited there by G. E. Moore, another Cambridge philosopher, and one of the leaders (Russell was another) of the revolt against Hegelianism which inaugurated analytic philosophy in the English-speaking world. Despite his seniority, Moore was not even an equal partner in their discussions: in fact, Wittgenstein used him to take down notes which he dictated. These *Notes Dictated to G. E. Moore in Norway* are also published as an appendix to the *Notebooks*.

In the summer of 1914, however, the First World War began, and Wittgenstein immediately joined up on the Austrian side. Wittgenstein did not shirk his military duties by any means — indeed, he was keen to be posted to the front and showed extraordinary courage when he was sent there — but he did not stop doing philosophy either. He worked in notebooks, some of which survive and are published as *Notebooks 1914–16* (though the last entry is dated January 1917). These begin with questions in the foundations of logic. The very first entry, indeed, reads:

Logic must take care of itself.

And for most of the first two years Wittgenstein's concerns are chiefly directed to difficulties which arise out of his worries about the work of Russell and Frege. But in June 1916 Wittgenstein's unit was in the midst of extremely heavy fighting, in which terrible casualties were suffered. At this point the notes lurch over to questions about the meaning of life — back, in fact, to questions which had pre-occupied him and his own older brothers, as well as much of a certain class in Vienna, in the first years of the century. From now on, the work he was writing began to be a unification of his approach to the foundations of logic with a certain attitude to problems of the meaning of life.

The *Tractatus* itself was put together from Wittgenstein's wartime notebooks over the next two years. There was an intermediate first draft, now known as the *Prototractatus*, and the final version was typed up in the summer of 1918. Wittgenstein did not find it easy to get it published, however, and in the end it was only under the auspices of Russell's name, and accompanied by Russell's own explanatory introduction — which Wittgenstein himself disliked — that the work finally came out in 1922. It was written in German, but appeared in a parallel text, alongside a translation which is presented as being by C. K. Ogden, but which seems largely to have been the work of Frank Ramsey, a brilliant mathematician and philosopher at Cambridge, who was not even twenty at the time.

After the appearance of the *Tractatus*, Wittgenstein withdrew from academic life — indeed from the ordinary intellectual life which would have been natural for a man of his background. He gave away his money, and became a teacher in a village school in Austria. Ramsey visited him there, and he gradually became engaged in philosophy again, both through Ramsey's questions about the *Tractatus*, and through the interest of a group of young philosophers in Vienna who were strongly influenced by the *Tractatus*, and formed the 'Vienna Circle' of logical positivists around it. (Rudolf Carnap was the member of this group to have the greatest influence in his own right.) Wittgenstein eventually returned to Cambridge in 1929, and began a re-examination of the issues of the *Tractatus* which gradually brought about a transformation in his views during the 1930s, until he reached the position of the great work of his later life, the *Philosophical Investigations* (the bulk of which was written by 1945, though it was not published until 1953, after Wittgenstein's death).

2 THE PROBLEMS FOR INTERPRETERS

Two things about the *Tractatus* make it peculiarly hard for interpreters — both professional scholars and students. The first is its style, and the second its content. Wittgenstein's stylistic intentions are declared in the Preface. Here is the opening paragraph:

> This book will perhaps only be understood by those who have themselves already thought the thoughts which are expressed in it — or similar thoughts. It is therefore not a textbook. Its object would be attained if it afforded pleasure to one who read it with understanding.
>
> (*TLP*, p. 27)

He is not going to make things easy for the reader. The thought here is echoed in the Preface of his later work, the *Philosophical Investigations*:

> I should not like my writing to spare other people the trouble of think-ing. But, if possible, to stimulate someone to thoughts of his own.
>
> (*PI*: x)

There is at least that much commonality between the early and the late Wittgenstein. In fact, the *Tractatus* is much harder to get a grip on than the *Philosophical Investigations*: there are times in the *Tractatus* when Wittgenstein seems to abbreviate his expression of points in order to make them harder, rather than easier, to understand. There is a strong contrast of tone here between the earlier and the later writing: the *Philosophical Investigations* is a work of great — sometimes even patronizing — patience; the *Tractatus* is, if anything, impatient. The point can be illustrated with an example. Much of the technicality of Whitehead and Russell's monumental *Principia Mathematica* is designed to deal with the paradox Russell found in Frege's system. Wittgenstein devotes just five paragraphs to this in the *Tractatus* (3.331–3.333), before concluding:

> Herewith Russell's paradox vanishes.
>
> (3.333)

The work seems to be deliberately difficult, made difficult in order to force the reader to think for herself. Sadly, this seems to have frustrated one of the book's ambitions. It is tempting to think that Wittgenstein hoped that Frege, in particular, would be 'one who read it with understanding', and he sent Frege a copy of the typescript before it was published. Unfortunately, Frege could make nothing of it. (Wittgenstein's hope was not altogether frustrated, however: he certainly found one person who read the book with understanding — and derived great pleasure from it — in Frank Ramsey.)

The difficulties created by the compression of style are severe. Those who begin to speak a foreign language are familiar with the dangers of 'false friends' — words which seem like words of our own language, and which we are therefore inclined to assume have a similar meaning, but which in fact mean something quite different. There are many false friends in the *Tractatus*, even — perhaps especially — for professional scholars. There are phrases and snatches of argument which are reminiscent of things we have come across elsewhere in other authors, and when we read them, we clutch at them, thinking that Wittgenstein must have in mind something similar to what those other authors had in mind; but often he does not.

It is not mere perversity which dictates Wittgenstein's style, however. His writing is guided by a certain austere poetic sense. Later in the Preface Wittgenstein writes:

> If this work has a value it consists in two things. First that in it thoughts are expressed, and this value will be the greater the better the thoughts are expressed. The more the nail has been hit on the head.
>
> (*TLP*, p. 29)

(We will return to the second thing in a moment.) Here we see Wittgenstein attending above all to the way in which the thoughts of the book are expressed — in fact, this comes before the issue of whether those thoughts are true (which Wittgenstein addresses in the next paragraph). His concern here is the concern of a poet (even if the image he uses is rather humdrum), and the *Tractatus* is meant to work poetically. There is, I think, a particular reason for that, apart from simple considerations of taste, as we will see in a moment.

Unfortunately for someone trying to make sense of the *Tractatus*, this poetic style is itself something of a false friend: the very cadence of some of the book's remarks seduces us into thinking that we know what is being said, when really we do not. The very first remark of the book — 'The world is everything that is the case' — is an example of this.

The other thing which is difficult about the book is its content — or, rather, one particular feature of its content. The book is certainly technical at times, and Wittgenstein's impatience in exposition does not help here, but this is not the deepest problem. The real problem is that the book seems, on the face of it, to be paradoxical: it seems to undermine itself. The book's penultimate section begins:

> My propositions are elucidatory in this way: he who understands me finally recognizes them as senseless, when he has climbed out through them, on them, over them.

> (6.54)

We will note, of course, that Wittgenstein cannot resist putting this poetically. But the key problem is that this remark seems to declare the sentences of the book ('my propositions') to be without any meaning at all.

To see the problem this causes for an interpreter, we need to reflect a little on the practice of interpretation. Interpretation is guided by what is known as a 'principle of charity'. The idea which this label enshrines is that we do not interpret someone well if our interpretation represents her as an idiot. But there is a simpler and deeper point here. It is that interpreting a text is a matter of making sense of it. And to make sense of a text is to represent it as making sense. In the general case, representing a text as making sense is representing it as saying something which is, in the context, a reasonable thing to say. But it is at least a minimal condition on doing that that one represents the text as, literally, making sense — that is to say, as not being meaningless. The penultimate section of the *Tractatus* now seems to put an impossible burden on an interpreter: in order to represent it as saying something which it is reasonable, in the context, to say, we seem to have to represent it as not saying anything at all.

This general problem also has particular applications. Usually, if we are interpreting a work, we have reason to think that the author is not saying something if we have clear evidence that he denies that very thing. Unfortunately, if a work declares itself to be paradoxical, that rule cannot be used without extreme caution. We have to make quite delicate judgements in deciding which denials indicate that the author does not mean something, and which do not. In the case of the *Tractatus*, one interpreter can take Wittgenstein to be saying something, while another can point to a piece of text and say, 'But look: he denies that here'. The first interpreter can still respond, 'Yes, indeed he does', and feel no pressure to revise her interpretation.

My own view is that the paradoxicality of the work is one of the reasons for the importance of its mode of expression — for the importance of the poetic in the way it is written. Because the work is paradoxical — because it is meaningless by its own lights — it cannot really be taken to be trying to say anything. And here the poetry of the language can be used to work in a different way, to achieve a different kind of purpose from the statement of truths. (But this is a matter for the final chapter.)

This connects with the second thing which Wittgenstein says gives value to the work. Wittgenstein does indeed claim that in it all the problems of philosophy 'have in essentials been finally solved' (*TLP*, p. 29). But it is not this which makes the work worthwhile. Rather, Wittgenstein continues:

> And if I am not mistaken in this, then the value of this work secondly consists in the fact that it shows how little has been done when these problems have been solved.
>
> (*TLP*, p. 29)

And this links with something which he had at one point thought of writing in the Preface. As he told a publisher, Ludwig von Ficker:

> What I meant to write then was this: my work consists of two parts: the one presented here plus all I have *not* written. And it is precisely this second part that is the important one.
>
> (*WSP*, 94–95)

This lies behind the cryptic and epigrammatic, poetic style of writing: the aim is to give a sense always of what has *not* been said, which is the most important thing.

3 *TRACTATUS* SCHOLARSHIP

We are currently in an exciting period in *Tractatus* scholarship — indeed in the scholarship of the early period of analytic philosophy in general. In part this is because the analytic tradition has just woken up to the fact that its own works are open to historical treatment — that is, to treatment by a philosophical historian of philosophy. (To put the matter a bit too simply, I take a *philosophical* historian of philosophy to be someone who postpones until the very last moment the abandonment of belief in the reasonableness of the views of the philosophers she studies; a piece of philosophical history of philosophy is an attempt to reconstruct the *justification* for a philosophical view. A non-philosophical intellectual historian, by contrast, will be happy to appeal to non-justificatory explanatory factors at a much earlier stage in her account of a view, or of a change of view.) The analytic tradition has recently noticed that its own core works are not merely contributions to a current debate: they express views that are peculiar enough to stand in need of justification from further out than that.

At the core of this burgeoning interest in philosophical scholarship of the analytic tradition has been a revival in interest in Bertrand Russell, in particular. This revival has been fed by — as well as feeding — the publication over the last few years of Russell's philosophical papers. Of particular importance for the *Tractatus* has been the publication of papers written both before and after the great paper 'On Denoting' of 1905, and of the manuscript entitled *Theory of Knowledge*, which was written in a few weeks in 1913, and then abandoned — apparently because Russell could not see how to get round Wittgenstein's criticism. At the same time, serious work has been continuing into the actual history of the composition of the *Tractatus* and its more informal predecessors, the *Notes on Logic* and the wartime *Notebooks*. More is now known about the views which Wittgenstein was reacting to, and the circumstances of his reaction, than perhaps has ever been known to anyone other than the work's author since the book was published.

In addition to the flourishing of scholarly work on early analytic philosophy, interest in the *Tractatus* has been galvanized recently by a dispute over the interpretation of the work. If one believes the popular accounts, the dispute is between two schools of interpretation: those who describe themselves as presenting a 'new Wittgenstein', or a 'resolute' reading, on the one hand, and those who are thought of as in some way 'traditionalists', on the other. In fact, there are more than two positions in play here, and they centre on different interpretative problems. At the core of all of them is the apparent paradox of the *Tractatus*, and the dismissal of philosophy as nonsense which forms part of that. One dispute is over exactly what is meant by 'nonsense' here: is there a distinction between *plain* nonsense and nonsense which is, somehow, significant? And is plain nonsense just *gibberish*? Another is over whether Wittgenstein in the *Tractatus* holds that there are ineffable truths — truths which cannot be stated, but whose communication might be thought to be the purpose of the work. Another again is concerned with the relation between Wittgenstein's attitude to philosophy in the *Tractatus*, and his attitude in the later work, in particular in the *Philosophical Investigations*. A good proportion of those who describe themselves as presenting a 'new Wittgenstein', or a 'resolute' reading, take the later work to embody a rejection of a particular kind of way of doing philosophy, which they call 'metaphysics'; and, furthermore, they tend to think that Wittgenstein is *right* in this rejection. They then read the *Tractatus* as if it were fundamentally in agreement with the *Philosophical Investigations* — and them — in this rejection of 'metaphysics'. Against these proponents of a 'new' or 'resolute' interpretation of the *Tractatus* there are those who think that there is a radical disagreement in view between Wittgenstein's early and later work.

4 THE APPROACH OF THE PRESENT WORK

It would be foolish to ignore the enormous amount of recent scholarship on the *Tractatus*, and impossible to avoid taking a stand on the large interpretative disputes. But my aim has been to avoid overloading the text with historical detail, and to present something which might be of use even to those who end up disagreeing with me on the major points of interpretative dispute. This book is designed, above all, to make comprehensible a text which is difficult to make any sense of at all. Its focus, therefore, is on the details of the text itself — and in particular, on those details which are initially (and often persistently) very puzzling.

The problems are presented by the poetic style of the work, which I have already remarked on, in conjunction with a very obvious fact: Wittgenstein continuously presents some epigrammatic claims as being logically dependent on others. If there is a logical dependence, there ought to be some argument which makes that dependence clear. But with Wittgenstein's impatience and his concern for poetic expression, the argument is very seldom expressed. It is this absence of expression of arguments which is the principal source of the work's difficulty. Accordingly, it has been my principal concern to express as clearly and explicitly as possible the arguments which everybody feels are there to be found. Clearly this will involve a loss of the work's poetry, and will sometimes also lead to a loss of subtlety and nuance. But there is a very fine line between subtlety and evasion, and whenever I felt that line was close, I have tried to be explicit and unambiguous, at the risk of being unsubtle. It seems to me that this is the best way of serving both students and scholars.

The arguments which I try to present explicitly have been the subject of scholarly dispute ever since the work was first studied. There is nothing which deserves to be called the 'standard' view of any of them, so it is impossible to avoid controversy in presenting an explicit interpretation. This means that this book cannot be merely introductory, as study guides are sometimes expected to be. But I have tried to make the steps in the argument as clear as students need them to be, while also indicating differences from other interpretations.

Of course, in presenting the arguments explicitly I take seriously — at least for the period of presenting them — the arguments which I present. This inevitably involves me in some of the issues which arise from the apparent paradoxicality of the book, but I do not dwell on those issues while laying out the arguments. Instead, their proper treatment is postponed until the last chapter, where they are dealt with at some length.

There is one question of interpretation which I have not pursued here in any depth. This concerns the relation between the early and the late Wittgenstein. The reason why this cannot be discussed properly here is that it is no easier to understand the later work than it is to understand the *Tractatus*, although the reasons for the difficulty are a little different. But even though this is not the place to argue for an interpretation, it may help readers to understand the orientation of this book if I say briefly what I am inclined to think. I am inclined to think, first, that Wittgenstein is less anti-philosophical in his later work than he is often taken to be. And, second, I am inclined to think there is at least one simple but decisive philosophical disagreement between the early and the later work: the early work endorses (though in a way made complicated by its paradoxicality) and the later work rejects the central thesis of the *Tractatus*'s philosophy of language, that the form of language is the same as the form of the world.

5 A KANTIAN OVERVIEW

In addressing a difficult work, a synoptic overview always helps. The *Tractatus* itself invites a particular kind of summary, because of the numerical arrangement of its remarks. The book presents itself as having seven key theses:

1 The world is everything that is the case.
2 What is the case, the fact, is the existence of atomic facts.

3 The logical picture of the facts is the thought.

4 The thought is the significant proposition.

5 Propositions are truth-functions of elementary propositions.
(An elementary proposition is a truth-function of itself.)

6 The general form of truth-function is: $[\bar{p},\bar{\xi}, N(\bar{\xi})]$.
This is the general form of proposition.

7 Whereof one cannot speak, thereof one must be silent.

Everything else in the book is presented as a comment on or explanation of one of these seven theses, or a comment on a comment, or a comment on a comment on a comment, and so on, according to the numbering scheme set out in a footnote to the first thesis.

The chapters which follow can be assigned roughly to these remarks, as follows. Chapter 1 is concerned with theses 1 and 2. The notion of a 'picture' which is used in thesis 3 is explained in Chapter 3, and its application to language in thesis 4 is the subject of Chapter 4. This treatment of language has a certain history, which is the subject of Chapter 2. Chapter 5 deals with theses 5 and 6. Wittgenstein thinks these claims have an important consequence for the issue of solipsism, and that is the topic of Chapter 6. The further consequences of thesis 6 for philosophy, as they lead up to thesis 7, are dealt with in Chapter 7.

But this kind of overview is unlikely to provide someone who reads the book for the first time with the help she needs. We want to know what the whole thing is really about, and these seven theses do not reveal that very clearly. Here it helps to remember that the project was first addressed in Wittgenstein's wartime notebooks with this remark:

Logic must take care of itself.

(*NB* 2; *TLP* 5.473)

I think the significance of this is most simply understood as deriving from a concern with a broadly Kantian problem with philosophy. (There is uncertainty about how much Kant — indeed, how much of anything — Wittgenstein had actually read; but there is little doubt that his approach to philosophy has a broadly Kantian orientation.) What follows is a brief overview of the *Tractatus* from this slightly different perspective. It is controversial, of course, like everything else in the interpretation of *Tractatus*. But those who read the work for the first time need it to be given some shape; and it is better that it should be given a shape which is later rejected as a caricature, than that it should have no visible shape at all.

Here, then, is a way of raising some of the issues that concerned Kant. A mathematician friend of mine once said to me something like this: 'Isn't it amazing that the numbers, which stand in all the complicated relations to each other that mathematicians are interested in, can be used to count ordinary things in the real world, like sheep and cows?' It seems immediately clear that there is something very odd about my friend's way of looking at things, but it is less easy to explain what exactly has gone wrong, and more difficult still to articulate what has to be accepted if we are to avoid going wrong in that way.

The first thing we are inclined to say is something like this: it is not any kind of accident that the numbers can be used to count ordinary things in the real world; rather, the moment we have *things*, we must be able to distinguish between different things, and hence distinguish between *one* thing and *two*, and this provides us with the possibility of counting them. In short, it is not that the numbers have a life of their own, and are then used to count things; it is rather that their origin lies in the counting of things, and only because of that do they get to have the interesting properties which are the mathematician's concern.

This reply is not altogether wrong, but it is inadequate in two crucial respects. First, just distinguishing between things is not enough for counting, and hence not enough for arithmetic. What we need is a crucial extra notion — that of a *successor* in a series of a certain kind. And then we can ask: where does that notion of a *successor* come from? And, secondly, it is all very well saying that the origin of numbers lies in the discrimination of *things*, but that now puts a certain pressure on our conception of *things*: the notion of a thing needs to bring with it the notion of identity (and, correlatively, distinctness). Furthermore, that notion of identity looks as if it is connected with *classification*: if we identify a thing, we have to identify it as a thing of a certain *kind*. And then we can ask: where does the notion of a *thing*, with these connected notions of identity and classification, come from?

Whatever we say about this, we need to take account of an important fact about these fundamental concepts (like all concepts): they bring with them certain commitments, which we are inclined to think of as necessary truths. Some things seem to be *necessarily* true of any relation which can be described as that of *succession*. Some things seem to be *necessarily* true of anything which can be counted as a *thing*. There seem to be some *necessary* truths about identity. And there seem to be some things which are *necessarily* true of anything which can be said to belong to a given *kind* of thing. It is tempting to say that what are revealed when we consider what is presupposed in the apparently simple practice of counting are nothing less than necessary truths about the world. The task of undermining the amazement of my mathematician friend seems to lead us to consider the necessary structure of the world — how the world absolutely *has* to be, if counting, or even talking, is to be possible at all.

And this — to put it very crudely — is how things struck Kant. There are some things which are necessarily true of the world, and these are revealed when we consider what is required for mathematics — indeed, thinking in general — to make sense. But this is puzzling in itself. It is natural to think that our understanding of what is true of the world is furnished by *experience* — by our perception of things around us using our senses. But experience seems only to present us with *contingent* truths: with things which are true, but not *necessarily* true. We observe the *actual* position of a sheep on a hill, or of a needle on a dial: we do not observe how sheep, hills, needles and dials *must* be. So how can we possibly have knowledge of how things *must* be in the world, of what is *necessarily* true of the world?

Kant's answer — still putting things crudely — was something like this. For a truth to be necessary, he thought, it had to be capable of being known without recourse to experience: that is, it had to be *a priori*. But for it to be a truth *about* the world, it had to run beyond what could be derived from a mere analysis of the concepts involved: it had to have something supplied by the world, rather than by our concepts. In his terms, this meant that it had to be *synthetic*, rather than *analytic*. So Kant thought that in order to deal with muddles like that of my mathematician friend, we need to appeal to truths of a special kind: those which are both *synthetic* and *a priori*. This is, in itself, a puzzling notion. It looks as if there needs to be some kind of encounter or acquaintance with the world, for the world to supply anything which outruns our concepts: Kant called such an acquaintance an *intuition*. But this acquaintance or intuition must not be allowed to compromise the fact that the truths which it delivers are *a priori*: it must not involve any recourse to experience. Kant accordingly thought that there had to be some kind of *a priori* acquaintance with, or intuition of, the world. The challenge is then to understand how such a thing is possible, and that is the beginning of Kant's own positive philosophy.

We can understand what Wittgenstein is doing in the *Tractatus* if we see him as reacting against this position — even if his reaction was not, or not initially, against Kant's own presentation of it. Necessary truth is the business of logic, on a view of logic which Wittgenstein inherited from Russell. To insist that 'logic must take care of itself' is to insist that necessity is, in a sense, independent of the world, and that we can have knowledge of what we think of as necessary or logical truths without any kind of acquaintance with, or intuition of, the world. What needs to be resisted, on this view, is the idea of synthetic *a priori* truth.

There is a way of avoiding appealing to synthetic *a priori* truths while still allowing both that there are necessary truths about the world and that we can have knowledge of them. We avoid appeal to *synthetic a priori* truths by insisting that *a priori* truths, insofar as we can speak of truths here at all, are known simply by understanding the system in which we represent the world to ourselves: if what we appeal to is simply the nature of the system of representation, then we are still within the realm of the *analytic*, in Kant's terms, rather than the synthetic. But this understanding of the system can, in effect, give us knowledge of the world if a certain condition is met. We need to insist that the way the system must be either mirrors, or is mirrored in, the way the world must be. If we have a correspondence of this kind between the system of representation and the world which is represented, we can have *a priori* knowledge of what are, in effect, necessary truths about the world, but without any *a priori* intuition of, or acquaintance with, the world.

What is crudely expressed here is, I think, the view presented in the *Tractatus* — insofar as the *Tractatus* can be said to present any view at all. At its core is a thesis about the relation between a system of representation — any system of representation — and the world: each must, in a certain sense, mirror the other. This is the assumption that a system of representation and the world must both have the same *form*. It is the central thesis of the philosophy of language presented in the *Tractatus*, the view which is somewhat misleadingly described as the 'picture' theory — which is expressed in theses 3 and 4 of the seven main claims of the book.

This assumption of sameness of form can only be true if both the world is a certain way and language is a certain way. The way the world has to be for the same-form assumption to be true is elaborated in theses 1 and 2, and their dependent comments and explanations. The way language has to be is worked out in theses 3, 4, 5, and 6, and the remarks which explain and develop them. But if the same-form assumption is true it turns out that there will be problems stating it: we cannot, as it were, use language to step outside the mirroring relation between language itself and the world. And that means that the whole Kantian philosophical enterprise turns out to be impossible; and the same goes for any philosophy which is concerned to say something about our relationship to the world — including the *Tractatus* itself. And that explains the later comments on thesis 6, as well as thesis 7. It turns out, then, that the only way of properly addressing the Kantian problem ends up demolishing all philosophy.

So much for an overview: the devil, of course, is in the detail, which the chapters which follow will try to explain.

6 NOTE ON TRANSLATION

Much of the time it is important to look at the very words Wittgenstein uses — or the closest you can get to them if you do not actually speak German. I quote the text in translation extensively in the chapters which follow. I therefore had to consider which translation to use for these quotations.

There are two well-established and authoritative translations currently in circulation. One is the translation which was originally published opposite Wittgenstein's German — the translation by C. K. Ogden (though largely the work of Frank Ramsey). A revised version of this is still available, still alongside the German in a parallel text. The other is the later translation by David Pears and Brian McGuinness, which appears without the German. Russell's original introduction to the work is printed before both translations.

The relative merits of the two translations are, briefly, these. The Ogden translation was actually approved by Wittgenstein, and its final form is the result of modifications made in the light of communications between Ogden and Wittgenstein himself. And the German is printed alongside the English. But the translation is clumsy, at times as a result of being dog-literal. It is also insensitive to some nuances (there is a famous failure to notice the difference between 'sinnlos' — without sense — and 'unsinnig' — nonsense). On the other hand, its literalness does some things nicely — for example the detailed progression of 6.54.

The virtues of the Pears and McGuinness translation are the opposite of those of Ogden's. Idiomatic German is rendered into idiomatic English, and the book can be read relatively easily. Moreover, some of the nuances of the original are properly marked (their treatment of 'sinnlos' and 'unsinnig' is a famous improvement over Ogden's). There are, however, places where their idiomatic English is misleading about what Wittgenstein means (for example, the statement of the general form of the sentence in 4.5). The index is more useful than Ogden's.

In the end I have chosen to use Ogden's translation when I quote from the text, both in the chapters which follow, and in this Introduction. I have chosen the Ogden largely because of its faults. Its very clumsiness and the fact that it is so unidiomatic mean that it offers relatively few of the 'false friends' which can so easily lure a reader into misunderstanding. Since I do not quote without commenting on what is quoted, I am able to draw attention to the more obvious ways in which Ogden's translation fails to capture something important in the text. And the fact that Wittgenstein himself approved Ogden's translation means that it can be treated, in the parallel text in which it appears, as part of a primary text.

For all that, a student should have no difficulty working through this book if she has either of these two translations: it is not difficult to find your place in the Pears and McGuinness translation if you have the Ogden translation and the number of the remark which is quoted. A serious student who reads English but not (or not yet) German will want to have both the Ogden and the Pears and McGuinness translations: use both to get a handle on what Wittgenstein is doing, playing idiomatic against unidiomatic English; use Ogden to key into the German; and use Pears and McGuinness for their index.

7 REFERENCES

Quotations from the main body of the *Tractatus* are referenced by section number — '4.0312' for example. References to works by Wittgenstein are in general made by means of abbreviations, the key to which is to be found in the Bibliography. References to the Preface of the *Tractatus* use both abbreviation and page number — the page number being the page number in the Ogden edition — as, for example '*TLP*, p. 29'.

1

THE NATURE OF THE WORLD

1A AN OUTLINE OF METAPHYSICS

The *Tractatus* begins with a famously gnomic pronouncement:[1]

1. The world is everything that is the case.

Most people, on first reading this, have no idea what to make of it. Is it supposed to be a definition, fixing the meaning of the term 'world'? Is it supposed to be just obvious? Or is it meant to be a contentious claim, a deliberate marking out of a position which Wittgenstein expects to be attacked, but which he is prepared to defend? Again, if it is a definition, what project might Wittgenstein have in mind, for which it was appropriate simply to define a word like 'world'? And if it is not a definition, what reason could Wittgenstein have had for thinking it is true?

The only reason for thinking that Wittgenstein's claim might be a definition is that he introduces it without justification. If a work of philosophy begins with a striking claim — and it is certainly that, whatever else it is — for which no justification is offered, we are inclined to assume that the claim itself is the basis of the philosophy which is to follow. But the opening claim of the *Tractatus* cannot, in fact, be read like that. If the claim were a definitional beginning to the philosophy of the *Tractatus*, we would expect the terms which are used to state the definition to be clear themselves, in advance of the philosophy which follows. But they are not. We do not yet understand what something 'that is the case' is. We will know very shortly (in 1.1) that it is a 'fact', and not a 'thing'; but at this stage we have little idea what the difference between 'facts' and 'things' is, and this is something which cannot really be made clear independently of the general conception of language which follows in later sections.

Furthermore, if the claim were a definition, it would immediately rob the work of much of its significance. Since Wittgenstein would no longer be making a claim about the world, as we normally understand the notion, we could simply respond to him: Yes, yes, this may all be true of the 'world', in your peculiar sense, but what about the *world*, as the rest of us use the term?

It is best to accept that the claim is not a definition. The term 'world' is here being used in a familiar sense. The opening claim of the *Tractatus* is supposed to be a substantive claim about the world we all know about, the world which we have experience of. And it is supposed to be contentious in at least this sense: Wittgenstein is here proposing a view of the nature of the world which has not been realized until now. He expects this view to be new and striking to many of us, even if he supposes that it will seem obvious enough once we have understood his reasons for it. He is here deliberately opposing himself to a long tradition of philosophy.

The opening claim begins the presentation of a very general account of the nature of reality as a whole, which extends from this first remark up until 2.063. (At least, a very general account of the nature of reality is what it seems to be: a worry about this is addressed at the end of section 1F below.) But although a general account of reality is presented here, no real argument for this account is presented in these sections. Some points are elaborated, and some arguments are presented which point forwards, beyond 2.063 — but it will only be in later sections that those arguments are completed. Why, then, does Wittgenstein hold the views which he presents about the nature of reality in these early sections of the *Tractatus*? Ultimately, because he thinks they are required by the very possibility of language: he thinks that language would not even have been possible if the world had not been as he presents it as being in these early sections.

But why, then, does he begin the *Tractatus* with this general outline of the nature of reality, if the reason for thinking that reality is like that is to be offered later? We can get a sense of what is going on in the early part of the *Tractatus* if we think in the following way. Philosophers are supposed to want to understand the nature of reality: this is the traditional task of philosophy, and above all, of the queen of all philosophy, metaphysics. It is the business of metaphysics to explain how the world must be. Very well, then: Wittgenstein will tell us how the world must be. He tells us in these first sections, up to 2.063. You will then wonder why we should accept this particular metaphysical view. The explanation will emerge gradually, as the nature of language — any possible language — is explained.

Even so, we may feel that we have not really understood why Wittgenstein should *begin* the book with an account of the nature of the world, of which he offers no explanation, and the justification for which he brings in only afterwards. The reason for this style of presentation will only emerge properly later, once we have worked through the whole book; but we can anticipate it a little here. The penultimate sentence of the book reads:

> He must surmount these propositions [i.e. the propositions of the *Tractatus*]; then he sees the world rightly.

We have here, in the opening sections of the *Tractatus*, an anticipation of the vision of the world which is only properly available to someone who has understood what Wittgenstein is doing in the book. And, as will be clear when we have worked through the whole book, it is important that there should be something mysterious (to use a crude term, for the time being) about the vision which is presented. The opening sections are designed to give us an imperfect glimpse of what a proper understanding of Wittgenstein's purpose will enable us to see rightly, and to give us a taste of the mystery which belongs with that vision. By presenting the outline of his view of the nature of the world with only minimal explanation and justification, Wittgenstein is able to generate something close to what he regards as a proper feeling for the world.

I will follow Wittgenstein's procedure in my own presentation in this chapter. In this chapter I will present very little in the way of justification for the metaphysical view which Wittgenstein propounds in the book's opening sections. I will dip into Wittgenstein's general conception of language only insofar as that is necessary to explain *what* Wittgenstein is claiming, rather than his reasons for claiming it (though at one point that will itself involve some quite extensive anticipation). I will aim to make clear exactly what Wittgenstein holds, and what he is disagreeing with in holding just that. This should give us a clear view of precisely what needs to be justified by the account of language which follows.

1B THE WORLD AS THE TOTALITY OF FACTS

Back to the beginning, then:

1. The world is everything that is the case.

What does this mean? What is being ruled out? The next remark explains it:

1.1. The world is the totality of facts, not of things.

A fact is something which is the case, so for the world to be everything which is the case is just for the world to be the totality of facts. But this still does not get us very far. In order to make sense of Wittgenstein's claim here, we need to understand two things: first, what the difference between facts and things is; and second, why the world should be said to be the totality of facts and *not* of things — as opposed, for example, to being the totality of facts *as well as* of things.

The difference between facts and things can best be understood — perhaps can *only* be understood — by means of a comparison, which will already require us to peep ahead into the later parts of the book. We are familiar with a distinction between words and whole sentences. Words are, in a certain sense, the basic components of sentences: they are naturally taken to be the smallest meaningful parts of sentences. Sentences are composed of words, but (as we naturally put it) in a special way. As we ordinarily understand things, the way in which a *sentence* is composed of words is different from the way in which a *list* is composed of words, for example. Consider the difference between these two strings of words:

    (S) Wittgenstein was rich;
    (L) Wittgenstein; was; rich.

(S) is a complete sentence, while (L) is just a list — even though both (S) and (L) consist of exactly the same words. The difference is that words can be added to or subtracted from (L) quite arbitrarily, without making any difference to whether we have a list; whereas only very particular subtractions from or additions to (S) would still leave us with a sentence. A sentence is a complete, organic unit, in a way that a list is not.

The relation between facts and things is exactly similar to that between sentences and words (or at least: certain basic words), according to Wittgenstein. Facts are composed of things; and a fact is not just an assemblage of things: it has a certain organic unity of its own. The fact that Wittgenstein is rich, for example, is not just an assemblage of Wittgenstein (the man) and the property of being rich. The reason for this precise correspondence between the sentence–word relation, on the one hand, and the fact–thing relation, on the other, will be explained by Wittgenstein's general account of language. But the parallelism is clear already, in these early passages, before the account of language is presented. Even here we have remarks about the nature of reality juxtaposed with remarks about language (see, e.g., 2.0122 and 2.02–2.0201).

What kind of entity is a fact? It is something which is essentially characterized by a whole sentence. A fact is, as it were, a *that* such and such is the case (that Wittgenstein was rich, that Russell lived to a great age, that Ramsey liked climbing mountains, and so on). An entity which is a *that* such and such is the case seems entirely different in kind from an entity which we might refer to with an ordinary name (an entity such as Wittgenstein, or Russell, or Ramsey). This difference extends to what we might think of as the *location* of facts. Ordinary things exist in space, and are distributed in space. That they are spatial is a fundamental condition of their nature. But it is hard to see what it would be for a *that* to have a spatial location. If facts exist in a space, we might expect it to be a different kind of space. Wittgenstein says:

1.13 The facts in logical space are the world.

What, then, is *logical* space? Logical space is a space of *possibilities*. It is a fact that Wittgenstein was rich; another fact that Russell lived to a great age; another that Ramsey liked climbing mountains. But Wittgenstein's parents might have lost their money; Russell might have died young; Ramsey might have had a searing experience which left him with a horror of the hills. There are, as it were, lots of other facts which *might* have existed, but do not. The actual facts are only some of the possible facts; they exist, in a sense, *among* all the possible facts. What is possible marks out the extent of logical space. Each possibility is, as it were, a location in a space of possibilities. Only some of these locations are actually occupied — by what is actually the case.

So facts are quite different from things. Why, though, should Wittgenstein have insisted that the world is the totality of facts, but *not* the totality of things? Why could the world not be thought to be fundamentally constituted by the things, even if these things themselves can be combined to form facts? It is sometimes suggested that the reason is that Wittgenstein is thinking of the world in a rather special sense: as what makes truths true.[2] Certainly very few truths are made true by the mere existence of things: the existence of Wittgenstein, the man, for example, makes true very few truths about him. It seems that to get all the truths fixed we need more than the things: we need, as it were, the *way things are* — that is to say, the facts.

I think, though, that this is not the real motivation for the claim that the world is the totality of facts, not of things. It has the disadvantage that it makes Wittgenstein seem to change the subject from what he seemed to be concerned with: it makes him stop dealing with the world, as we ordinarily understand it, and start considering instead some conception of the world which suits philosophers. And if that is what he is doing, then, as in the case of the earlier suggestion that the opening claim is merely definitional, we want to respond: Yes, yes, that's all very well for your special notion of 'world' — but what about the world as we ordinarily think of it? Moreover, we only think that Wittgenstein takes the world to be, by definition, what makes truths true, because we cannot think of any other reason for him to say that the world is the totality of facts, not of things. And the response to that is just: be patient; the real reason will emerge soon enough.[3]

Indeed, the reason for thinking that the world is the totality of facts, not of things, begins to emerge in the immediately following remark, which is parallel to 1.1, and itself is part of the explanation of the opening claim that the world is everything that is the case:

1.2 The world divides into facts.

That remark in turn is elaborated as follows:

1.21 Any one can either be the case or not be the case, and everything else remain the same.

What Wittgenstein has in mind here is a kind of conception of things which forms part of an ancient (originally Aristotelian) view of the most basic entities.[4] The traditional Aristotelian metaphysical system supposes that the world is made up of entities of various kinds, beginning with the most basic, and including those whose existence is in some way dependent on or derivative from the existence of the most basic entities.

What must an entity be like if it is to qualify as one of these basic entities? The conception of the most basic entities in traditional metaphysics combines a number of features (and did even in Aristotle). Here is one natural condition, a condition of independence of existence:

(Ind) A basic entity is something which does not depend for its existence on the existence of any other entity.

(Ind) is a central feature of broadly Aristotelian metaphysics and theology, right up until the modern era (until roughly the eighteenth century).[5] According to Leibniz, for example, the universe is filled with an infinite number of independent entities, or monads, none of which is causally related to any other (since causal relations involve a kind of dependence). According to Spinoza, on the other hand, there is really only one such independent entity, God, since everything but God depends on God for its existence, while God depends on nothing.

It is something like (Ind) which is in play in the opening claim of the *Tractatus*. What Wittgenstein seems to be claiming is that it is only of *facts* that we can make anything like the claim of independent existence which is expected of the fundamental constituents of reality (though we will see in the next section that this claim will have to be qualified a little). No fact — strictly, no *basic* fact (we will come to this shortly) — depends for its existence on any other fact. Things, by contrast, can only exist with some qualities: there cannot be a *thing* which has no qualities (this would be like having Russell, the man, with no characteristics at all). For a thing to have qualities, on Wittgenstein's view, is for it to exist as part of a *fact*: the fact that it has those qualities. And for it to exist as part of a fact is, according to Wittgenstein, for it to exist in combination with *other* things. That means that there cannot be any one thing without some other thing existing.

What Wittgenstein is doing here is taking a traditional kind of view, and radicalizing it. We can give a flavour of this by considering a parallel move which we ourselves might be tempted to make. In a traditional Aristotelian metaphysics (on one orthodox interpretation), the basic entities were individual things: things like Wittgenstein (the man), or the table in my room, or the Leaning Tower of Pisa. These individual things have qualities: Wittgenstein had the quality of being rich ((S) is true); my table has the quality of being messy; the Leaning Tower of Pisa has the quality of being very famous. Individual things, on the one hand, and qualities, on the other, correspond to linguistic expressions which belong to different grammatical categories. Individual things correspond to singular terms (expressions which function like proper names). Qualities correspond to predicates (for the time being, we can take a predicate to be what you have left when you knock one or more singular terms out of a sentence). The traditional Aristotelian view is that individual things are basic, and do not depend for their existence on anything else. Qualities, however, are taken to be *dependent* beings: a quality cannot exist except as the quality of some individual thing. Other philosophers (Hume is an example) have adopted an opposite priority: they have supposed that individual things are just bundles of qualities. On this view, qualities are the basic entities, and individual things are dependent on them.

It is natural to respond to both of these views that the dependence is mutual: it is exactly as hard for an individual thing to exist with no qualities, as it is for a quality to exist except as the quality of some individual thing. We may hesitate to say that Wittgenstein makes precisely this move, because it is quite hard to understand Wittgenstein's view of qualities (we will return to this topic in section 4F below). But what he does is at least similar to this: individual things can only exist somehow qualified, and this will require them to exist in combination with other things. If there is to be anything which is a really basic being, in anything like the sense of (Ind), it cannot be either what we antecedently think of as an individual thing or a quality: it can only be a fact. Here is the point of the opening remark, then. If we are trying to characterize the constitution of the world, we want to understand the basic entities of which it is composed. When we are talking of basic entities, we are interested in entities which are independent of each other. The only entities which meet that condition are facts of a certain kind. So the world is fundamentally composed of facts.

This, in turn, means that we need to revise our intuitive or traditional understanding of what the world itself is. If we think that the world is fundamentally composed of individual things, we will think that the world itself is a large composite thing — perhaps something like the physical universe, as we ordinarily think of it, bound by the limits of space and time. But if the world is the totality of *facts*, the world itself will be a large compound fact, the conjunction of all the other facts. The world will be, as it were, a grand *that*. It is perhaps for this reason — to emphasize that the world is not any kind of thing — that Wittgenstein chooses to begin the book with remark 1, rather than 1.1: even to talk of 'facts', in the plural, suggests that facts are a kind of thing. If the world is a great *that*, rather than an all-encompassing object, it will be delimited by the facts, together with the fact that they are all the facts, and not by the limits of space and time, as Wittgenstein says in 1.11. The world is an altogether different kind of entity from *things* (though even to say that is problematic).

1C FACTS AND THINGS

It is not, however, that there are facts and not things. Facts are composed of things, and, as we will see, this complicates the picture which seems to be presented in 1–1.21: in fact,

1.1 may end up looking like an overstatement. The composition of facts can be broken down into two stages. First, we should note:

2 What is the case, the fact, is the existence of atomic facts.

The claim here is that all facts are composed of certain basic facts, called 'atomic facts' in Ogden's translation. Some facts are just atomic facts; others are compounds of several atomic facts. It is these 'atomic facts' which are the basic constituents of the world, the entities into which the world 'divides' (1.2), the entities of which Wittgenstein says:

1.21 Any one can either be the case or not be the case, and everything else remains the same.

These atomic facts are the fundamental organic unities in the world, the entities whose existence depends on no other entity of the same kind.

But a word on the translation here. 'Atomic fact' is Ogden's translation of Wittgenstein's German word 'Sachverhalt'. 'Sachverhalt' means, etymologically, something like: comportment or arrangement of things. Pears and McGuinness's alternative translation of the term — *state of affairs* — is therefore, much closer to the sense of the German word. As a result, in some places in the text — for example the very next remark, 2.01 — Pears's and McGuinness's translation does something which Ogden's does not do. But the movement of philosophy since the *Tractatus* makes their translation awkward in other ways. The phrase 'state of affairs' is now sometimes used to mean *possible fact*, including, therefore what *might* have been the case, as well as what actually is the case. So, on this use, 'state of affairs' has a wider application than 'fact'. But Wittgenstein means his term to have a *narrower* application than 'fact': a *Sachverhalt* is a fact of a very special kind, one which is basic in the constitution of the world. And although Ogden's term 'atomic' reflects no element of the German word, it does capture something of Wittgenstein's reason for singling out *Sachverhalten*. To be 'atomic', etymologically, is to be indivisible. When Wittgenstein says that the world 'divides' into facts, he means that it divides into *Sachverhalten*, and no further. I will continue to use Ogden's translation — Wittgenstein himself approved it after all — but it is as well to be aware both of what it omits and of what it interpolates.

What are atomic facts? Wittgenstein gave the following explanation in a letter to Bertrand Russell:

> Sachverhalt is, what corresponds to an Elementarsatz if it is true.
>
> (*CL*: 125)

An 'Elementarsatz' is an elementary proposition, or basic sentence. This tells us that the notion of an atomic fact is tied to language, just as the notion of fact, in general, is.[6] And it also emphasizes the basicness of atomic facts. But beyond this the explanation relies on the full conception of language which is elaborated later in the *Tractatus*.

Facts, in general, are compounds of atomic facts. And atomic facts, Wittgenstein continues (2.01), are combinations of objects. The notion of an object will shortly be given fuller elaboration, but, for the time being, Wittgenstein is happy to take it to be equivalent to 'entity' ('Sache') or 'thing' ('Ding'). Things enter the *Tractatus*'s picture of the world only when combined — bound or linked — with one another to form atomic facts. The remainder of the 2.01s (up until 2.0141) are concerned with the relation between objects and atomic facts; and Wittgenstein returns to the topic in the 2.03s. Wittgenstein is concerned to explain here certain complicated relations of dependence and independence. Objects are both, in one sense, dependent on, and, in another sense, independent of, atomic facts. Atomic facts are, in a sense, dependent on objects, despite themselves being the most basic organic unities in the world.

Objects have to be, in a sense, independent of atomic facts, if we are to make sense of the idea that atomic facts are composed of objects. They are independent of atomic facts in the following sense. Objects appear in combination with one another, in atomic facts, but the very same objects *could* have existed even if those particular atomic facts had not existed. Suppose that there is an atomic fact that Bill is to the left of Ben, in which the objects Bill and Ben stand in relation to each other. Bill and Ben could have existed, even if they had not stood in that particular relation to each other (if Bill had been to the right of Ben, for example). The crucial point here is that atomic facts are *contingent*: they are what is *actually* the case, but might not have been. The independence of objects from atomic facts consists in this: the existence of objects does not depend on what is *actually* the case, but simply on what is *possible*.

But Wittgenstein is concerned to insist that this independence should not be overstated or misunderstood. It is not that the objects might have lain around uselessly, uncombined with each other. For if that had been possible, we would have needed some kind of special glue, to join objects tightly enough together to form the organic unities which are atomic facts. But no glue is needed:

2.03   In the atomic fact the objects hang one in another, like the links of a chain.

There are two separate points here. First, the objects are built to link up, to be combined in atomic facts. And, second, their combination does not require any extrinsic joining agent: the objects always come in particular combinations; they are always already joined, with no external assistance.

This means that objects cannot be thought of as self-standing entities which just happen to be joined together in states of affairs. This is what Wittgenstein is ruling out when he says:

It would, so to speak, appear as an accident, when to a thing that could exist alone on its own account, subsequently a state of affairs could be made to fit.

(2.0121)

And the reason there cannot be such an accident is this:

2.012   In logic nothing is accidental: if a thing *can* occur in an atomic
fact the possibility of that atomic fact must already be prejudged
in the thing.

And again:

(A logical entity cannot be merely possible. Logic treats of every
possibility, and all possibilities are its facts.)

(2.0121)

What is Wittgenstein's point here? In saying that in logic
nothing is accidental, or that a logical entity cannot be
merely possible, Wittgenstein seems to be ruling out the
idea of something which *is* possible, but might not have been
possible. That is, he seems to be insisting on this principle:

(NP) Whatever is possible is *necessarily* possible.

(NP) is a basic and intuitive principle of modal logic: it is the
core principle of the modern modal logical system (S5). It
seems clear that Wittgenstein commits himself to it.

(NP) has a counterpart which relates to what is essential to
things, provided we are prepared to countenance the very
idea of things having essences.[7] The essence of something is
— or at least entails — whatever is necessary to that thing's
existence. If we accept both (NP), and that things have
essences, we will accept this:

(NPE)   If something *can* be true of an object, it is essential to the
object that that can be true of it.

We can see (NPE) at work in one of Wittgenstein's fundamental
claims about objects:

2.011   It is essential to a thing that it can be a constituent part of an
atomic fact.

These points are then elaborated in the following remarks:

2.0123   If I know an object, then I also know all the possibilities of its
occurrence in atomic facts.
(Every such possibility must lie in the nature of the object.)
A new possibility cannot subsequently be found.

And that lies at the heart of a distinction which Wittgenstein
makes between 'internal' and 'external' qualities:

2.01231   In order to know an object, I must know not its external but
all its internal qualities.

The external qualities of a thing are those qualities which it
has only contingently; the internal qualities are what is
essential to it. In our trivial example, it is an external quality
of Bill that he is to the left of Ben, because he need not have
been to the left of Ben. But it is *internal* to Bill that he *can*
be to the left of Ben: this is part of his essence.

The same points are used again to introduce for the first
time one of the crucial notions of the *Tractatus*, the notion
of *form*:

2.0141   The possibility of its occurrence in atomic facts is the form of
the object.

The notion of form is one with a huge philosophical resonance. It harks back to Plato and Aristotle: in Aristotle, for
example, the form of a thing is what is essential to it, what
makes it the thing it is.[8] And it recalls Kant, for whom space
and time were the *forms* of intuition (roughly: basic experi-
ential awareness of things), which means (at least) that they
are presupposed in all intuitions (of the relevant kinds). In
fact, Wittgenstein's concerns are even closer to Kant than
this. Kant says:

[T]hat which allows the manifold of appearance to be intuited as
ordered in certain relations I call the **form** of appearance.[9]

Wittgenstein's claim is that what is essential to an object is just the fact (as we might put it) that it *can* combine with other objects to form a particular range of atomic facts: that is the form of the object.

This is in itself a dramatic claim about objects: there is no more to their essence, or to what is internal to them, than which other (kinds of) objects they *can* combine with, to form atomic facts. This leads Wittgenstein to say:

2.0232 Roughly speaking: objects are colourless.

Which picks up an earlier point:

A speck in a visual field need not be red, but must have a colour; it has, so to speak, a colour space around it.

(2.0131)

The point is not that objects do not have any more material qualities than the fact that they can combine with particular ranges of other objects to form particular ranges of atomic facts: it is not that they do not actually have any colour (literally speaking) — although that may be true. It is just that these material qualities are not part of the form or essence of the objects. Material properties, he says, 'are first presented by the propositions — first formed by the configuration of objects' (2.0231).[10]

This is what lies behind the limits of the independence of objects from atomic facts:

The thing is independent, in so far as it can occur in all *possible* circumstances, but this form of independence is a form of connexion with the atomic fact, a form of dependence.

(2.0122)[11]

There are two things worth noting about this claim. First, the word translated 'connexion' here is 'Zusammenhang': this is an ordinary word, meaning *connection* or *context*, but etymologically it means a *hanging together*. It thus employs the very image of hanging together which Wittgenstein uses to explain the relation of objects to one another in an atomic fact, which we have already seen in 2.03 (it also appears in 2.032). Second, this remark about the independence of objects actually being a form of dependence is justified by the following parenthesis:

(It is impossible for words to occur in two different ways, alone and in the proposition.)

Here we see an explicit appeal to the nature of language to justify Wittgenstein's metaphysical claim about the nature of the world. The claim is, apparently, that we can see that objects must be dependent on atomic facts, because words essentially occur in sentences.

It is important, however, to recognize that the dependence of objects upon atomic facts does not require there to be any actual atomic facts. All that is needed is that the relevant atomic facts be *possible*. This is the point Wittgenstein is making in this remark:

2.013   Every thing is, as it were, in a space of possible atomic facts. I can think of this space as empty, but not of the thing without the space.

This is a clear echo of Kant. Here is what Kant says, in support of the claim that space is *a priori*:

One can never represent that there is no space, although one can very well think that there are no objects to be encountered in it.[12]

There is a risk of being misled by this echo, however. If we have Kant in our ears when we read 2.013, we might take Wittgenstein to be claiming in the second sentence that we could have a space of possible atomic facts, even if that space were empty of objects. He would then be claiming that those atomic facts would have been possible even if the objects had not existed, but there could not have been those objects without those atomic facts being possible. But this is inconsistent with Wittgenstein's own theory. He does not think that the very same atomic facts could have been possible without the objects existing. As we will see, his view is that nothing at all would have been possible if the objects which constitute atomic facts had not existed.

Wittgenstein does not mean what the Kantian echo might lead one to think he means. He does not mean that the space of possible atomic facts could have been empty of *objects*, but that it could have been empty of *atomic facts*. That is to say, it might have been that none of the atomic facts were *actual*, or *actually existed*. This would not be a situation in which there were no actual *facts*, of course: it would simply be a situation in which none of the actual facts was atomic. As we know from 1.21, each atomic fact can either be the case or not be the case. If an atomic fact is not the case, then there is a fact all right: the fact that the atomic fact is not the case. But this fact (which Wittgenstein calls a 'negative fact' in 2.06) is not an atomic fact. Wittgenstein's point in 2.013 is that the existence of an object does not require that any atomic fact be *actual*: it simply requires that the relevant atomic facts be *possible*.

Furthermore, although there is a clear echo of Kant in 2.013, the relations of dependence and independence between objects and atomic facts are more complex than any simple parallel with Kant's conception of empirical space would suggest. Atomic facts are, of course, the basic organic unities of the world, and objects can only exist, combined with other objects, in atomic facts. But beyond that, there is really a mutual dependence. Thus, Wittgenstein claims, on the one hand, that the thing's capacity to occur in all possible circumstances is a form of dependence of object upon atomic fact. But, on the other hand, the fact that the possibility of its occurrence in atomic facts must be 'prejudged' in an object means that this is true:

> 2.014 Objects contain the possibility of all states of affairs.[13]

And this gives us a sense in which objects are basic: they are, in a sense, the ground of all possibilities. This basicness of objects is further elaborated in Wittgenstein's claim that 'objects form the substance of the world' (2.021). I will turn to that claim in the next section. But we can note now that the picture we began with has been complicated. It remains true that the world is the totality of facts, and not of things (1.1), because the things do not appear in the world as self-standing entities; but it is clearly the case, on Wittgenstein's view, that objects are just as basic in one way as facts are in another.

1D THE SUBSTANCE OF THE WORLD

We have seen that Wittgenstein begins the *Tractatus* with a general contrast between *fact* and *thing*. At the outset the contrast is quite schematic, and the terminology not used with great precision. Thus some of his core claims (for example, 1.2 and 1.21) are made in terms of *facts* (*Tatsachen*), when they are strictly true only of facts of a special kind, the atomic facts (*Sachverhalten*). Similarly, he begins with relatively vague talk of *things* (*Dingen*), apparently swapping the notion easily with that of an object (*Gegenstand*) or an entity (*Sache*). But it becomes gradually clear that the things which are his principal focus have to meet certain quite demanding conditions. Two remarks in particular are striking:

2.0232   Roughly speaking: objects are colourless.
2.0233   Two objects of the same logical form are — apart from their external properties — only differentiated from one another in that they are different.

By this stage it is clear that we are dealing with things which are not at all like the things we usually take ourselves to have experience of. These are the things which Wittgenstein calls *objects* (*Gegenständen*).

Wittgenstein makes the following central claim about objects:

2.02   The object is simple.

That is to say, objects have no parts; they are not composed of things; they are not complex. This means that Wittgenstein's objects cannot be anything like the 'things' which we ordinarily take ourselves to experience and to understand. They are not like people, or tables, or roads, or cities: all of these 'things' are compound; they have parts. Strictly speaking, there are no such things, on Wittgenstein's view. Sentences which seem to refer to such 'things' need to be re-understood, so that we do not let ourselves admit that there are complex objects:

2.0201 Every statement about complexes can be analysed into a statement about their constituent parts, and into those propositions which completely describe the complexes.

Where we might have thought that we had a complex object, according to Wittgenstein there is nothing but the *fact* that its constituent parts are related to each other in a certain way.

This is striking enough, but it is no more striking than the reason Wittgenstein offers for the claim that objects are simple:

2.021 Objects form the substance of the world. Therefore they cannot be compound.

What does Wittgenstein mean by 'substance'? His answer is this:

2.024 Substance is what exists independently of what is the case.

Here we can see that Wittgenstein is appealing to a key strand in the traditional (Aristotelian) notion of substance.[14] We might express it as follows:

(Sub) A substance is something which remains the same thing through change.

But Wittgenstein is not concerned with anything so vulgar as *change* in the empirical world. His concern is with alternative *possibilities*, with the full range of possible atomic facts.

Wittgenstein's conception of substance is expressed, not by the traditional (Sub), but by something like this:

(Sub*) Substance is what is constant across all possible differences in the atomic facts.

There is a significant claim embodied in this: that there must *be* something which is constant, fixed, across all possible variations in what is contingent. Wittgenstein does, indeed, make this substantial claim:

2.022 It is clear that however different from the real one an imagined world may be, it must have something — a form — in common with the real world.[15]

Every possible world must share a form with the actual world. Wittgenstein continues:

2.023 This fixed form consists of the objects.

And he says of substance:

2.025 It is form and content.

The thinking here is something like this. There must be something common, something constant across all possible alternative scenarios. This is (at least close to) what is known traditionally as *substance*. But what is actually required, according to Wittgenstein, is a common form. What might be meant by 'form' here? The notion of form has already been introduced in the idea of the form of an object: it is the ways in which that object can combine with other objects to form atomic facts. Wittgenstein introduces a related notion in connection with atomic facts:

2.032 The way in which objects hang together in the atomic fact is the structure of the atomic fact.
2.033 The form is the possibility of the structure.

The structure of an atomic fact is something contingent: it is the fact that its constituent objects are actually combined in the way they are. The atomic fact's form is quite different: it is (as it were — the reason for this caution will have emerged by the time we have reached the end of the book) the fact that the constituent objects *can* be arranged like that. This latter 'fact' — the form of the atomic fact — clearly has its roots in the form of the constituent objects, since 'objects contain the possibility of all states of affairs' (2.014). So there can only be a fixed form, common to all possible worlds, if the objects whose form is the root of the form of atomic facts are also common to all possible worlds. This is why substance is both form and content. It is form, because the form of atomic facts — the possibility of there being such facts — is what is common to all possible worlds. And it is content, because the form of atomic facts is carried in the form of their constituent objects, so there must be *things* as well as forms, if there are to be the appropriate forms. Hence Wittgenstein says:

2.026 Only if there are objects can there be a fixed form of the world.

2.027 The fixed, the existent and the object are one.

We have here a dramatic conception of objects. It turns out that the world is made up of atomic facts whose constituents are entities which exist *necessarily*, in every possible world. The objects can only be independent of what is the case, in the way they have to be to form the substance of the world, if they exist no matter what: if, that is, they are necessary existents, not depending for their existence on any contingent fact. And this is why objects must be simple: an object's being compound requires it to be *possible* for it not to exist (before its components are combined, for example, or after they are broken apart).

This conception of objects may be dramatic and clear, but the reasoning which underlies it is not entirely obvious. For the sake of simplicity I will just present my own reading here — leaving the difficulties of interpretation to be considered more fully in the Appendix.

As I understand it, then, the *Tractatus*'s conception of objects depends on the following two claims:

> (FF) There must be a fixed form which is common to all possible worlds;
>
> (FO) There can only be such a fixed form if there are objects common to all possible worlds.

Why might we hold (FF)? (FF) is a way of stating the modal principle (NP) (that whatever is possible is *necessarily* possible), which is itself natural and intuitive: we have already seen this principle in play in Wittgenstein's conception of the essence of objects (as (NPE)). But does Wittgenstein have an independent reason for holding (FF)?

Well, he certainly produces an argument:

2.0211 If the world had no substance, then whether a proposition had sense would depend on whether another proposition was true.

2.0212 It would then be impossible to form a picture of the world (true or false).

The wording of 2.0211 suggests that what Wittgenstein wants to insist on is that the *sense* of all propositions must be independent of the *truth* of any of them. This is reminiscent of the following remark from the *Notebooks*:

> A statement cannot be concerned with the logical structure of the world, for in order for a statement to be possible at all, in order for a proposition to be CAPABLE of making SENSE, the world must already have just the logical structure it has. The logic of the world is prior to all truth and falsehood.

> (*NB*: 14)

In 2.0212 Wittgenstein insists, in effect, that it must be possible to form a 'picture' of the world. The central claim of the theory of language which is developed later in the

Tractatus is that sentences are *pictures* or *models*. It is natural, therefore, to take the use of 'picture' ('Bild' — picture or model) in 2.0212 to be an anticipatory reference to that theory. We will consider the theory itself in detail in Chapters 3 and 4; for the moment, however, I will anticipate that explanation, and say that the theory involves a commitment to these three claims:

(a) In the basic case, a sentence is a combination (a hanging in one another) of symbols (names);

(b) In the basic case, for a sentence to have sense is for two conditions to hold:
  (i) Its symbols are correlated with objects in the world;
  (ii) It is possible for the symbols to be combined in the way in which they are actually combined in the sentence;

(c) It is possible for the constituent symbols of a sentence to be combined in the way they are, and be correlated with the objects with which they are correlated, if and only if it is possible for the corresponding objects to be combined in the same way in reality.

Armed with these assumptions, we can reconstruct an argument for the key assumption (FF) which it is natural to think lies behind 2.0211 and 2.0212.

We may begin with a general modal assumption:

(1) If any possibility is a necessary possibility, then every possibility is a necessary possibility.

This is extremely natural: it simply insists on a uniform approach to modality. Given (1), we can pick on an arbitrary possibility and try to argue for (FF) for that case. Let us take a sentence of the kind which Wittgenstein will regard as basic: according to assumption (a), it consists just of a combination of names. We can use the letters '*a*', '*b*', '*c*', etc., as sample names, and we can just write such letters in a string to indicate their being combined. A basic sentence, then, might look like this:

(P₁) *abcde*

(P1) asserts that something is the case: it asserts that *abcde*. We assume that (P1) states a genuine possibility (some sentences must, and this can be taken to be an arbitrarily chosen example of one which does). Given (1), we can now assert:

> (2) If the possibility expressed by (P1) is a necessary possibility, then every possibility is a necessary possibility.

Our aim will then be to show that the possibility expressed by (P1) is indeed necessarily possible (granted that it is at least possible). Consider, first, the statement that the possibility asserted by (P1) is indeed a possibility. We might write it like this:

> (P2) It is possible that *abcde*.

If what is expressed by (P1) is possible, but not necessarily possible, then (P2) must be contingent. So in order to prove (FF) we need to show that (P2) is not contingent.

Now here is a natural principle about contingency:

> (3) If a sentence is contingent, its having sense must not depend upon its being true.

This is natural, because it is natural to think that if a sentence is contingent, its truth could not be *worked out* just from its meaning.

At this point, we should recall assumption (b) of the *Tractatus*'s general theory of language. It follows from this that (P1) has sense if and only if '*abcde*' is a possible combination of symbols, provided that the names are correlated with objects in reality. But by assumption (c) of the *Tractatus*'s general theory of language, '*abcde*' is a possible combination of symbols if and only if the corresponding objects can be combined in the same way — that is, just in case (P2) is true. So the *Tractatus*'s theory of language entitles us to claim:

(4) (P1) has sense if and only if (P2) is true.

But now look at (P2): the sentence '*abcde*' occurs within it — and in its own right, not merely quoted. It is clear that (P2) cannot have sense if this integral part of it has no sense. Furthermore — if we assume for the moment that it is legitimate to talk about possibility at all — there can be no other problem about (P2)'s having sense. That means that we can assert this:

(5) (P2) has sense if and only if (P1) has sense.

But from (4) and (5) together we can derive this:

(6) (P2) has sense if and only if (P2) is true.

But by (3), the natural principle about contingency, (6) implies this:

(7) (P2) is not contingent.

But we already know:

(8) If (P2) is not contingent, what is asserted by (P1) is necessarily possible.

Putting this all together with (2), we can conclude:

(9) Every possibility is a necessary possibility.

Which is, in effect, the fixed-form assumption (FF).

How, precisely, does this argument relate to the text? The suggestion is that 2.0212, in effect, brings in assumptions (a), (b), and (c) from the *Tractatus*'s general theory of language — the so-called 'picture theory'. And the argument can be seen as showing that it is impossible for the sense of one sentence to depend on the truth of another (which is what 2.0211 says is problematic). (P2) asserts a certain possibility. By assumptions (b) and (c) from the picture theory, its asserting that possibility is the same thing as (P1)'s having sense. So (P2) is tantamount to an assertion that (P1) has sense: on this interpretation, (P2) is the 'other proposition' on whose truth the sense of (P1) depends. But of course (P2)'s truth is not independent of its own sense, which means that it cannot be contingent, as it would have to be for the world not to have a 'fixed form'. We may also note, moreover, that the reasoning from step (4) to step (5) is reasoning which is naturally attributed to Wittgenstein. As we will see in the next chapter, Wittgenstein objected to Russell's 'multiple-relation' theory of judgement on the following ground:

5.5422   The correct explanation of the form of the proposition "A judges *p*" must show that it is impossible to judge a nonsense. (Russell's theory does not satisfy this condition.)

The point here is at least close to the thought that a sentence which contains a piece of nonsense as an integral part must itself be nonsense.[16]

The argument is clearly valid, and seems close to Wittgenstein's thought, but is it sound? The most obviously questionable assumptions — apart from those which derive from the *Tractatus*'s theory of language — are the general modal principles (1) and (3). I will not question (1) here, but it is worth pausing for a moment over (3). What (3) assumes, in effect, is that there cannot be contingent *a priori* truths. Now this was standardly assumed by philosophers: it is connected with Kant's insistence that philosophy and mathematics are *a priori*, and therefore with his claim that they involve synthetic *a priori* knowledge. It is also natural to think that it is connected with Wittgenstein's own interest in the *a priori*. But it has been questioned by Saul Kripke, in his groundbreaking lectures on naming and necessity (Kripke 1980).

Kripke points out that the two distinctions — between the *a priori* and the *a posteriori*, on the one hand, and between the necessary and the contingent, on the other — are made in quite different ways. The distinction between the *a priori* and the *a posteriori* is an *epistemic* distinction: it concerns ways in which truths can be *known*. But the distinction between the necessary and the contingent is *metaphysical* or *ontological*: it is concerned with whether things could *in fact* have been otherwise. We would probably reject the argument I have presented here, therefore, whatever our view of the *Tractatus*'s theory of language, but this is no reason not to ascribe some such argument to Wittgenstein: Wittgenstein would certainly have assimilated the two distinctions.

All our effort so far has been directed towards the fixed-form assumption (FF). But what about the other key assumption, (FO), the assumption that a fixed form requires objects which are common to all possible worlds? Wittgenstein's views here have a certain history.[17] Russell at one point thought that the form of a basic kind of sentence was expressed in a very general statement: so the form of a sentence such as '*Fa*' would be captured in the very general statement '$(\exists x, \varphi). \varphi x$' (there is a φ and there is an x such that x is φ; or: there is at least one object, and at least one property, such that the object has the property).[18] And Wittgenstein seems at one point to have agreed (*NB*: 17).[19] Unfortunately, that general statement seems to be true only if some particular sentence of the appropriate form is true. So one sentence's having the form it has seems to depend on either it or another (of the same form) being true.[20] This seems arbitrary in itself, and it violates Wittgenstein's general insistence that questions of sense must be settled in advance of questions of truth and falsity.

Wittgenstein seems to have thought that the only way of avoiding this problem was to say this:

> The logical form of the proposition must already be given by the forms of its component parts.

> (*NB*: 23)

And since, according to the *Tractatus*'s general conception of language, the logical form of a proposition (sentence) is the same as the logical form of any reality it can represent, the form of atomic facts must be given by the forms of *their* component parts — which is to say, the objects. There might seem still to be a gap, however, between this and what Wittgenstein claims about objects:

2.027   The fixed, the existent and the object are one.

This seems to commit Wittgenstein unambiguously to the idea that genuine objects exist independently of what is the case — that is, necessarily. But it might seem that what Wittgenstein needs in order to establish the possibility of 'forming a picture of the world', while grounding the forms of propositions in the forms of their parts, could be granted him without admitting this strong conclusion, that the objects which embody the form of the world exist necessarily. For his main purposes, Wittgenstein needs the following three claims:

    (d) The form of the world (the ways in which objects can be combined) is independent of what is the case;
    (e) The form of the world is contained in the forms of objects (the ways in which they can combine with one another);
    (f) The forms of objects are essential to them.

And it might seem that (d), (e), and (f) could all be true, even if the objects themselves were not necessarily existent entities. It might seem that what is necessary is just that there should be *some* objects in each world — perhaps just this number of objects — with just the forms of the objects which actually exist. But then it is not at all obvious that there could not have been other objects which had essentially the forms which the objects which actually exist have. And, as we have seen, Wittgenstein himself seems to allow just this possibility:

2.0233 Two objects of the same logical form are — apart from their external properties — only differentiated from one another in that they are different.

In fact, however, it is not clear that Wittgenstein's actual commitments really do outrun what his philosophy of language requires. This only seems to be the case if we misunderstand what (d) here involves.[21] In requiring the form of the world to be independent of what is the case, Wittgenstein is requiring the *possibilities* to be independent of what is the case: that is to say, however else things might have been, there must at least have been the *same possibilities*. But according to the philosophy of language to be expounded later in the book, the possibilities are just ways in which the objects correlated with the names might have been arranged. So we would not have the *same* possibilities unless we had the *same* objects. With different objects, we might have formally parallel possibilities, but they would not strictly have been the *same* possibilities. So it seems that if we grant Wittgenstein his philosophy of language, together with his general principles of modality, he really does have an argument for the claim that the fundamental objects exist necessarily.

1E THE WORLD AS A WORLD OF FACTS: A RECAPITULATION

Wittgenstein completes his outline of the nature of the world by restating the points of 1–1.21 explicitly in terms of atomic facts. Thus he says:

2.04 The totality of existent atomic facts is the world.

This looks like just a restatement of 1, but things are not quite so simple. The reason is that there are facts other than the actual atomic facts. In particular, we need to bear in mind that there are a lot of atomic facts which *might* have existed, but do not. If we consider an atomic fact which might have existed, but does not, and say that it does not exist, we seem to have reported another fact. Facts of this kind — facts that such and such (something atomic) is *not* the case — Wittgenstein calls 'negative' facts:

> The existence of atomic facts we also call a positive fact, their non-existence a negative fact.

> (2.06)

Negative facts will not be included in the list of all the existent atomic facts, but they will be included in 'everything that is the case'.[22] What this reveals is that it is not at all straightforward to restate the opening claim of the *Tractatus* just in terms of atomic facts.

But there seems to be a way around the difficulty, for the case of negative facts, at least. This is because, if we have a list of all the existent atomic facts (the positive facts), we will have fixed the full list of negative facts as well. Once we have fixed which of all the possible atomic facts actually exists, we must also have fixed which do not exist — all the rest. That is to say:

2.05 The totality of existent atomic facts also determines which atomic facts do not exist.

Once we fix all the positive facts, we have thereby fixed all the negative facts as well. So we now have, as it were, a much larger list of facts: all the atomic facts and all the facts which are, as it were, negations, of possible but not actual atomic facts. But is even this larger list enough to fix all the existent facts there are? Only if it is can the claim of 2.04 hold good.

It is one of Wittgenstein's distinctive claims that this larger list — the list of all the atomic facts and all the negations of possible but not actual atomic facts — suffices to fix the full range of facts. Since that larger list is fixed by fixing which atomic facts exist, the claim is that once we have fixed which of all the possible atomic facts actually exist, we will have fixed all the facts there are. I think that it is to make precisely this point that Wittgenstein introduces the notion of 'reality', as the Ogden translation has it ('Wirklichkeit').

But we face a puzzle, created by three sentences which are almost next to one another in the text:

2.04   The totality of existent atomic facts is the world.

2.06   The existence and non-existence of atomic facts is the reality ... .

2.063   The total reality is the world.

Why does Wittgenstein not simply use the word 'world' in place of 'reality' in 2.06, and dispense with 2.063 altogether? It is only if there is a difference in the meaning of the words that there can be any point in using both of them; but how, then, can the claim of 2.063 be true? The problem is that 2.04 suggests that the world is restricted to the *existent* atomic facts, whereas 2.06 and 2.063 together seem to require that the world also include (in some sense) the *non*-existent atomic facts.

I think that the Wittgenstein's point here is made more obscure than it need be by an awkwardness of translation: 'Wirklichkeit' would be better rendered *actuality*, rather than *reality*. 'Die Wirklichkeit' is what is *actually* the case — as opposed to what is merely *possible*. If we adopt this suggestion, 2.04–2.063 can be seen to constitute an argument: or, rather, 2.05–2.063 can be seen to constitute an argument for 2.04. Once it is determined which of the possible atomic facts actually exist it is also determined which do not exist (2.05). The substantial claim of 2.06 is then that listing which atomic facts exist, and which do not exist, is enough to determine completely what is actually the case — which of all the possible facts of any kind (not just atomic facts) is actual. And 2.063 can then be seen as making the simple point that this means that we will have delimited the whole world: the world is, after all, the totality of what is actually the case (as 1 claims).

I think this must be Wittgenstein's argument, but it is not enough to solve our problem with 2.04, 2.06, and 2.063: how can the world consist *both* just of the existent atomic facts *and* of the existent together with the non-existent atomic facts? The best that can be said, I think, is that Wittgenstein's writing here is loose. He seems to be conflating these two claims:

(i) The totality of existent atomic facts is (constitutes) the world (everything that is the case);
(ii) The totality of existent atomic facts, together with these being all of the existent atomic facts, *determines* everything that is the case (the world).

(ii) is what he must mean; but (i) is what he actually says, at 2.04. This kind of looseness is actually not uncommon in the *Tractatus*. It is, I think, part of what in the Introduction I called the 'poetic' character of the work. We should simply accept it, and make the minor modifications needed to deal with the puzzles it creates.

The puzzle of 2.04, 2.06, and 2.063 should not distract us from the substantial claim that Wittgenstein makes here — the claim that fixing which possible atomic facts do and do not exist is enough to fix which possible facts of any kind exist. There seems to be a connection between this substantial claim and the claim of the mutual independence of atomic facts. For in the midst of this argument Wittgenstein writes:

2.061 Atomic facts are independent of one another.
2.062 From the existence or non-existence of an atomic fact we cannot infer the existence or non-existence of another.

This is, of course, a restatement of the early claim which lay at the heart of the idea that facts — atomic facts, at least — are the basic organic unities in the world:

1.21 Any one can either be the case or not be the case, and everything else remains the same.

But what is the claim doing here, right in the middle of the argument for the point that fixing which atomic facts exist is enough to determine all the facts?

There is a reason: it is only if atomic facts are independent of each other that it can be plausible to make the substantial claim which Wittgenstein makes at 2.06. For suppose that some atomic facts did depend on other atomic facts. Then there would be facts of the following form, where '*p*' and '*q*' express atomic facts:

> (D) Its being the case that *p* depends on its being the case that *q*.

We might call facts of this form *dependence facts*. The obvious examples of dependence facts would be *explanatory* facts: facts expressed by sentences of the form '*p* because *q*'. There could only be a point in making dependence claims or explanatory claims if dependence relations and explanatory relations held between some pairs of facts and not others. For example, suppose that 'The house caught fire', 'The circuit blew', and 'Gary dropped his cigarette' all express atomic facts. We only have reason to say that the house caught fire *because* the circuit blew if we are concerned to rule out other dependence relations — such as that the circuit blew because the house caught fire, or that the house caught fire because Gary dropped his cigarette. If dependence relations hold between some pairs of facts and not others, then whether or not a particular dependence fact exists — whether or not the relevant dependence claim is true — will not depend just on whether the atomic facts involved actually exist. It can be true that the house caught fire, that the circuit blew, and that Gary dropped his cigarette, and still not be true that the circuit blew *because* the house caught fire, or that the house caught fire *because* Gary dropped his cigarette. So if some atomic facts depended on others, there would be some further facts — *dependence facts* — whose obtaining was not determined by the existence and non-existence of the atomic facts. That is to say, if some atomic facts depended on others, the claim of 2.06 would not be true.

It turns out, then, that the fundamental metaphysical claim of the opening sections of the *Tractatus* — that it is

THE NATURE OF THE WORLD

facts which are the basic organic unities in the world — is interconnected with the substantial claim of 2.05 and 2.06, that once it is determined which atomic facts exist, all of the facts are determined. It is only because of the claim that the atomic facts are independent of one another that Wittgenstein can restate the opening statement of the *Tractatus* in terms of atomic facts, and claim that the totality of existent atomic facts is the world.

1F THE METAPHYSICAL COMMITMENTS OF THE *TRACTATUS*

As we will see, the metaphysics of the *Tractatus* is justified — insofar as it is justified at all — by the theory of language which follows it in the text. Let us take stock here of what we will have to find support for in that theory of language:

(T1)   The basic organic unities of the world are facts;

(T2)   Facts are different in kind from things (objects);

(T3)   Facts are either atomic facts or combinations of atomic facts;

(T4)   The existence of any atomic fact is independent of the existence of any other atomic fact;

(T5)   Atomic facts are combinations of objects;

(T6)   Which atomic facts are possible is determined by the nature of objects;

(T7)   It is essential to an object that it can combine with other objects, in the ways it can, to form atomic facts;

(T8)   Nothing is essential to an object beyond the fact that it can combine with other objects, in the ways it can, to form atomic facts;

(T9)   Objects exist necessarily;

(T10)   It is necessary that just those atomic facts are possible which are, in fact, possible.

(T6), (T7), (T9), and (T10) have already been shown to follow (given a small pinch of salt) from the theory of language — provided that that theory of language turns out to require the truth of the following claims:

(a) In the basic case, a sentence is a combination (a hanging in one another) of symbols (names);

(b) In the basic case, for a sentence to have sense is for two conditions to hold:

    (i)   Its symbols are correlated with objects in the world;

    (ii) It is possible for the symbols to be combined in the way in which they are actually combined in the sentence;

(c) It is possible for the constituent symbols of a sentence to be combined in the way they are, and be correlated with the objects with which they are correlated, if and only if it is possible for the corresponding objects to be combined in the same way in reality.

We need then to ensure that (a)–(c), together with (T1)–(T5) and (T8), can be extracted from the account of language which the *Tractatus* provides. That account of language will be the topic of Chapters 3, 4, and 5. But before we turn to it, we need to understand something of the philosophical background from which the theory sprang, which will be our concern in Chapter 2.

Even before turning to that, however, it is as well to raise — if only to postpone — an issue which has struck several people in connection with these opening sections. It is commonly assumed that taking Wittgenstein to be presenting a metaphysical account of the nature of the world in the opening remarks of the *Tractatus* requires us to attribute to him a form of *realism*.[23] And this is sometimes felt to be a falsification of Wittgenstein's views.[24] We need to be clear, at least, about what is being suggested here. First, here is a statement of realism:

(R)   The nature of the world as it is in itself is altogether independent of anything to do with any thought or representation of it.

Any reluctance to accept (R) is a form of *anti*-realism. A positive denial of (R) (involving an assertion of some dependence of the world upon something to do with thought or representation) is a form of idealism.

Second, here is a definition of metaphysics, as I have been using the term so far:

> (M) Metaphysics is concerned with the ways in which the world must, can, and cannot be.

That is to say: metaphysics is concerned with the modality of the world. Just as (R) is a relatively traditional statement of realism, so (M) is a fairly conventional definition of metaphysics.

What is the connection between metaphysics and realism? Some are tempted to make this simple connection:

> (MR) Only a realist can engage in metaphysics.[25]

Given the definitions of realism and metaphysics which I have offered (and which, as I say, are quite uncontroversial), (MR) should seem unobvious, to say the least. In fact, on the face of it, idealism (as I have defined it) is likely to be a metaphysical thesis (on the definition of metaphysics provided by (M)). The idealist holds that there is some dependence of the world upon something to do with thought or representation, and is unlikely to think that this dependence is accidental: idealism is itself likely to be a statement of how the world must be (viz., dependent on something to do with thought or representation).

I think (MR) is false. We should also beware of a claim which might seem to run in the other direction. I have said that the metaphysics of the opening pages of the *Tractatus* is justified, insofar as it is justified at all, only by the conception of language which is presented later. Someone might suppose that this requires some form of idealism. That is, someone might think that *this* was true:

> (MLI) If a metaphysical theory is justified by a philosophy of language, then the way the world must, can, and cannot be (which is described in the metaphysical theory) must depend on the nature of language (which is described by the philosophy of language).

But (MLI) is false too: the direction of justification need not mirror the direction of any real dependence. This point about the separability of the direction of justification from the direction of dependence is very obvious in science: a reading on an instrument will justify a judgement about the current flowing through a wire, even though the instrument reading obviously *depends upon* the current, rather than vice versa (the current *causes* the reading). There is no more reason to expect the direction of justification to match the direction of dependence in philosophy than there is in science.

Someone might react to this, however, and take the parallel I have just drawn between philosophy and science to show something else, namely this:

(MLR) If a metaphysical theory is justified by a philosophy of language, then the nature of language (which is described by the philosophy of language) must depend on the way the world must, can, and cannot be (which is described in the metaphysical theory).

This might be reasonable if the nature of language were merely *evidence* for a metaphysical theory, but the relation between the philosophy of language and metaphysics need not be thought of in this way. So (MLR) — which is another way of trying to get realism out of the general shape of the *Tractatus* — is not true either.

What this all means is that at least one set of worries about the attribution to Wittgenstein of any substantial metaphysical views can be set aside. The grand description of the structure of reality with which the *Tractatus* begins can be accepted at face value, without prejudging the question whether Wittgenstein was a realist or not. These remarks are simply neutral on the issue. I will address the general question of realism and idealism directly in Chapter 6, as part of a discussion of the issue of solipsism in the *Tractatus*. And in the meantime, I will note how views to be found in the *Tractatus* fit with realist and anti-realist interpretations, as those views are encountered.

2

THE LEGACY OF FREGE AND RUSSELL

2A THE IMPORTANCE OF LANGUAGE

The *Tractatus* begins with a vision of the nature of the world. That vision depends on the conception of language which is elaborated in the work's main body. But what has language got to do with it? Why should a philosophy of *language* have anything to contribute to a view of the nature of reality?

What makes language relevant is something which is naturally thought to define what is distinctive about language — in contrast, for example, with any other kind of representational or expressive system. Almost everyone thinks that languages are systems of signs which are arbitrary in the following sense: whatever any particular sign does, a different sign could have done just as well (so it is, in a sense, arbitrary that this particular sign, rather than another, is actually used). The view that languages are systems of arbitrary signs is interdependent with a very general conception of what it is for languages to be meaningful, which is seldom formulated explicitly, but can be traced back through the whole history of philosophy. This general approach to linguistic meaning, with slight variations, continues to shape both philosophical and non-philosophical conceptions of language.

We can attempt to express this approach to linguistic meaning as a matter of being committed to a certain assumption, which we might call the *correlation* assumption:

(Corr) Languages depend for their meaningfulness on correlations between certain linguistic items, on the one hand, and extra-linguistic items, on the other.

If this is to express an attitude to language which is almost universal, we need to take some care about what is meant by 'correlation'. Here is a natural characterization:

(C) A *correlation* is any pairing of items which meets this condition: it does not matter for the purposes of the pairing how the pairing is achieved.

The correlation assumption, with correlation understood in the manner of (C), clearly supports the view that languages are systems of arbitrary signs.

It is worth dwelling a moment on the formulation of (Corr) and (C). First, we should note that (C) explicitly allows the relevant correlations to be made in any number of ways. Some will think of them being made deliberately and self-consciously: 'Here is a sign,' we might imagine someone saying, 'and there an extra-linguistic item; let me correlate the one with the other.' Others, however, will think of the correlations as no more than assignments of meaning which are recognized explicitly only after the fact, in order to make sense of those who speak some language (and the speakers themselves may have no conscious conception of the correlations which give meaning to their words). (C) is neutral on this. In a similar spirit, some views might hold that the extra-linguistic items with which linguistic items are correlated can be recognized as having the character they have, quite independently of thinking of them *as* correlates of the relevant linguistic items. Other views, on the other hand, might deny this, supposing that we can only be in a position to identify the correlates of linguistic items in virtue of speaking a language of an appropriate kind.[1] Both kinds of view can be understood to accept (Corr) with correlation understood as it is characterized in (C). Further, (C) allows that there may be what we might call *derived* correlations: the obvious examples would be correlations between complex linguistic items and extra-linguistic items which are simple *consequences* of antecedent pairings of the components of those complex linguistic items with certain other extra-linguistic items. That a correlation is *actually* established in a particular way does not mean that it is essential to the purposes of the correlation that it be established in that way. Finally, it is worth pointing out that (Corr) does not hold that the meaningfulness of *every* linguistic item depends on a correlation with some extra-linguistic item: it merely requires there to be *some* such correlations for a language as a whole to be meaningful. (Corr) allows, in particular, that some linguistic items might be meaningful, even though they themselves are not correlated with anything extra-linguistic, just in virtue of *other* linguistic items being correlated with extra-linguistic items.

With correlation understood in this way, (Corr), I think, is almost universally accepted — or at least *was* until relatively recently.[2] But it is comparatively unspecific. We get something more substantial if we specify the kind of thing we might include as the relevant extra-linguistic items with which linguistic items need to be correlated. The interpretation of (Corr) which underlies Wittgenstein's conception of language in the *Tractatus* can be formulated as a commitment to the following *objectivity* assumption:

(Obj) The extra-linguistic items with which linguistic items have to be correlated for languages to be meaningful are items in the world (objects).

(Obj) seems more obviously deniable than the correlation assumption, (Corr): indeed, a whole tradition in the philosophy of language has denied it. John Locke, for example, held that linguistic items were meaningful in virtue of a correlation with something extra-linguistic (in line with (Corr)), but thought that the extra-linguistic items in question were things in the mind of each speaker — the speaker's 'ideas' (Locke 1700: III, ii). Wittgenstein's great predecessors and philosophical inspirations, Gottlob Frege and Bertrand Russell, played a decisive part in the turn towards the world, away from the mind, which (Obj) represents; almost everyone since has followed them.

The correlation and objectivity assumptions ((Corr) and (Obj)) together express the general approach to language which Wittgenstein took over from Frege and Russell. And these two assumptions, taken together, make language immediately and directly relevant to an understanding of the nature of reality. To see why, we need first to recognize how little mere correlation (as characterized by (C)) can achieve. Correlation is not a process of transformation: if we merely *correlate* linguistic items with something extra-linguistic, the extra-linguistic is not thereby reconfigured as it is in itself. All that we can do is get linguistic items to *reflect* certain properties of the extra-linguistic — whichever properties are not lost in a process of correlation. Of course, if linguistic items *reflect* certain properties of the extra-linguistic, language must *reveal* something of the nature of the extra-linguistic. We can explain this a little more carefully. If we accept the correlation assumption, (Corr), we can divide the properties of language in use into three categories. First, there are the core intrinsic properties of the most basic linguistic items themselves — typically, their shape and sound. These we can simply set aside, as irrelevant to the significance of language. Second, there is the mere fact that the basic linguistic items are correlated with the extra-linguistic items with which they are, in fact, correlated. And then, third, there is everything else: if we are right in our determination both of the philosophically irrelevant intrinsic properties of the linguistic items, and in our account of which extra-linguistic items they are correlated with, everything else about language in use must in some way be a reflection of the extra-linguistic, and must, therefore, show us something about the true nature of the extra-linguistic.

If we add the objectivity assumption, (Obj), to this picture, we ensure that the extra-linguistic whose true nature language can reveal is nothing less than the world. It then appears that any feature of language which cannot be set aside as philosophically irrelevant, and which is not just the fact of certain linguistic items being correlated with items in the world, must itself be in some way a reflection of the true nature of reality.

Once we acknowledge these two core assumptions, we can see why the philosophy of language might play such a central role in the *Tractatus*. But (Corr) and (Obj) are more deeply embedded in the book than that suggests. They are not mere background assumptions. In fact, the whole conception of language which forms the heart of the *Tractatus* can be seen as nothing more than a working out of (Corr) and (Obj), in the light of difficulties which Wittgenstein found with the views of Frege and Russell.

The importance of the work of Frege and Russell for an understanding of the *Tractatus* is hard to exaggerate. Most of the rest of this chapter will be concerned with the background which their work provides for the philosophy of language of the *Tractatus*.[3] Frege and Russell were decisive in forming Wittgenstein's view of the way in which (Corr) and (Obj) must be true. Their work — whether directly or indirectly[4] — led him to consider the range of linguistic expressions which are meaningful in virtue of a correlation with something extra-linguistic, the nature of the extra-linguistic items with which they are correlated, and the manner of the correlation. But the influence of Frege and Russell was also crucial in shaping the larger philosophical motivations for the overall view of the *Tractatus*. Their work in the philosophy of mathematics engaged explicitly with Kant's conception of the task of philosophy,[5] and this Kantian background intersects with Wittgenstein's longer-standing philosophical interests.[6]

2B THE OBJECTIVE TURN

I have already remarked that Frege and Russell played a decisive role in the establishment of the objectivity assumption, (Obj). In adopting (Obj) Frege and Russell were rejecting a long-standing alternative interpretation of the correlation assumption, (Corr). The simplest version of this alternative interpretation of (Corr) is to be found in Locke's claim that 'words in their primary or immediate signification, stand for nothing, but the ideas in the mind of him that uses them' (Locke 1700: III, ii, 2). This looks like a completely general claim — it seems to be meant to apply to all words — but as we will see in section 2D, Locke does make some exceptions.

The word 'idea' is a technical term for Locke: he takes it to mean 'whatsoever is the object of the understanding when a man thinks' (Locke 1700: I, 8), with the 'object of the understanding' being assumed to be something in the mind. The crucial thing about Locke's view, for the tradition of which he was a part and which followed him down to the nineteenth century, is that words signify (in the first instance, at least) items in the mind. These mental items are components of thoughts — which on this view will be taken to be composite mental items — and it is thought which language is (in the first instance, at least) about.

If words signify mental items which are components of thoughts, whole sentences — the things of which words are components — will signify (in some sense) whole thoughts. And relations between whole sentences will have to be explained in terms of relations between whole thoughts. Some of these relations are of particular interest to philosophers. Consider, for example, the following linguistic sequence:

Bertie loved Ottoline. So Bertie loved someone.

If the sentences here signify (in some sense) whole thoughts, the relation between them — which is embodied in the word 'so' — will naturally be taken to express a relation between thoughts. The relation here is a logical relation; logical relations will then be relations between thoughts. Since thoughts are here being understood to be composite mental items, on this view logic will be concerned with the relations between composite mental items. It will then be tempting to take these relations to be the business of psychology, and to treat the laws of logic as psychological laws.

Frege objected to every part of this view, which he referred to as *psychologism*. He had two reasons for thinking that words were not meaningful in virtue of correlations with ideas. First, because ideas (he assumed) are private to each individual, so that one person's ideas are not accessible by another, ideas must be irrelevant to the meaning of the words of public languages, which we can all understand (Frege 1884: vi). Second, he took it that our words are meaningful in virtue of correlations with what we are concerned with when we use them, and we are almost never concerned with ideas (Frege 1892a: 28, 31–32). In the area in which he had a particular interest, mathematics, Frege claimed that we are concerned with *numbers*, and not with the ideas of numbers (Frege 1884: v). In general, our concern is with things in the world, rather than things in the mind, and it must be things in the world which linguistic items are correlated with.

As to the idea that the laws of logic might be psychological laws, Frege takes it to derive from an ambiguity in the notion of a law. There are, on the one hand, laws which prescribe what one should do, and there are, on the other, laws which describe what is the case. It is in the latter sense that laws of nature are laws. If we describe the laws of logic as 'laws of thought', we will be tempted to take them as laws in this descriptive sense. They will then become psychological laws. But psychological laws can only be concerned with what is *held* as true, whereas logic is concerned with *truth*. Treating the laws of logic as 'laws of thought' — as psychological laws — forces us to conflate being *held* true with being *true* (Frege 1893: xv).

Frege's hostility to the psychological interpretation of (Corr) was part of his lifelong attempt to set mathematics straight and give it rigorous foundations. A similar concern motivated Russell, though he came at it differently. In the first instance, he approached the problems of coherence which seemed to infect the foundations of mathematics in the expectation of finding them insoluble. Their insolubility was to be part of the motive for the reinforcement of the neo-Hegelian philosophy in which he was first schooled. But further research showed him that many of these problems had, in fact, been solved by a number of German mathematicians whom he had not previously studied; and reading the works of Hegel himself seems to have left him disillusioned.

The mention of Hegel is relevant here, because the neo-Hegelian view which was dominant in Russell's circle during the early part of his academic career was certainly at least continuous with Locke's in its approach to language. And the particular neo-Hegelian views of F. H. Bradley were the subject of criticism by G. E. Moore at just the moment when Russell's commitment to neo-Hegelianism had been weakened (Moore 1899). Moore points to the confusing fact that Bradley uses the term 'idea' in two different senses: to refer to a kind of state of mind, on the one hand; and to a 'universal meaning', on the other. Moore takes Bradley to be confusing these two senses when he takes ideas in the second sense — that is, 'universal meanings' — to be dependent on our states of mind, and when he consequently thinks that truth involves some relation between our states of mind and reality (Moore 1899: 177). To avoid such a confusion, Moore replaces the use of the word 'idea' in the second sense — referring to 'universal meanings' — with the word 'concept'. Concerning 'concepts', so understood, Moore says this:

> Concepts are possible objects of thought; but that is no definition of them. It merely states that they may come into relation with a thinker; and in order that they *may* do anything, they must already *be*

something. It is indifferent to their nature whether anybody thinks them or not.

(Moore 1899: 179)

If we understand 'concepts' (in this sense) to be what are meant by words, we have here a first move away from psychologism about meaning. And, in some sense, this move away from psychologism is a move towards the world. Moore says: 'It seems necessary ... to regard the world as formed of concepts' (Moore 1899: 182). Likewise, he takes his view to be a way of holding that 'the relation of premisses to conclusion is an objective relation' (Moore 1899: 183) — that is, that it does not depend at all on the conclusion and premises being connected in our thoughts. Moore here rejects psychologism about logic.

This early theory of Moore's does give some endorsement to (Obj), but it is an odd kind of endorsement, since it depends crucially on an unorthodox conception of the world — as something 'formed of concepts'. And Moore's 'concepts' are peculiar entities. According to Moore, 'concepts' are 'incapable of change' (Moore 1899: 179). He describes it as 'perfectly obvious' that 'the concept can consistently be described neither as an existent, nor as part of an existent, since it is presupposed in the conception of an existent' (Moore 1899: 181). Moreover, according to Moore, concepts 'cannot be regarded fundamentally as abstractions either from things or from ideas; since both alike can, if anything is to be true of them, be composed of nothing but concepts' (Moore 1899: 182).

In this respect, Russell's view was clearer, and more clearly distinct from any form of idealism. His view changed over time, and several times, but in all the versions of his view which had some bearing on Wittgenstein's philosophy in the *Tractatus*, he seems to have held that linguistic items are correlated with things which are *objects in the world* in a relatively unproblematic sense. The range of these objects may change: early on the range is extremely extensive — 'a man, a moment, a number, a class, a relation, a chimaera, or

anything else that can be mentioned' (Russell 1903: 43) —
whereas later it seems to be restricted to things with which a
subject may be acquainted (Russell 1984). But these changes
may be understood as changes of view about what objects
there are in the world: the sense in which the objects are
objects, the world is the world, and the objects are in the
world, seems constant and relatively orthodox.

Frege and Russell both endorse (Obj) as well as (Corr); and
once (Obj) is accepted — once it is accepted that words are
meaningful in virtue of a correlation between linguistic
items and items in the *world* — it is hard to retreat from. As
Frege insisted, it is so obviously items in the world which are
the objects of our concern, rather than anything in our
minds. But, for all that, acceptance of (Obj) is not pain free.
It brings with it two large problems, in particular. These will
be the subjects of the following sections.

2C THE OBJECTIVE TURN AND THINNESS OF MEANING

Frege and Russell held (Obj), that languages are meaningful
in virtue of correlations between linguistic items — signs —
and things in the world. The first problem this view faces is
that it seems to make meaning too *thin*: it seems to allow too
little to be involved in the meaning of words. If — in the
basic case, at least — words are meaningful in virtue of
being correlated with things in the world, it seems that any
two words which are correlated with the same thing in the
world will have the same meaning, and any word with which
nothing in the world is correlated will have no meaning. But
this is, on the face of it, implausible. Consider the following
two sentences:

(1) Everest is the highest mountain in the world;
(2) Chomolungma is the highest mountain in the world.

It is natural to think that these two sentences differ in
meaning, because someone could understand both and yet

think that one of them was true and the other false. And yet the only difference between them is that one has the name 'Chomolungma' where the other has the name 'Everest', and these two names in fact refer to the same mountain. Again, consider this sentence:

(3) Green kryptonite is fatal to Superman.

We are likely to think that this sentence is meaningful — perhaps even true — even though it seems that there is no object at all with which the name 'Superman' is correlated.

This thinness of meaning was especially problematic for Frege, whose view combined three things: a very simple view of the grammar of sentences; a relatively unrestricted conception of the kinds of linguistic item whose meaningfulness depends on their being correlated with something extra-linguistic; and a very austere view of the things with which different kinds of linguistic item are correlated. At base, his theory recognizes three classes of expression: singular terms, sentences, and predicates (the result of removing one or more singular terms from a sentence). He is very generous in what he counts as a singular term: any expression at all which picks out an individual object counts as a singular term. By this criterion, ordinary proper names (such as 'Everest' and 'Chomolungma') are singular terms; but so are more complex expressions, like 'the least rapidly converging series', 'whoever discovered the elliptic form of the planetary orbits', and '$(2 \times 2^3) + 2$'.

The three basic kinds of expression are correlated with three distinctive kinds of item in the world, on Frege's theory. Singular terms refer to objects, which may be of various kinds: people, series, numbers (for example). Sentences refer to entities of a very special kind: truth values. All true sentences refer to the True, and all false sentences refer to the False. Sentences, in fact, become a special kind of name, on Frege's theory, with the True and the False being objects of a special kind. Predicates refer to entities which are different again: according to Frege, they refer to a kind of incomplete entity which he calls a *concept*. This is another confusing use of a difficult word: for Frege, a 'concept' is a function, which yields a truth-value (either the True or the False) as output, given a particular object, or class of objects, as input. On Frege's view, it seems that all predicates which are true of exactly the same objects will refer to the same 'concept', the same function from objects to truth-values.

These basic assumptions make the problem of thinness of meaning very sharp for Frege. The expressions '$(2 \times 2^3) + 2$' and '18' refer to the same thing, on his view: the number eighteen. But surely they differ in meaning? He holds that all true sentences refer to the same thing — the True — as do all false sentences — to the False: but surely different true sentences, and different false sentences, can differ in meaning? And surely two predicates could be true of exactly the same things without having the same meaning?

Frege introduced a technical notion, which he called *sense*, precisely to deal with this difficulty (Frege 1892a). Fregean 'sense' is defined precisely to be whatever it is that marks a difference in meaning between such pairs of sentences as (1) and (2), despite the fact that, on Frege's theory, the words in them (and, indeed, the sentences themselves) all refer to the same things. The 'sense' of an expression is supposed to be determined by the way in which the entity with which the expression is correlated is given to one — by, as the technical terminology has it, the 'mode of presentation' of the entity the expression refers to. So the names 'Everest' and 'Chomolungma' express different ways in which the same mountain is presented to us; similarly, the expressions '$(2 \times 2^3) + 2$' and '18' present the same number in different ways.

And Frege claimed that an expression could have 'sense' even if there was in fact nothing with which it was correlated. So the phrase 'the least rapidly converging series' has 'sense', according to Frege — and therefore a kind of meaning — even though there can be no such series. And sentence (3) can have 'sense' — and therefore still be meaningful — even though there is not really such a person as Superman, and consequently (according to Frege) the sentence as a whole is neither true nor false. All kinds of expression have 'sense' (in his sense), according to Frege. He gives a particular name to the 'sense' (in his sense) of sentences: the 'sense' of a sentence is a *thought* (in the sense of *what is thought*, rather than the thinking of it).

On Frege's view the 'sense' of an expression is distinct from its reference — distinct from the entity in the world with which it is correlated. But it is still both public and objective: it is not meant to be psychological in any way. So Fregean 'thoughts' — the 'senses' of sentences — are unlike thoughts as Moore understood the term, in two crucial respects: if two people think that $(2 \times 2^3) + 2 = 18$, they both think the same thought; and that thought — the thought that $(2 \times 2^3) + 2 = 18$ — existed, and was there to be thought, even before anyone entertained it. Fregean 'sense' is meant to be objective and non-psychological in much the same way as Moore's 'concepts' are.

Frege's response to the problem of thinness of meaning is, then, to offer a rather richer account of what is involved in (Corr) and (Obj). At base, languages depend for their meaningfulness on linguistic items being correlated with items in the world. But the correlations are made in different ways — the items in the world are given to us in different ways — and these differences in *manner* of correlation are reflected in an aspect of meaning which goes beyond the mere fact of correlation.[7] Indeed, in some cases this aspect of meaning can be present even when no actual correlation has been made.

Russell distrusted Frege's notion of 'sense'. His attitude is made clear in a letter to Frege written at the end of 1904:

> In the case of a simple proper name like 'Socrates', I cannot distinguish between sense and [reference]; I see only the idea, which is psychological, and the object. Or better: I do not admit the sense at all, but only the idea and the [reference]. I see the difference between sense and [reference] only in the case of complexes whose [reference]

is an object, e.g., the values of ordinary mathematical functions like ξ + 1, ξ^2, etc.

(Frege 1980: 169)[8]

And within a year he had given up the appeal to Fregean 'sense' even in the case of the 'complexes' he mentions here. His revised view made no appeal to Fregean 'sense' at all. His response to the problem of thinness of meaning had, therefore, to be quite different. In essence, it involved changing those features of Frege's theory which made the problem peculiarly sharp for him. He took a much less simple view of grammar, and distinguished as belonging to fundamentally different grammatical categories expressions which Frege had grouped together. He took a more restrictive view of the range of linguistic items whose meaningfulness depends on their being correlated with something extralinguistic. And he had a less austere conception of the nature of the entities in the world with which linguistic items may be correlated.

Russell's crucial advance came with his invention of his theory of descriptions, presented for the first time in his classic paper, 'On Denoting' (Russell 1905). This theory involved making a radical distinction between singular terms properly so called (what Russell himself would later call 'logically proper names') and definite descriptions. Definite descriptions are complex expressions which serve to pick out particular individual things: expressions such as 'the least rapidly converging series', 'whoever discovered the elliptic form of the planetary orbits', and '$(2 \times 2^3) + 2$'. Whereas Frege had treated these as singular terms, on a par with semantically simple proper names, Russell took them to be quantifier expressions. If we take the standard form of definite description to be given in a phrase of the form 'The F', we can present Russell's view of them, as they occur in sentences of the form 'The F is ... ', as being that they are paraphrasable with something of this form: 'There is exactly one object which is an F, and that object ... '. Thus, 'the least rapidly converging series' can be rendered (as it occurs in appropriate sentences) as 'There is exactly one object which is a least rapidly converging series, and that object … '. And '$(2 \times 2^3) + 2$' becomes something like 'There is exactly one object which is a result of taking the cube of 2, multiplying it by 2, and adding 2 to the product, and that object … '.

So understood, the meaningfulness of a definite description (or of a sentence in which such a description occurs) does not depend in any way on the description's being correlated with an object. Whereas on Frege's view a correlation with an object is presupposed, and there is something defective about the meaning of a description when there is no object with which it is correlated, on Russell's view descriptions to which no objects correspond are fully and unproblematically meaningful. Their use simply involves the assertion (rather than merely the presupposition) that exactly one thing satisfies a certain condition. This theory enabled Russell to explain differences in meaning between different definite descriptions, and between definite descriptions, on the one hand, and semantically simple proper names, on the other. Different descriptions will involve the assertion that different conditions are uniquely satisfied; and semantically simple proper names will not involve the assertion that any condition is uniquely satisfied. Much of the problem of thinness of meaning — at least as it applies to what Frege counted as singular terms — is thus avoided.

Part of this problem still remains, however. What are we to do about the apparent difference of meaning between (1) and (2), which differ only in the different apparently simple proper names which they contain? Hints of Russell's approach to such sentences are to be found in the closing paragraphs of 'On Denoting'. Russell saw that he need not count any expression as depending for its meaning on a correlation with an object, unless the object and our mode of access to it meet whatever theoretical conditions our philosophy might demand. For example, our philosophy might involve denying that there are any unreal objects; in that case we will not count the apparently simple proper names to be found in fiction as depending for their meaning on correlations with objects. Instead, they will be regarded as being equivalent to definite descriptions, and will be meaningful in just the same way as definite descriptions are, on Russell's account.

What Russell's account allows is that we may set aside the indications of surface grammar, and take a linguistic expression to function in whatever way our underlying philosophy requires. Russell himself married his theory of descriptions to a broadly Cartesian epistemology. At the end of 'On Denoting' we find him proposing that we need only regard an expression as meaningful in virtue of a correlation with an object, if the object in question is one with which we are 'immediately acquainted' — where 'immediate acquaintance' is restricted to things whose existence we cannot doubt (principally qualitative features of our experience). All other expressions, whatever their apparent form, can be treated as equivalent to definite descriptions.

It is arguable that this method enables Russell to deal even with problems such as those raised by (1) and (2), which turn on apparent differences of meaning between sentences which involve different, but apparently unstructured, proper names. Different proper names can be regarded as being equivalent to different definite descriptions, and the different descriptions will involve the assertion that different conditions are uniquely satisfied. So the name 'Everest' in (1) might be taken to be equivalent to the description 'the mountain named after a Surveyor-General of India', and the name 'Chomolungma' in (2) might be taken to be equivalent to the description 'the mountain revered by Tibetans as the mother of the world'. If we only regard an expression as meaningful in virtue of a correlation with an object if the object in question is one with which we are 'immediately acquainted', and we count every other expression as equivalent to some compound of such basic expressions, it is not implausible that we will be able to deal with the problems of thinness of meaning which arise for expressions which Frege would have counted as singular terms.

But the problem of thinness of meaning affects more than just *those* linguistic expressions. How does Russell deal with it elsewhere? Here the crucial feature of Russell's account is its rejection of Frege's account of the reference of sentences. Frege took the full meaningfulness of sentences to depend on their being correlated with a special kind of object — a truth-value, either the True or the False. (A sentence which has no truth-value must be defective in meaning, having sense, but no reference.) Russell rejected this view for two reasons (Russell 1903: 504). First, it could be seen by 'direct inspection' that the relation between a sentence and a truth-value was quite different from that between an ordinary singular term and an object. And, second, Frege's view must find insufficient distinction between all true sentences, or, alternatively, between all false sentences. But although he rejected Frege's account of the entity with which sentences are correlated, he agreed with Frege — early on, at least — that whole sentences were indeed correlated with entities. While he held this theory, he called the entities in question *propositions*: they are supposed to be some kind of objective correlate of whole sentences.

Propositions, in this sense, the objective correlates of whole sentences, are composed of the objective correlates of the words of which sentences are composed. The objective correlates of words are constituents of the propositions which are the objective correlates of whole sentences. Thus Russell wrote to Frege (in the letter from which I have already quoted):

> I believe that in spite of all its snowfields Mont Blanc itself is a component part of what is actually asserted in the proposition 'Mont Blanc is more than 4000 metres high'. We do not assert the thought, for this is a private psychological matter: we assert the object of the thought, and this is, to my mind, a certain complex (an objective proposition, one might say) in which Mont Blanc is itself a component part.
>
> (Frege 1980: 169)

In his early work Russell says that the objective correlates of words in general are *terms* (Russell 1903: 43). 'Terms' clearly belong to the world: they are whatever can be counted as *one*, and are also describable as *units*, *individuals*, or *entities*. Russell describes 'terms' as follows:

> A term is, in fact, possessed of all the properties commonly assigned to substances or substantives. Every term, to begin with, is a logical subject: it is, for example, the subject of the proposition that itself is one. Again every term is immutable and indestructible. What a term is, it is, and no change can be conceived in it which would not destroy its identity and make it another term.
>
> (Russell 1903: 44)

Among 'terms' in general, Russell distinguishes two kinds. On the one hand there are *things* (what we have been calling *objects*), which are correlated with the expressions we call singular terms (such as proper names); on the other hand there are what Russell calls *concepts* (yet another use of that slippery word), which are the correlates of other words (Russell 1903: 44). What Russell here calls *concepts* include entities which are more familiar as *qualities* and *relations*, the objective correlates of predicates. A crucial difference from Frege emerges here: although neither Russellian 'concepts' nor qualities and relations are very tightly defined by Russell, it seems clear that there can be distinct 'concepts', qualities, and relations correlated with different predicates which are true of exactly the same things. Frege seems to have taken predicates which are true of exactly the same things to be correlated with the *same* 'concept' in *his* sense (a function from objects to truth-values). But with his richer conception of the entities correlated with whole sentences and predicates, Russell is not open to such acute embarrassment over the problem of thinness of meaning as Frege would have been if he had not posited 'sense' as an extra dimension of meaning. There is no suggestion in Russell's view that all true sentences (or all false sentences) have the same meaning, nor that all predicates which are true of exactly the same objects have the same meaning.

Russell certainly has something to say in response to the general problem of thinness of meaning, both because of his theory of descriptions, and because of his richer conception of the entities with which sentences and predicates are correlated. Whether what he has to say is finally adequate is a matter for further debate. We have seen, for example, that the problem led Russell to posit an explicit version of the description theory of names, according to which every ordinary proper name ('Socrates', 'Everest', and 'Chomolungma' are examples) is equivalent in meaning to some definite description. This theory has been subjected to serious criticism, and is now generally rejected.[9] But some version of this theory was accepted almost without question for more than half a century: it would be no surprise if Wittgenstein (for example) thought it was obviously correct.

2D THE OBJECTIVE TURN AND THE UNITY OF THE PROPOSITION

There is a very obvious fact about language which is easily missed if we begin from the correlation assumption, (Corr), which holds that the meaningfulness of languages depends on correlations between linguistic items and something extra-linguistic. The obvious fact is that words can be combined to form sentences, but sentences are not just lists of words. The crucial difference between a sentence and a list is this: words can be added to or subtracted from a list quite arbitrarily, while still leaving us with a list; but only very particular additions of words to a sentence, or subtractions of words from a sentence, will leave us with a whole sentence. Sentences have a kind of completeness or unity which lists do not have. We might call this the unity of the sentence.

(Corr) forces us into a certain difficulty over the unity of the sentence. According to the picture which (Corr) expresses, languages are composed, at base, of intrinsically meaningless things (marks or sounds), which are in some way given meaning by being correlated with something extra-linguistic. But since these most basic linguistic items are intrinsically meaningless, the special unity and completeness of a sentence cannot be explained by their core intrinsic nature. Rather, the unity of *sentences* must be some kind of reflection of an *extra*-linguistic unity.

This seems (initially, at least) relatively unproblematic in a theory like Locke's. When he first introduces his theory, Locke seems to suggest that all words are meaningful in virtue of being correlated with items in the mind, but this is an oversimplification. Some words, he thinks, work quite differently:

> The mind, in communicating its thought to others, does not only need signs of the *ideas* it has then before it, but others also, to shew or intimate some particular action of its own, at that time, relating to those *ideas*. This it does several ways; as, *Is*, and *Is not*, are the general marks of the mind, affirming or denying.
>
> (Locke 1700: III, viii, 1)

The claim here is that the combination of words in a sentence is an expression of an act of the mind in combining the mental correlates of those words in the mind. In effect, the unity of the sentence is an expression of the unity of a certain kind of mental item — we might call it a *judgement*. The unity of the sentence is therefore explained in terms of the more basic unity of judgements, where judgements are thought to be things in the mind. Something like this theory held sway well into the nineteenth century. Among its famous adherents was Kant, whose 'transcendental deduction of the categories' depends on something very close to this thought.

But it looks difficult to hold any such view once we have taken the objective turn — once we have determined that words are meaningful in virtue of correlations with something objective, rather than something in the mind of particular individuals. It is then hard to see how the unity of the sentence can be an expression of an *act* of unification: it looks as if it must be an expression of the completeness of some *objective* unity. What might that objective unity be?

Frege's view must be that the crucial objective unities are *thoughts*, the objective entities which he took to be the 'senses' of whole sentences. Thoughts, like sentences, have components: the 'senses' of subsentential expressions. And just as sentences are not simply lists of words, so thoughts are not mere aggregates of the 'senses' of subsentential expressions. But Fregean thoughts are, in fact, very odd candidates for being the basic unities whose completeness is expressed in the unity of the sentence. The reason is that it is hard to understand their unity as being independent enough of the unity of sentences to be capable of being merely *reflected* in sentences. Let us ask: is a thought *essentially* the 'sense' of a sentence? That is: could there be thoughts without the sentences which express them? If thoughts are essentially the 'senses' of sentences, then they are clearly not independent enough of sentences for the unity of sentences to be a reflection of their unity. If they are not essentially 'senses' of sentences, then the nature of thoughts, and of 'sense' more generally, depends on the notion of a mode of presentation, which we will then want some independent grasp of. In general, 'sense' is, or is dependent on, the *way* in which some item in the world — the referent of the relevant expression — is given or presented. Sentences refer to truth-values, the True and the False. So if it is the unity of Fregean thoughts which is reflected in the unity of sentences, the unity of sentences will have to be explained as a reflection of the unity which is required of something if that thing is to be mode of presentation of the True or the False. But what kind of unity is required of something which is a mode of presentation of the True or the False? We have no grip on this other than as the kind of unity which is expressed in sentences.

This makes it look as if the prospects of explaining the unity of the sentence within a Fregean theory — at least, in a way which is compatible with (Corr) — are poor. We seem forced, then, to try to explain the unity of the sentence in terms of the prior unity of something like Russellian *propositions*, the objective correlates of sentences. If they are to do the work that is here required of them, Russellian propositions must themselves be unities: they cannot be mere aggregates of the objective correlates of parts of sentences; they cannot be just collections of objects and relations.

But this creates a problem. Suppose that there is a Russellian proposition correlated with sentence (1). We might refer to it as follows:

(1p) Everest's being the highest mountain in the world.

If the nature of this proposition is to explain how it is that (1) is a complete sentence, and not a mere list, it must be different from the mere aggregate of the object, Everest, and the quality of being a man, which we might refer to by means of the following list:

(1a) Everest, being the highest mountain in the world.

What is the difference between the unified proposition and the mere aggregate? The natural thought is that in the proposition the elements — Everest and the quality of being the highest mountain in the world — are somehow *joined* together. But what might such 'joining together' amount to? Again, the natural thought is this: the object, Everest, must actually *possess* the quality; that is, Everest must actually be the highest mountain in the world.

But now consider *this* sentence:

(4) Everest is a lake.

We might refer to the Russellian proposition which is correlated with this sentence as follows:

(4p) Everest's being a lake.

And if Russellian propositions are complete unities — as they have to be, if they are to be capable of explaining the unity of sentences — the proposition (4p) must be distinct from the mere aggregate of its parts, which we might refer to as follows:

(4a) Everest, being a lake.

But what could that difference be? If we follow the natural thought we used in connection with (1p) and (1a), the difference is that the proposition (4p) consists of Everest's actually being a lake. But, of course, (4) is false: Everest is not actually a lake. So it seems that there is no such proposition as (4p): there is no such thing as Everest's actually being a lake.

We might ourselves suggest a possible way out of this difficulty: perhaps, we might say, sentences are correlated with *possible* situations — *possible* combinations of objects and qualities or relations. When the sentence is true, the possible combination is actual, and not *just* possible; and when it is false, the combination is merely possible. (4p) might indeed be thought to represent a possible combination of things, and this might seem to solve our problem. Russell himself seems not to have considered this solution, however, and there are strong hints that he would not have favoured it (Russell 1910: 152). It also faces a further difficulty, whose seriousness depends on the way in which the correlation of linguistic items with the extra-linguistic is understood.

Frege and (early) Russell both seem to have held that among the expressions for which some kind of correlation conception of meaningfulness applies are (at least some) *sentences*. (It is as well to remember here the liberality of the conception of correlation expressed in (C), in section 2A above.) For Frege, the full meaningfulness of sentences depends on their being correlated with truth-values: truth-values are objects (of a distinctive kind), and a sentence which has no truth-value is at best defective in meaning. For (early) Russell the meaningfulness of sentences depends on their being correlated with propositions. There seems no clear reason why the meaningfulness of true sentences should be more basic than the meaningfulness of false sentences. In that case, if any sentences are meaningful in virtue of correlations with extra-linguistic items, both true and false sentences will have to be meaningful in virtue of such correlations. And that means that there will have to be extra-linguistic items which are the correlates of false sentences. If we hold this view, we can only adopt the proposed solution to the problem raised by false sentences for Russell's account of the unity of sentences if we can make sense of sentences being *correlated* with merely possible combinations of objects, qualities, and relations. But can we make sense of sentences being correlated with something which is merely possible?

That depends on the kind of correlation we have in mind. In discussing the characterization of the notion of correlation provided by (C) in section 2A, above, I said that (C) was consistent with some correlations being *derived*, dependent on other, antecedent correlations. Derived correlations can obviously be contrasted with *non-derived* correlations. Frege seems not to have been much concerned with the distinction between derived and non-derived correlations, and it is quite implausible to suppose that the correlation of sentences with truth-values is a non-derived correlation: if it were, it would be impossible to understand a sentence without knowing whether it was true. Russell, however, *is* plausibly understood as having been concerned with this contrast, and as having thought that at least some correlations of sentences with propositions would be non-derived. And it seems that a *non-derived* correlation can only intelligibly be made between a linguistic item and something non-linguistic which *actually* exists, rather than one which is merely possible.[10] Russell seems to have thought that there can only be an appropriate correlate of a sentence if the relevant proposition actually exists — that is to say, if the sentence is true. And this means that he had to give up the theory which provided him with an account of the unity of sentences.

The problem here can be rephrased like this. Despite the fact that Russell himself restricted the class of singular terms, properly so-called, to linguistic expressions whose meaning really does depend on their being correlated with an object — thereby preventing definite descriptions from counting as genuine singular terms — he seems, in effect, to have treated whole sentences as complex singular terms whose meaningfulness is to be explained in fundamentally the same way as the meaningfulness of genuine singular terms — that is, in terms of a non-derived correlation. It looks as if the natural solution to Russell's problem with the unity of the proposition is to reject this approach to whole sentences, and deny that their meaningfulness depends on correlations with extra-linguistic items. As we will see in Chapter 4, this is indeed the approach Wittgenstein adopted.

2E THE UNITY OF THE PROPOSITION AND THE MULTIPLE-RELATION THEORY OF JUDGEMENT

In the face of the difficulty with false sentences — as well as some others[11] — Russell himself seems, in effect, to have reverted to something akin to the Lockean account of the unity of sentences.[12] In *Principia Mathematica*, written with Alfred North Whitehead, we find him denying that propositions are among the basic unities of the world — even when the sentences they correspond to are true. One reason for holding the early account of propositions is that it supplies a pleasantly simple account of propositional-attitude constructions. For example, suppose we say:

(5) Othello believes that Desdemona loves Cassio.

This is naturally parsed as involving a two-place, or 'dual', relation (believing) which holds between a thinker, Othello, and the object of his belief, *that Desdemona loves Cassio*. Russell's theory of propositions gives us precisely this analysis: the object of belief is the proposition that Desdemona loves Cassio — or, in the phrasing we used before, *Desdemona's loving Cassio*. In *Principia Mathematica*, Russell and Whitehead reject this simple view:

> When a judgment occurs, there is a certain complex entity, composed of the mind and the *various* objects of the judgment.
>
> (Whitehead and Russell 1927: 44; my emphasis)[13]

There is not a *single* object of judgement; there is rather a relation between a thinker and the *components* of possible propositions — in our case, between Othello, on the one hand, and the three entities, Desdemona, Cassio, and the relation of loving. Judgements involve *multiple* relations, rather than merely 'dual' relations (between a thinker and a single object of judgement). Russell and Whitehead remark:

> It follows from the above theory that a 'proposition', in the sense in which a proposition is supposed to be *the* object of a judgement, is a false abstraction, because a judgement has several objects, not one.
>
> (Whitehead and Russell 1927: 44; original emphasis).

And they continue:

> Owing to the plurality of the objects of a single judgement, it follows that what we call a 'proposition' (in the sense in which this is distinguished from the phrase expressing it) is not a single entity at all. That is to say, the phrase which expresses a proposition is what we call an 'incomplete' symbol; it does not have meaning in itself, but requires some supplementation in order to acquire a complete meaning.[14]
>
> (Whitehead and Russell 1927: 44)

What kind of supplementation might be provided? Russell and Whitehead say this:

> [W]hen I judge 'Socrates is human', the meaning is completed by the act of judging.
>
> (Whitehead and Russell 1927: 44)

This is Russell's famous 'multiple-relation' theory of judgement. It may have solved the problem of sentences to which no actual combination of extra-linguistic entities corresponds, but it brought other difficulties in its place. One is a problem of *order*.[15] There is a clear difference between (5) — which might explain Othello's jealousy — and the following claim:

(6) Othello believes that Cassio loves Desdemona.

Without something like (5), this would explain only pride or pity on Othello's part, not his jealousy. But if belief — like all judgement, on Russell's theory — involves a relation just between a believer and the various things, including relations, which the belief concerns, how are we to understand the difference? We can hardly say 'Othello stands in the believing relation to Cassio, loving, and Desdemona, *in that order*': words may have an order in any writing or speaking of them, but it is hard to make sense of judging itself ordering things.[16] And, in any case, the ordering even of words leads us back to the problem of the unity of the sentence. Words may be ordered in two ways: either for some extraneous purpose — as in alphabetical ordering, or ordering by number of letters — or because of the demands of grammar. Clearly the ordering of the words in (5) and (6) is not designed to suit any extraneous purpose: the ordering is here required by the grammar of English if we are to say precisely that. But grammatical requirements are always requirements for the construction of complete, unified sentences; this suggests that we will only be able to make sense of this kind of ordering of words insofar as we can make sense of the unity of sentences.

The multiple-relation theory of judgement faces difficulty on this score in any case, because it attempts to combine a Lockean, mental-act conception of the unity of sentences with an objective, world-oriented conception of the meaning of (most) words. As Russell himself later said:

> Suppose we wish to understand 'A and B are similar'. It is essential that our thought should, as is said, 'unite' or 'synthesize' the two terms and the relation; but we cannot *actually* "unite" them, since either A or B are similar, in which case they are already united, or they are dissimilar, in which case no amount of thinking can force them to become united.
>
> (1984: 116)

This confirms the initial thought (see section 2D) that it is difficult to combine an objective conception of the meaning of words with this subjective conception of what makes sentences unities.

One final difficulty for the multiple-relation theory is worth noting. At the time when he proposed it, Russell did not want to insist that there were, fundamentally, altogether different logical categories of thing. (This is something to which we will return in the next section.) So Desdemona, Cassio, and the relation of loving are all entities which are capable, in principle, of being *named* (by the names 'Desdemona', 'Cassio', and 'Loving', for example): they are all, in Russell's early terminology, *terms*. While we may think the relation of loving as being a fundamentally different type of entity from Desdemona and Cassio, on Russell's theory they are treated as being, in a sense, grammatically on a par. One advantage of the multiple-relation theory of judgement, from Russell's point of view at the time, is that it does not need there to be differences of logical type between the entities correlated with different kinds of word. These entities fit together, not because they belong together in unified, complete propositions, but because they are brought together by a mental act of a judging subject. In principle, a judging subject can unite or synthesize any group of entities whatever — or, at least (bearing in mind the last criticism mentioned), its ability to unite or synthesize groups of entities does not depend at all on their logical type.

Wittgenstein thought this consequence was unacceptable. He put the point in this way in his 1913 *Notes on Logic*:

> Every right theory of judgement must make it impossible for me to judge that 'this table penholders the book' (Russell's theory does not satisfy this requirement).
>
> (*NL*: 96)

The point recurs, slightly differently formulated, in the *Tractatus*:

> 5.5422 The correct explanation of the form of the proposition 'A judges p' must show that it is impossible to judge a nonsense. (Russell's theory does not satisfy this condition.)

What this shows is that something like the unity of the proposition must be accepted as a basic given, prior to any intervention by judgement. Some, but not all, combinations of words make up whole sentences, and only a whole grammatical sentence can be put in the 'p' position of a sentence of the form 'A judges p'.[17] This is a constraint on the possibilities of judgement which is quite independent of anything to do with the character of the judging subject; and it requires a notion of sentential or propositional unity which is independent of any consideration of acts of judgement.

The precise details of the history of Russell's view and the interpretation of various points of his work are a matter of some controversy, but it looks as if Russell was at least on the way to abandoning the multiple-relation theory of judgement in the face of such difficulties as these. In 1913 he set to work on a manuscript, provisionally entitled *Theory of Knowledge*, which incorporated what I think amounts to at least the beginnings of a revised theory of judgement, whatever Russell thought its status was.[18] In essence, this new theory does to sentences something akin to what the theory of descriptions does to singular terms. It suggests that, in many cases at least, sentences should not be regarded as *names* of combinations of entities. Instead, they implicitly involve existential quantifiers. As Russell puts it:

> The proposition [here: sentence[19]] 'a is before b' must be interpreted as meaning 'there is a complex in which a is earlier and b is later'.
>
> (1984: 135)

This brings with it what looks like a new theory of judgement: to judge that a is before b is really to judge that there is a complex in which a is earlier and b is later.

On the face of it, this seems a neat resolution of the problems which faced Russell's earlier two theories. We do not have the problem of falsity which faced the early account of propositions: sentences in general do not name complexes in which entities are combined, and judgements do not involve us directly in relations to such entities. A sentence can meaningfully assert the existence of a combination of entities, even if there is in fact no such combination; and a subject can believe that there is a certain combination of entities, even if there is none. And the unity of complexes is not dependent on our judgement: rather, we judge that there are such complexes, whose unity is wholly independent of any act of ours. Nor do we have the problem of ordering which afflicted the multiple-relation theory: where the order of singular terms matters in language, this can be taken to be an expression of the objective difference of position (in space and time, for example) of the correlative objects in a complex.[20]

Despite these attractions, Russell abandoned all attempts to provide a theory of judgement, including this proposal which I think amounts to a new theory. From all accounts, it appears that what made him abandon the subject was a criticism of Wittgenstein's. The criticism was made in person, but Wittgenstein later reformulated it in a brief letter dated June 1913:

> I can now express my objection to your theory of judgment exactly: I believe it is obvious that, from the prop[osition] 'A judges that (say) a is in the Rel[ation] R to b', if correctly analysed, the prop[osition] 'aRb. v.~aRb' must follow directly *without the use of any other premises*. This condition is not fulfilled by your theory.

> (CL: 29)

It is possible to understand this criticism as no more than a reformulation of the criticism we have already encountered, which was directed specifically against the multiple-relation theory of judgement. Interestingly, though, the criticism in the letter of June 1913 certainly applies to Russell's new theory, which the other does not obviously do. Intuitively, what someone judges when she judges that *aRb* is *that aRb*, and *that aRb* is, so to speak, something which can either be the case or not. But on Russell's new theory (as I take it to be), when someone judges that *aRb*, what she really judges is that there is an *R*-complex in which *a* fills one position and *b* fills the other. It is immediately clear that *that there is an R-complex in which a fills one position and b fills the other* is something which can either be the case or not; but we need a further premise — to the effect that an *R*-complex is a propositional complex — for it to be clear that the *complex itself* is something which can either be the case or not.

Is Wittgenstein's criticism (on this interpretation of it) sound? As will become clear in later chapters, Wittgenstein came to have reasons for objecting to accounts of language which required the logical or grammatical status of linguistic expressions to be specified. But there are reasons for thinking that, independently of those considerations, there is even more reason to be worried about Russell's new view than Wittgenstein makes explicitly clear. To see this, we need to introduce the notion of an atomic sentence. An atomic sentence is one which involves no logical connectives ('and', 'or', 'not', 'if ... , then ... ', and their formal counterparts, and the quantifiers). Russell notes a striking consequence of his theory (perhaps after reflection on an early form of Wittgenstein's criticism):

> The proposition [here: sentence] '*a* is before *b*' must be interpreted as meaning 'there is a complex in which *a* is earlier and *b* is later'. This involves the word 'and', which is one of the words that indicate *molecular* [i.e., non-atomic] complexes ... . This result is curious, for the *complex* '*a*-before-*b*' is atomic, and yet the corresponding *proposition* [i.e., sentence] is not atomic. It is not very easy to believe that such a difference can exist, and perhaps some other theory of 'sense' [i.e., direction] can be found which would avoid such a difference.
>
> (1984: 135)

A little reflection suggests that on Russell's new theory no sentence can be genuinely atomic.[21] That means that no apparently atomic sentence (such as Wittgenstein's '*aRb*') can have the form it seems to have, and we cannot define an atomic complex (such as the supposed *R*-complex in which *a* fills one position and *b* the other) as being propositional in form by saying that it is expressed by an atomic sentence of that form.[22] But if it is not propositional in virtue of having the form of a sentence, in what way can it be propositional? This makes the difficulty raised by Wittgenstein (if I have understood that correctly) look very deep. The problem is not merely that an extra premise needs to be added to ensure that the complex in question is propositional. The difficulty is that it is unclear what the complex's being propositional amounts to, if there is no sentence which can express it. It is not just that an extra premise is needed: it looks as if no extra premise will, in the end, be capable of doing the job.

It is worth dwelling for a moment on Russell's disquiet over the asymmetry between the atomicity of the complex and the molecularity of its expression. What Russell is here finding difficulty in swallowing is the suggestion that, for the case of atomic complexes, the form of language does not match the form of the world. As we will see, Wittgenstein's account in the *Tractatus* precisely does not face this difficulty.

2F THE UNITY OF THE PROPOSITION, THE CORRELATES OF WORDS, AND THE CONTEXT PRINCIPLE

If the unity of sentences is secured by an act of the mind, as it is on Locke's theory and on Russell's multiple-relation theory of judgement, then the grammar of words — how they combine to form sentences — is not of fundamental importance. What this means is that words do not need to be of fundamentally different kinds: or, at least, the difference of kind among words need only be a superficial difference. And if we have a conception of language according to which the fundamental linguistic expressions are meaningful in virtue of correlations with something extra-linguistic, there need be no fundamental difference in kind between the extra-linguistic items which are correlated with different kinds of word. This was both the decisive difficulty with the multiple-relation theory for Wittgenstein (as we have seen), and a crucial advantage in the theory for Russell.

Throughout the period of his most advanced technical work in philosophy, it is plausible to claim that Russell attempted to maintain the idea that there were not fundamental differences of logical category among the entities with which words are correlated. This can be seen as being central to the ramified theory of types, on which his logical construction of mathematics depended (at the time of *Principia Mathematica*, on which he collaborated with Whitehead).[23] But it is also to be found in his early work, *The Principles of Mathematics*. Recall the terminology of that work: the correlates in the world of linguistic expressions are *terms*; and among terms Russell distinguishes between *things* (the terms correlated with proper names) and *concepts* (the correlates of other expressions, including predicates). In the first place, Russell says:

> Every term, to begin with, is a logical subject: it is, for example, the subject of the proposition that [it] itself is one.
>
> (Russell 1903: 44)

A logical subject is an entity which a sentence may be *about*; it is something that may be referred to with a name. A little later Russell considers the following issue:

> It might be thought that a distinction ought to be made between a concept as such and a concept used as a term, between, *e.g.*, such pairs as *is* and *being*, *human* and *humanity*, *one* in such a proposition as 'this is one' and 1 in '1 is a number'.
>
> (Russell 1903: 45)

This is a little difficult to construe, but I take it that the entities Russell is considering here are all entities in the world, rather than linguistic items. So the question is whether 'is' and 'being', for example, are correlated with the *same* entity: whether, that is, *is* and *being* (the entities) are the same. Similarly, the proposition which Russell here refers to as the proposition 'this is one' is a unified entity in the world: in the style I used earlier, it is *this being one*. Note that Russell is here using the notion of a 'term' to refer to entities in the world only when they are acting as 'logical subjects'. In this use of 'term', an entity's being a term is contrasted with its being an *adjective*: and again, being an 'adjective' is not being a certain kind of *linguistic* entity; rather this is a way of referring to a worldly entity when that entity is playing a certain 'adjectival' — that is, qualifying — role.

Should, then, *one* (the entity which may figure as a qualifier, an 'adjective') be distinguished from 1 (the entity which may figure as a logical subject, a 'term')? Russell says that 'inextricable difficulties will envelop us' if we say that it should (1903: 45). Here is the argument:

> For suppose that *one* as adjective differed from 1 as term. In this statement [i.e., the statement made by this last sentence], *one* as adjective has been made into a term [because it is the logical subject]; hence either it has become 1, in which case the supposition is self-contradictory; or there is some other difference between *one* and 1 in addition to the fact that the first denotes a concept not a term while the second denotes a concept which is a term. But in this latter hypothesis, there must be propositions concerning *one* as term, and we shall still have to maintain propositions concerning *one* as adjective as opposed to *one* as term; yet all such propositions must be false, since a proposition about *one* as adjective makes *one* the subject, and is therefore really about *one* as term.
>
> (Russell 1903: 46)

This, therefore, is a fundamental reason for thinking that there are no fundamental differences in logical or grammatical kind between the entities which are correlated with different kinds of words. So long as they are entities, they must be capable of being logical subjects — what propositions are about — and that requires that they be what Russell calls *terms*.

This assimilation of all correlates of linguistic expressions to the same fundamental logical kind — they are all terms — can also be seen in the new theory of judgement of the 1913 manuscript (Russell 1984). The very idea of a *complex* is the idea of an entity, which may be a logical subject, which is in some way — even if it is, as we have seen, a curious way — a correlate of whole sentences. The same insistence on uniformity of logical type is found late as well as early in Russell's logical work.

In this, Russell's view is strikingly opposed to Frege's. Frege held that different kinds of subsentential expression correspond to entities in the world of radically different kinds. Singular terms (such as proper names) refer to *objects*, according to Frege: objects are distinctive in being 'saturated', or complete. On Frege's view, predicates refer to a special kind of function, which he called a 'concept'. Fregean 'concepts' are 'unsaturated', or incomplete — in just the same way as a predicate may be thought to have one or more gaps which can be filled by singular terms to form whole sentences.[24] This led Frege into a paradox which is not unlike the paradox which we have just seen leading Russell to insist that there are no fundamental differences of logical type between the entities which different kinds of expression are correlated with. Frege wants to insist that 'concepts', the correlates of predicates, are wholly different in kind from objects, the correlates of singular terms. Consider, in particular, the case of the 'concept' *horse* — the correlate of the predicate '*x* is a horse'. Frege seems committed to *this*:

(CH1) The concept *horse* is not an object.

The problem is that the phrase 'the concept *horse*' functions grammatically like a singular term (at least on Frege's grammar). But that means that, if it refers to anything at all, what it refers to is an *object*, not a 'concept'. It thus becomes impossible for Frege to state truly the fundamental distinction between objects and 'concepts'. In fact, so long as predicates are taken to refer to entities at all, it looks as if it will be difficult for Frege to say *what* predicates are correlated with, and hence to say what predicates mean.[25] The following, for example, cannot truly say what Frege wants it to say:

(CH2) The predicate '*x* is a horse' refers to the concept *horse*.

For the phrase 'the concept *horse*' can only refer to an object, if it refers to anything at all; and no object can be what the predicate '*x* is a horse' refers to.

Frege's response to this problem is infamous:

> By a kind of necessity of language, my expressions, taken literally, sometimes miss my thought; I mention an object, when what I intend is a concept. I fully realize that in such cases I was relying upon a reader who would be ready to meet me half-way — who does not begrudge a pinch of salt.

> (Frege 1892b: 204)

Russell was dismissive of this: he says, 'Frege's theory ... will not, I think, bear investigation' (Russell 1903: 510).

But Frege's commitment to his view, despite its paradoxical nature, is not unmotivated. It derives from the following claim about linguistic items and the entities with which they are correlated — a claim of *correspondence of grammar*:

> (CG) The different grammar of different categories of linguistic expression must be matched by differences between the entities with which they are correlated.

(CG) is bound to create difficulties, since the expressions 'the concept *horse*' and '*x* is a horse' are themselves grammatically different, but both expressions must be correlated with the same entity if the meaning of predicates is to be explained by their being correlated with entities in the first place. But as long as we hold that the meaning of both singular terms and predicates essentially involves some correlation with non-linguistic entities, it is hard to see how we can abandon (CG) — at least for the case of some expressions for which the same problems will arise — without adopting some quasi-Lockean account of the unity of sentences.

On a view like Locke's, the unity which underlies the unity of a sentence is created by an act of judgement: the words themselves need contain nothing which makes them suited to fit together in the way they do; and nor does any comparable suitability for combination need to be found in the correlates of those words. To put the point a little crudely, the grammar of sentences is not to be explained by what is to be found in either the words themselves or their extra-linguistic correlates: it derives just from the act of judgement. Once we abandon that kind of view, however, we have to accept that parts of sentences can only combine together grammatically if they are, in some way, fit by nature to be so combined. If we think the parts are meaningful only in virtue of a correlation with something extra-linguistic, it is natural to think that it is only in the correlation, or else in what is required for the correlation to be possible at all, that the various linguistic items come to be suited to their various grammatical roles. But correlation itself is so brute an association that the correlating itself cannot provide grammar. Rather, we must suppose that grammar involves some kind of relation between linguistic items which are suited to form whole sentences, and non-linguistic items which have a matching capacity to fit together.

What we have here is, of course, just a particular application of the general point about the correlation assumption, (Corr), which was made when that assumption was first introduced (in section 2A, above). Since correlation cannot be a process of transformation, all it can do is enable linguistic items to *reflect* features of the extra-linguistic entities with which they are correlated. This means that features that we find in language in use must be either (i) irrelevant to meaning (because intrinsic features of intrinsically meaningless entities — marks and sounds), (ii) the mere fact of the signs being correlated with extra-linguistic entities, or (iii) reflections, in some way, of the nature of those extra-linguistic entities themselves. Grammar cannot be regarded as simply irrelevant to meaning; nor is an expression's having a particular grammar the mere fact of its being correlated with a particular entity. Consequently, the grammar of an expression must be a reflection of the nature of the extra-linguistic entity with which it is correlated, if there is one — or of the nature of the extra-linguistic entities with which it *can* be correlated, if no correlation has yet taken place.

Now that we have, in grammar, a specific instance of the way in which the correlation assumption, (Corr), entitles us to suppose that language reveals the nature of the world, it is as well to confront explicitly an issue which will have occurred to many when the idea was first broached. I have suggested that (Corr) requires that language *reflect* certain fundamental features of the world. It might be thought that this commits anyone who accepts (Corr) to a simple form of realism, where realism is understood in line with the definition I gave in Chapter 1, as a commitment to the following thesis:

(R) The nature of the world as it is in itself is altogether independent of anything to do with any thought or representation of it.[26]

But — focusing for the moment on the case of grammar — it is important to recognize that the idea of extra-linguistic categories being *reflected* in the grammar of language may be understood in any one of at least three ways. The first way is the most obvious one: we suppose that the world as it is in itself comes composed of items which are already, as it were, suited to be combined in certain ways with each other (grammatically, as it were). On this view, we suppose that correlating linguistic items with these items in the world enables the antecedently meaningless linguistic items simply to *borrow* from the items in the world their capacities for combination. On this first account, the grammar, so to speak, of the world, is basic, and language does no more than copy that.

This is the most obvious view, but it is possible to construct an alternative to it. On this alternative, we begin, as it were, with mere marks and sounds. Something has to happen to these to make them into meaningful words. What happens, on the alternative view, is that they are (either simultaneously or successively)[27] provided with a grammar and projected onto the world. This projection is, in effect, the projection of a grammar onto the world. The world as it is in itself has no grammar, on this second view, but in the establishment of mere marks and sounds as meaningful words, what we do is read a grammar into the world. And having read that grammar into the world, we find in this now grammatically viewed world items which can be proper correlates of the grammatical words which we have just created, and whose objective grammar (so to speak) the words themselves can now reflect.

Both of these two views are realist, on the conception of realism which I defined in the last chapter (commitment to (R)). In the case of the first view, the nature of the world as it is in itself includes a worldly correlate of grammar, from which the grammar of language can just be derived. In the case of the second view, the world as it is in itself does not contain any correlate of grammar: it is grammatically amorphous. But the second view permits us to make sense of what we might call a 'world of language' — not the world as it is in itself, but the world as it is reconceived by us in our construction of language, precisely to be a correlate for language. If we start to think of this 'world of language' as in some sense a real world, a separate entity, as it were, from the world as it is in itself, then we seem to have found something for which a realist view is inappropriate: the nature of this 'world of language' will not be altogether independent of anything to do with any thought or representation of it.

This second view is recognizably Kantian: it is realist with respect to the world as it is in itself, and idealist with respect to the 'world of language'.[28] But we can now imagine someone being sceptical about the possibility of describing the world as it is in itself, within this Kantian second view. If language can only talk about items which are suitable correlates for its grammatical categories, how can we talk about the world as it is in itself? And if we cannot even talk about the world as it is in itself, how can we even formulate this Kantian position? So we may be inclined to erase the Kantian world-as-it-is-in-itself from the picture, leaving ourselves just with the 'world of language', which now becomes the only world which we can describe as the world 'as it is in itself'. But since, on this third picture, the only world which we can think of as the world as it is in itself is still just the 'world of language', we now seem to be committed to a straight denial of (R): the nature of the world as it is in itself is *not* altogether independent of anything to do with any thought or representation of it. On the contrary: its nature is shaped by the projection of our grammar.[29]

We have here three completely different conceptions of the relation between language and the world. But they have this in common: they are all committed to (CG), for all its paradoxicality. (CG) itself is neutral between realist, Kantian, and idealist approaches to language.

Whichever way we turn on the question of realism, however, we have to recognize that whole sentences are, in a certain sense, basic in the nature of language. If the meaning of words has to include their grammar, the meaning of words must include the way in which they are capable of combining with other words to form whole sentences, since there is nothing to the grammar of words *other* than their capacity to combine in certain ways with other words to form whole sentences. So the whole sentence has to be presupposed in any account of the meaning of words. This led Frege to insist on his famous 'context principle'. He formulates this in various ways. Here is one version:

> [N]ever to ask for the meaning of a word in isolation, but only in the context of a proposition [i.e., sentence].[30]

And here is another:

> [It] is only in the context of a proposition [i.e., sentence] that words have any meaning.[31]

It's not entirely clear what this principle amounts to, or what, exactly, Frege needs for his arguments to work,[32] but it is possible to understand Frege as wanting to insist just on this:

(CP) There is no more to the meaning of a word than its contribution to the meanings of legitimately constructed sentences in which it may occur.

As we will see, Wittgenstein understood the basicness of the whole sentence more literally and more radically than Frege himself did.

2G LOGICAL FORM AND LOGICAL CONSTANTS

Frege and Russell, in their different ways, accepted versions of the two core assumptions about language, (Corr) and (Obj), which I identified in section 2A, and applied them to each of the three kinds of linguistic expression which it is natural to think are basic, on the Frege–Russell logical grammar. Singular terms are correlated with objects (Russell's 'things'), and predicates with 'concepts' (qualities and relations, according to Russell). The case of sentences is different, and more complicated, but surprisingly analogous claims are held here too. They are correlated with truth-values, according to Frege,[33] or propositions, according to the early Russell. And even in 1913, Russell seems to have thought that the world contained what we might think of as *counterparts* — if not, precisely, correlates — of whole sentences: when a sentence of the form 'aRb' is true, there will exist a *complex*, a-bearing-R-to-b, which is propositional in form.

But a whole category of expressions seems here to have been omitted from consideration. This is the category of expressions commonly referred to as 'logical constants' — such expressions as 'it is not the case that ... ', 'either ... or – ', 'if ... , then – ', ' ... and – '. An understanding of these expressions is crucial to the understanding of logic, which itself was a crucial concern of both Frege and Russell. Are these expressions to which (Corr) applies? Are they meaningful in virtue of a correlation with something extralinguistic, some entity in the world?

On Frege's mature view, these expressions are treated as being remarkably like predicates. As we have seen, on

Frege's view, the meaningfulness of predicates depends on their being correlated with a special kind of item in the world — what he calls *concepts*. These are essentially 'unsaturated' or incomplete entities. In fact, they are a special kind of function. A function, in general, is something which takes one or more objects as input (or *argument*), and yields a single object as output (or *value*). Different kinds of expression can refer to functions of different kinds. Thus 'the father of x' refers to a function (of being x's father): if you take a particular object (say Queen Elizabeth II) as input, or argument, you get a particular object (King George VI) as output, or value. The function referred to by the predicate 'x is a monarch' is of a particular kind, on Frege's view: if you take a particular object as argument, you get a very special kind of object — either the True or the False (according to whether the argument is a monarch or not) — as value. The 'logical constants' of Frege's logic — the formal counterparts to such expressions as 'it is not the case that ... ', 'either ... or – ', 'if ... , then – ', ' ... and – ' — also refer to functions, of another special kind. These functions are called *truth-functions*: they take the truth-values of one or more sentences as arguments, to yield the truth-value of a compound sentence as their value. On Frege's view, function-expressions in general are meaningful in virtue of being correlated with a particular kind of entity — an entity which is 'unsaturated' or incomplete. The same will then be true of the 'logical constants': they will be correlated with similarly incomplete entities, the truth-functions.

This kind of view is the direct provocation for some of Wittgenstein's most fundamental thoughts (including the one which he himself calls his 'fundamental thought': *TLP*: 4.0312). And it has deep roots, with a very general philosophical significance. Logic is naturally thought to be an *a priori* discipline in the following sense: we do not find out by experiment or experience what follows from what. It is tempting to suppose that this epistemic point — which concerns how we *know* about logic — is underpinned by a metaphysical claim, which we might call the thesis of the *world-independence* of logic. We might formulate that metaphysical thesis as follows:

(WIL) Logic does not depend on anything in particular being the case.

(WIL) might also be thought to explain the apparent *necessity* of logic: what holds in logic holds in every possible world. Both (WIL) and the claim that logic is *a priori* are concerned with the status of what we might call logical *truths*: they are not truths *about* the world, and we do not need to *experience* their truth in order to know that they are true. But these claims are naturally thought to require a more radical kind of independence from the world: they cannot depend on any kind of acquaintance with the world.

The issues here reach right back into the philosophical tradition: we will be looking at those links further in the next section. But enough has already been said to make Frege's view of the 'logical constants' seem puzzling. Frege's view seems to make logic depend on something in the world: the special entities known as truth-functions. And our understanding of logic seems bound then to depend on some kind of intuition of, or acquaintance with, these entities.

Russell was certainly exercised over these issues. He seems to be advocating a version of the world-independence thesis, and rejecting Frege's theory, in this remark in his 1913 *Theory of Knowledge* manuscript:

A proposition which mentions any definite entity, whether universal [such as a quality or relation] or particular, is not logical: no one definite entity, of any sort or kind, is ever a constituent of any truly logical proposition.[34]

This seems clearly to deny that there are any 'logical' entities. What are we to make of the so-called 'logical constants', then? Here is what Russell says:

'Logical constants', which might seem to be entities occurring in logical propositions, are really concerned with pure *form*, and are not actually constituents of the propositions in the verbal expression of which their names occur.[35]

We might note a certain ambivalence here. 'Logical constants' are not entities, are not constituents of propositions, but are nevertheless named. We will see this ambivalence recurring later.

What is this 'pure form'? Russell considers the following 'pure logical proposition', derived by removing the reference to its constituents from 'if Socrates is human, and whatever is human is mortal, then Socrates is mortal':

Whatever x and α and β may be, if x is α and whatever is α is β, then x is β.

And he comments:

Here there is no longer any constituent corresponding to Socrates and humanity and mortality: the only thing that has been preserved is the pure *form* of the proposition, and the form is not a 'thing', not another constituent along with the objects that were previously related in that form.
(Russell 1984: 98)

And he continues a few sentences later:

It is obvious, in fact, that when *all* the constituents of a complex have been enumerated, there remains something which may be called the 'form' of the complex, which is the way in which the constituents are combined in the complex. It is such pure 'forms' that occur in logic.
(Russell 1984: 98)

And he suggests a possible way of characterizing such pure forms:

Take, for example, the proposition 'Socrates precedes Plato'. This has the form of a dual complex: we may naturally symbolize the form by 'xRy' .... When we have reached the form 'xRy', we have effected the utmost generalization which is possible starting from 'Socrates precedes Plato'.
Russell 1984: 98

There are two crucial things to note about this. First, forms are not *entities*, and are therefore naturally represented by means of variables (one in place of each singular term, and one in place of each predicate: we should note, though, the oddity of describing variables as involving 'generalization'). Second, forms are forms of *complexes*: that is to say, they are forms of the propositional entities which are, in some sense, the counterparts of sentences. (The complex, *Socrates preceding Plato*, will be the counterpart of the sentence 'Socrates precedes Plato', although it will not be the correlate of the sentence, in the way that objective propositions would have been on Russell's original view — for reasons which we considered in section 2E.) The idea seems to be to secure the world-independence of logic by claiming that logic is concerned with forms of complexes, and not with entities of any kind.

Unfortunately, Russell seems not to have been able to hold on to this view. What caused him trouble was a certain epistemological fact: we know (to take the latest example) how Socrates, Plato, and precedence can be combined to form a complex. Russell thinks that we could not possibly know that, unless we were *acquainted* with the form of the complex (Russell 1984: 99). Russell accepts that 'acquaintance' may here be being used in an 'extended sense' (Russell 1984: 99), but it is unclear that this 'extension' of sense is enough to remove the difficulty which is brought in with the introduction of the notion of acquaintance. The difficulty is that for Russell acquaintance is the relation which holds between a person, on the one hand, and the objective correlate of some fundamental feature of language, on the other, in virtue of which the person is able to understand the meaning of the feature of language. By supposing that we are acquainted, even in an 'extended sense', with the forms of complexes, Russell seems forced to treat these forms as a kind of very abstract object.

It is hard not to read Russell's description of the acquaintance involved here as expressing an awkward half-consciousness of this point. When he says that 'acquaintance' may be being used in an 'extended sense', the extension seems to be needed because we are dealing with 'something as abstract as the pure form' — that is, because of the *abstractness* of the object of acquaintance, not its not really being an object. And the following remark is also revealing:

> As a matter of introspection, it may often be hard to detect such acquaintance; but there is no doubt that, especially where very abstract matters are concerned, we often have an acquaintance which we find it difficult to isolate or become acquainted with.
>
> (Russell 1984: 99)

There is no hint here that the object of this 'extended' acquaintance is any less of an object than the acquaintance itself is.

This pressure exerted by the notion of acquaintance is naturally understood as the reason for Russell changing his canonical way of expressing form. Whereas before, as we have seen, the form of 'Socrates precedes Plato' is given by an expression involving variables, 'xRy', Russell soon makes the form a *fact* — 'the fact that there are entities that make up complexes having the form in question' (Russell 1984: 114). His final expression of the form no longer involves *variables*, but *quantifiers*: instead of 'xRy' we have 'something has some relation to something' (Russell 1984: 114).[36]

What is here implicit becomes explicit when Russell returns to the notion of form a few pages later:

> It will be remembered that, according to our theory of the understanding of propositions, the pure form is always a constituent of the understanding-complex, and is one of the objects with which we must be acquainted in order to understand the proposition ... . Since we desired to give the name 'form' to genuine objects rather than symbolic fictions, we gave the name to the 'fact' 'something is somehow related to something'. If there is such a thing as acquaintance with forms, as there is good reason to believe that there is, then a form must be a genuine object; on the other hand, such absolutely general 'facts' as "something is somehow related to

something" have no constituents, are unanalyzable, and must accordingly be called simple.

(Russell 1984: 129)

Here, unambiguously, forms are constituents on a par with the ordinary objects and relations which we expect to find in a Russellian analysis of judgement. And Russell himself has already offered what looks a decisive objection to any such theory:

[The form] cannot be a new constituent, for if it were, there would have to be a new way in which it and the other two constituents are put together, and if we take this way as again a constituent, we find ourselves embarked on an endless regress.

(Russell 1984: 98)

Russell seems to have ended up in a predicament not wholly unlike Frege's predicament with concepts and objects. The character of the notion of acquaintance, which Russell introduces to deal with a striking epistemic fact, seems to have forced him to treat forms as objects — even though he has compelling reason not to think of them in that way.

And forms are not the only objects which Russell finds himself led to introduce by the requirements of the notion of acquaintance, in order to make sense of logic:

Besides the forms of atomic complexes, there are many other logical objects which are involved in the formation of non-atomic complexes. Such words as *or*, *not*, *all*, *some*, plainly involve logical notions; and since we can use such words intelligently, we must be acquainted with the logical objects involved.

(Russell 1984: 99)

This treatment by Russell of the logical constants combined with his treatment of 'pure forms' to provoke Wittgenstein to some of the most striking and fundamental claims of the *Tractatus'* conception of language.[37] He thought that no kind of acquaintance was needed for logic, and that there were no 'logical objects' which corresponded to the logical constants. This is all part of his commitment to what we have called the thesis of the *world-independence* of logic.[38] That thesis is also connected with the project in the philosophy of mathematics which Russell took over from Frege: indeed, its motivation can be more clearly shown in that context.

2H FREGE AND RUSSELL ON MATHEMATICS

Russell's treatment of logical constants and forms — as objects of a special kind of acquaintance — is, in fact, in tension with the approach to the philosophy of mathematics which he took over from Frege. Russell and Frege shared a commitment to *logicism* about mathematics — the view that mathematics depends on nothing but logic. This view, and the large philosophical issues with which it is concerned, can be seen as the original root of the general philosophical outlook presented in the *Tractatus*. Indeed, it is not unnatural to think that the problems arising through this approach to mathematics played a significant role even in Wittgenstein's adoption of the conception of language which eventually came to shape the book. The *Notebooks*, in which the thoughts which were to find expression in the *Tractatus* were first worked out, begin not with any general thoughts about language, but with this famous remark:

> Logic must take care of itself.
>
> (*NB*: 2; *TLP*: 5.473)

This remark can be seen as an expression both of the world-independence thesis (WIL), which we considered in the last section, and the view that logic is an *a priori* discipline, requiring no experience of the world. Wittgenstein's concern with these issues arises directly from the context of Frege's and Russell's logicism about mathematics. Logicism about mathematics is the link between Wittgenstein's conception of logic and the whole philosophical tradition.

The significance of logicism about mathematics can be traced back to Kant. Kant was concerned to defend the possibility of metaphysics, on a certain understanding of that notion. On this understanding, metaphysics is the study of how the world must be: that is, it aims to provide truths which are both necessary and genuinely about the world. In order to be necessary, Kant thought they had to be *a priori*: presupposed, in some way, in all thought. But in order to be genuinely about the world, they could not be simply the product of the analysis of the concepts which we bring to the world: they could not, that is, be *analytic*. So the possibility of metaphysics seemed to Kant to depend on the possibility of there being truths which were both *synthetic* (not analytic, not simply the result of analysing the concepts involved) and *a priori*. In insisting on truths of this kind Kant was opposing Hume, for whom necessary truths simply reflected our concepts, and were (when seen from an appropriately lofty point of view) ultimately trivial.

It was not just on theoretical grounds that Kant thought that there could be synthetic *a priori* truths: he thought that there were actual examples. He thought that mathematical truths were clear examples of such truths, since, on the one hand, they were both necessary and not known by experiment, and, on the other, they both had clear application to the real world (we can count real things; we can apply geometry to items in the space around us), and were non-trivial. Kant's philosophy of mathematics was therefore central to his general conception of the relation between thought and the world. On Kant's view, mathematical truths depended on a co-operation between two faculties: the faculty of sensibility, which provides one with a kind of acquaintance ('intuition') of the world (even if it is a kind of pre-experiential *a priori* intuition, and of no more than the world as a spatio-temporal entity); and the faculty of understanding, which contributes the laws of thinking.

Frege, in opposition to Kant, aimed to show that mathematics (or rather, arithmetic: he was not opposed to Kant on geometry) did not depend on any kind of intuition or acquaintance: he claimed that it depended on nothing but logic, with something like the thesis of the world-independence of logic being simply assumed. Frege took his view to mean that arithmetic was analytic, rather than synthetic. Of course, his view required an enrichment both of the notion of the analytic — it can no longer be thought of as a realm of ultimately trivial truths — and of logic. Frege developed a new logical system, which is now, in effect, modern logic: he claimed that this logic alone was enough to generate all of arithmetic.

Arithmetic is based on a small set of axioms. These were first formalized by Richard Dedekind, and a little later by Giuseppe Peano, after whom they are now named. Here is an informal expression of the version of these axioms which is now generally used:[39]

> (Pe1) 0 is a natural number;
> (Pe2) The successor of any natural number is a natural number;
> (Pe3) 0 is not the successor of any natural number;
> (Pe4) No natural number is the successor of more than one natural number;
> (Pe5) If 0 has a property, and the successor of any natural number with that property also has it, then all natural numbers have it.

There are two basic things to note about these axioms. The first is that at their core is a description of the formal pre-suppositions of the procedure of counting (the natural numbers are the counting numbers), which brings with it the notion of a *successor*. And the second is that, in the form they have here (and were taken to have by Frege and Russell), they imply a simple (if extensive) ontology: the natural numbers are taken to be objects. If we accept these basic points at face value, showing that arithmetic derives from logic alone is going to involve the following task: we will need to show that there are some objects (the natural numbers) whose existence depends on logic alone (which would make them 'logical objects'[40]), and which have the properties necessary to underwrite the procedure of counting.

How could there be objects which depended on logic alone, and which had the crucial properties necessary to underwrite arithmetic? Frege's answer depends on the following thought: at the heart of logic is the notion of predication, and predication itself is enough to generate objects of the appropriate kind. The idea (in modern terminology) is that every predicate defines a class: the class of things of which the predicate is true (so, for example, the predicate 'x is a pen' defines the class of pens). This class in turn is an object to which predicates apply. So predication alone is enough to introduce a special kind of object, a class; and the notion of a class can be used to generate arithmetic. In the first place, it is possible to construct a series of classes with increasing numbers of members. Here is one way (close to Frege's own[41]), characterized intuitively. Let us define a class as the class of those objects which are not identical with themselves, the class of those objects of which the predicate '$x \neq x$' is true; there are no such objects, so this class is an (the) empty class. Importantly, this class can be recognized as having no members without recourse to experience: it is a matter of logic alone that that there can be nothing which is not identical with itself. Once we have this first class, constructed, apparently, from logic alone, we can proceed with the construction of a whole series of classes. That first class, although empty, is itself an object; there is a predicate 'x is the empty class' which applies to it. That predicate can be used to define a class, the class whose sole member is the empty class. We have now introduced two classes: the empty class, and a class with just one member. These two classes themselves are objects, and can be collected together to form a third class — a class with two members. It is intuitively clear that this series can be extended indefinitely, with each item in the series being a class with one more member than the item which precedes it.

Such a series provides us with something which at least mirrors the basic arithmetical notion of succession, but it is not the series of numbers themselves. What we want is not the class itself, at each stage in the series, but the number of items in the class — what we might call the *number of the class*. In order to capture this, Frege exploits the notion of equinumerousness, or same-numberedness. We can ask of two classes whether they have the same number of members as each other, or are equinumerous. The notion of equinumerousness can, in fact, be defined without talking about numbers at all: two classes are equinumerous if it is possible to pair each member of one class with exactly one member of the other, and vice versa; and this is something that can be explained entirely in terms of quantificational logic together with the notion of identity. If we return to our original series of classes with increasing numbers of members, we can obviously associate with that series a series of collections of classes — the classes which are equinumerous with the classes in the original series. It is, in effect, this latter series — the series of collections of classes which are equinumerous with the original series — that Frege identifies with the series of natural numbers. The number of a class, on Frege's view, is the class of classes which are equinumerous with the appropriate class in the original series. So the number 0 is the class of classes which are equinumerous with the first class in our original series (the class of things which are not identical with themselves). The number 1 is the class of classes which are equinumerous with the second class in our original series. And so on. The series of natural numbers, according to Frege, is a series of classes of classes.

By this means Frege took himself to have vindicated the claim that numbers are objects. First, he has given a meaning to phrases of the form 'the number of ... ', so as to conform to the following equivalence:

(E) The number of class C_1 = the number of class C_2 if and only if class C_1 is *equinumerous* with class C_2.

Phrases of the form 'the number of ... ' have the grammar of singular terms, on Frege's theory. Since a properly meaningful singular term must refer to an object, there must be objects referred to by phrases of the form 'the number of … '; and these objects must be numbers. Second, he has actually identified a range of objects for numbers to be: it is a range of classes, with classes being objects whose existence depends on nothing more than the meaningfulness of the predicates which define them.

Whatever its artificiality (do we really think that numbers are classes?), Frege's definition of number seems enough to form the basis of a complete construction of arithmetic: we can use it to derive the Peano axioms. Unfortunately for Frege, at the very moment when his logicist project was coming to formal fruition, Russell pointed out to him that his system was contradictory (Frege 1980: 130–31). The problem was with one of the key assumptions designed to show that the whole construction depends just on logic, the assumption that any predicate could be used to define a special kind of object, a class. The problem comes from the fact that there is nothing in Frege's system to stop the predicate which defines a class being applied to that class itself, and, as Russell showed, this leads to a paradox. To see this, consider first the predicate 'is a member of itself'. If we accept this as a coherent predicate, it applies truly to classes which are members of themselves — the class of things which are not pens, for example (since that class is not itself a pen) — and falsely to everything else. Those other things seem to be picked out by a different predicate — the predicate 'is not a member of itself'. Now suppose this last predicate defines a class: the class of things (classes) which are not members of themselves. Call this class S. Let us ask: is S a member of itself? That is: does the predicate 'is a member of itself' apply truly or falsely to the class S? Suppose, first, that S *is* a member of itself: since to be a member of itself it must meet the condition imposed by the predicate 'is not a member of itself', it must then *not* be a member of itself. So if it *is* a member of itself it is *not* a member of itself. So suppose, instead, that S is not a *not* a member of itself. But not being a member of itself is enough to meet the condition imposed by the predicate 'is not a member of itself', which means that S qualifies as a member of itself. So if S is *not* a member of itself, then it *is* a member of itself. We have a contradiction. It seems that the moment we allow ourselves to formulate a predicate such as 'is not a member of itself', and allow such a predicate to define a class, we are going to be in trouble.

Russell himself did not abandon either the logicist project in general, or, in particular, the attempt to ground mathematics in the theory of classes: instead he tried to deal with the paradox by restricting the manner of construction of classes, and the range of admissible predicates. More specifically, he took classes to be constructed in a hierarchy: at the base were individuals; at the next stage were classes of individuals; at the next stage, classes of classes of individuals, and so on. Classes could only have members from lower stages in the hierarchy, so the idea of a class either being or not being a member of itself became simply unintelligible. Correlatively (since exactly similar paradoxes arise with the notion of a property of not being possessed by itself, or with the notion of a predicate such as '*x* does not apply to itself'), predicates could only be meaningfully applied to objects at lower levels in a hierarchy of objects; so the predicate '*x* does not apply to itself' is counted as simply meaningless. This theory — Russell's 'theory of types' — may have avoided the paradoxes, but it had the result that features common to different levels of the hierarchy became uncapturable (since any attempt to capture them would involve a predicate which disobeyed the hierarchy restrictions). And it also meant that extra axioms, of uncertain status, had to be introduced to generate all of arithmetic.[42] These extra axioms are not obviously a matter just of logic; so the final status of the construction, as a defence of logicism about mathematics, is correspondingly unclear.

Wittgenstein was clearly convinced of the central tenet of logicism about mathematics: that mathematics depended on no intuition of or acquaintance with the world, however general or abstract such an intuition might be; and consequently that mathematical truths were not synthetic, in Kant's sense. This is an application to the case of mathematics of the general view of necessity which underlies the thesis of the world-independence of logic. But he was not impressed by the attempt to construct a pseudo-world of 'logical objects', which seemed to provide one with something which only intuition could offer, though without appealing to intuition. His rejection of the class-theoretic construction of arithmetic was at least parallel to his rejection of the idea of special logical objects of acquaintance which were counterparts to the familiar logical constants.

If we think of the *Tractatus* as being motivated in part by a desire to maintain some form of the logicism which he inherited from Frege and Russell, and with it a rejection of the idea of mathematics as a realm of synthetic *a priori* truth, we can see a larger, and more generally philosophical purpose to the work. Just as Kant tried to make sense of metaphysics, in general, as requiring synthetic *a priori* truths, so we can see the *Tractatus* as an attempt to make sense of what is necessarily true of the world — in general, and not just in the mathematical case — *without* appealing to synthetic *a priori* truths. If we pursue this line of thought, the *Tractatus* begins to look like a work whose concern is with the same field of problems, broadly speaking, as Kant's work is, although it offers a radically different solution to them.

3

THE GENERAL THEORY OF REPRESENTATION

3A WITTGENSTEIN'S STARTING POINT

The grand metaphysical theory with which the *Tractatus* begins is nothing but what is required, on Wittgenstein's view, by the very possibility of language. But what, exactly, does that require? In the light of the work of Frege and Russell, Wittgenstein will have found himself with two fundamental assumptions and a pair of problems. The two fundamental assumptions are the *correlation* assumption and the *objectivity* assumption which were identified in the previous chapter:

(Corr) Languages depend for their meaningfulness on correlations between certain linguistic items, on the one hand, and extra-linguistic items, on the other.

(Obj) The extra-linguistic items with which those linguistic items have to be correlated for languages to be meaningful are items in the world (objects).

(Corr), or something very close to it, seems just obvious:[1] it is what underlies the claim, which has been accepted almost without question at least since Aristotle, that languages are systems of signs. And (Obj) seems forced on us once we accept the general orientation towards the world which comes with Frege's rejection of psychologism: it is correlations with items in the world which make languages meaningful, not associations with things in speakers' minds.

And the two problems which Wittgenstein faced are these:

(P1)   Which linguistic items need to be correlated with things in the world for languages to be meaningful?

(P2)   How is the unity of the sentence to be explained?

These problems need a little explanation. In the case of (P1), an issue arises for each of the three basic kinds of expression in a Fregean grammar: singular terms, predicates, and sentences. Singular terms are naturally just defined to be terms whose meaningfulness depends on their being correlated with particular, individual objects. The question then is which, if any, expressions of ordinary language (and other symbol systems) should be counted as singular terms. Frege had been generous in his inclusion of ordinary expressions: in particular, he counted ordinary proper names and definite descriptions as singular terms. The problem, then, was to understand how an expression of this kind could have meaning, if there was no real object with which it was correlated. Frege's use of his technical notion of 'sense' provided a solution to the problem whose merits were, at best, unclear. With his theory of descriptions, Russell found a way to be more sparing in what he counted as a singular term. In fact, neither definite descriptions nor ordinary proper names were included. The category of singular terms — what Russell himself would call 'logically proper names' — was restricted to those terms which are correlated with items with which we are acquainted. These will be items about whose existence we cannot be mistaken, so an expression will only be counted as a singular term when we can be sure that there really is an object with which it is correlated.

The problem with the case of predicates is clear from Frege's difficulty with the concept *horse*, together with the difficulties which seem to face Russell's alternative approach. Predicates are naturally understood to be in some sense incomplete, to contain in them a gap where a singular term may be placed. This thought reflects the fact that the predicate in Frege's grammar contains the copula, or the verb, which has traditionally been seen to be what is responsible for the binding together of the parts of a sentence to form a single unity. The difficulty can be seen if we consider whether, *if* predicates are meaningful in virtue of being correlated with some entity in the world, the entity in question itself incorporates some counterpart to the sentence-unifying grammar which predicates are traditionally understood to have. If it does — if the worldly counterpart to a predicate is itself an incomplete entity — we have Frege's problem with the concept *horse*: it will, at best, be impossible to say what the predicate refers to, by actually using the concept of reference, since every attempt to do that will inevitably treat the worldly counterpart to the predicate as a *complete* entity.[2] If, on the other hand, we adopt Russell's solution, and treat the worldly counterparts of predicates as being no different at the level of the most fundamental logical category from the worldly counterparts of singular terms — they will all just be *objects* (Russell's 'terms') — then we seem unable to make sense of the grammar of predicates: how do these linguistic items have the sentence-unifying grammar which they seem to have? It looks, on the face of it, as if any way of correlating predicates with items in the world will lead to serious problems, so long as we continue to think that predicates are the agents of the unification of sentences.

As for sentences themselves, the differing views of Frege and Russell again serve as a warning. Frege and Russell both at some point took the meaningfulness of sentences to require correlations with entities in the world.[3] In Frege's case, the entities were odd in themselves — the True and the False — and provided no distinction in meaning among all the true sentences, on the one hand, or all the false sentences, on the other. In his early theory, Russell took sentences to be correlated with 'propositions' — sentence-like worldly counterparts of sentences. But this faced the difficulty that it was hard to make sense of there really being such sentence-like counterparts of false sentences.[4] In response to this, Russell moved to his 'multiple-relation' theory of judgement, thereby abandoning the thought that sentences need to be correlated with entities in the world — and he then faced difficulties making sense of the unity of sentences.

In addition to the versions of problem (P1) which arise in the case of singular terms, predicates, and sentences, there is another class of expressions which is crucial to Frege's system, but about which neither Frege nor Russell had anything very significant to say. What are we to make of the logical constants — the formal counterparts of such expressions as 'if', 'not', 'and', and 'or' — or the quantifiers (which correspond to 'all' and 'some')? In the *Theory of Knowledge* manuscript, Russell at least acknowledged that some explanation needed to be given of the meaning of these expressions, and quickly (if rather vaguely) assumed that there must be 'logical objects' with which they are correlated. But this is problematic, for reasons which will be considered in some detail in Chapter 5.

So much for the various forms of problem (P1). Problem (P2) — over the explanation of the unity of the sentence — is not wholly unconnected with them. If languages are meaningful in virtue of a correlation between linguistic items and something extra-linguistic, it is natural to think that the distinctive unity and completeness of sentences must mirror some extra-linguistic unity (even if the extra-linguistic unity is itself no more than a projection of a linguistic unity).[5] But where is that extra-linguistic unity to be found? It seems that it cannot be something created by an act of judgement — as Locke, and the Russell of the 'multiple-relation' theory held — since that looks incompatible with the generally world-directed conception of language enshrined in (Obj). And it is not immediately obvious how it can be anything in the world, since it is hard to see how there could be any appropriate extra-linguistic unities in the case of *false* sentences. In fact, it seems that this problem lies behind the form of problem (P1) which arises in the case of predicates. Finding a counterpart in the world to the sentence-unifying grammar which is traditionally assigned to predicates belongs with the early Russell's solution to the problem of explaining the unity of the sentence — and therefore seems to require the postulation of objective sentential counterparts even to false sentences. On the other hand, supposing that the worldly correlates of predicates have nothing in them which corresponds to the distinctive grammar of predicates seems — on the face of it, at least — to force us to adopt the Lockean, act-of-judgement account of the unity of sentences.

We can take it that Wittgenstein adopted (Corr) and (Obj) as the only thing to think about language, and that, as a result, he faced problems (P1) and (P2) in these uncomfortable forms. The theory of language of the *Tractatus* can then be seen as his solution to them. That theory is the application to language of a general theory of representation. The rest of this chapter will be concerned with the general theory; we will deal with the application of the general theory to the case of language in the next chapter.

3B THE PARIS COURTROOM MODEL

The core of Wittgenstein's new theory of language is presented in this famous remark in the notebook he was writing in September 1914:

> In the proposition a world is as it were put together experimentally. (As when in the law-court in Paris a motor-car accident is represented by means of dolls, etc.)

> (*NB*: 7)

The reference in the parenthesis is apparently to something which Wittgenstein read about in a magazine.

This courtroom model seems to have been the inspiration for what has come to be known as Wittgenstein's 'picture' theory of language. But the term 'picture' here can be misleading. It translates the German 'Bild', which does not mean quite the same. 'Bild', like 'picture', is applied primarily to visual representations, but it gets there by a different route: 'picture' is linked etymologically with painting, while 'Bild' is connected with the more general notions of composition and formation. This means that 'Bild' is naturally applied to models, which 'picture' is not. And, indeed, Wittgenstein is quite happy to use the word 'model' (German 'Modell') in presenting the 'picture' theory (*TLP*: 2.12). In describing Wittgenstein's theory, I will mostly talk of 'pictures or models', in order to prevent too easy an assimilation between the German word 'Bild' and the English word 'picture'.

In fact, if we are to understand what Wittgenstein is proposing, it is crucial to see that his account of language is really *rooted* in thought about models — like the model in the Paris courtroom. He was not struck by the so-called 'picture' theory after going to an art gallery, or looking at a book of sketches. It is significant that in his presentation of the theory of language in the *Tractatus* he says this:

3.1431 The essential nature of the propositional sign becomes very clear when we imagine it made up of spatial objects (such as tables, chairs, books) instead of written signs.

In understanding Wittgenstein's theory, we should not be looking for analogies between paintings or photographs, on the one hand, and sentences on the other. We should be trying to understand what is important about the kind of model in which we might be naturally described as 'putting a world together experimentally'.

So what exactly was it that suddenly struck Wittgenstein when he read about the courtroom model?[6] Well what might strike us? Let us imagine the model in a little detail. We can suppose that it might include something like a map or plan of the layout of the streets, painted on a large board; perhaps, even, some blocks (of wood, say) might be included to show the location of buildings, if these are relevant to what happened in the accident. All this is, as it were, the fixed part of the background. Now suppose that the accident involved three vehicles and two pedestrians. We will want some kind of model for each of the vehicles, and a little doll, or some other figure of an appropriate scale, for each of the pedestrians. These models are, as it were, loose: their position is not fixed in advance. What we do is put them in appropriate places on the model streets and model pavements, in order to indicate where the real cars and the real pedestrians were located on the real streets and pavements at the time of the accident.

When we consider such a model in this kind of detail, the most obvious thing about it is that the model cars and people are *movable*: we can put them in different places on the model streets and pavements. Now of course the way we move them — by lifting them up with our hands and putting them down somewhere else — is quite different from the way in which the real cars and people can move. But the positions they can end up in are not so different, once we allow for scale. The model cars and people are solid, spatial objects, describable by the geometry and general physics appropriate to such things; and so are the real cars and people. The range of positions on the base board in which the model cars and people can end up is exactly the same — allowing for a certain loss of detail due to the change of scale — as the range of positions on the real streets and pavements in which the real cars and people could have ended up. The possibilities of arrangement of the movable bits of the model are exactly the same as the possibilities of arrangement of the movable things — the real cars and people — in reality. This makes it possible for us to use the model to construct, experimentally, a way in which the real things might have been arranged.

This is the core of Wittgenstein's observation. The model is composed of a number of movable things arranged in a certain way. Each of the movable things in some sense stands for, or represents, a movable thing in the real world. And the range of ways in which the movable things in the model might be arranged is exactly the same — allowing for scale — as the range of ways in which the movable things in the real world might be arranged.

Movability is just possibility made vivid: what is movable *can actually* be differently located. And this vividness is what accounts for the inspiration provided by the courtroom model. But there are alternative possibilities even for what is fixed in a model: even what is fixed *could have* been differently located. So the actual location of the fixed parts of the courtroom model — the layout of the model streets and buildings — *could have* been otherwise. And the same morals, broadly speaking, apply to the fixed parts of the model as to the moving parts. Each of the fixed parts of the model stands for, or represents, a fixed thing in the real world. And the range of ways in which the fixed parts *could have* been arranged is the same — allowing for considerations of scale — as the ways in which the fixed things in the world *could have* been arranged. At this point, we can see that what holds most obviously for models with movable components might also be thought to apply to a very broad class of representations — including pictures as those are standardly understood. A painting from life, for example, may be composed of marks made with coloured paint on a sheet of canvas. Each of those marks, though not movable now, *could have* been placed differently on the canvas. And it is at least not absurd to suppose that each mark (of a certain size, at any rate) stands for, or represents, something in the real world. And then the range of ways in which the marks could have been arranged, while still counting as representing the same things in the world, might be thought to be the same as the range of ways in which the relevant things in the world could have been arranged.

This, I suggest, is exactly the reasoning which led Wittgenstein to the theory of language which is usually referred to as the 'picture theory', but which I prefer to describe as the theory that sentences are *models*. The Paris courtroom model is naturally taken to be capable of representing or depicting the traffic accident in virtue of the following three facts:

(PM1)   The model has movable components, and the real situation involves movable objects;

(PM2)   The movable components of the model can be correlated with the movable objects of the real situation;

(PM3)   The range of ways in which the movable components of the model can be positioned is the same as the range of ways in which the movable objects in reality are capable of being positioned.

If we generalize from movability to the more general notion of possibility, this suggests the following general conception of models:

(M1)   A model has components which could have been arranged otherwise, and real situations involve objects which could have been arranged otherwise;

(M2)   The components of a model can be correlated with objects in reality;

(M3)   The range of ways in which the components of a model could have been arranged is the same as the range of ways in which the correlated objects in reality could have been arranged.[7]

And this general conception of models is then taken by Wittgenstein to apply to all kinds of representation, including representation by what we ordinarily think of as pictures.

This is the core of Wittgenstein's view. But it is as well to note one peculiarity of Wittgenstein's use of language in the presentation of his theory, which will have some significance when we consider the case of language in the next chapter. So far we have rather loosely characterized Wittgenstein's view by using a more-or-less everyday notion of 'representation'. But Wittgenstein himself uses two distinct ranges of words in (broadly) systematically different ways. On the one hand are words linked with the German 'Darstellung':

these are naturally translated by means of some form of the English 'represent'. On the other hand, there are words linked with the German 'Bild' (picture, model). What is the point of Wittgenstein's difference of use?

Put simply, the point is this. The relationship between a picture or model (*Bild*) and reality is generally described by means of a cognate of the word 'Bild' itself, and is most naturally translated in English by means of some cognate of 'picture' (for example, 'pictorial', 'depict'). In these terms, the relationship between a model and reality is *pictorial*; the model *depicts* reality — and it may depict reality correctly or incorrectly. On the other hand, cognates of the word 'Darstellung' are used to describe *the way a model depicts reality as being*. If we use some cognate of the word 'represent' for this notion, we will say that a model *represents* that things are a certain way.[8] On this use of the notion of representation, no picture or model can represent something *incorrectly*: rather, *what* it represents may be correct or incorrect about the reality which the model depicts. Wittgenstein is generally (though not always) careful to use the two ranges of German words in these systematically different ways (an exception can be found at 2.173, and there are others at 4.04 and 4.12), but Ogden does not observe the difference in his translation (on this point the Pears and McGuinness is preferable). In quotations from the text I will continue to use the Ogden translation, although I will reformulate it (in the spirit of the Pears and McGuinness version) to take account of the actual German words involved, recording in the notes when I have done so. The point is not crucial for the purposes of this chapter, but will take on some importance when we consider the application of the general theory of representation to language, in the next chapter (see Chapter 4, section 4C).

3C THE GENERAL THEORY OF REPRESENTATION

The 2.1s and 2.2s present Wittgenstein's general theory of representation — that is to say, they present the application of the insights gained from the Paris courtroom model to the general category of representations or 'pictures'. They seem, then, to be broaching a new subject, something different from the grand metaphysical theory which occupies the 1s and early 2s. But, of course, the numbering of these remarks — the fact that they are in the 2s at all — indicates that in Wittgenstein's mind they belong with the general elaboration of the nature of facts which is the primary business of these sections. This is something we need to explain.

2.1 presents us with a summary statement of our relation to the world. It will be helpful to present this remark in both of the two classic translations. Ogden puts it like this:

> We make to ourselves pictures of facts.

Whereas Pears and McGuinness put it like this:

> We picture facts to ourselves.

As is often the case, Ogden's translation is word-for-word literal, while Pears and McGuinness give more of the colloquial flavour of the original. The German expression which Ogden translates so literally has a colloquial force which is much more nearly captured by Pears and McGuinness: it is a perfectly ordinary way of saying that we visualize facts — even, perhaps, just that we have facts in view.[9] As such it seems undeniable, once we have accepted that the world itself consists of facts. What the Ogden translation brings out is that, if we take it literally, the everyday German way of describing this almost undeniable thing actually suggests that we construct something — some *thing* — when we view the world. The everyday German suggests that viewing the world is a matter of constructing pictures or models.

We get the real force of what Wittgenstein is claiming here when we put together what we gather from these two translations. If we once grant that the world consists of facts — which, after all, has been one of the central assertions of the 1s and early 2s — it seems undeniable that, in some sense, we picture facts to ourselves. This is just to say that we have access to the world. But the everyday German way of describing this suggests that our having access to the world involves us constructing something, a picture or model of the world. Wittgenstein's point is just that this literal implication of the everyday German is entirely correct: our access to the world does involve our constructing pictures or models of it.[10] What this will mean is that the conception of representation derived from the Paris courtroom model — the conception enshrined in (M1)–(M3) — applies to our most fundamental engagements with the world.[11]

The bulk of the remarks between 2.11 and 2.174 can be seen as elaborations of the model conception of representation, but they also draw out some consequences of that conception which are crucial both for Wittgenstein's response to the difficulties he found in Frege and Russell and for the status of the *Tractatus* as a whole. Sections 2.13 and 2.131 are expressions of (M2). Section 2.14 presupposes at least half of (M1): the fact that the elements of a picture are combined in a definite (particular, determinate) way presupposes that they could have been combined otherwise. Moreover, this phrase echoes 2.031, where it is claimed that in an atomic fact objects are combined in a definite (particular, determinate) way: and that gives us the other half of (M1).

What Wittgenstein says about the *form* of a picture gives us (M3). Recall, first, the introduction of the notion of form in relation to objects (the ultimate constituents of facts):

2.0141   The possibility of its occurrence in atomic facts is the form of
the object.

That is to say: the form of an object is the range of ways in which that object can combine with other objects to form atomic facts. Next consider the application of the notion of form to atomic facts:

2.032   The way in which objects hang together in the atomic fact is the
structure of the atomic fact.

2.033   The form is the possibility of the structure.

The form of an atomic fact is its being possible for its constituent objects to be arranged in the ways in which they can be arranged. It is, as it were, the form of all of the constituent objects taken together, seen from the point of view of the atomic fact of which they are constituents.

The notion of form is then applied to pictures in a way which is precisely parallel to this:

> This connexion of the elements of the picture is called its structure, and the possibility of this structure is called the form of depiction of the picture.[12]

(2.15)

And this is the basis of what is, in effect, an assertion of (M3), the claim that the range of ways in which the components of a model could have been arranged is the same as the range of ways in which the correlated objects in reality could have been arranged. Here is how Wittgenstein puts it first:

2.151 The form of depiction is the possibility that the things are combined with one another as are the elements of the picture.[13]

The word 'as' here ('so ... wie' in German) means: *in the same way as*. The model conception requires something to be the *same* — the ranges of possibilities of arrangement of the components of both model and reality must be the *same*, according to (M3). Wittgenstein expresses the point in terms of form, which we have seen is just the notion of possibilities of arrangement:

2.161   In the picture and the pictured there must be something identical in order that the one can be a picture of the other at all.
2.17   What the picture must have in common with reality in order to be able to represent it after its manner — rightly or falsely — is its form of depiction.[14]

This is really just (M3), expressed in terms of form.

Wittgenstein makes three important further claims about representation in general in these sections (the 2.1s and 2.2s): two of them take on their full significance only when this general theory is applied to language, while the final ramifications of the third are not realized until the very end of the whole book.

The first claim is expressed in these two remarks:

2.14 The picture consists in the fact that its elements are combined with one another in a definite way.

2.141 The picture is a fact.

Strictly speaking, 2.14 is over-translated here: there is no word in this German sentence corresponding to the English 'fact'. The German just means 'The picture consists in this, that its elements ... '. But this does not make this way of putting the claim altogether wrong: after all, a fact is precisely a *that* — a *that* things are arranged in a certain way. And the claim is, of course, summarized in precisely the manner of Ogden's translation in the following remark (2.141 does contain a German word corresponding to 'fact' — the familiar 'Tatsache').

The claim is a striking one. We naturally think of a picture or a model as a complex object: an object with component parts — movable parts in the case of the Paris courtroom model. Wittgenstein here denies this: a picture or a model is not an object at all, and what we usually think of as its component parts are not related to the picture or model as parts to a whole. Rather, a picture or model is a *that*, and what we think of as parts are really just 'elements'. Instead of being an object with parts, a picture or model is a *that* certain elements are arranged in a certain way.

That pictures or models are facts is required by (M3), if pictures or models are to be capable of representing facts; (M3) requires that the components of the model and the components of the corresponding reality should be capable of being arranged in the same ways. If the relevant reality is a fact whose constituents are combined in the ways appropriate to facts, then any representation which is capable of representing that fact must also be a fact. Hence Wittgenstein writes:

> *That* the elements of the picture are combined with one another in a definite way, represents *that* the things are so combined with one another.
>
> (2.15; my emphasis)

At this point the claim that pictures or models are facts has not been justified. Indeed, Wittgenstein never gives any explicit justification for it. But a justification can be offered on his behalf, once we see the significance of the claim for the philosophy of language. At that point we will see how it is the basis of Wittgenstein's solution to problem (P2), the difficulty of explaining the unity of the sentence (see Chapter 4, section 4G, below).

The second important claim that Wittgenstein makes about pictures or models — whose full significance again can only be seen once the theory is applied to the case of language — is embedded in these remarks:

2.1511   Thus the picture is linked with reality; it reaches up to it.

2.1512   It is like a scale applied to reality.

2.15121   Only the outermost points of the dividing lines *touch* the object to be measured.

2.1514   The depicting relation consists of the co-ordinations of the elements of the picture and the things.[15]

2.1515   These co-ordinations are as it were the feelers of its elements with which the picture touches reality.

The basic view expressed here is this: a picture or model gets to be a picture or model in virtue of its elements being co-ordinated with the components of the reality which it represents. The idea is that it is the correlations whose possibility is declared by (M2) which make a picture a picture. In the case of the Paris courtroom model, the model gets to be a depiction of the traffic accident in virtue of the model cars and people being correlated with — taken in some way to stand for — the real cars and people which were involved in the accident. As Wittgenstein comments:

2.1513   According to this view the depicting relation which makes it a
picture, also belongs to the picture.[16]

The crucial claim Wittgenstein is making is that the correlations between picture and reality need only be correlations between *elements* of the picture and *things* in reality: it is not also required that there be a correspondence between the picture as a whole — the fact that the elements are arranged in a particular way — and a fact in reality — the fact that the things in reality are arranged in a particular way. This means that there can be representations which depict things incorrectly, or falsely — which represent things as being otherwise than they actually are. This will have an obvious significance when the theory is applied to language. It means that Wittgenstein is taking a particular stand on the issues raised by problem (P1), the problem of deciding which linguistic items need to be correlated with items in the world for languages to be meaningful. He is going against the view of Frege and the early Russell, and denying that the meaningfulness of sentences requires them to be correlated with anything in the world. He is claiming that we do not need to make peculiar objects of truth-values, as Frege did; nor do we need to posit 'objective falsehoods' — false facts, as it were — as the early Russell did. According to Wittgenstein, the only correlations which are required are between *elements* of the picture (eventually: the sentence) and *things* in reality, not between the whole picture (sentence) and something in reality which might be taken to be the correlate of a picture (sentence).

It is worth pausing for a moment here over the picturesque image of 2.1512 and 2.15121. The image is of an ordinary ruler or measure, marked out with lines at intervals (millimetres and centimetres in a metric system; quarter-inches, half-inches, and inches in an imperial system): these are the 'dividing lines' Wittgenstein speaks of. Wittgenstein says that it is only the ends of these lines — the ends by the edge of the measure — which touch the object to be measured. What point is being made here? It may be that the point is the one we have just explained: there only need to be correlations between the *elements* of a picture and the *things* in reality, not between a picture as a whole and something corresponding to it in reality. But the image of the ruler falls apart on this reading. What Wittgenstein says is that the rest of the dividing line — the part which runs away from the edge of the measure — does not touch reality. The suggested reading has to suppose that the whole picture is here likened to the whole dividing line. But the difficulty is that the picture consists in the fact that its elements are arranged in a certain way; in the terms of our image, these elements are the dividing lines; and that means that the fact which constitutes the picture has to be a fact about all the dividing lines on the measure (which are each correlated with something in reality), and not a fact about the relation between the different parts of each dividing line. So it is hard to see how this image can be making the point that there need be no correlate in reality to the whole picture — even if that is a point which Wittgenstein wants to make.

We get a more satisfying interpretation of the image if we consider 2.1512 and 2.15121 in their context. The context is Wittgenstein's version of claim (M3), his claim that a representation must have the same *form* as the reality it depicts. The claim of 2.15121 then becomes something like this: nothing matters about the elements of a picture or model other than that they have the same ranges of possibilities of combination as the items in reality with which they are correlated. No further similarity is required. And this amounts, in effect, to the claim that the elements of a picture or model are arbitrary signs: whatever representational work the elements of a picture may do, it can be done by quite different things, provided that those different things have the same possibilities of combination with other things. The point of the remark, on this interpretation, is to insist that representation only requires a very abstract kind of similarity between representation and reality: nothing more than sameness of form.[17]

If this is right, the clear connection between 2.15121 and 2.1515 — they both contain the idea of the elements of a picture *touching* reality — makes a further point. 2.15121, on the interpretation which I have suggested, claims that all that is required for a picture to be a picture is that the *form* of the picture be the same as the *form* of reality; and 2.1515 claims that what is required is for the elements of a picture to be correlated with things in reality. Putting the two together seems to amount to making the following claim: it is only possible for the elements of a picture to be correlated with things in reality, if the items on each side of such a correlation can be combined in the same ways with other items. That is to say, the claim which is being made here is that what is asserted by (M2) — the possibility of correlation — requires what is asserted by (M3) — sameness of form. It is not that we might correlate elements of a model with items in reality, and *then* decide how the elements of the model can be moved around: it is only if the elements of the model *already*, or *thereby*,[18] have the same ranges of possibility of combination as the items in reality that the correlation can have been set up in the first place.

3D THE IMPOSSIBILITY OF DEPICTING FORM

The third important claim about representations, which Wittgenstein takes to follow from his overall account, emerges in these sections:

2.172 The picture, however, cannot depict its form of depiction; it shows it forth.[19]

2.173 The picture represents its object from without (its standpoint is its form of representation), therefore the picture represents its object rightly or falsely.[20]

2.174 But the picture cannot place itself outside of its form of representation.[21]

The claim of 2.172 will turn out to have absolutely funda-mental significance for the whole *Tractatus*: this claim entails that the *Tractatus* itself is meaningless, on its own terms. And here, in 2.173 and 2.174, we get Wittgenstein's argu-ment for that claim. A case can be made for saying that these two short sections are the pivotal sections of the whole work.

Unfortunately, the argument is not completely clear. The crucial steps seem to be these:

(1) A picture can only depict something (its 'object') if it can depict it correctly or incorrectly;
(2) A picture can only depict something correctly or incorrectly from a position *outside* what it depicts;
(3) A picture cannot occupy a position *outside* its own form; so
(4) A picture cannot depict its own form.

To begin with, we need to be clear that when he talks about the picture's 'object' in 2.173, Wittgenstein is not talking about the objects which are the fundamental constituents of facts, and hence, in the end, of the world. His term for object in *that* sense (the necessary existents whose form is the form of the world) is 'Gegenstand'; but here the term is 'Objekt'. The object of a representation in this sense (the 'Objekt' sense) is *what is depicted*: that is, according to Wittgenstein, a certain situation in reality. (Pears and McGuinness actually translate 'Objekt' here as *subject*.)

As we know, the form of a representation is its being possible for the elements of the representation to be com-bined in the way they are: for example, its being possible for the model cars and people in the Paris courtroom model to be arranged in the way they are. The claim of 2.172 is, then, that a picture which represents *that* things are a certain way cannot represent that it is possible for its own elements to be the same way. The reason is, apparently, that a picture cannot 'place itself outside' its own form of representation. So the argument clearly turns on what it is for a picture to be 'outside' what it represents. A slightly later section suggests a natural interpretation:

2.22   The picture represents what it represents, independently of its
       truth or falsehood, through its form of depiction.[22]

I suggest that for a picture to be occupying a place 'outside'
what it represents is for its being a picture (and, indeed, its
being the picture it is) to be independent of whether it
represents things correctly or incorrectly. If we adopt this
interpretation, then we can rewrite the whole argument as
follows:

(1*)   A picture can only represent that p (for a given 'p') if it can
       represent that p correctly or incorrectly;

(2*)   A picture can only represent that p correctly or incorrectly, if
       its being a picture is independent of whether or not it is true
       that p;

(3*)   A picture's being a picture cannot be independent of whether
       it is possible for its own elements to be arranged as they are
       arranged (or that it is possible that things in reality are so
       arranged); so

(4*)   A picture cannot represent that it is possible for its own ele-
       ments to be arranged as they are arranged (or that it is pos-
       sible that things in reality are so arranged).

Premise (3*) here must be accepted once we accept the central claim of Wittgenstein's conception of representation:
that is, once we accept (M3). But what is going on in (1*)
and (2*)? It is sometimes suggested that Wittgenstein's reasoning in the *Tractatus* turns fundamentally on a principle
known as the Principle of Bipolarity. According to this
principle, in its most general form, every meaningful sentence must be capable both of being true, and of being false.
It is not enough merely that every sentence must be either
true or false: that is the principle known as the Principle of
Bivalence. The Principle of Bipolarity demands, not merely
that each proposition must fall into one of the two categories, but that both categories must be, as it were, live
options for every proposition. If we think that Bipolarity is
the basic assumption of the argument of 2.173 and 2.174, we

may be tempted to read that principle explicitly into 2.173, and hence into premise (1*): the condition on a picture's representing that *p* will be that *both* correctly representing that *p and* incorrectly representing that *p* must be live options.

The Principle of Bipolarity is certainly something which Wittgenstein accepted at some points during the composition of the *Tractatus* (*NL*, pp. 98–99, 101–02). But although I think that something *like* the Principle of Bipolarity — at least in a qualified form — is involved in the argument, I think that this principle itself does not have the fundamental role which this kind of reasoning ascribes to it, and it arises in 2.173 in a slightly different way from that which this reasoning suggests. If we take the phrase 'can represent that *p* correctly or incorrectly' (or the phrase 'represents its object rightly or falsely' in 2.173) as being itself an expression of the Principle of Bipolarity, it will mean, in effect: is capable *both* of being correct *and* of being incorrect in representing that *p*. Premise (1*) will then be the substantial claim, and premise (2*) will be trivially true. But this surely misrepresents the shape of the argument (and of 2.173), which requires (2*) to be the substantial claim, with (1*) being, on reflection, undeniable, even if not quite trivial.

I suggest that the basic reason for accepting (2*) can be approached as follows. Consider again the courtroom model. Suppose that it misrepresents the real traffic accident very badly: the model cars and people are in altogether the wrong places. And now imagine someone saying, 'Still, the model has got something right.' We wonder what this might be. 'Well, it's right about its own geometry, at least,' comes the reply. This reply is surely absurd, and its absurdity is the basis of 2.173.

What is absurd about this reply? It seems to be something like this. The whole business of representation is to portray something which is independent of the representation itself. This has always been the point of representation. What is it for something to be *independent* of a representation? The natural suggestion is this: something is independent of a representation, in the relevant sense, if the representation might be wrong about it. Putting this all together, we reach the thought that a representation can only depict something which it might be wrong about. And that means that no representation can depict something which is presupposed in its being the representation it is. Since no representation can be the representation it is without its own existence being at least *possible*, no representation can count as either representing or depicting its own possibility, which means that no representation can represent or depict its own form, in Wittgenstein's sense.

If this is the core of Wittgenstein's reasoning, then it does involve something like the Principle of Bipolarity — though in a rather different form — but that principle is not the most fundamental thing about the reasoning. The most fundamental thing is the simple thought about representation, that representation is essentially representation or depiction of something independent of the representation. And the form of the Principle of Bipolarity which follows from this is both more general and more restricted than the original statement suggested. The original formulation involved the claim that every meaningful sentence must be capable both of being correct and of being incorrect. The principle which Wittgenstein is committed to (effectively (2*)) is more general than this, in that it applies to representations which are not sentences. But it also seems, on the face of it, to be more restricted, since, among sentences, it applies only to those which are representations, and it is not obvious that Wittgenstein assumes that all sentences are representations.[23]

Wittgenstein's argument here seems to have a very significant consequence for issues of possibility and necessity. He seems to be committed to this claim:

(NF) No representation can be necessarily correct or necessarily incorrect just in virtue of its form.

For if a representation were necessarily correct or incorrect just in virtue of its form, then it would be correct or incorrect just in virtue being the representation it is; which contradicts (2*). And (2*) also seems to be the basis for the following remarks:

2.224   It cannot be discovered from the picture alone whether it is true or false.

2.225   There is no picture which is a priori true.

All of these claims will have considerable significance when we turn to the status of philosophy.

There is another extremely important point about the claim of 2.172. Although it claims that no representation can *depict* its own form, it does not claim that the form of representation is invisible. It is, rather, visible in a different way: a representation does not depict its own form, but it 'shows it forth' (or, as Pears and McGuinness put it, it 'displays it'). We see here the first appearance of a contrast which is central to the *Tractatus*, and to its view of the status of philosophy: between what can be *represented* (ultimately, what can be *said*), on the one hand, and what can only be *shown*, on the other. We see here that what is depicted is always a *that* — *that* something is the case (*that* things are arranged in a certain way); whereas (in this case at least) what is shown is *form* — the possibilities of combination of things.

3E THOUGHTS AND LOGICAL FORM

Wittgenstein offers us a general conception of representation. Its central thesis is that representation requires an identity of form — an identity of possibilities of combination of components — between a representation and the reality which it depicts. This general conception of representation is applied to the case of sentences, in particular, by way of two crucial notions: the notions of *logical* form, and of *thought*. I will close this chapter by considering these notions.

The notion of logical form is introduced in section 2.18:

What every picture, of whatever form, must have in common with reality in order to be able to represent it at all — rightly or falsely — is the logical form, that is, the form of reality.

And the point is elaborated two sections later:

2.182 Every picture is *also* a logical picture. (On the other hand, for example, not every picture is spatial.)

A number of claims are being made here, both in the characterization of logical form, and in the description of it as, precisely, *logical* form.

In the first place, logical form is the most general form which may be common between a representation and what it represents. This point is most naturally explained in terms of possibilities of combination or arrangement (which are, after all, what Wittgenstein's notion of form is about). There may be possibilities of spatial arrangement. There may be possibilities of temporal arrangement. There may be possibilities of arrangement in terms of pitch, or on a spectrum. Each of these kinds of possibility of arrangement is different from the others, but they are all, according to Wittgenstein, possibilities of *logical* arrangement. The significance of this point will be clear later, when we consider the following striking claim which Wittgenstein makes towards the end of the *Tractatus*:[24]

There is only *logical* necessity.

(6.37)

The universality of logical form can be expressed in terms of the notion of a *space*. We can think of a space as defined by what is possible and what impossible within it. So we can imagine a Euclidean space and a non-Euclidean space, while still remaining within the bounds of geometry. We can talk of the space of colours, or the space of tonality. If we express the universality of logical form in these terms, we will say that all these spaces are part of, or lie within, *logical* space. Hence Wittgenstein is able to say:

2.202 The picture [i.e., *every* picture] represents a possible state of affairs in logical space.

And this, of course, recalls the following remark, made very early on in the *Tractatus*:

1.13 The facts in logical space are the world.

The first point about logical form, then, is that logical form is the most general form which a representation may share with reality. The second point is clearly connected with this, although it might seem to run beyond it: it is that logical form is the form of reality (2.18). The reason why this might seem to run beyond the first point is that it might seem that the following claim (of the unrepresentability of some aspects of reality) could be true:

(UR) There are aspects of reality which cannot be represented.

Clearly, if (UR) were true, this would mean that there were ways in which objects can be combined which outrun what any representation could match. There would, then, be possibilities which could not be reflected in any representation.

Since Wittgenstein insists here (2.18) that the most general form which a representation may share with reality is just the form of reality, he cannot be accepting (UR). Here, though, it is important to distinguish between two different ways of not accepting (UR):

(i) One might think that (UR) was *false* — that is, that there are no aspects of reality which cannot be represented;
(ii) One might just decline to accept (UR), without asserting that there are no aspects of reality which cannot be represented.

It is important to distinguish between (i) and (ii), because there is at least the smell of a threat of paradox about (i): it looks as if, in even contemplating the possibility of aspects of reality which cannot be represented (in order to deny that possibility), we need, at least, to get towards representing them (as those aspects which cannot be represented). It may be that there is no real paradox here, but we should at least be aware of the possibility of a less committal position than (i); we should be aware that someone might simply decline to countenance a reality which contained aspects which cannot be represented.

It is tempting to think that any view which refrains from accepting (UR) must be *anti-realist*, in some way. In Chapter 1 (section 1F) I offered this statement of *realism*:

> (R) Reality as it is in itself is altogether independent of anything to do with any way of representing it.

We might think that (R) would make the denial of (UR) look unmotivated, and hence that it would be odd for a realist to deny (UR): surely if reality as it is in itself is altogether independent of anything to do with any way of representing it, we should expect there to be aspects of reality which are not representable? In fact, there is no such obvious connection between (UR) and anti-realism. These are issues we will look at in some detail in Chapter 6.

So much, then, for Wittgenstein's positive claims about logical form. But what is the significance of Wittgenstein's decision to use the term '*logical* form' to describe the most general form which can be common to representations and reality, the form of reality itself? The first and most obvious reason for this choice of term is that Wittgenstein will later be using this most fundamental form of the world as part of his account of the nature of logic, and of the way in which the so-called 'logical constants' (which are normally expressed by 'only if', 'not', 'and', 'or', and so on) function in sentences. Wittgenstein's account of logic and the logical constants will be explained in Chapter 5.

But the description of the form of reality as *logical* form has a further point. Logic is the study of validity. Validity is the property an argument has when its conclusion really follows from its premises. And the premises and conclusions of arguments are things that can be expressed in sentences. If form is concerned with possibilities of arrangement, *logical* form must be concerned with possibilities of arrangement within and between *sentences*. That is to say, the identification of the form of reality as logical form is already the identification of the form of reality as the form of what can be expressed or represented in sentences. In effect, to say that the form of reality is logical form is to say that there is nothing in reality which is not *describable*, in the words of some language.

The stage is thus set for the application of Wittgenstein's general theory of representation to the apparently special case of language, through the suggestion that language is not so much a special case as the general case. But the actual application is indirect:

3   The logical picture of the facts is the thought.

Wittgenstein is here clearly distancing himself from Frege's conception of thought. For Frege, as we have seen, a thought is *what* someone thinks: it is the *object* of thinking, something *grasped* in thinking. On his account of meaning, it is the 'sense' of a sentence (in his technical sense of 'sense'). For Wittgenstein, on the other hand, a thought is a representation, an arrangement of pictorial elements which are correlated with items in the world. It is not an object of thinking, something *grasped* in thinking, but something *produced* in thinking. Wittgenstein applies the point in the very next remark, which Ogden translates as follows:

3.001   'An atomic fact is thinkable' — means: we can imagine it.

This is a rare case where the Ogden translation prefers the colloquial to the literal, with some loss of significance.[25] A more literal translation, following Ogden's own example from the parallel section 2.1, would read as follows:

'An atomic fact is thinkable' means: we can make to ourselves a picture of it.

The point seems to be this. Everything which can be represented at all can be represented in a picture we make to ourselves: and a picture which we make to ourselves is what Wittgenstein calls a *thought*.

3.001 has a striking consequence, give.ι Wittgenstein's general conception of representation as modelling:

What is thinkable is also possible.

(3.02)

If we can think that something is the case, we can form a picture or model which represents that it is the case. But a picture or model can only represent that something is the case in virtue of having its elements arranged in a way in which the corresponding items in reality *could* be arranged. But if the items in reality *could* be arranged like that, then what the picture or model represents as actually being the case must at least be possible; which is what Wittgenstein claims at 3.02.

This means that we cannot represent an impossible state of affairs, a way things in reality *could* not be arranged. We cannot even do that in order to say that things could not be arranged like that. It seems, then, that we cannot truly say:

(5) It is impossible that *p*.

For if (5) is true, the '*p*' here will have to represent an impossible state of affairs.[26] And that makes it look as if it will be equally impossible for us to say truly:

(6) It is impossible that *not-p*.

But this latter is equivalent to 'It is necessary that *p*'. That means that we can say truly neither that it is impossible that *p*, nor that it is necessary that *p*.

If we can say truly neither that it impossible that *p*, nor that it is necessary that *p*, we might wonder whether we could truly say even this:

(7) It is possible that *p*.

After all, there is a sense in which we cannot be ruling out anything substantive in saying that: there is no substantive — imaginable, picturable, modellable — alternative which we are ruling out when we say that it is possible that *p*. And if we are ruling out nothing substantive, it may be hard to see how we can be *asserting* anything in using (7).

Wittgenstein does, indeed, seem to have thought that we cannot truly say that some state of affairs is even possible. The issue will be discussed in some detail in Chapter 6. But in order to see why he thinks this, we first need to see how his general theory of representation is applied to language; and that is the topic of the next chapter.

4

SENTENCES AS MODELS

4A PRELIMINARY EXPOSITION

The *Tractatus*'s theory of language is at base the application to language of the general theory of representation which was examined in Chapter 3 — the theory that representations represent in the same way as the Paris courtroom model. Accordingly, the basic claim of the theory of language of the *Tractatus* is what is stated at 4.01:

> The proposition is a picture of reality.
> The proposition is a model of the reality as we think it is.

But 'propositions' are first mentioned at 3.1: what has been going on in the sections from 3.1 to 4.0031? Very roughly, these intervening sections do two things: they justify the very idea that propositions might be models of reality; and they develop that idea in such a way as to justify the metaphysics of the 1s and early 2s (the metaphysics which was outlined in Chapter 1). The sections which follow 4.03 elaborate some of the consequences for philosophy of the claim that propositions are models, and introduce the theory of logic. (I will be considering the theory of logic in Chapter 5, and the account of philosophy in Chapter 7.)

Language is introduced with this remark:

3.1 In the proposition the thought is expressed perceptibly through the senses.

The point is a little clearer in the Pears and McGuinness version:

In a proposition a thought finds an expression that can be perceived by the senses.

This remark raises two questions immediately. First, what is a 'proposition'? The word is a translation of the German 'Satz'. It is not entirely clear how we should understand it, however. It is most naturally understood as being used to refer to a *sentence* — or, rather, a particular kind of sentence: a *declarative* sentence, one which is grammatically suited to say something true or false. But even to say that a *Satz* is a declarative sentence does not settle matters finally: after all, what is a sentence? Wittgenstein seems mostly to use the word 'Satz' to refer to a sentence *with* a meaning (as in 3.12), but there are places where he cannot mean that (6.54, for example). This is a point which I will return to (in section 4C below): for the moment, it is enough just to be aware of the issue.

The other question raised immediately by 3.1 is exactly what claim Wittgenstein means to be making here. He might be taken to be making either or both of the following claims:

(i) Every sentence is an expression of a thought;
(ii) Every thought is expressed (i.e., expressible) in a sentence.

I suggest that Wittgenstein is actually concerned to assert both (i) and (ii). It is (ii) which is crucial to the sequence of thought of the following remarks:

3   The logical picture of the facts is the thought.

3.1 In the proposition the thought is expressed perceptibly through the senses.

3.2 In propositions thoughts can be so expressed that to the objects of the thoughts correspond the elements of the propositional sign.

It is only if 3.1 includes the assertion of (ii) that we have any reason to think that every thought can be expressed in a notation which reveals its true form (which is what 3.2 claims). On the other hand, it is only if 3.1 includes the assertion of (i), that the *Tractatus*'s general theory of representation can be applied to language in general, and hence, in particular, to attempts to say something philosophical (whose significance will be clear in Chapter 7 below).

To begin with, I will present just an outline of Wittgenstein's application to sentences of his general theory of representation. But there is one thing to be clear about from the start: the application is meant to be completely literal. Wittgenstein is not claiming that sentences are somehow *like* pictures or models; nor is his claim that sentences are pictures *metaphorical*. His claim is that the analysis of models which he provides in the 2.1s and 2.2s applies completely straightforwardly and literally to sentences — or, at least, to certain basic sentences. Sentences just *are* models, strictly and literally.

Recall the core commitments of the general theory of representation:

(M1) A model has components which could have been arranged otherwise, and real situations involve objects which could have been arranged otherwise.

(M2) The components of a model can be correlated with objects in reality.

(M3) The range of ways in which the components of a model could have been arranged is the same as the range of ways in which the correlated objects in reality could have been arranged.

If sentences are to be pictures or models, it follows from (M1) and (M2) that they must have elements; accordingly, Wittgenstein says:

> The proposition is a picture of its state of affairs, only in so far as it is logically articulated.

(4.032)

And, given this, (M3) requires this:[1]

4.04 In the proposition there must be exactly as many things distinguishable as there are in the state of affairs, which it represents.
They must both possess the same logical (mathematical) multiplicity (cf. Hertz's Mechanics, on Dynamic Models).[2]

After all, different numbers of components cannot have precisely the same possibilities of combination.

But a sentence is not just a *mixture* of the words which are its pictorial elements. In a formulation which echoes 2.14, Wittgenstein says:

> The propositional sign consists in the fact that its elements, the words, are combined in it in a definite way.

(3.14)

That is, just as pictures or models in general are facts (2.141), so are sentences:

> The propositional sign is a fact.

(3.14)

As Wittgenstein recognizes, we do not readily think of sentences as facts: instead, we are inclined to think of them as complex objects. I take it that this is one of the key 'misunderstanding[s]' of the logic of our language' which lie at the heart of the problems of philosophy, according to the Preface (*TLP*, p. 27).[3] But Wittgenstein thinks that the true nature of sentences becomes clearer if we imagine them having something other than a written form:

3.1431   The essential nature of the propositional sign becomes very clear when we imagine it made up of spatial objects (such as tables, chairs, books) instead of written signs.

     The mutual spatial position of these things then expresses the sense of the proposition.

Here we see a sentence taking on the explicit appearance of a model, like the Paris courtroom model. And later on he uses exactly the language he used when he first (in *NB* 7) referred to the courtroom model:

In the proposition a state of affairs is, as it were, put together for the sake of experiment.

(4.031)

Of course, if we insist that sentences are *facts*, and not complex objects, that makes a difference to how we can talk about them. That is part of the point of the following remark:

3.1432   We must not say, 'The complex sign "*aRb*" says "*a* stands in relation *R* to *b*"'; but we must say, '*That* "*a*" stands in a certain relation to "*b*" says *that aRb*'.

(Though this remark is important in other ways, to which I will return in section 4F.)

In fact, if sentences are facts, and not complex objects, there will be some difficulty in talking *about* them at all:

States of affairs can be described but not *named*.

(3.144)

This last point is of crucial importance in the general motivation for the theory that sentences are pictures or models. Wittgenstein here makes a radical distinction between the relation which holds between a name and the object for which it stands, on the one hand, and the relation between a sentence and the fact which obtains if the sentence is true, on the other. A sentence is not any kind of name: to suppose that it is would be to treat sentences — which, like all pictures or models, are facts — as complex objects. That difference is reflected in many ways in language, but among the most important is this. It is a fundamental fact about language that every language contains an indefinite number of sentences which any competent speaker of that language can understand without having previously encountered them. Wittgenstein seems to have taken this fundamental fact to *prove* that sentences are pictures or models:

> 4.02 This [i.e., that the proposition is a picture of reality: 4.01] we see from the fact that we understand the sense of the propositional sign, without having had it explained to us.

Wittgenstein certainly has a case here, though I think he is overstating it. What is correct is that the theory that sentences are pictures or models can *explain* how it is possible for someone to understand a sentence which she has not previously encountered, without having had it explained to her. The reason is this. As we saw in the last chapter, a model's being the model it is cannot, according to Wittgenstein, depend on its being correct. If sentences are pictures or models in the same way, then the meaningfulness of a sentence — or, at least, of a sentence which is a representation — must be independent of whether it is true. Wittgenstein holds the following view of what it is to understand a sentence:

> To understand a proposition means to know what is the case, if it is true.
>
> (4.024)

And he concludes, correctly:

> One can therefore understand it without knowing whether it is true or not.
>
> (4.024)

We can have this understanding because the following is true:

One understands [the proposition] if one understands its constituent parts.

(4.024)

This falls directly out of the claim that sentences are pictures or models, on the general conception of representation which we considered in the previous chapter. For on that conception, sentences are not meaningful because of any correlation between the sentences themselves and any facts in the world: if we are not to follow the early Russell down the path to objective falsehoods (false facts), that would make the meaningfulness of a sentence — its being the representation it is — depend on its being true (see Chapter 2, section 2D). Instead, sentences, like all pictures or models, are meaningful in virtue of their *elements* being correlated with items in the world. Consequently, all one needs in order to understand the meaningfulness of a sentence is to know which items in reality its *elements* are correlated with.

The way in which I think Wittgenstein overstates his case in 4.02 amounts to this. What he offers is a plausible — one might think compelling — case for thinking that the view that sentences are pictures or models provides a good (perhaps even the best) explanation of the fact that we can understand sentences we have not encountered. But even that falls short of *proving* that sentences are models, given just the fact that we can understand sentences we have not come across before, which is what 4.02 seems to claim. In general, inferences to the best explanation make it *rational to believe* something: they do not prove that thing to be *true*.

The important final point of the application to sentences of the general account of pictures or models is this. Sentences, like pictures or models generally, have the following limitation: whatever else they may represent or depict, they cannot represent or depict their own form. In the general account of representation, Wittgenstein explains this point in terms of the impossibility of a picture standing 'outside' ('ausserhalb') its own form — outside the possibility of its components being arranged in the way they are (2.173, 2.174). That spatial metaphor is re-used in the theory of sentences in connection with the mathematical multiplicity which model and reality must share:

4.041 This mathematical multiplicity naturally cannot in its turn be depicted. One cannot get outside ['heraus'] it in the depiction.[4]

And it returns in 4.12, in a clear echo of 2.172–2.174:

Propositions can represent the whole reality, but they cannot represent what they must have in common with reality in order to be able to represent it — the logical form.

To be able to represent the logical form, we should have to be able to put ourselves with the propositions outside ['ausserhalb'] logic, that is outside the world.[5]

We saw earlier that a certain notion of 'showing forth' or 'displaying' is used in connection with form in the general case of representations:

2.172 The picture, however, cannot depict its form of depiction; it shows it forth ['weist sie auf'].

A similar notion is now used in connection with the *sense* of a sentence:

4.022 The proposition *shows* ['zeigt'] its sense.
The proposition *shows* ['zeigt'] how things stand, *if* it is true.
And it *says*, that they do so stand.

And it is used quite explicitly in remarks about form which are precisely parallel to those made in the general theory of representation:

Propositions cannot represent the logical form: this mirrors itself in language.

The propositions *show* ['zeigt'] the logical form of reality.
They show it forth ['weist sie auf'].[6]

(4.121)

An even more dramatic conclusion, however, is drawn here than was drawn explicitly for the general case of representations:

4.1212　What *can* be shown *cannot* be said.

This is more dramatic, because of the implicit claim it makes about the form of each sentence. What the general theory of representation tells us is that no representation can represent its own form; but that seems to leave it open for the form of one representation to be represented by another representation. Accordingly, we might think that, although no sentence could represent its *own* form — state its *own* sense — it might be possible for the form of one sentence to be represented by another. But this possibility is what is explicitly ruled out by 4.1212: no sentence can state the form of any sentence. This claim is only legitimate if every sentence has the same form. We will consider what that means in a little more depth in section 4E below, and again when we consider the theory of logic in Chapter 5.

We therefore see here the general theory of representation applied explicitly, literally, and in careful detail to the case of sentences. Sentences, like pictures or models generally, represent in virtue of having elements which can be correlated with items in reality, and in virtue of those elements having the same ranges of possible combination as the corresponding elements of reality — that is to say, the same form as reality. But this brings with it a necessary limitation, with sentences as with pictures or models in general: no sentence can represent or depict its own form. So much for the outline of Wittgenstein's account of sentences as models of reality. Now we need to look at it in a bit more detail, in order to understand how it answers the problems about language which Wittgenstein inherited from Frege and Russell, and how it generates the metaphysics of the 1s and 2.1s.

4B SAMENESS OF FORM AND RULES OF TRANSLATION

The central claim of the *Tractatus*'s view of language is that sentences have the same form as the reality they depict. As we have seen, this claim about form is really just a claim about possibilities of arrangement. The crucial claim of sameness of form in the case of sentences is this variant of the general claim about models, (M3):

> (SM3) The range of ways in which the components of a sentence could have been arranged is the same as the range of ways in which the correlated objects in reality could have been arranged.

This may strike us as a strange claim: if we consider the arrangement of words in a sentence, on the one hand, and the arrangement (for example) of furniture in a room, on the other, it might seem to us that there is no similarity at all in the possibilities which are available. Wittgenstein clearly felt this too:

> 4.011 At the first glance the proposition — say as it stands printed on paper — does not seem to be a picture of the reality of which it treats. But nor does the musical score appear at first sight to be a picture of musical piece; nor does our phonetic spelling (letters) seem to be a picture of our spoken language. And yet these symbolisms prove to be pictures — even in the ordinary sense of the word — of what they represent.[7]

And yet in some cases Wittgenstein thought that (SM3) was obvious:

> 4.012 It is obvious that we perceive a proposition of the form *aRb* as a picture. Here the sign is obviously a likeness of the signified.

This might seem sheer bravado, but in many cases of sentences involving two-place predicates, (SM3) is indeed quite intuitive. Consider this sentence, for example:

John hates Mary.

It is hard not to think of this sentence in the kind of way Wittgenstein does: we imagine John on the one side, and Mary on the other, and a shooting of dagger looks from one to the other expressed by the word 'hates'. The difficulty is to see how the possibilities of arrangement of the words on the page can strictly be the *same* as the possibilities of interrelation between John and Mary with respect to dagger looks.

I think the solution is that just as the bald statement 'John hates Mary' does not capture everything about the relationship between John and Mary, even if it is true, so the possibilities of arrangement of the words on the page do not have to encompass *all* the possibilities of interrelation between John and Mary with respect to dagger looks — since even dagger looks are richer in information than the simple word 'hates'. We have all that Wittgenstein needs for (SM3) if the possibilities of arrangement of words are the same as *some* of the possibilities of arrangement of the corresponding items in reality.

That this solution is Wittgenstein's own is suggested by his use of the geometrical image of *projection* to explain the relation between language and reality (3.11–3.13; 4.0141). In a geometrical projection (for example, of a three-dimensional object onto a two-dimensional screen), we expect some properties of the object projected to be lost and others to be transformed — as with perspective — but some will be preserved. Often what remains invariant will be extremely abstract. Wittgenstein's thought seems to be that if we find ourselves thinking that there is no similarity of form between a representation and what it depicts, we are simply looking for too wholesale and too concrete a similarity.

Wittgenstein's view of the issues is expressed in this reaction to cases where the relevant similarity is not obvious.

4.0141   In the fact that there is a general rule by which the musician is
         able to read the symphony out of the score, and that there is a
         rule by which one could reconstruct the symphony from the

> line on a gramophone record and from this again — by means
> of the first rule — construct the score, herein lies the internal
> similarity between these things which at first sight seem to be
> entirely different. And the rule is the law of projection which
> projects the symphony into the language of the musical score.
> It is the rule of translation of this language into the language of
> the gramophone record.

The claim being made here is a strong one: it is not that the existence of a certain kind of rule of translation is *evidence* of sameness of form; nor that the existence of such a rule somehow *expresses* an underlying sameness of form. The claim is that sameness of form between a model and reality is *nothing but* there being a rule of translation between the two. This is, in effect, a maximally abstract conception of similarity. A translation of a text from one language to another produces something which is in a certain way *equivalent* in the second language to what the original text was in the first. Such a notion of equivalence is what the demand of sameness of form eventually amounts to: a sentence has the same form as what it depicts if it is, in the language, equivalent to it in a certain respect; which is to say that what is depicted can be recovered from it, as the symphony can be recovered from the score.

The important thing about the notion of translation in play here is that it does not involve piecemeal translation, of a single text or sentence of one language into another language: it is the idea of one whole language being translated into another:

> The translation of one language into another is not a process of
> translating each proposition of the one into a proposition of the
> other, but only the constituent parts of the proposition are translated.
>
> (4.025)

On this conception, the constituent parts are correlated with each other, just as the constituents of sentences in general are correlated with the constituents of facts in reality. It is because the notion of translation involved here is fundamentally concerned with the translation of *constituents* of propositions that it is plausible to say that sameness of form essentially *consists in* the presence of a rule of translation: sameness of form is sameness of possibilities of combination, and that requires a certain equivalence among constituents.

Furthermore, the notion of translation also provides a plausible elaboration of the metaphor of sameness of form. 'Form' literally means *shape*: to say that language has the same form as the world is to say that language has the same *shape* as the world. This is evidently a metaphorical claim: how would we naturally understand it? What might it be for sentences to have the *shape* of the world? Here is a natural thought: for sentences in a language to have the same *shape* as the world is for it to be possible for someone, who was acquainted with the world but did not yet understand the language, to come to understand the language simply on the basis of an experience of the world which is available without understanding the language, together with the use of reason — at least, insofar as the language is intelligible at all. This makes sense of the idea of a mapping of the world by a language: such a mapping presupposes that the world is intelligible independently of the language in question, insofar as it is intelligible at all, and that the language is then intelligible (insofar as it is intelligible at all) just on the basis of understanding the mapping relation.[8]

This conception of the relation between language and the world is most naturally understood in a realist way. Recall that I formulated realism as the acceptance of this claim:

> (R) The nature of the world as it is in itself is altogether independent of anything to do with any thought or representation of it.

Any substantial denial of that claim counts as a form of idealism. The natural, realist way of reading the rule-of-translation conception of sameness of form seems to be found in Wittgenstein himself. Thus in notes taken of lectures which he gave in 1930, soon after his return to philosophy, we find these remarks:[9]

> But grammar is not entirely a matter of arbitrary choice. It must
> enable us to express the multiplicity of facts, give us the same degree
> of freedom as do the facts.
>
> (WLC 8)

> Grammar is a mirror of reality.
>
> (WLC 9)

The first of these remarks suggests that objective possibility
constrains grammar, which suggests that objective possibility is independent of grammar; this also is suggested by the
'mirror' image.

Of course, these remarks are rather later than the
Tractatus itself, and Wittgenstein might by this time have
forgotten some of the philosophy which originally motivated him. But in any case, although they are naturally
understood in a realist way, they can be made compatible
with a form of idealism. The key is to note that in my elaboration of the rule-of-translation conception of sameness
of form, it became natural to talk about 'a language' —
rather than just *language*. When we talk about translation,
we have in mind translation between *one* language and
another, and not some translation between language in
general and the world as it is in itself, taken neat.[10] Once we
take proper account of this, a non-realist understanding of
the rule-of-translation conception of sameness of form
becomes available — and, indeed, natural as an interpretation of the *Tractatus*.

Suppose that someone is able to think about the world. On
the account of thought which is presented in the *Tractatus*,
this means that she is able to form for herself pictures or
models of the world. Someone could be in this position
without yet having the ability to speak a particular language (English or German, say), or to use a certain notation. But her ability to form pictures or models for herself
can itself be counted as knowledge of a kind of language.
Note what Wittgenstein says in response to a question from
Russell:

Does a Gedanke [thought] consist of words? No! But of psychical constituents that have the same sort of relation to reality as words.

(CL 125)

Our subject's position is, then, that she can operate with a kind of language — which uses what we may call the symbols of thought — while not yet being able to use any familiar, everyday language or notation.

Now suppose that we understand the relation between this thought-language and the world in an idealist way. That is, we imagine our subject as projecting the structure of her thought-language onto the world, so that its grammar is visible in the nature of the objects which are reflected back, as it were, to her. (For this idea, recall the discussion of realism and idealism in Chapter 2, section 2F, above.) The world which is a proper correlate of her thought-language is now understood to be dependent, in part, on the way in which it is represented in her thought-language. Of course, our subject now has a kind of access to the world which is independent of understanding any familiar language (such as English or German), or any familiar notation. The conception of language which is enshrined in the rule-of-translation understanding of sameness of form (which underlies 4.0141) says simply that there is some kind of rule of translation which can take someone from this thought-language access to the world into understanding any familiar language or notation. And we can read the remarks from 1930 in the same way: grammar will present itself as 'not entirely a matter of arbitrary choice' to someone who already has *some* conception of the world — the conception provided by her own thought-language. Even these remarks do not require a realist reading.

What this means is that even the rule-of-translation conception of sameness of form, which seems at first sight to require some form of realism, is in fact compatible with an idealist view of the fundamental relation between language or representation, on the one hand, and the world, on the other.

4C SAMENESS OF FORM, SENSE, AND NONSENSE

For all the abstractness of the conception of sameness of form which Wittgenstein embraces, there is a further reason why it might seem that the world could not have the same form as language. Form is a matter of possibilities of combination, on Wittgenstein's view. But it might seem that the notion of combination which applies in the case of language was quite different from the one which applies in the case of the world. In the case of language, it might seem that the crucial notion we are really interested in is essentially *normative*: we are concerned with *grammatical* combinations, combinations which are *legitimate,* which result in a *well*-formed rather than an *ill*-formed string, which generate *proper* sentences. There are other possible combinations, we are inclined to think — combinations which are *illegitimate* or *ungrammatical,* which do not result in proper sentences. In the case of the world, on the other hand, there is no such normativity involved in the notion of combination of elements: there is no contrast between legitimate and illegitimate combinations — there are just the *possible* combinations. How, then, can we say that the possibilities of combination in language are the same as the possibilities of combination in reality, without involving ourselves in an ugly equivocation over the notion of possibility of combination?

Wittgenstein solves this problem by simply blocking any distinction between normative and non-normative conceptions of possible combination in the case of language:

5.4733 Frege says: Every legitimately constructed proposition must have a sense; and I say: Every possible proposition is legitimately constructed, and if it has no sense this can only be because we have given no *meaning* to some of its constituent parts.

(Even if we believe that we have done so.)

Thus 'Socrates is identical' says nothing, because we have given *no* meaning to the word 'identical' as *adjective*. For when

> it occurs as the sign of equality it symbolizes in an entirely dif-
> ferent way — the symbolizing relation is another — therefore
> the symbol is in the two cases entirely different; the two symbols
> have the sign in common with one another only by accident.

We will return to the contrast with Frege in the next section. The point which Wittgenstein is making in 5.4733 turns on a contrast between *signs* and *symbols*. The notion of a *symbol* is introduced, along with that of an *expression*, in this remark:

> Every part of a proposition which characterizes its sense I call an
> expression (a symbol).

(3.31)

But this is still quite obscure, because it is not obvious what 'characterizes' means here. Our best bet is to look more particularly at the meaning of 'proposition', and at Wittgenstein's conception of *sense*. The notion of sense — in relation to pictures in general — is introduced in the following remark:

2.221 What a picture represents is its sense.

Understanding this remark depends on recalling the contrast between the terms 'represent' ('darstellen') and 'depict' ('abbilden'), as they are generally used by Wittgenstein.[11] What is depicted is reality — nothing less than what is actually the case. What is *represented*, on the other hand (as Wittgenstein generally uses the term), is a way reality might be. Consider the sentence 'John hates Mary', and suppose that, in fact, John does *not* hate Mary. The actual fact, the real state of relations between John and Mary, is *depicted* by the sentence; but what the sentence *represents* is just that John hates Mary; and this — *that John hates Mary* — is what Wittgenstein counts as the *sense* of the sentence.

This use of the notion of sense is quite different from Frege's.[12] On Frege's view, every meaningful linguistic expression has a sense (as he uses the term): the sense of an

expression is just a matter of the way in which the referent
— the entity whose correlation with the expression makes it
meaningful — is presented. On Wittgenstein's use, by contrast, only whole sentences can have sense, and the sense of
a sentence is just the possible fact which it represents.
Wittgenstein has no use for the Fregean idea of sense as an
extra *dimension* of meaning — a layer of cognitive significance
over and above an expression's reference. Wittgenstein's
contrast between sense and reference is not between different dimensions of meaning which the *same* expression
might have: rather it is between the different kinds of
meaning which *different* kinds of expression may have.
Names have reference, but sentences have sense.[13] The point
of choosing different words is to emphasize the radical difference in kind between names and sentences, a difference
which Frege's theory obscures.

With this in mind, we can go on to consider the way in
which Wittgenstein characterizes propositions:

3.11　We use the sensibly perceptible sign (sound or written sign, etc.)
　　　of the proposition as a projection of the possible state of affairs.
　　　The method of projection is the thinking of the sense

3.12　The sign through which we express the thought I call the propo-
　　　sitional sign. And the proposition is the propositional sign in its
　　　projective relation to the world.

3.13　To the proposition belongs everything which belongs to the pro-
　　　jection; but not what is projected.
　　　Therefore the possibility of what is projected but not this itself.
　　　In the proposition, therefore, its sense is not contained, but the
　　　possibility of expressing it.
　　　("The content of the proposition" means the content of the sig-
　　　nificant proposition.)
　　　In the proposition the form of its sense is contained, but not its
　　　content.

These remarks are not without internal tension, but the
main thought seems to be this. The mere sounds or written
marks (the signs, on Wittgenstein's account) do not

themselves determine grammar — what we think of, antecedently, as the legitimate ordering of words. That is to say, the mere signs do not determine the range of ways in which grammatical combinations can be made. But it is only once the range of grammatical combinations is fixed that we can even think of setting up correlations with the world. The proposition is what we have when we have a string of signs *with the range of possible grammatical combinations fixed.* It is, therefore, only the constituents of a *proposition* — rather than a mere propositional *sign* — which can be correlated with items in reality. In effect, a proposition is a certain kind of sign *with the syntax fixed.* Contrary to some modern uses,[14] syntax brings in more than what we are given with the mere signs: we can have two examples of the same sign, which have different syntax; syntax provides us with the range of combinations.

A symbol is a part of a proposition in this sense: it is a sign which has a syntax. Just as a propositional sign is 'sensibly perceptible' (3.11), so 'A sign is the part of the symbol perceptible by the senses' (3.32). And just as signs, in general, are not enough for syntax —

3.321　Two different symbols can therefore have the sign (the written sign or the sound sign) in common — they can signify in different ways.

For two symbols to signify in different ways (see also 3.322) is just for them to have different syntax — that is, to be different symbols. And Wittgenstein makes it clear that this is more than just having different meanings:

In the proposition "Green is green" — where the first word is a proper name and the last an adjective — these words have not merely different meanings but they are *different symbols.*

(3.323)

But there is still some uncertainty over what the notion of a symbol involves; and the same applies to the notion of a proposition. This is worth considering in a little more detail, since it has some importance for the interpretation of the *Tractatus* as a whole, as well as for 5.4733 itself. We have already seen that the point of introducing the notion of a symbol is to focus on the syntax of an expression: the point of 3.323 is that the proper name and the adjective differ in *syntax*, and not just in meaning (not just in the objects assigned to them). And it is natural to take this as presupposing that there can be expressions with the same syntax, but with different meanings (just as there can apparently be different objects with the same form — see 2.0233). But there are two questions which are still not finally resolved here. First, could there be an expression which had a syntax but *no* meaning — with no object having been assigned to it? (Or is it only in giving meaning to a sign that we fix its syntax?) And, second, where exactly do the notions of *symbol* and *proposition* fit in here? That is, even if it is possible for syntax to be fixed independently of meaning, is fixing the syntax enough to give us a *symbol* or *proposition*, or do we only have a symbol or proposition once the meaning is given, as well as the syntax?

Let us deal with the first question first. If a symbol is a component of a proposition, 3.13 strongly suggests that the syntax of a symbol can be fixed without giving it a meaning, without assigning an object to it. For Wittgenstein says there that the proposition contains 'the form of its sense, but not its content' — that is, surely, its syntax, but not what is actually represented. And again, the proposition is said to include 'everything which belongs to the projection' — that is, the possibilities of combination, the syntax — 'but not what is projected' — that is, not the particular aspects of the world which are depicted in a proposition which has meaning. And the point seems to be put beyond doubt by this remark from a little later on:

3.33 In logical syntax the meaning of a sign ought never to play a rôle; it must admit of being established without mention being thereby

> made of the *meaning* of the sign; it ought to presuppose *only* the
> description of the expressions.

3.33 looks unambiguous here. It seems clearly to present the official view of the *Tractatus* on our *first* question — the question whether syntax can be fixed without fixing meaning.[15] In principle — and ideally — syntax can be fixed in advance of assigning meaning. This will be done simply by fixing the rules for combining signs with other signs in whole sentences — which, of course, will then make symbols of those signs. The reason for thinking that this is the official view of the book is that this is what is required if the account of sentences as models is strictly to follow the example set by the general account of representation as modelling, for which the Paris courtroom model does indeed provide a clear and useful paradigm. The general account of representation imagines two parallel systems — the representational system, on the one hand, and reality, on the other — which are both subject to the same necessities, and which therefore permit the same possibilities of arrangement. If the two systems are parallel, each must be, to some degree, independent of the other. And it is important to insist on this literal understanding of the view that sentences are models, because it makes all the difference to the kind of answer which the *Tractatus* provides to the Kantian question of how metaphysics is possible. I sketched out what I take Wittgenstein's answer to be in section 5 of the Introduction. I will return to it in Chapter 5, section 5E, below. The idea that language and reality constitute two systems which are parallel but subject to the same necessities seems to require that syntax be, in principle, independent of correlations between language and the world.

I suspect that the principal reason for resisting this interpretation is the thought that it involves a commitment to realism,[16] as I have defined it earlier — that is, as acceptance of the following claim:

> (R) The nature of the world as it is in itself is altogether independent
> of anything to do with any thought or representation of it.

And it is reasonable to doubt that Wittgenstein was a realist. (This is an issue which will be considered properly in Chapter 6.) But I have been interpreting the conception of sentences as models all along as involving parallel systems subject to the same necessities, and I have already argued that commitment to such a parallelism is not enough in itself to commit Wittgenstein to realism (see section 4B, above; as well as section 2F of Chapter 2).

We seem to have a clear answer to our first question, whether syntax can be fixed without fixing meaning. But this still leaves open our second question: whether fixing the syntax is enough to give us a *symbol* or a *proposition*. On this question, it looks as if the evidence is not decisive — indeed, it is contradictory. As we have already seen, 3.13 seems clearly to say that propositions are defined by syntax, independently of meaning. But there is this apparently contradictory statement:

3.326   In order to recognize the symbol in the sign we must consider
         the significant [*sinnvollen*] use.

And the history of this last statement makes the appearance of contradiction here even starker. The thought of 3.326 first appears in a relatively early remark in the *Notebooks*:

In order to recognize the sign in the sign we have to attend to the use.

(*NB*: 18)

There are just two differences between these two versions in the German.[17] The first is that Wittgenstein has introduced the new, technical notion of *symbol* by the time of the *Tractatus*.[18] The second is that 'sinnvollen' — senseful, significant, meaningful — is inserted to qualify 'Gebrauch' (*use*). Why should Wittgenstein have bothered to insert that, if there could be symbols (including propositions, sentences) with no meaning?

Moreover, later on Wittgenstein says (as we have seen):

> To understand a proposition means to know what is the case, if it is true.
> (4.024)

And it is hard to see how we could understand something which had no meaning.

3.326 is a remark whose translation Wittgenstein commented explicitly on, in a letter to Ogden. His comment is not altogether unambiguous, however. Here it is in full:

> I think 'significant' is al[l]right here. The meaning of this prop[osition] is: that in order to recognize the symbol in a sign we must look at how this sign is *used* significantly in propositions. I.e., we must observe how the sign is used in accordance with the laws of logical syntax. Thus 'significant' here means as much as 'syntactically correct'.
> (*LO*: 59)

We might take the last sentence here to be asserting that in 3.326 'significant' ('sinnvollen') means just *syntactically correct*. But this is itself problematic: that is just not what 'sinnvollen' means. The term means *senseful* or *having sense*, and being 'sinnvollen' contrasts with having *no* sense (which is the very notion which is at issue in 5.4733). And, as we will see in a moment, it is used in 3.14 to mean, precisely, *senseful, meaningful*. This actually makes it quite tempting to interpret Wittgenstein's comment to Ogden on 3.326 as an attempt to rewrite 3.326 in a way which makes it more obviously consistent with 3.14. Seen in this light, the comment as a whole would look as if it is a gradual massaging of the text of 3.326 towards the view of 3.14.

But, in fact, the appearance of contradiction between 3.326 and 3.14 need be no more than an appearance anyway. Although in principle, and ideally, a symbol can be introduced in advance of any assignment of meaning, in practice both tasks will often be done at once, and what we are usually confronted with are symbols which already have some meaning assigned to them. And we can take 3.326 to be concerned just with this last kind of case. It is easy to be misled about the syntax of expressions in actual use (3.324). In particular, when the same sign — the same type of mark or sound — is used, it is easy to suppose that we have the same syntax (this is the worry of 3.323). To avoid that, we ought ideally to set up an unambiguous symbolism (3.325). But for the words we already have, the key is to attend properly to the way they are used (3.326). In practice, this will be the only way of getting clear about their syntax (hence the 'must' in 3.326).

As for 4.024, it looks as if Wittgenstein has already anticipated the temptation to think of a proposition as something which has a meaning, in the following remark which is added as a parenthesis in 3.13:

> 'The content of the proposition' means the content of the significant [*sinnvollen*] proposition.

In the context of 3.13, which seems concerned to say that a proposition is a merely *syntactic* entity, this has to be understood as saying that 'the content of the proposition' means the content of the proposition *once a meaning has been assigned to its parts*.

Accordingly, I think the official view of the *Tractatus* is that symbols in general, and therefore propositions (sentences), in particular, are defined by their syntax, independently of their meaning, but less hangs on this answer to our second question than hangs on the answer to our first.

It also seems to me that taking symbols — and therefore propositions — to be defined by their syntax makes the most natural sense of the passage we set out to address at the beginning of this section: 5.4733, where Wittgenstein draws a contrast between his own view of nonsense and the one he finds in Frege.[19] Recall that it is here that he blocks the possibility of a distinction between normative and non-normative conceptions of the possibility of linguistic combination, and thereby allows the possibilities of combination in language to be the same as the possibilities of combination in reality. Wittgenstein puts his point as follows:

> Every possible proposition is legitimately constructed, and if it has no sense this can only be because we have given no *meaning* to some of its constituent parts.

> (5.4733)

(We might note that once again Wittgenstein seems explicitly to endorse the view that syntax is independent of meaning. What he seems to countenance is something which is 'legitimately constructed' — that is, 'syntactically correct' (*LO*: 59) — which has no sense, because no meaning has been given to some of its parts.) The two different conceptions of propositions — as being defined by syntax alone, or as having their meaning essentially — give different construals of the first clause here. On the merely syntactic conception of propositions, that clause just says this:

> There cannot be illegitimately constructed propositions.

The rest of the remark then allows that there can be propositions with no meaning. On the syntax-plus-meaning conception of propositions, on the other hand, the first clause means something like this:

> Nothing which is illegitimately constructed can be an entity of the category *possible proposition*.

And the rest of the remark allows merely that there can be *possible* propositions with no meaning (that is to say, they are not actual propositions). The first reading strikes me as much the most natural.

Wittgenstein's point in 5.4733 can be explained as follows, in line with that first reading (it is easy enough to vary this for the other reading). The general theory of propositions (sentences) as models requires that the elements of any possible sentence must be capable of being combined in exactly the same ways as those in which the corresponding elements of reality can be combined. Suppose we allowed that there can be ungrammatical sentences — syntactically illegitimate combinations of sentential components. That would mean that the possible ways of combining sentential components would include *both* the legitimate *and* the illegitimate combinations. If we are still to maintain that sentences are models, we would therefore have to suppose that it was this larger range of possibilities — including the illegitimate as well as the legitimate ones — which coincided with the range of possible combinations of objects in the world. But that would make the capacity of sentences to be models of reality entirely independent of their syntax: syntax would now be irrelevant to the representational capacity of sentences. Sentences would be, in effect, a kind of natural entity.

On the other hand, if we allow that syntax is relevant at all to the representational capacity of sentences, we cannot allow the possibility of ungrammatical, syntactically illegitimate sentences. For if there were illegitimate sentences, they would have to represent *impossible* combinations of objects, and if we allowed that a sentence could represent an impossible combination of objects, we would be allowing that the components of sentences can be combined in ways in which the corresponding elements of reality *cannot* be combined — which contradicts the thesis that sentences are models. Accordingly, what we might antecedently have thought of as illegitimate combinations of symbols can really be no more than strings of marks or sounds. We only have a *proposition*, in the sense of 5.4733, on what I think is its natural reading — something capable of representing the world, rather than a mere string of marks or sounds — if we have something which is a syntactically possible combination of symbols: that is, something which is *legitimately* constructed. Such a thing, obviously, cannot be meaningless — nonsense — in virtue of being ungrammatical. Consequently, it can only be meaningless if, despite its being in good order syntactically, no objects have been assigned as the meaning of some of its parts. And that is the claim of 5.4733.

5.4733 has a large significance for an important aspect of the interpretation of the *Tractatus* as a whole — an issue we will return to in Chapter 7. We see here Wittgenstein clearly advocating part of what has been called an 'austere' conception of nonsense (Conant 2000: 176). The 'austere' conception consists of two central claims:[20]

> (Au1) What is nonsense fails to have any sense; it does not have an incoherent kind of sense;
>
> (Au2) What fails to have sense fails to have sense because meaning has not been assigned to it or to some part of it.

Section 5.4733 is an explicit statement of (Au2): Wittgenstein here contrasts his view with a view which he ascribes to Frege, which would allow that a proposition could fail to have sense through being illegitimately constructed. It seems clear that the reason why Wittgenstein adopts (Au2) is that this is what he needs to do, if he is to maintain the same-form thesis, (SM3), which is at the heart of his account of language, without depending on an awkward equivocation between normative and non-normative conceptions of possible combination. And the same same-form thesis, (SM3), also generates a commitment to a form of (Au1): it rules out the idea of a nonsense proposition somehow representing an impossible state of affairs — as we saw at the end of Chapter 3.

4D THE CONTEXT PRINCIPLE AND THE GENERAL FORM OF THE SENTENCE

The conception of nonsense expressed in 5.4733 is linked with Wittgenstein's understanding of a famous principle of Frege's — the Context Principle. This principle is enunciated in various ways in Frege's early work, *The Foundations of Arithmetic*. Here are two formulations:

> (CP1) never to ask for the meaning of a word in isolation, but only in the context of a proposition.

> (Frege 1884: x)

> (CP2) it is only in the context of a proposition that words have any meaning.
>
> (Frege 1884: §62)

The general point of Frege's insistence on this principle, as he first introduces it, is to enable him to reject decisively any suggestion that meaning might be something psychological — that the meaning of words might be a matter of 'ideas' in the minds of speakers, for example. The minimal claim of the Context Principle is that the meaning of words must always either include or depend on their grammar, so that words with quite different syntax must have different kinds of meaning. As we saw in Chapter 2 (section 2D) this is essential if we are to accommodate the unity of sentences without making meaning psychological. If we suppose that the grammar of words is irrelevant to their meaning, the unity and completeness which is the distinctive mark of sentences cannot be thought to arise naturally out of the components of sentences — it has to be imposed on them. And if it is imposed on them, the unity of sentences has to be the product of an act of the mind; and if the unity of sentences is a product of an act of the mind, it looks as if the unity which is created has to be a unity *in* the mind; at which point it is hard to see how meaning could be non-psychological.

But what exactly does Frege need for this point? It is arguable that he needs no more than this:

> (CP) There is no more to the meaning of a word than its contribution to the meanings of legitimately constructed propositions in which it may occur.

This seems to be the reading of Frege which Wittgenstein expresses at 5.4733, and, certainly, the (CP1) formulation requires no more than this (although it can also be read as an expression of the same thought as appears in (CP2)). It is important to be clear that, although this suggests — just by seeming to open a space for *illegitimately* constructed propositions — a conception of nonsense which is at odds with clause (Au2) of the 'austere' view of nonsense considered in the last section, even on that reading it does not lead to any violation of (Au1). After all, it is natural to ascribe to Frege, as well as some form of the Context Principle, a principle which we might call the Principle of Compositionality:

> (PC) There is no more to the meaning of a proposition than is determined by the meaning of its parts, together with their mode of combination.

It would follow from this, in combination with (CP), that an *illegitimate* combination of words would have no meaning at all — not some kind of incoherent meaning; it is thus entirely in line with clause (Au1) of the 'austere' conception of nonsense.

Although a version of the Context Principle in line with (CP) would seem to be enough for the purposes which Frege uses to justify the principle's introduction,[21] it will not do for Wittgenstein's. As we have seen, Wittgenstein's insistence on sameness of form — sameness of possibilities of combination — between language and the world requires him to remove any space for a contrast between legitimate and illegitimate combinations of words. He has to hold that there are only legitimate combinations: the putative illegitimate combinations are not really combinations of those words at all — they are merely assemblages of marks or sounds. Consequently, he seems to endorse the (CP2) formulation on its strongest (most literal) interpretation:

> 3.3 Only the proposition has sense; only in the context of a proposition has a name meaning.

The first clause here expresses Wittgenstein's divergence from Frege over the notion of sense (which we saw earlier, in section 4C): sense is the kind of meaning whole sentences have — it is not a dimension of meaning, as it was for Frege. The second clause expresses the strong version of the Context Principle.

Why does Wittgenstein insist on this version? The reasoning might be this. What he cannot allow is that there might be *illegitimate* combinations of words. But it is plausible that if words could appear in isolation — not in legitimate propositional combinations — then they could appear in illegitimate combinations. After all, what is an illegitimate combination of words other than a string of isolated occurrences of those words? So it is plausible to think that Wittgenstein has to deny that words can occur in isolation.

This might seem absurd: surely words can occur in isolation — just on their own? In particular, it might seem that such isolated uses are presupposed by the very fact that gives the unity of the sentence its point. What matters about sentences, as such, is that they are distinct from mere lists of words: they have a completeness and unity which a mere list does not. But to say that seems to presuppose that there can be occurrences of words which are not in sentences — as words in a list, in particular. And isn't it just obvious that words can occur in lists, and therefore not in whole sentences?

This is a powerful point, but it looks as if there is something which Wittgenstein can say against it. Here is what Wittgenstein says about *expressions* (words, symbols):

3.311 An expression presupposes the forms of all propositions in which it can occur. It is the common characteristic mark of a class of propositions.

3.312 It is therefore represented by the general form of the propositions which it characterizes.
And in this form the expression is *constant* and everything else is *variable*.

Wittgenstein here enunciates a conception of the relationship between words and sentences which is distinct from the one which is presupposed in the objection. According to Wittgenstein, words are not *ingredients* in sentences: they are *common characteristic marks* of classes of sentences. A word is not something which is taken from elsewhere and combined with other such things to form a sentence: it is always just something which a range of sentences have in common. If this is what a word is, then when a word occurs in a list, it does not occur outside a sentence: rather, the writing of a word in a list is a way of gathering together all the sentences in which the word occurs. As Wittgenstein puts it:

> An expression is thus presented by a variable, whose values are the propositions which contain the expression.

(3.313)

On this account, when we see just the expressions in a list, we are inclined to misunderstand what we are seeing: really we are seeing only part of what is being presented to us — the part which is common to all the sentences of which the expression can be a part, and not the fact that there are always the other parts of those sentences. To make this explicit, we might use the form of expression ' … E … ' as a way of indicating any sentence of which the expression 'E' may form a part. In that case, whenever we come across the expression 'E' apparently in isolation (as in a list), what we really have is something of the form ' … E … '. Consider, then, the list of words which might normally be written as follows:

'Socrates'
'is'
'identical'.

If that list really is a list of *words* (*expressions* or *symbols*, as Wittgenstein understands these notions), it is the same list as would be written in our new notation like this:

' … Socrates … '
' … is … '
' … identical … '.

If we think of lists of words in this way, they are not examples of places where words appear in isolation, outside the context of sentences. Rather, listing words is just a way of listing ranges of sentences.

It is worth pausing for a moment on the notion of 'context' in play in 3.3. When Frege writes that 'it is only in the context of a proposition that a word has any meaning', the word translated 'context' here is 'Zusammenhange', which means, literally, *hanging together*. And Wittgenstein uses the same word in his formulation of the Context Principle in 3.3. Wittgenstein is attentive to the etymology here. Recall that in his account of the relationship between objects and atomic facts, in the basic structure of the world, Wittgenstein writes:

2.03 In the atomic fact objects hang ['hängen'] in one another, like the links of a chain ['Kette'].

And when he gets to the linguistic counterpart of atomic facts — so-called *elementary* sentences — he writes:

4.22 The elementary proposition consists of names. It is a hanging together ['Zusammenhang'], a linking in a chain ['Verkettung'], of names.[22]

We have just seen that Wittgenstein thinks that all expressions can be presented as variables: that is to say, each expression is what is common, or constant, across a range of sentences, the rest of which is variable. Every expression can therefore be presented as a *propositional* variable — where the variable indicates the range of sentences ('propositions') which have that expression in common (3.313–3.314). (Note that Wittgenstein's use of the notion of 'propositional variable' differs from the contemporary one. We now use the term for a range of letters which we have set aside to replace whole sentences in formalizations of arguments — standardly 'p', 'q', and 'r'. Wittgenstein, however, thinks every ordinary expression is itself a 'propositional variable' (3.313).)

Consider, for example, the name 'Socrates'. This name can occur in combination with a one-place predicate (examples might be 'is ugly', 'is wise', 'is waspish') to form a simple kind of sentence.[23] We can indicate the whole range of such sentences — all the sentences which combine the name 'Socrates' with a one-place predicate — by using a variable in place of the one-place predicates. We might then indicate that whole range with the expression 'f Socrates': this whole expression is a propositional variable. The values of this variable are all the sentences in which the name 'Socrates' occurs in combination with a one-place predicate. Obviously, we could also replace the name 'Socrates' here with a variable — whose function will be to represent, as it were, the whole range of names. We might write the resulting expression 'fx'. This whole expression is once again a propositional variable: it indicates the whole range of sentences which consist of a single name in combination with a one-place predicate. All the sentences in that range are the values of this variable.

This is the kind of process which is described in the following remark:

3.315   If we change a constituent part of a proposition into a variable, there is a class of propositions which are all the values of the resulting variable proposition. This class in general still depends on what, by arbitrary agreement, we mean by parts of that proposition. But if we change all those signs, whose meaning was arbitrarily determined, into variables, there always remains such a class. But this is no longer dependent on any agreement; it depends only on the nature of the proposition. It corresponds to a logical form, to a logical prototype ['Urbild': pre-model].[24]

All of the sentences which are values of a propositional variable of this kind are sentences of specific type: for example, sentences consisting of a one-place predicate in combination with a name, or sentences consisting of a two-place predicate in combination with two names, or sentences consisting of two sentences joined by 'and' — and so on. But it seems that we ought to be able to specify something more general than this — something which is common to *all* sentences. Without this, we might be doubtful about the coherence of the very idea of a sentence, just as such.[25] This would be the *general* form of the sentence.

That there is such a general form of the sentence is of central importance to the *Tractatus*. Wittgenstein discusses the issue in the context of his account of logic, and we will consider it in that context in the next chapter. But it is worth anticipating that discussion a little, in order to link it back to the remarks about the context principle which introduce the idea of a propositional variable. In that later discussion, Wittgenstein says the following things:

(G1) The general form of [the] proposition is: Such and such is the case. (4.5)

(G2) The general propositional form is a variable. (4.53)

(G2) is an expression of the same point as the one which Wittgenstein makes about expressions in general, in 3.311–3.316. The general propositional form — the general form of the sentence — is what is common to every sentence. And what is common to every sentence can be represented by a variable which can be replaced by any sentence.

In this context, it is worth remarking on the difference between Ogden's translation of (G1) and this alternative, provided by Pears and McGuinness:

The general form of a proposition is: This is how things stand.

Ogden's translation is clearly preferable here: its 'such and such' is a close translation of the German 'so und so', and gives precisely the idea of a variable.[26] 'Such and such' (like the German 'so und so') is an expression which is meant to be replaced by a more precise specification: it is an ordinary-language variable.[27]

Wittgenstein offers an argument for the claim that there is a general form of the sentence (at 4.5). It is an argument which appears to be distinct from the simple thought that without such a general form the idea of the sentence, in general, would be incomprehensible. And it seems to depend on the precise claims he makes about logic, so we will consider it in detail in that context. But something of the significance of the claim can be seen in the context of the *Tractatus*'s general theory of language — the theory that sentences are models. For if there is a general form of the sentence — a form which is common to all sentences — then that will be something which no sentence can depict, since, in general, no picture can depict its own form. Similarly, it will follow from the general account of language that nothing which can only be described by describing the general form of the sentence will be describable. This will take on a fundamental importance when Wittgenstein turns to the status of philosophy.

4E ANALYSIS AND ELEMENTARY SENTENCES

The central claim of the *Tractatus*'s conception of language is that sentences are models, like the Paris courtroom model. This means, in particular, that the elements of sentences must have the same possibilities of combination as the corresponding items in reality. But is Wittgenstein really claiming that *all* sentences are models? And does he think that every part of every sentence is correlated with something in reality which shares the same possibilities of combination?

The answer to both questions is *No*. His claim that sentences are pictures or models (at 4.01, for example) should be compared with his claim (at 1.21) that any fact can either be the case or not, while everything else remains the same. The claim at 1.21 seems to apply unrestrictedly to every kind of fact; but really Wittgenstein only takes it to hold for *atomic* facts: it was just that the more general notion of fact had to be used in the first instance. In the same way, although the apparently unrestricted claim that sentences are pictures or models might seem to apply to every sentence, really Wittgenstein does not need it to hold for every kind of sentence, and I think it is clear that he does not hold it. He really needs it to hold — and means it to hold — just for a very limited class of sentences, those which he calls *elementary* sentences. For most purposes, we can treat the 'picture theory' — the theory of sentences as models — strictly speaking, as a theory only of elementary sentences. This explains the following sequence of remarks:

3.2 In propositions thoughts can be so expressed that to the objects of the thoughts correspond the elements of the propositional sign.

3.201 These elements I call 'simple signs' and the proposition 'completely analysed'.

3.21 To the configuration of the simple signs in the propositional sign corresponds the configuration of the objects in the state of affairs.

3.21 is, in effect, a statement of the crucial sameness-of-form assumption (SM3); the context makes it clear that it is only supposed to apply to sentences which consist solely of 'simple signs'. 3.201 also indicates that not all of the single words in a sentence will count as 'simple signs': for some sentences, it seems, will not be 'completely analysed', and these will contain components which stand in need of analysis. That is to say, some of the single words in an unanalysed sentence will not count as 'simple signs'.

Wittgenstein claims here that it is possible in principle for there to be sentences which consist wholly of 'simple signs'. Only these sentences will be models in the strict sense, although the possibility of describing the world in language at all will depend on the possibility, in principle, of analysing familiar sentences in terms of these basic, elementary sentences which consist just of 'simple signs'. But what is a 'simple sign'? The answer to this question is contained in the following two sections:

3.23 The postulate of the possibility of the simple signs is the postulate of the determinateness of the sense.

3.24 A proposition about a complex stands in internal relation to the proposition about its constituent part.

A complex can only be given by its description, and this will be either right or wrong. The proposition in which there is mention of a complex, if this does not exist, becomes not nonsense but simply false.

That a propositional element signifies a complex can be seen from an indeterminateness in the propositions in which it occurs. We *know* that everything is not yet determined by this proposition. (The notation for generality *contains* a prototype.)

The combination of the symbols of a complex in a simple symbol can be expressed by a definition.

Here we see Wittgenstein committing himself to the following claims:

(i) Sense must be determinate.
(ii) Sense can only be determinate if there are simple signs.
(iii) Sentences which contain signs which stand for complexes are evidently indeterminate.

There are three things which are not quite clear about this, however. First, it is not immediately clear what the 'determinateness' which Wittgenstein speaks of is. Second, it is not quite obvious what 'complexes' are. And, third, the character of the argument involved in claims (i)–(iii) is not completely clear.

The kind of indeterminacy which is Wittgenstein's concern here can be discovered by reflecting on the remark in parentheses: 'The notation for generality *contains* a prototype'. The obviousness of this — indicated by the emphasis on *'contains'* here — is clearly supposed to underline the obviousness of the indeterminacy of sentences which contain signs for complexes. Since we considered 3.315 in the last section (strictly speaking, out of order), we have already come across the notion of a 'prototype', or pre-model ('Urbild'). A prototype in this sense is something like '*x* is wise' or '*fx*', which results from replacing some or all of the different parts of a sentence with variables. The standard (logical) notation for generality does indeed contain a prototype in this sense. For example, 'Everything is *F*' is rendered

'$\forall x \; Fx$' (or '$(x)Fx$'); and 'Something is F' is rendered '$\exists x \; Fx$'. The prototypes involved here are indeterminate in the sense of being *unspecific*: 'x is wise' does not say who, in particular, is wise'; 'fx' does not say what particular object has what particular quality. It is, in fact, this unspecificity which ensures that sentences involving generality are not literally pictures or models: they do not consist of elements which are correlated with items in reality (nor, as we will see in Chapter 5, section 5C, are they simply compounds — conjunctions or alternations — of sentences which consist of elements which are correlated with objects in reality).

Claim (i), then, must be the claim that sense cannot be unspecific in the way in which 'prototypes', in Wittgenstein's sense, are. But what might *that* mean? The natural interpretation is that it means that uses of such unspecific prototypes — for example, in expressions of generality — can only have sense in virtue of those prototypes being variables which can in principle be replaced by *specific* sentences. That is to say, the use of these prototypes is only really a way of indicating a range of specific sentences. This roughly coincides with the more everyday thought that general claims like 'Everything is F' or 'Something is F' can only really be true in virtue of more specific claims of the form 'a is F'.

Wittgenstein seems to think that the obvious lack of specificity of expressions of generality *shows* that sentences which 'mention' complexes lack specificity in the same way. This seems to require that sentences which 'mention' complexes must themselves involve expressions of generality. And this has only one natural interpretation, in the historical context of the *Tractatus*. An expression which mentions a complex must be being treated in a similar way to a definite description, something of the form 'The F' (where 'F' is singular). Frege treated such expressions as singular terms — that is to say, as expressions which are only meaningful in virtue of being correlated with something in the world. But Russell, in his theory of descriptions, treated them as involving quantifier expressions; that is to say, as involving generality (see Chapter 2, section 2C, above).[28] He treated an expression of the form 'The *F*' as equivalent in meaning to 'There is exactly one thing which is *F*, and that thing … '. It is a feature of Russell's theory that when there is nothing which satisfies the description — when there is no *F* — the sentence which contains the phrase is not meaningless — as it would have been on Frege's view (leaving aside the notion of Fregean 'sense') — but false (because there just is *not* exactly one thing which is *F*). This coincides precisely with what Wittgenstein says here:

> The proposition in which there is mention of a complex, if this does not exist, becomes not nonsense but simply false.
>
> (3.24)

And the connection with Russell is made even clearer later in the book:

> 5.526 One can describe the world completely by completely general-ized propositions, *i.e.* without from the outset co-ordinating any name with a definite object.
> In order then to arrive at the customary way of expression we need simply to say after an expression 'there is one and only one *x*, which … ': and this *x* is *a*.

So Wittgenstein seems simply to assume that expressions which appear to stand for complexes are properly treated as Russell treats definite descriptions — though perhaps with a slight qualification. The qualification is that Wittgenstein is unlikely to have been happy to regard a 'complex' as a thing at all. It seems more plausible to attribute to him the view that where the layperson might see a 'complex', Wittgenstein sees only the components and facts about their arrangement — or rather: only that there are *some* components arranged in certain ways. Thus he says:

> 2.0201 Every statement about complexes can be analysed into a statement about their constituent parts, and into those pro-positions which completely describe the complexes.

Wittgenstein seems, then, to assume without argument that sentences about 'complexes' need to be analysed by means of some use of generality. Because the notation for generality always involves the inspecificity of 'prototypes', and the inspecificity of 'prototypes' is itself an indication of the possibility of their being replaced by specific expressions, the fact that expressions which stand for complexes are to be analysed by means of generality is taken to show that there must be 'simple signs'. And since 'simple signs' are here contrasted with expressions which stand for complexes, 'simple signs' must be expressions which stand for simple entities — that is to say, *objects*.

If this is right, there is no argument here for the existence of simple entities — the *objects* introduced in the early 2s. The argument we have here seems to *presuppose* a contrast between 'complexes' and simple entities, and then to be concerned to show, merely, that it must be possible in principle for there to be *signs* for the simple entities: that is, the names from which fully analysed sentences are constructed. That means that the argument for the existence of objects, in the sense of the early 2s, must depend just on general features of the *Tractatus*'s theory of language — in particular, on the assumption that language and the world must share a common form. And, in fact, on my interpretation the argument for substance in 2.02 and the following sections does indeed depend just on general features of the *Tractatus*'s theory of language. (See Chapter 1, section 1D.)

Sections 3.23–3.24 must then be concerned to address a different worry. And it is not hard to see what that worry must be. It is the worry that the words of our ordinary sentences simply do not stand for items in the world which have the same ranges of possible combination as the words do, and whose ranges of possible combination constitute the form of the world itself — that is to say, the ultimate possibilities of combination of things. In fact, we have very little idea of the objects with which words would have to be correlated for there to be this kind of match. The point of 3.23–3.24 is, then, simply to claim that the failure of the surface grammar of our everyday language to meet the demands of the theory that sentences are models is no objection to the theory itself — or indeed to the meaningfulness of our everyday language. In fact, Wittgenstein thinks that our everyday language is perfectly meaningful:[29]

> All propositions of our colloquial language are actually, just as they are, logically completely in order.
>
> (5.5563)

Instead of giving up the theory of sentences as models, or doubting the meaningfulness of our everyday language, Wittgenstein thinks that we need to understand our everyday words as involving implicit generalizations, whose instances, ultimately, will consist entirely of signs for simple objects, hanging in one another like the links of a chain. Wittgenstein summarizes his approach to everyday languages in this remark:

> 4.002 Man possesses the capacity of constructing languages, in which every sense can be expressed, without having an idea how and what each word means — just as one speaks without knowing how the single sounds are produced.
>
> Colloquial language is a part of the human organism and is not less complicated than it.
>
> From it it is humanly impossible to gather immediately the logic of language.
>
> Language disguises the thought; so that from the external form of the clothes one cannot infer the form of the thought they clothe, because the external form of the clothes is constructed with quite another object than to let the form of the body be recognized.
>
> The silent adjustments to understand colloquial language are enormously complicated.

4F PREDICATES AND RELATIONS

We are now in a position to understand Wittgenstein's general theory more clearly. Language is capable of representing reality in virtue of the possibility of there being sentences which consist wholly of simple signs — names — of the objects whose possibilities of arrangement constitute the ultimate possibilities of the world. Wittgenstein scornfully dismisses questions about the nature of these objects — beyond what his theory requires — but there is one question which might seem to be pressing for him, and on which there is some doubt whether he had a settled view. Do Wittgenstein's objects include qualities and relations? In the terms of an ancient debate, was Wittgenstein a 'realist' or a 'nominalist' about qualities and relations?[30] (In the traditional debate on this issue, a *realist* holds that 'universals' — qualities and relations — exist, in the sense of being things — objects — whereas a *nominalist* denies this, hoping to explain language which seemed to refer to universals as involving nothing more than a complicated way of dealing with the use of linguistic expressions. Note that this use of the term 'realism' is only tangentially connected with the use of the term in which it contrasts with 'idealism', as in Chapter 1, section 1F, for example.)

Wittgenstein's views on this issue might appear at first sight to be confused and inconsistent. The difficulty is revealed by what he says in texts outside the *Tractatus*, which are nevertheless clearly relevant to it. In 1913 he wrote:

(a) I have changed my views on 'atomic' complexes: I now think that qualities, relations (like love) etc. are all copulae!

(*CL*: 24)

And again:

(b) Indefinables are of two sorts: names and forms. Propositions cannot consist of names alone, they cannot be classes of names.

(*NL*: 96)

But in 1915 he wrote:

(c) Relations and properties, etc. are *objects* too.

(*NB*: 61)

And soon after he returned to philosophy (some time in 1930–31), he is recorded as saying this in explanation of *Tractatus* 2.01 ('A state of affairs (a state of things) is a combination of objects (things)'):

(d) Objects etc. is here used for such things as a colour, a point in visual space etc. ... . 'Objects' also include relations; a proposition is not two things connected by a relation. 'Thing' and 'relation' are on the same level. The objects hang as it were in a chain.[31]

(*WLC*: 120)

The puzzle is this. As texts (a) and (b) show, in 1913 he seems to have thought that qualities and relations were *not* objects, and that something other than names was needed for there to be whole sentences. But in 1915, and again long after the writing of the *Tractatus,* he seems to have decided that qualities and relations *are* objects. This could be put down to a simple change of mind, were it not for a crucial text in the middle of the *Tractatus* itself:

3.1432 We must not say, 'The complex sign "*aRb*" says "*a* stands in relation *R* to *b*"'; but we must say, '*That* "*a*" stands in a certain relation to "*b*" says *that aRb*'.

This seems to express (among other things) exactly the doctrine of text (b): it seems that the symbol '*R*' does not function as a *name* of a relation, but as a way in which the two names '*a*' and '*b*' can be related — something which the two names can be written each side of. And, indeed, 3.1432 is verbally very close to this remark of 1913, from which it seems ultimately to derive:

In '*aRb*', '*R*' looks like a substantive, but is not one. What symbolizes in '*aRb*' is that R occurs between *a* and *b*.

(*NL* 98)

At this point we seem to have a truly bizarre historical sequence. We seem to find Wittgenstein endorsing one view in 1913, changing his mind over it in 1915, changing it back again in the final version of the book (around 1918), only for him to change his mind yet again (while still making use of the imagery of the *Tractatus* itself) in the academic year 1930–31. This looks like a level of vacillation and uncertainty over a major issue which it is very hard to attribute to Wittgenstein.

In fact, there is no such very serious anomaly, even if the interpretation of what Wittgenstein is doing is not altogether obvious. I will start by trying to get clear about the position of the *Tractatus*, before going back to consider the stages in the process by which Wittgenstein reached this position. It will turn out that the process does not involve any very peculiar vacillation.

To begin with, we should recall what qualities and relations are traditionally taken to be. They are entities which are correlated (in some way) with predicates: one-place predicates, in the case of qualities; and many-placed predicates, in the case of relations. In the light of that, the first thing we need to do is distinguish between two questions, a semantic question and an ontological one, even if they are bound to be related:

(SQ)   Are there any predicates in elementary sentences?
(OQ)   Are there some qualities and relations among the fundamental objects?

Let us begin with the semantic question, (SQ). In order to answer this, we need to know what a predicate is. In the most neutral sense, a predicate is what is left of a sentence containing names once one or more names have been removed.[32] Clearly there must be predicates, in this minimal sense, among elementary sentences, if elementary sentences include names at all. For a sentence must be *more* than just a single name, so there must be something left of a sentence once a name has been removed. It is clear from this that anyone who raises (SQ) at all must have a less minimal sense of 'predicate' in mind. We might call this a *rich* sense of the term 'predicate', and explain it as follows: a predicate (in this rich sense) is a *non-namelike basic component of sentences, which yields a whole sentence when combined appropriately with one or more names.* Those who think that there is a fundamental linguistic contrast between names and predicates (between 'subject' and predicate in an older terminology) hold that even the most basic sentences include predicates in this rich sense.

Wittgenstein clearly disagrees:

4.22 The elementary proposition consists of names. It is a hanging together ['Zusammenhang'], a linking in a chain ['Verkettung'], of names.

The whole point of 4.22 (as text (d) confirms) seems to be to say that we do not need anything other than names to glue a sentence together: the names hang in one another on their own. So there are no predicates in elementary sentences, if 'predicate' is understood in the rich sense, as a *non-namelike* basic sentential component.

This might seem puzzling, since Wittgenstein is clearly happy to use the familiar predicate *letters* of modern predicate logic (in 3.1432, for example). But the use of those familiar predicate letters requires nothing more than the *minimal* sense of 'predicate'. We can spell the point out explicitly as follows. Suppose that elementary sentences are just strings of names, such as these three:

(1) *abcdef*
(2) *nbcdef*
(3) *mbcden*

(1) and (2) can be seen to share a common form: they both represent a combination of an object (*a* and *n*, respectively) with the objects *b, c, d, e,* and *f*. We can perfectly well use the letter '*F*' to symbolize what they share, and then, following the familiar modern ordering, represent that fact by rewriting them as follows:

(1a)   *Fa*
(2a)   *Fn*

Both sentences can now be said to have the form '*Fx*'. Again, we can see that (1) and (3) share a common form: they both represent combinations of pairs of objects (*a* and *f*, and *m* and *n*, respectively) with the further objects *b*, *c*, *d*, and *e*. Again, we could use '*R*' to symbolize what they share, and rewrite (1) and (3) as follows:

(1b)   *aRf*
(3b)   *mRn*

Both (1) and (3) can now be seen to have the form '*xRy*'. In (1a), (2a), (1b), and (3b), the letters '*F*' and '*R*' do not function as names. Rather, they are functional expressions in a very particular sense: they represent whole sentences as being functions of certain selected names. Thus '*Fa*' represents the sentence '*abcdef*' as a function of the name '*a*', and '*aRf*' represents '*abcdef*' as a function of the two names '*a*' and '*f*'.[33] (For this idea of a sentence being a function of one or more names within it, see 3.318 and 4.24: this issue is considered further in Chapter 5, section 5B, below.) The use of '*R*' in 3.1432 is quite compatible with this: it figures there as no more than a way of symbolizing a commonality sharable by other sentences — even if it is one which could, in principle, be spelled out as consisting just of a string of names.

Does this mean that sentences using predicate letters cannot be elementary sentences? Must we say that '*aRb*', as it occurs in 3.1432, for example, is not an elementary sentence? There is a slightly tricky issue here about the relationship between sentences and notations. If we look at the way '*F*' was introduced on the basis of (1) and (2), and '*R*' on the basis of (1) and (3), we can see that these predicate letters are no more than convenient ways of writing chunks of sentences — ways designed to make commonalities obvious. So we might regard (1a) and (2a) as just ways of writing (1) and (2), and (1b), and (3b) as just ways of writing (1) and

(3). Since, by hypothesis, (1), (2), and (3) are themselves elementary sentences, (1a), (2a), (1b), and (3b) would all be elementary sentences too, though they are not written in ways that show all the names of which they are composed. As long as we are clear about what we are doing, this seems a perfectly legitimate way of describing them.

So even if there are no predicates in elementary sentences, in the *rich* sense of 'predicate' (a non-namelike basic sentential component), there can still be a legitimate use of the predicate letters of standard predicate logic, as functions of the relevant kind from names to sentences. And it seems perfectly legitimate to count at least some sentences in which the familiar predicate letters are used as elementary sentences.

Now let us turn to the ontological question (OQ). Just as the answer to (SQ) depends on what is meant by 'predicate', so the answer to (OQ) depends on what, precisely, is meant by 'quality' and 'relation'. It is natural to take qualities and relations to be the ontological correlates of predicates, understanding 'predicate' in the *rich* sense: that is, we might define qualities and relations as the correlates of appropriate *non-namelike* basic sentential components. If we define 'quality' and 'relation' in this way, and we take what counts as *non-namelike* to be determined by *Wittgenstein's* conception of names, Wittgenstein's answer is unequivocal, since he clearly does not accept that there are such non-namelike basic sentential components.

But a different conception of names would generate a different conception of what counts as *non-namelike*. And we need look no further than to Frege to find such a different conception of names. Frege reserved the term 'name' ('proper name', strictly speaking) for one of two basic kinds of sub-sentential expression; as we saw in Chapter 2, he contrasted names in *his* sense with 'concept-expressions' or predicates. This contrast between basic kinds of sub-sentential expression is parallel to a contrast between basic kinds of entity. Frege reserved the term 'object' for the referents of names (in his sense of 'name'), and used the term 'concept' for the referents of predicates. Frege took objects (in his sense) to be 'saturated' or complete, and 'concepts' (in his sense) to be 'unsaturated' or incomplete. If these two contrasts — between names (in Frege's sense) and predicates, and between 'saturated' and 'unsaturated' entities — can be made good, we can define qualities and relations in their terms. Qualities and relations can still be defined as the referents of predicates in the *rich* sense: that is, they will be the referents of *non-namelike* basic expressions (as before), but the conception of what counts as *non-namelike* will be determined by *Frege*'s conception of names, rather than by Wittgenstein's. That is to say, we can define qualities and relations as *unsaturated* entities, in whatever sense of 'unsaturated' it is that Frege is concerned with.[34]

Whether some of Wittgenstein's names refer to such 'unsaturated' entities is at least not immediately ruled out by 4.22 (which is parallel to the explicitly ontological 2.01 and 2.03). There is no immediate reason why a Tractarian name should not be *non-namelike* in *Frege*'s terms. For it might be that the expressions which Wittgenstein counts as names can in fact be divided into exactly two types, and types of exactly the right kinds: those which Frege would count as namelike, and those which Frege would count as non-namelike. And it might be that a corresponding simple distinction can be made among the entities which Wittgenstein counts as objects: some would be counted as 'saturated' by Frege, and some as 'unsaturated'.

What *is* immediately ruled out by 4.22 is the idea that all Tractarian names might be namelike in *Frege*'s sense, and that all of the objects to which Wittgenstein's names refer might be *saturated* entities. For that would involve making the following three assumptions simultaneously:

(i) A sentence might be composed just of *names*;

(ii) All names are *namelike* in the Fregean sense; and

(iii) No sentence can be composed just of *namelike* expressions, in the Fregean sense of 'namelike'.

And these three assumptions quite obviously form an inconsistent set.

On the Fregean picture, there is a single crucial distinction to be made between the entities correlated with different components of the most basic sentences; and we only get a whole sentence of the most basic type, when we have something made in an appropriate way from both kinds of component expression. But, although Frege thought that the most basic sentences are constructed, ultimately, of components of just two fundamental kinds, this is not the only way in which we might think sentences were constructed. We might suppose that there was a greater variety of fundamental kinds of component of basic sentences than this simple Fregean asymmetry allows. Different kinds of fundamental expression might take quite different kinds of complements to form whole sentences. But even this more variegated conception of the composition of sentences is compatible with counting qualities and relations among Wittgenstein's objects, given a suitable modification of our conception of what qualities and relations are. For we might suppose that among the large variety of different kinds of object which are correlated with the various different kinds of fundamental expression, there was a principled reason to single out two in particular; and because (as it might turn out) the linguistic expressions which correspond to these two particular kinds of object stand in close proximity to certain everyday quality-words and relational expressions, we might legitimately call objects of these two kinds *qualities* and *relations*. This would mean breaking or qualifying the traditional connection between the concepts of *quality* and *relation*, on the one hand, and the relatively simple grammatical category of predicates, on the other. But it might nevertheless provide another way of allowing qualities and relations to be included among the objects of the *Tractatus*. And this, too, would be consistent with 4.22 (as well as 2.01 and 2.03).

We seem, then, to have at least two ways in which Wittgenstein could hold a 'realist' position — that is, accept that the objects of the *Tractatus* include qualities and relations — consistently with his claim that the most basic sentences are composed just of names. He could adopt the Fregean view, according to which the unity of sentences depends on a single, particular kind of asymmetry; or he could suppose that there is a variety of different kinds of complementarity, which permits the unity of sentences to be realized in a variety of different ways, with the notions of quality and relation doing no more than mark out distinctive commonalities within that variety.[35]

The *Tractatus* itself is neutral between these two views. Perhaps, indeed, it is deliberately neutral: it is quite plausible to suggest that Wittgenstein took the final determination of the nature of objects to be something that could not be settled *a priori* — that is, before a detailed analysis of language had actually been carried out. This seems to be the view of the text held by Frank Ramsey (hinted at in Ramsey (1923), and argued for explicitly at (1925b: 133)). And it seems to have been endorsed openly by Wittgenstein himself in 1929 (*WVC*: 42).[36]

Furthermore, it is not just that the *Tractatus*, in general, is neutral on the fundamental nature of the objects to which the names in elementary sentences refer: there is nothing in 3.1432 which disrupts this neutrality. In particular, there is nothing here which involves *denying* that there are qualities and relations among the objects — provided merely that qualities and relations are not defined as the referents of expressions which are non-namelike in *Wittgenstein's* terms. For all we know, '*a*' or '*b*' may refer to a quality or a relation; and '*R*' itself may be a replacement for a common component of sentences which includes names for qualities and relations.

Bearing all this in mind, what story can we tell of the history of Wittgenstein's thought? In 1913 he seems to have thought that qualities and relations were not included among the objects referred to by names: instead, qualities and relations seem to be *forms*.[37] (This view was a significant change in itself, as text (b) suggests: by making qualities and relations themselves 'copulae' or forms, Wittgenstein aimed to remove the need to add an *extra* copulative component to glue them onto objects.[38]) But by 1915, and apparently thereafter — with no interruption in the *Tractatus*, as far as can be seen from the text — he seems happy to count qualities and relations as objects. It looks as if a significant stage in this transition is marked by the following text (also from the 1913 *Notes on Logic*):

> But the form of a proposition symbolizes in the following way: Let us consider symbols of the form 'xRy'; to these correspond primarily pairs of objects, of which one has the name 'x', the other the name 'y'. The xs and ys stand in various relations to each other, among others the relation R holds between some, but not between others. I now determine the sense of 'xRy' by laying down: when the facts behave in regard to 'xRy' so that the meaning of 'x' stands in the relation R to the meaning of "y', then I say that the [the facts] are 'of like sense' with the proposition 'xRy'; otherwise, 'of opposite sense'; I correlate the facts to the symbol 'xRy' *by* thus dividing them into those of like sense and those of opposite sense. To this correlation corresponds the correlation of name and meaning. Both are psychological. Thus I understand the form 'xRy' when I know that it discriminates the behaviour of x and y according as these stand in the relation R or not. In this way I extract from all possible relations the relation R, as, by a name, I extract its meaning from all possible things.[39]

> *(NL: 104)*

Two things are striking about this passage. One is that Wittgenstein draws a close parallel between the definition of the meaning of names and the definition of the meaning of 'forms': each kind of sentential element is meaningful in virtue of an arbitrary psychological correlation. The other is the idea that at least some parts of sentences have their meaning defined in terms of a correlation between sentences, on the one hand, and facts which are specified as being 'of like sense' and 'of opposite sense', on the other. Let us consider these two striking things in turn.

Earlier in the *Notes on Logic* (*NL*: 96; text (b) above) Wittgenstein had insisted that there are two sorts of 'indefinables': names and forms. This is a single fundamental distinction between kinds of basic expression, which is parallel to, even if not quite the same as, Frege's distinction between complete and incomplete expressions.[40] But the observation in this later passage (*NL*: 104) that there is a fundamental similarity between the two kinds of 'indefinable' encourages one to think that that distinction might not be as fundamental as it seemed. In that case, we might assimilate these two kinds of 'indefinable' to a single category, and call them all just *names*. And that seems to be just what Wittgenstein did.

But if this is what Wittgenstein did, we should be careful not to exaggerate the magnitude of the transition which is involved here. It is not that Wittgenstein maintained the same (basically Fregean) conception of both names and objects from early 1913 onwards, with the difference being that he later came to think that some expressions which he had earlier counted as 'copulative' were, after all, names in that original sense, and that some 'unsaturated' entities were included among the ('saturated') objects. It is rather that he changed his conception of names and objects: he came to think that, for his purposes at least, there was not a fundamental difference between those expressions which he originally counted as names, and those which he originally counted as 'copulative'. And he came to think that there was not a fundamental difference, for his purposes at least, between the entities which he originally counted as objects, and those which he was previously inclined to distinguish from objects. It is slightly exaggerating the point to say that the change in Wittgenstein's views is verbal rather than substantial; but at least there is not the kind of substantial difference which there is usually taken to be between traditional 'realists' and 'nominalists' about universals.

Wittgenstein may have been encouraged to change his conception of the nature of names and of objects by the substance of his own suggested account of the meaning of forms in the later passage from the *Notes on Logic* which I have quoted. A remarkable feature of this account is that it explicitly and deliberately explains the meaning of forms in terms of their contribution to whole sentences of which they can be part. It was, of course, an important part of Frege's view that the same holds for *every* kind of subsentential expression: indeed, he emphasized the point in particular in connection with singular terms (what he called 'proper names'). If Wittgenstein was not particularly concerned with the point of Frege's contrast between 'saturated' and 'unsaturated' entities (whatever, exactly, that may have been), we can imagine him reflecting further on Frege's Context Principle, and coming up with the following thought. The account which is here (in *NL*: 104) provided of the meaning just of forms could be generalized to provide us with the basis of an account of the meaning of *all* fundamental expressions — including those which were previously called 'names' *in contrast* with those called 'forms'. That is, we can imagine Wittgenstein assimilating Frege's Context Principle more thoroughly than he had before, and taking *all* fundamental expressions to have their meaning in virtue of a distinction between those facts which are 'of like sense' and those which are 'of opposite sense'.

There are two further features of the account of the meaning of forms in the *Notes on Logic* which are worth noting. The first is its conception of the relation between the meaning-determining subject and the world. The meaning-determining subject seems to be imagined as seeing the world, on the one hand, there with all its facts, independently of language, while having whole sentences, on the other hand, ready to correlate with those facts. This idea of a kind of language-independent access to the facts, just as such, seems to be derived from Russell: it does not survive into the *Tractatus*.[41]

The other notable feature of the account of the meaning of forms does survive, however. This is that the meaning even of parts of the most basic sentences is explained in terms just of the difference they make to the truth or falsity of whole sentences in which they may occur. The facts 'of like sense' are those which make the relevant sentences *true*, and the facts 'of opposite sense' are those which make the relevant sentences *false*. And this difference is supposed to be enough to establish completely the meaning of the relevant expressions. This is the deep underlying link between the account of elementary sentences as models, and the account of compound sentences as truth-functions of elementary sentences, which is the topic of much of Chapter 5.[42]

4G THE SOLUTION OF THE PROBLEMS INHERITED FROM FREGE AND RUSSELL

The so-called 'picture theory' — the theory that sentences are models, like the Paris courtroom model of the traffic accident — is designed to deal with the problems in the philosophy of language which faced Frege and Russell. Wittgenstein clearly felt that it was the only possible solution to those problems: this conviction underlies his confidence that there is no way of doing philosophy at all without being undermined by the paradoxes which face the picture theory.

Recall from the last chapter that Wittgenstein was operating with these two fundamental assumptions:

> (Corr) Languages depend for their meaningfulness on correlations between certain linguistic items, on the one hand, and extra-linguistic items, on the other.
>
> (Obj) The extra-linguistic items with which those linguistic items have to be correlated for languages to be meaningful are items in the world (objects).

And in the light of these, he faced two fundamental problems:

> (P1) Which linguistic items need to be correlated with things in the world for languages to be meaningful?
>
> (P2) How is the unity of the sentence to be explained?

Problem (P1) relates in particular (in the context of the new logic developed by Frege and Russell) to three categories of linguistic expression: apparent singular terms, predicates, and whole sentences. In the case of apparent singular terms, the difficulty is to deal with the fact that certain apparent singular terms can seem to be meaningful, even though there is no real object in the world with which they are correlated. (This is part of what I called the problem of *thinness of meaning* in Chapter 2, section 2C.) Wittgenstein here follows Russell, in restricting the range of genuine singular terms to those for which the problem cannot arise. His singular terms — the names which are combined in elementary sentences — are correlated with objects which exist necessarily. Other apparent singular terms are not really singular terms, but they are meaningful in the same way as definite descriptions are, on Russell's account of definite descriptions: sentences containing them involve assertions of existence, so the sentences are simply false, rather than meaningless.

A problem arises if predicates are correlated with items in the world. If the items in the world have a distinctive character, in order for them to be capable of explaining the grammar of the corresponding predicates, then we face difficulties in counting these items as objects — the difficulties which faced Frege over the concept *horse*. On the other hand, if we follow Russell and treat predicates in very much the manner in which names had been treated, we will be at a loss to explain how predicates are capable of combining with singular terms to form whole sentences. Wittgenstein's solution, I think, is to be quite explicit in thinking of the meaning of *all* expressions as being no more than the difference they make to the truth or falsity of sentences in which they occur.

As for whole sentences themselves, if we take them to be correlated with objects in the world, we seem to have a choice between two odd theories. On the one hand is Frege's theory, which correlates sentences with truth-values — the True and the False — and these are very odd entities. On the other hand there is Russell's early theory which correlated sentences with propositions: the sentence 'Ottoline loves Bertie' will be correlated with the proposition that Ottoline loves Bertie, for example. The problem then is to explain what it is for that proposition to exist when the sentence is false, since the actual existence of the proposition seems to depend on Ottoline's actually loving Bertie. Once again,

Wittgenstein avoids these problems by denying that sentences are correlated with anything. All that needs to be common between a sentence and the reality it depicts is a *form*: that is, its elements must be capable of the same ranges of possible combination as the corresponding objects are. There need be no false fact corresponding to a false sentence.

So much for problem (P1). The *Tractatus*'s solution to problem (P2) is devastatingly simple. The difficulty for both Frege and Russell was that they had to explain the distinctive unity and completeness of whole sentences in terms of something external to language. But Wittgenstein does not. This is because, for Wittgenstein, sentences themselves — like all pictures — are *facts*. A fact is an entity in the world which has a distinctive unity: exactly the kind of unity which sentences possess, to be precise. But Wittgenstein does not need to explain the unity of sentences in terms of the supposedly prior unity of facts: instead, sentences themselves have this unity, because they are themselves facts, in just the same way as any fact in the world is. That means that the unity of sentences does not need to be explained by anything else.

Nor is the unity of a sentence something constructed. This is where Wittgenstein's hard-line insistence on the letter of the Context Principle comes into play. Since, for Wittgenstein, words strictly do have meaning only in the context of a sentence, it turns out that those very words cannot occur except within sentences. So sentences are not constructed from parts which might occur in isolation. Sentences are composed of parts which are always already part of them. There is therefore no need to understand how the parts of a sentence can be joined together in a way which ensures the completeness and unity of the result: they only occur within an entity which already has the required completeness and unity.

4H THE METAPHYSICS OF THE *TRACTATUS*

In Chapter 1 we discerned the following major metaphysical commitments of the *Tractatus*:

(T1)   The basic organic unities of the world are facts;

(T2)   Facts are different in kind from things (objects);

(T3)   Facts are either atomic facts or combinations of atomic facts;

(T4)   The existence of any atomic fact is independent of the existence of any other atomic fact;

(T5)   Atomic facts are combinations of objects;

(T6)   Which atomic facts are possible is determined by the nature of objects;

(T7)   It is essential to an object that it can combine with other objects, in the ways it can, to form atomic facts;

(T8)   Nothing is essential to an object beyond the fact that it can combine with other objects, in the ways it can, to form atomic facts;

(T9)   Objects exist necessarily;

(T10)   It is necessary that just those atomic facts are possible which are, in fact, possible.

The bulk of these commitments derive directly from the theory that sentences are models. (T1) is ultimately a consequence of the same-form assumption, (SM3). As we saw (section 4C), that assumption leads Wittgenstein to insist that names cannot be combined in ways which are not matched by the ways in which the corresponding objects can be combined: there can be no illegitimate combinations of words. And it seems hard to insist that there can be no illegitimate combinations of names without insisting that names can only occur at all in legitimate combinations — that is to say, in whole sentences. But if names can only occur in whole sentences, and the range of possible combination of names must be the same as the range of possible combination of objects (as (SM3) requires), then objects can only occur in combination with other objects in whole facts. That means that objects cannot exist independently of all other objects, or of facts; if any entities at all can exist independently of other entities of the same kind, it is only facts which can do that. So if there are any basic organic unities, in this sense, they must be facts. We therefore get a conditional confirmation of (T1): (T1) is true *if* there are any basic organic unities.

That facts — or, at least, atomic facts — actually are such basic organic unities requires them to be independent of one another. The claim that they are independent of one another is tied up with two other basic commitments of the metaphysics of the *Tractatus*: (T3) and (T4). The vindication of these two commitments depends, strictly speaking, not simply on the theory that sentences are models — since that theory applies directly only to elementary sentences — but to the *Tractatus*'s account of logic. Accordingly, these two commitments will be considered in the next chapter. That there is *some* contrast, however, between atomic facts and facts of other kinds is required by the idea that not every sentence is 'completely analysed': that is to say, not every sentence of everyday language consists wholly of names for objects whose possibilities of combination are the fundamental possibilities of the world.

(T2) and (T5) are reflections of the fact that there is a distinctive issue about the unity of the proposition. This issue presented Frege and Russell with one of the principal difficulties which any theory of language of their world-oriented kind had to deal with: the unity of a sentence is different from the unity of any other kind of thing, and seems to need a special kind of explanation. In the theories of the early Russell and of the *Tractatus*, the unity of sentences needs to be understood in terms of the unity of a special kind of entity in the objective world — objective 'propositions' in Russell's early theory, and facts in Wittgenstein's. The problem disappears on Wittgenstein's account, as we have seen, in the insistence (deriving from (SM3)) that sentences themselves are facts. For all that, he still offers some account of what it is for a fact to be unified. The unity of a fact does not consist, according to Wittgenstein, in the presence of a special copulative element — a kind of predicative glue, as it were — in a fact which binds the other elements together. Rather the unity of the fact simply consists of the objects appearing, as they always do, in the special kind of combination with other objects which facts are. This is the significance of (T5), which is the metaphysical counterpart of 4.22.

(T6) follows from the *Tractatus*'s commitments about the nature of substance, combined with the thought that the fundamental possibilities are simply the possibilities of combination of the objects which correspond to names in fully analysed sentences. The *Tractatus*'s theory of representation requires that the only possibilities which can be represented are the possibilities of combination of the objective counterparts to the elements of models: alternative arrangement is just the theory's conception of alternative possibility. And the theory of substance is what generates (T7)–(T10).

We considered the argument for the conception of substance in Chapter 1. As we saw there (section 1D), the specific assumptions which the argument needs are these:

(a) In the basic case, a sentence is a combination (a hanging in one another) of symbols (names);
(b) In the basic case, for a sentence to have sense is for two conditions to hold:
  (i) Its symbols are correlated with objects in the world;
  (ii) It is possible for the symbols to be combined in the way in which they are actually combined in the sentence;
(c) It is possible for the constituent symbols of a sentence to be combined in the way they are, and be correlated with the objects with which they are correlated, if and only if it is possible for the corresponding objects to be combined in the same way in reality.

What we have here is just the basic conception of models applied to the case of sentences. And, in fact, as we saw in Chapter 1, the text of that argument itself adverts to the theory of representation; what apparently requires that there be objects which satisfy the requirements of (T7)–(T10) is the following alleged consequence of there being none:

2.0212 It would then be impossible to form a picture of the world (true or false).

It seems, then, that all of the ten basic metaphysical commitments of the *Tractatus*, with the exception of (T1), (T3), and (T4), follow from the book's theory of the way in which the most basic sentences represent the world. And it will be clear in the next chapter that (T1), (T3), and (T4) follow from the book's account of logic.

It also seems clear that the metaphysics of the 1s and early 2s can be grounded in the philosophy of language of the 3s and 4s without itself being obviously *either* realist *or* idealist. In fact, the symmetry of any notion of sameness, including the one in play in the same-form assumption, (SM3), suggests that the co-ordination of language and world is itself neutral on the issue of realism.

5

LOGIC AND COMPOUND SENTENCES

5A THE PROBLEMS

The theory that sentences are models seems to offer an account of language which solves a large number of the problems which Wittgenstein inherited from Frege and Russell. It also seems to vindicate a distinctive metaphysics, and so to contribute decisively to what has seemed to be a central task of philosophy, throughout its history. For all that, the theory as it stands is incomplete, even as an account of language, in two very obvious ways.

First of all, the theory that sentences are models seems to apply so far only to basic non-compound sentences. It seems not to apply straightforwardly to any compound sentences — sentences which have whole sentences as parts — or to any of the sentences of our everyday languages, which Wittgenstein seems to regard as general statements whose instances would be elementary sentences. So it seems that the theory that sentences are models applies straightforwardly only to sentences which Wittgenstein thinks must be possible, in principle — not to the sentences we actually have.

And, second, no account has yet been given of a large class of subsentential expressions. We know that sentences are taken to be facts, and describe facts (correctly or incorrectly); they are not objects themselves, and are not meaningful in virtue of being correlated with objects. We know that genuine singular terms — the names of which elementary sentences are formed — are held to be meaningful in virtue of being correlated with objects. It is plausible to suggest that this correlation between names and objects is simply a matter of there being a rule which correlates whole sentences in which the names appear with certain types of fact. And this allows at least some expressions which we might previously have regarded as predicates to be classed as names. What we do not know is how Wittgenstein thinks that the so-called 'logical constants' should be treated. We do not know how he thinks the negation sign is meaningful, or how the connectives which are at the basis of modern logical systems — connectives which translate ordinary-language terms like 'if', 'and', and 'or' — are supposed to work. And we do not know yet what his view is of signs of generality — in particular, 'all' and 'some'. Since almost all sentences of everyday language are to be understood in terms of generality, on Wittgenstein's view, this is a very significant lacuna in the theory so far.

Furthermore, in addition to these two ways in which the account of language is incomplete, the *Tractatus* has not yet addressed another major concern which Wittgenstein inherited from Frege and Russell, a concern which might indeed be thought to underlie his whole attitude to philosophy: to show how logic (and with it mathematics) was independent of everything to do with intuition or acquaintance, and thereby reject the Kantian commitment to synthetic *a priori* truths.

5B WITTGENSTEIN'S 'FUNDAMENTAL THOUGHT'

The second paragraph of 4.0312 reads:

> My fundamental thought is that the 'logical constants' do not represent. That the *logic* of the facts cannot be represented.

The German word translated as 'represent' here ('vertreten') is also standardly translated 'stand for' or 'deputise'. (Pears and McGuinness write 'My fundamental idea is that the logical constants are not representatives'.) The point is that the 'logical constants' do not function as names, and there are consequently no 'logical objects' which correspond to them. Wittgenstein puts the point like this a little later:

> 5.4 Here it becomes clear that there are no such things as 'logical objects' or 'logical constants' (in the sense of Frege and Russell).

As we saw in Chapter 2 (section 2G), this is something which Russell seems to have vacillated over, but his final view seems to be presented in this remark which was quoted there:

> Such words as *or, not, all, some*, plainly involve logical notions; and since we can use such words intelligently, we must be acquainted with the logical objects involved.
>
> (Russell 1984: 99)

And Frege seems to have regarded words like 'or', 'not', 'all', and 'some' as names of functions of a special kind: so, although they do not strictly stand for *objects*, on Frege's view, they are nevertheless exactly what Wittgenstein thinks they are not — *names* or *representatives* of entities in the world (Frege 1893: 28).

Wittgenstein offers what looks like a decisive argument for his view that the 'logical constants' are not names of constituents of facts:

> And if there was an object called '~', then '~ ~ p' would have to say something other than 'p'. For one proposition would then treat of ~, the other would not.
>
> (5.44)

This disappearance of the apparent logical constants also occurs if '~ ($\exists x$). ~ fx' says the same as '(x). fx' ['$\forall x.fx$' in some notations], or '($\exists x$). fx. $x = a$' ['$\exists x$ (fx & $x = a$)' in some notations] the same as 'fa'

(5.441).

The key assumption here is that 'p' and '~ ~ p' *say* the same thing. What is the justification for that? Wittgenstein gives this account of what a sentence *says*:

4.022   A proposition *shows* its sense.
A proposition *shows* how things stand, *if* it is true. And it *says*, that they so stand.

In the basic case, what a sentence *shows* is just a certain possible arrangement of the objects which its constituent names refer to. What it *says* is, then, just that the objects are, in fact, arranged in that way. What matters here is that two sentences which represent the same possible arrangement of objects will have the same sense, and will therefore *say* the same thing. It is important to note here that Wittgenstein's notion of sense is not an epistemic notion, like Frege's: it is concerned just with objective possibilities.

We get from this thought to what we need for the argument of 5.441 by recalling that, for Wittgenstein, all possibility is ultimately a matter of the possible arrangements of objects (see Chapter 1, section 1D, above). If two sentences are true in exactly the same possible situations, they must represent the same possible arrangement of objects, and therefore must say the same thing. Evidently, 'p' and '~ ~ p' are true in exactly the same possible situations: consequently, they must say the same thing.

Once this is granted, the point has much wider application. In fact, all the different logical connectives (apart from negation) which are in use in standard modern logic can be defined using another of them, together with negation. So '$p \supset q$' is equivalent (for example) to '~ p v q'; 'p v q' is equivalent to '~ (~ p & ~ q)'; and 'p & q' is equivalent to '~

$(p \supset \sim q)'$. Indeed, Henry Sheffer (1913) had already proved that a single connective was enough.[1] This can either be 'alternative denial', sometimes known as NAND ('not both p and q'), or 'joint denial', also known as NOR ('neither p nor q'). It is now quite common to express the first by means of '|' ('$p \mid q$') and refer to it as the *Sheffer Stroke*, and the latter by '$\downarrow$' ('$p \downarrow q$') and refer to it as the *Sheffer Dagger* (although originally the Sheffer Stroke was used for joint denial, as in Sheffer's paper and *Tractatus* 5.1311, and this practice is still sometimes followed).[2] I will follow the now common practice of using the Sheffer Dagger for joint denial.

Wittgenstein's claim is this: if the logical constants functioned like names, then there would be objects corresponding to them, and the truth of sentences involving those constants would depend on how things were with those objects. This would mean that the reality depicted by '$\sim \sim p$' would have to be a matter of the way in which the object, $\sim$, was related to the other objects correlated with the names in 'p'. 'p' and '$\sim \sim p$' would then have to have a *different* 'logical multiplicity' (see 4.04).

The same problem holds for the interdefinability of the other connectives. A formula involving one connective would inevitably have a different logical multiplicity from that of its translation in terms of another connective, if the connectives were treated as names. (The translation of negation in terms of either the Sheffer Stroke (alternative denial) or the Sheffer Dagger (joint denial) is particularly striking here: '$\sim p$' is rendered as '$p \mid p$' or '$p \downarrow p$'; which makes 'p' equivalent to '$(p \mid p) \mid (p \mid p)$' or '$(p \downarrow p) \downarrow (p \downarrow p)$'.)

Wittgenstein also offers another argument for the claim that the familiar logical constants are not correlated with any kind of 'logical object':

4.0621   That, however, the signs 'p' and '$\sim p$' *can* say the same thing is important, for it shows that the sign '$\sim$' corresponds to nothing in reality.

That negation occurs in a proposition, is no characteristic of its sense ($\sim \sim p = p$).

> The propositions '*p*' and '~ *p*' have opposite senses, but to them corresponds one and the same reality.

How is it that '*p*' and '~ *p*' can say the same thing? The clue lies in the phrase 'opposite senses', which is reminiscent of the account of the relation between sentences and reality which was originally offered as an account of the meaning of 'forms':

> But the form of a proposition symbolizes in the following way: Let us consider symbols of the form 'xRy'; to these correspond primarily pairs of objects, of which one has the name 'x', the other the name 'y'. The x's and y's stand in various relations to each other, among others the relation R holds between some, but not between others. I now determine the sense of 'xRy' by laying down: when the facts behave in regard to 'xRy' so that the meaning of 'x' stands in the relation R to the meaning of 'y', then I say that the [the facts] are 'of like sense' with the proposition 'xRy'; otherwise, 'of opposite sense'; I correlate the facts to the symbol 'xRy' *by* thus dividing them into those of like sense and those of opposite sense. To this correlation corresponds the correlation of name and meaning. Both are psychological. Thus I understand the form 'xRy' when I know that it discriminates the behaviour of x and y according as these stand in the relation R or not. In this way I extract from all possible relation the relation R, as, by a name, I extract its meaning from all possible things.
> (*NL* 104)[3]

The crucial sentence here is this one: 'I correlate the facts to the symbol "xRy" *by* thus dividing them into those of like sense and those of opposite sense'. There is no independent notion of similarity between the arrangement of names around the symbol '*R*', on the one hand, and the arrangement of objects in the world, on the other. The similarity of form is constituted by determining that some arrangements of objects count as being 'of like sense' with sentences of the appropriate form. This means that those arrangements of objects which we now count as being 'of opposite sense' *could* have been counted as being 'of like sense' with sentences of the form '*xRy*'.

I suggested in Chapter 4 that this account of the meaning of so-called 'forms' was not abandoned by Wittgenstein in the *Tractatus*, but generalized to include every kind of expression — although without the commitment which is found in this passage from the *Notes on Logic* to the idea that one could, as it were, have access to the world and all its facts *neat*, independently of already possessing a language. If the account of the meaning of 'forms' in the *Notes on Logic* is now functioning (without commitment to the possibility of neat access to the facts) as the general account of the meaning of expressions in elementary sentences — in effect, as the account of the correlation of a name with its object — we can readily understand how '*p*' and '~ *p*' can say the same thing: the basic correlation of symbols with reality already presupposes the possibility of a converse correlation, with what is taken to be 'of like sense' on one assignment counting as being 'of opposite sense' on the other, and vice versa.

What, then, is the function of '~' on this picture? Its function is simply to switch the 'senses' of a sentence: that is, what counts as being 'of like sense' with a sentence is determined as being 'of opposite sense' with its negation, and vice versa. And essentially the same account is provided of the familiar 'logical constants' in general. The other familiar logical constants do not modify the 'sense' of just a single sentence, of course: what they do (to put it crudely) is combine a number of sentences with each other. Wittgenstein's idea is just this: the business of the familiar logical constants is simply to determine which facts count as being 'of like sense' and which 'of opposite sense' with compound sentences, given that it is fixed which facts count as being 'of like sense' and which 'of opposite sense' with the sentences which are their components.

The notions of likeness and oppositeness of 'sense' are obviously linked with the notions of truth and falsity. The facts which are 'of like sense' with a class of sentences are the facts which make those sentences *true;* and those which are 'of opposite sense' are those which make them *false*. Since the familiar logical constants can be explained in terms of what they determine to be 'of like sense' and 'of opposite sense' with a compound sentence, given which facts count as being 'of like sense' and 'of opposite sense' with its components, it is clear that their meaning can be characterized in terms of truth-tables of a kind which is now familiar.

Wittgenstein is sometimes credited with inventing the truth-table as we now know it, although this is also sometimes questioned (Landini 2007: 118–24).[4] However that may be, Wittgenstein certainly does use truth-tables in the *Tractatus*. Using a truth-table, we can define negation, '$\sim p$' as follows:

p	$\sim p$
T	F
F	T

And we can define '$p \supset q$' like this:[5]

p	q	$p \supset q$
T	T	T
F	T	T
T	F	F
F	F	T

This truth-table gives us the rule for computing the truth-value of compound sentences of the form '$p \supset q$', given just the truth-value of the component sentences. By the same token, it provides the rule which determines what it is for such compound sentences to be 'of like sense' with the facts.

If the truth-table gives us a rule which explains the way in which, as Wittgenstein would put it, '$p \supset q$' 'symbolizes', we can use the truth-table to reveal that explicitly, and remove the temptation to think of the sign '$\supset$' as a name:

> If the sequence of the truth-possibilities in the schema [the truth-table] is once for all determined by a rule of combination [that is, if we have settled the order in which we write down the rows on the left of the truth-table], then the last column is by itself an expression of the truth-conditions. If we write this column as a row the propositional sign becomes: ... '(TTFT) (p, q)'.
>
> (The number of places in the left-hand bracket is determined by the number of terms in the right-hand bracket.)

(4.442)

The suggestion is that we might simply use '(TTFT) (p, q)' to express what we normally express by means of '$p \supset q$'.

Any expression whose meaning can be defined using a truth-table is commonly called a *truth-function* (because its meaning consists in the fact that its output has certain truth-values given the truth-values of the inputs). Wittgenstein himself preserves this use of the term 'truth-function', even though (as we will see in a moment) his view is that truth-functions are not properly called *functions* at all. We can use Wittgenstein's rotated-truth-table notation (as in '(TTFT) (p, q)') to show the way in which any truth-functional way of combining sentences symbolizes, no matter how many sentences are involved — provided that we are dealing with a finite number of sentences, expressing a finite number of possible atomic facts. Wittgenstein has already given the formula which defines the number of rows we need in our truth-tables. If we are dealing with n possible atomic facts, each of which might or might not obtain independently of all the others, we are dealing with K_n possibilities, on the characterization of K_n which is provided in 4.27.[6] Given that there are just two possibilities for each atomic fact — obtaining or not obtaining — K_n will be equal to 2^n. And since these possibilities of existence and non-existence of atomic facts are expressed in the truth and falsity of elementary sentences, the same formula applies to the rows we need in our truth-tables. If we are giving a truth-table for a truth-functional combination of n elementary sentences, we will need K_n (i.e., 2^n) rows in our truth-table. So if we are dealing with a truth-functional combination of two sentences, our truth-table will need to have 2^2 (= 4) rows; if with one which combines three sentences, we will need 2^3 (= 8) rows; if with one which combines four sentences, 2^4 (= 16) rows; and so on.

Once we have Wittgenstein's account of the familiar logical constants, together with this device for replacing the familiar symbols by means of a rotated-truth-table column, we should have removed any temptation to think of the logical constants as names which are correlated with a special kind of entity in the world. But it is worth taking a little care over how they should be understood. We will remember Russell starting off with similar intentions:

> 'Logical constants', which might seem to be entities occurring in logical propositions, are really concerned with pure *form*, and are not actually constituents of the propositions in the verbal expression of which their names occur.
>
> (1984: 98)

But we saw that he found himself driven, by various epistemological considerations, to consider these 'pure forms' as objects of acquaintance, and hence, ultimately, as 'logical objects' (1984: 99).

Wittgenstein, however, rejects Russell's conception of logical constants as 'pure forms'. The application of a logical constant to a sentence he calls an *operation*; and concerning such operations he says this:

> 5.241 The operation does not characterize a form but only the difference between forms.

And we can understand why Wittgenstein was so keen to insist on this, if I am right in my interpretation of him as generalizing his earlier account of the meaning of forms, so that it becomes a general account of the meaning of expressions from which elementary sentences are composed. It is obvious even in the characterization in the *Notes on Logic* that there is at least a very close parallel between the correlations set up between names and objects, on the one hand, and those between 'forms' and the facts which count as being of like and of opposite sense with them, on the other. If we simply counted logical constants as 'forms' we would not have prevented their understanding being a matter of understanding a correlation between sentences and the world. We would not have removed the temptation to think that some kind of intuition or acquaintance is needed to understand them.

Wittgenstein's description of a truth-functional operator as simply characterizing a 'difference between forms' is both sufficient to avoid this temptation, and precise in its description of their role, on Wittgenstein's own theory. What such operators do is simply determine likeness and oppositeness of 'sense' for compounds, *given* the determination of likeness and oppositeness of 'sense' for their components.

What Wittgenstein is doing here belongs with his rejection of the temptation to assimilate sentences to names, which is one of the cornerstones of the *Tractatus*. This leads him to adopt an important distinction of terminology. Although Wittgenstein continues to use the already familiar term 'truth-function', his view is that truth-functions should not really be regarded as functions at all. We need to recall some of the historical background to understand the point being made. On Frege's theory, functions are the referents of certain kinds of expression: in effect, they are 'unsaturated' or incomplete referents — the referents of (things referred to by) expressions which are themselves visibly incomplete. They thereby contrast for Frege with *objects*, which, on his theory, are 'saturated' or complete. In the simplest case, a function takes one or more objects as input (or argument), and yields a single object as output (or value). So 'x is ugly' is a function for Frege: supply an object for x, and the result is another object — either the True or the False, depending on whether x is or is not ugly. And again '$\sim p$' (where 'p' is strictly a variable) is a function: supply an object — in this case either the True or the False — as the referent of 'p', and the result is, once again, an object — either the False or the True.

The whole of this apparatus needs to be changed, on Wittgenstein's account. First of all, we will not want to count such expressions as '*x* is ugly' as *referring* to functions, because the point of that is to make a contrast between functions and objects among the items correlated with basic expressions in elementary sentences; and Wittgenstein's view is that the items correlated with basic expressions in elementary sentences are all *objects* (though, of course, that means that he can no longer regard all objects as unproblematically 'saturated' or complete). And, second, he will not want to regard such expressions as '~ *p*' as referring to anything: that misconceives the way they work altogether, on Wittgenstein's account.

So Wittgenstein reserves the word 'function' for something which is not the *referent* of any basic expression of elementary sentences. The kind of function which concerns him is a *propositional* function in the following sense. Instead of being something which an expression *refers* to, it is itself an *expression* — more particularly, an expression which takes another expression to form a proposition or sentence. For example, the *expression* 'ξ was rich' is a *function* which takes the name 'Wittgenstein' as input (or argument) to yield the *sentence* 'Wittgenstein was rich' as output (or value). That is to say, to call an expression a function is to say something about its grammar, not about its referent. A function in Wittgenstein's terminology is what we now call a predicate: something which takes one or more *names* (or singular terms) to form a sentence.[7] For this point see, for example, these two remarks:

3.318 I conceive the proposition — like Frege and Russell — as a function of the expressions contained in it.
The elementary proposition I write as function of the names, in the form '*fx*', '*φ* (*x, y*)', etc.

(4.24)

An *operation* (we often call it an *operator*), on the other hand, is an expression with a quite different grammar. At least for the case he has in mind here (the so-called truth-functions), the difference can be characterized very simply. Whereas a function takes one or more *names* to form a whole sentence, what an *operation* does is take one or more whole *sentences* to form another whole sentence. Thus Wittgenstein says that we can present 'a proposition as the result of an operation which produces it from other propositions (the bases of the operation)' (5.21). And again:

5.23   The operation is that which must happen to a proposition in order to make another out of it.

Given that the distinction between names and sentences is fundamental for Wittgenstein, it is not surprising that he says this:

Operation and function must not be confused with one another.

(5.25)

And the next sentence marks an important respect in which Wittgenstein thinks that operations and functions differ:

5.251   A function cannot be its own argument, but the result of an operation can be its own basis.

As we will see, this will be crucial for Wittgenstein's treatment of arithmetic.

5C THE *N*-OPERATOR

There is an obvious lacuna in Wittgenstein's treatment of the 'logical constants' so far: what about the quantifiers — and, indeed, generality in general? How do the quantifiers work? We have already seen that Wittgenstein took the equivalence of '$\sim (\exists x). \sim fx$' and '$(x). fx$' ('$\forall x.fx$' in some notations) to show that the symbols here do not function as names. But how can we understand them as characterizing 'differences between forms'? The answer is that Wittgenstein offers a truth-functional account even of the quantifiers.

The truth-functional operators of standard logical systems either take just one sentence to form a sentence (in the case of negation) or just two sentences to form a sentence (in the case of the others). But Wittgenstein's rotated-truth-table notation can be adapted to provide a uniform treatment of combinations of any number of sentences. Wittgenstein's account of the quantifiers — and his final account of the whole range of logical constants — depends on an adaptation of this thought.

Recall the Sheffer Dagger, '$p \downarrow q$', which represents joint denial ('neither p nor q'). It is possible to define all of the standard truth-functions in its terms. The Sheffer Dagger, like most standard connectives, takes two sentences (the 'p' and the 'q') to form a sentence. Wittgenstein first introduces a generalized variant of the Sheffer Dagger using his rotated-truth-table notation:

5.5 Every truth-function is a result of the successive application of the operation $(- - - - -T)(\xi,....)$ to elementary propositions.

This operation denies all the propositions in the right-hand bracket and I call it the negation of these propositions.

Here the notation in the first bracket — '$(- - - - -T)$' — is meant to indicate that the operation yields the value *true* only at the last line of the truth-table — the line at which all of the component sentences are given the value *false*. (There is an intuitive oddity about this expression, since it is unclear how its *beginning* is to be written, until it has been determined how many elementary sentences we are considering.)

Wittgenstein then takes the basic idea of the generalized Sheffer Dagger and provides a more perspicuous notation for expressing it. First (in 5.501), he introduces a variable, 'ξ', which can take as values any of a pre-determined range of sentences. Then he writes a line above it — '$\bar{\xi}$' — to indicate that *all* of the sentences in that pre-determined range are to be treated together. Finally, he introduces a symbol — '$N(...)$' — which expresses the joint denial of any sentences indicated within the brackets. The result is that '$N(\bar{\xi})$'

expresses the joint denial of all of the sentences in the range of values for the variable 'ξ':

5.502   Therefore I write instead of '$(- - - - -T)(\xi,....)$', '$N(\bar{\xi})$'.
            $N(\bar{\xi})$ is the negation of all the values of the propositional variable ξ.

We can obviously express all of the standard sentential constants using this operator, by careful pre-determination of the range of sentences which can be values of the variable 'ξ', and repeated applications of the 'N'-operator. To make this clear, it will be convenient to have a way of indicating the range of values of 'ξ' which we can keep tabs on. So, for example, if the range of 'ξ' is restricted to just the single sentence 'p', we can replace '$\bar{\xi}$' with just 'p'; if it is the three sentences 'p', 'q', and 'r', we might replace '$\bar{\xi}$' with 'p, q, r'. (This is the notational rule Wittgenstein himself provides in 5.501.) Thus, if we restrict the range of 'ξ' to the single sentence 'p', '$N(\bar{\xi})$' — '$N(p)$' here — is equivalent to '$\sim p$' (5.51). And we can express '$p \supset q$' by several applications of 'N', as follows. First, we restrict 'ξ' to the single sentence 'p', and apply 'N' to that — as '$N(p)$'. Then we let the range of the variable be the two sentences '$N(p)$' and 'q', and apply 'N' to those — as '$N(N(p), q)$'. And then we let the range of the variable be just the result of that — '$N(N(p), q)$' — and apply 'N' to that. We end up with a sentence — '$N(N(N(p), q))$' — which means *not: neither not-p nor q*, and is equivalent to '$p \supset q$'.

Wittgenstein then uses the N-operator to explain quantification:

5.52   If the values of ξ are the total values of a function fx for all values
            of x, then $N(\bar{\xi}) = \sim (\exists x). fx$.

What is going on here? In the first place, it is important to be clear that Wittgenstein is not here proposing to define universal quantification simply in terms of conjunction — '$(x) fx$' as equivalent to 'fa & fb & fc & fd & ... ' — or existential quantification simply in terms of disjunction —

'$(\exists x)$ fx' as equivalent to 'fa v fb v fc v fd v ... '. At 5.501 Wittgenstein distinguishes between three different ways of determining the range of values of the variable 'ξ':

1. Direct enumeration. In this case we can place simply its constituent values instead of the variable.
2. Giving a function fx, whose values for all values of x are the propositions to be described.
3. Giving a formal law, according to which those propositions are constructed. In this case the terms of the expression in brackets [in the construction '$N(...)$'] are all the terms of a formal series.

The direct-enumeration method is the one we have already encountered in explaining the standard truth-functional connectives in terms of the N-operator: this is what would, in effect, be in play if universal quantification were being defined simply in terms of conjunction and existential quantification simply in terms of disjunction. But in 5.52 Wittgenstein is obviously adopting method 2 — defining the range of the variable 'ξ' as the range of values of a function.

There are two obvious problems with defining universal quantification in terms of conjunction and existential quantification in terms of disjunction. The first is that general statements are *unspecific*: they do not actually say *which* things have the relevant property; indeed, they do not actually mention those things at all. This is a point Wittgenstein has already made (3.24), and it constitutes his argument for the claim that it must be possible for there to be simple signs, and elementary sentences which consist solely of them (as we saw in Chapter 4, section 4E). The second problem is that if generalizations are defined in terms of conjunctions or disjunctions, it is hard to see how the generalizations can range over an *infinite* number of objects: after all, a conjunction or disjunction can only be finitely long.

Does Wittgenstein's account avoid these problems? A little explanation is needed before this can be settled. First we need to recall what Wittgenstein means by 'function', as the term is used in 5.52. What he has in mind is what he sometimes calls a 'propositional function': that is, it is something which yields a whole sentence when a particular name, or set of names is specified. Working from the other end, it is the result of replacing one or more names in a sentence with a variable. The function '*fx*' is, then, presumably something which yields a sentence when a particular name is put in place of the '*x*'; and the range of values (outputs) of that function is all the sentences which result from replacing the '*x*' with a name.

Suppose, then, that there are just three sentences which might be considered here: '*fa*', '*fb*', and '*fc*'. Those three sentences can be picked out as values of the variable 'ξ' for the *N*-operator *either* by direct enumeration, or, simply, as the values of the *function* '*fx*'. In the explanation of how the *N*-operator can be used to give the meaning of '*p* ⊃ q', we found it convenient to indicate which sentences we were taking as values of the variable 'ξ' at different points, by adopting a notational rule which allowed us to write something other than '$\bar{\xi}$' within the brackets in '*N* (...)'. For the case of '*p* ⊃ q', the range of values of the variable could be indicated by simple enumeration (method 1), so I followed Wittgenstein's own device (specified in 5.501, under method 1) of simply listing the sentences within the brackets. We need to adopt some other device when the values of the variable 'ξ' are determined by a function, as in the case of Wittgenstein's account of quantification: Wittgenstein does not himself offer any suggestion.[8] We can get what we want by adapting Wittgenstein's notation for functions slightly, and use expressions of the form '*x*: φx' according to the following rule:

> (F) When used within the brackets in '*N* (...)', '*x*: φx' indicates the whole range of sentences which are values of the function 'φx' for all values of '*x*'.[9]

Adopting this notational rule, we can use '*x*: *fx*' within the brackets of '*N* (...)' to indicate the values of the function '*fx*'.

So we can use 'N (x: fx)' to say that all the sentences of the form 'fx' — all the sentences which are formed by replacing the 'x' in 'fx' with a particular name — are false. This is what Wittgenstein takes to be equivalent to '~ ($\exists x$) fx' in 5.52. If we then apply the N-operator to this sentence in turn, we end up with 'N (N (x: fx))', which, according to Wittgenstein, will be equivalent to '~ ~ ($\exists x$) fx', or '($\exists x$) fx'. This gives us an account of existential quantification. We have here something which is, in a sense, equivalent to the disjunction 'fa v fb v fc', in the imagined situation where there are only three sentences of the relevant form, although it differs from it in not explicitly mentioning any of the objects a, b, or c.

Let us try to use the same procedure to provide an account of universal quantification. Again, for simplicity, suppose that we have just three sentences of the form 'fx': 'fa', 'fb', and 'fc'. Each of these can be negated using the N-operator: as 'N (fa)', 'N (fb)', and 'N (fc)'. These negations all have a common form: they are values of the function 'N (fx)'.[10] Using our rule (F), we can use the expression 'x: N (fx)' within the brackets of 'N (...)' to indicate the whole range of values of the function 'N (fx)'. The expression we end up with, 'N (x: N (fx))', says that none of the negations — none of the values of the function 'N (fx)' — is true. That is to say that all of the negated sentences — all of the values of the function 'fx' — are true. So 'N (x: N (fx))' seems to be equivalent to '(x) fx', and we have an account of ordinary universal quantification. We have something which is, in effect, equivalent to the conjunction of the sentences 'fa', 'fb', and 'fc' in the peculiar circumstances we have imagined; but it differs from the conjunction in explicitly mentioning none of the objects a, b, or c.

This explanation has already shown us how Wittgenstein's account of quantification differs from one which defines existential quantification in terms of disjunction, and universal quantification in terms of conjunction, in that it allows that quantified sentences do not involve explicitly mentioning any of the objects in the domain of quantification. Does his method allow us to quantify over infinite numbers of objects — the other crucial point of difference between quantification, as ordinarily understood, and disjunction and conjunction? I think this too is relatively unproblematic.[11] Wittgenstein seems quite happy to suppose that there are infinitely many names in a language:

> What the axiom of infinity [the assumption that there are infinitely many individual objects] is meant to say would be expressed in language by the fact that there is an infinite number of names with different meanings.

> (5.535)

And this will mean that there are infinitely many 'values of x' to generate 'values of a function fx'. How can we suppose that there are infinitely many names in a language? It is natural to think that this supposition amounts to nothing grander than the supposition that there is already, within the language, a mechanism for generating an infinite number of names with different meanings. (Standard numeral systems might be taken to be examples of such mechanisms.)

This point serves to lessen the importance of an issue which arises in connection with Wittgenstein's account of quantification: are Wittgenstein's quantifiers *objectual* or *substitutional*? We can explain the difference as follows.[12] Suppose we start with an anglicized quantifier-variable sentence:

(B) For some x, x is beautiful.

To treat this *objectually*, we proceed as follows. We take ourselves to have some relatively well-defined domain of objects. Then (B) is *true* if the predicate 'x is beautiful' is *true of* at least one object in the domain. Conversely, to treat this *substitutionally*, we say simply that (B) is true if there is at least one true *substitution-instance* of 'x is beautiful': that is to say, that at least one sentence which results from replacing the variable 'x' in 'x is beautiful' with a name is true.

'Ganymede is beautiful' might be such a substitution-instance; if it is true, then (B) is true, on the substitutional reading.

The difference between these two readings looks less severe when we ask what it is for a predicate to be *true of* an object in a domain. The answer which it is natural to give, for the case of 'x is beautiful' is this: 'x is beautiful' is true of an object just in case, if we treat the 'x' in 'x is beautiful' temporarily as a name of that object, 'x is beautiful' so understood is a true sentence.[13]

Even so, the two interpretations of the quantifiers do differ significantly, if we make one of two assumptions. One assumption is that there are some objects which have no names: in that case, those objects will be beyond the reach of substitutional quantification. The other assumption is that there are some meaningful names which are correlated with no objects (we might think that this is true of fictional names, for example). If we make this second assumption, there may be some true substitution-instances of a predicate, even when the predicate is not *true of* any object.

But Wittgenstein makes neither of these assumptions. First, as we have just seen, he seems happy, in principle, to accept the existence of infinitely many names, and this seems to ensure that it will be possible for any object to have a name.[14] And, second, he does not allow names to be meaningful unless they are correlated with objects. This means that the difference between objectual and substitutional readings is not very significant for him. Which reading is truer to what he says? I think it is clear that the substitutional reading is closer. The key terms are those of 5.52:

the total values of a function *fx* for all values of *x*.

As we have seen, functions for Wittgenstein are *propositional* functions: that is, they are *expressions* of a certain kind; they are expressions which take names as arguments to yield whole sentences as values. So where he writes 'a function *fx*' he should, strictly, have written 'a function "*fx*"'. The values of this kind of function are whole sentences: these are precisely sentences ascribing the predicate to some given object. As for the phrase 'values of x', something similar applies. He should, strictly, have written 'values of $"x"$', and the values of 'x' will then be substitution-instances of 'x' — that is, names which could be put in place of the variable.

There is a further advantage to the substitutional interpretation of Wittgenstein's quantifiers. It removes the problem of quantification into a non-name position. This is something which Wittgenstein seems happy to do; see, for example, the use of this expression at 5.5261:

$(\exists x, \varphi). \varphi x.$

In general, one-place predicates ('propositional functions', in Wittgenstein's terminology) in the *Tractatus* should not be assumed to be names: rather, they are simply that part of a sentence which takes a single name to form a sentence (see Chapter 4, section 4F). But if a one-place predicate is not a name, then there cannot be an object to which it refers; and that means that an objectual reading of quantification into a one-place-predicate position — such quantification as we find at 5.5261 — cannot be legitimate.

Let us return to Wittgenstein's general approach to quantification. Is it acceptable? Even if quantification over infinite numbers of things is unproblematic, it is arguable that Wittgenstein's account faces a different problem. We can, with relative ease, say that a language contains an infinite number of names with different meanings, provided that we have, now, the means to generate this infinity of names. And this may indeed be possible in certain cases. But it is not so obviously possible in certain more mundane cases. When he returned to the *Tractatus*'s treatment of generality in the 1930s, he thought it had certain obvious problems:

> But for cases like 'all men die before they are 200 years old' my explanation is not correct.

(*PG* 268)

It is not quite clear what Wittgenstein thinks the problem with this case is, but it is not implausible to describe it as a difficulty with simply generating names for all the individuals in question. In part, he seems to have thought that the problem lay with difficulties in determining precisely which individuals fall under the head of 'all men'. The concept *man*, he seems now to think, is not just a method for collecting together a group of previously identified individuals. It is, rather (he seems to think), a concept which has a life of its own and may lead to indeterminate results in certain cases.

This is a problem raised for the *Tractatus* from the period when Wittgenstein's view of things was undergoing quite a radical transformation. But we might think that the *Tractatus*'s account of quantification faced a problem in the book's own terms. In the *Tractatus*'s system, quantification over infinite domains would require there to be an infinite number of sentences of the same form (an infinite number of sentences — or possible sentences — of the form 'fx', for example, for the case of '$(\exists x)\,fx$', or of the form 'fxy' for the case of '$(\exists x,\,y)\,fxy$'). But for the case where there is an infinite number of sentences of the same form (and where this includes the full range of forms we might expect for standard predicate logic), it seems that we cannot strictly *define* the N-operator in terms of a truth-table — as equivalent to '$(\text{- - - - -}T)(\xi,....)$'. For if it had been possible strictly to define the N-operator in terms of a truth-table, for the case where an infinite number of sentences (including those involving many-placed predicates) are jointly negated, there would have been a mechanical decision-procedure for determining which sentences formed by means of the N-operator are tautologies (true whatever the truth-values of the sentences to which the operator is applied). But there is a well-known formal result, according to which there can be no such decision-procedure.[15] It seems to follow that the N-operator can only be strictly defined in terms of a truth-table if it is applicable only to finite domains.

It seems clear that Wittgenstein had hopes (to put it no more strongly) of a mechanical decision procedure of the kind which has turned out to be unavailable for logical systems involving quantification over infinite domains:[16] this is something to which we will return in section 5E below. But if we leave those hopes to one side, does it matter to Wittgenstein whether the N-operator is strictly definable in terms of a truth-table — as equivalent to '(- - - - -T)(ξ,....)'? It is not clear that it does. For his larger philosophical purposes, all that matters is that every possible sentence is expressible as being the result of successive applications of the N-operator to elementary sentences — or collections of elementary sentences. And the truth of that is quite independent of how we happen to come to *understand* the N-operator.

It is important to be clear about this point, if we are to avoid misunderstanding the central philosophical purpose of the N-operator. Recall that the N-operator was originally introduced with these words:

5.502   Therefore I write instead of '(- - - - -T)(ξ,....)', 'N($\bar{\xi}$)'.
        N($\bar{\xi}$) is the negation of all the values of the propositional variable ξ.

The second line here makes explicit use of the concepts both of negation and of generality ('all'). So if the N-operator is to be intelligible independently of those concepts, it must be by means of the rotated-truth-table formulation '(- - - - -T) (ξ,....)'. But that expression itself was introduced earlier with these words:

5.5   Every truth-function is a result of the successive application of the
      operation (- - - - -T)(ξ,....) to elementary propositions.
      This operation denies all the propositions in the right-hand bracket
      and I call it the negation of these propositions.

And here the rotated-truth-table formulation is itself explained in terms of the concepts of negation and generality. From this it seems clear that the N-operator cannot be designed to provide a grasp of truth-functions and generality which is wholly independent of truth-functions and generality. It is not supposed to provide an *epistemic* foundation either of logic or of the construction of sentences. Rather, the point is to show that all the apparently different ways of constructing sentences, and all the apparently different ways of representing logical relations, have something in common. What they all have in common is represented in the fact (as Wittgenstein takes it to be) that every sentence can be expressed as a result of successive applications of a single operation to elementary sentences. This is enough to show that there is a general form of sentences — and, further, what that general form is. For this purpose it simply does not matter whether the N-operator is intelligible independently of the concepts of negation and generality.

5D LOGIC AND THE GENERAL FORM OF THE SENTENCE

Wittgenstein introduces the N-operator in order to secure the following two claims:

6   The general form of truth-function is: $[\bar{p}, \bar{\xi}, N(\bar{\xi})]$.
    This is the general form of proposition.

He explains this himself in the following remark:

6.001   This says nothing else than that every proposition is the result
        of successive applications of the operation $N(\bar{\xi})$ to elementary
        propositions.

The square-bracket notation employed in the first line of 6 is an adapation of the notation which is explained in 5.2522, where it is used to describe, in general, the term of a series:

5.2522   The general term of the formal series a, O' a, O' O' a ... I write
        thus: '$[a, x, O' x]$'.
        This expression in brackets is a variable. The first term of the
        expression is the beginning of the formal series, the second the
        form of an arbitrary term x of the series, and the third the form of
        that term of the series which immediately follows x.

A *term* of a series is simply an *item* in the series: so the first four terms of the series 2, 4, 6, 8 ... are 2, 4, 6 and 8. 5.2522 presents a way of characterizing any term in a formal series which is the result of applying an operation O, beginning from a certain starting point (the first term). The series is characterized as beginning from that first term, and each later term is simply the result of applying the operation O to the previous term.

Unfortunately, the use of this notation in section 6 is not immediately obvious. The variable 'p' ranges over elementary sentences — the sentences which consist wholly of names in relation to each other. But this variable has a line over it, and it has not been made clear how this is to be understood in connection with the square-bracket notation. Following the practice of 5.501, the variable with a line over it should stand for *all* the values of the variable — in this case, all the elementary sentences. The natural way of reading 6 is then that the first term of the series in question is the *totality* of elementary sentences. The suggestion, then, seems to be that every possible sentence will figure somewhere in a single series of sentences formed by successive applications of the N-operator to the totality of elementary sentences.

It is very quickly obvious that this will not work.[17] A single application of the N-operator to the totality of elementary sentences yields a sentence which says that none of the elementary sentences is true. If you apply the N-operator to that, you get a sentence which says that at least one of the elementary sentences is true. If you apply the N-operator to that, you get, once again, a sentence which says that none of the elementary sentences is true — and so on. By this means you can only say one of two things: either that none of the elementary sentences is true, or that at least one of them is. This is inadequate in two very obvious respects. First, it leaves out a large number of truth-possibilities. And second, it leaves out the elementary sentences themselves — at least, if there is more than one elementary sentence: for if there is more than one elementary sentence, no single elementary sentence is the result of any number of applications of the N-operator to the totality of elementary sentences.

In fact, if we read the square-bracket formulation in 6 in this way, it says much more than 6.001. For the square-bracket formulation 6 seems on this reading to say that every possible sentence appears somewhere in a single series of successive applications of the N-operator, with the first term being the totality of elementary sentences. But 6.001 is more modest in two respects: first, it does not say that every possible sentence appears somewhere in a *single* series of successive applications of the N-operator; and second, it does not say that the first term in any series of applications of the N-operator is the *totality* of elementary sentences. And, in fact, both of these points of extra modesty are points in favour of 6.001, since each of these demanding conditions is failed by some possible sentences.[18] This leaves us with a minor interpretative quandary: do we take Wittgenstein to be saying what is strictly meant by the natural interpretation of the square-bracket notation of 6, on its most natural reading, so that 6.001 expresses his point rather carelessly — or do we take 6.001 to express what he really wants to say, with the square-bracket notation of 6 being an inept or lazy way of formulating it? My preference is for the latter: I take the introduction of the line over the variable in 6 to be a lazy way of indicating a range of series of applications of the N-operator, beginning with any number of elementary sentences as the first term.

Suppose we have a way of describing a term in any one of a number of series of successive applications of the N-operator, beginning with any number of elementary sentences. Why should this be the 'general form of truth-function', as Wittgenstein claims in the first sentences of 6? Note that the term 'function' has two related uses. On the one hand, it may be used to describe something which takes a certain input (one or more 'arguments') to yield a certain output (a 'value'). In this sense of 'function', the familiar logical constants of sentence logic — '~', '⊃', '&', and 'v' — or such things as the Sheffer Stroke or Dagger, or Wittgenstein's own 'N(ξ)' are truth-functions (*operations*, or *operators* in the kind of use Wittgenstein really prefers). And on the other hand, it may be used to describe the value of a function (in the first sense) for a given argument (or arguments): such a value of a function (in the first sense) may be described as a *function* (in this second sense) *of* a given argument. It is this second sense which is in play in 6: he is using the term here to describe the *result of applying truth-operators* to other sentences: so '~ p' is a 'truth-function' of 'p', and 'p ⊃ q' is a 'truth-function' of 'p' and 'q'. (See Russell 1922: 13.) The first sentence of 6 — understood in the way 6.001 suggests — therefore makes a relatively modest claim: the claim is just that every 'truth-function' of sentences (in this sense) can be expressed as the result of successive applications of the *N*-operator to elementary sentences. And this claim amounts to little more than the claim that the *N*-operator — like the Sheffer Stroke and the Sheffer Dagger — can be used as the single primitive logical constant.

The really significant claim, however, is the *second* sentence of 6, with its paraphrase in 6.001. We can, in fact, separate two distinct claims that Wittgenstein is committed to:

(F1) All sentences share a common form;

(F2) The common form shared by all sentences consists in the fact that each one is the result of successive applications of the *N*-operator to elementary sentences.

I will return to (F2) in section 5F below. The significance of (F1) lies in the fact that it marks a point of distinction between sentences and other types of expression. Wittgenstein does not think that there is a common form shared by all names, for example; nor that there is a common form shared by all predicates. One clear reason for thinking that predicates, in particular, do not all have the same form is that otherwise we are liable to be stuck with a version of Russell's paradox.

Recall that Russell's paradox arose in connection with Frege's attempt to ground arithmetic in classes: in this form, the problem is with the idea of a class being (or not being) a member of itself. (This issue was considered briefly in section 2H of Chapter 2, above.) Analogous paradoxes arise if we allow properties to be (or not be) possessed by themselves, or predicates to be true (or false) of themselves. Russell's solution was to establish a hierarchy of predicates (and correlatively of classes), and rule that predicates could only meaningfully be applied to objects at lower levels in the hierarchy.

Wittgenstein himself deals with the problem in 3.333; here is the paragraph which is crucial for our present purposes:

> If, for example, we suppose that the function $F(fx)$ could be its own argument, then there would be a proposition '$F(F(fx))$', and in this the outer function F and the inner function F must have different meanings; for the inner has the form $\varphi(fx)$, the outer the form $\psi(\varphi(fx))$. Common to both functions is only the letter 'F', which by itself signifies nothing.

The precise background to this remark is the rule introduced by Whitehead and Russell to prevent the formulation of Russell's paradox. Here it is, in the form in which they state it:

> [T]he functions to which a given object a can be an argument are incapable of being arguments to each other, and ... they have no term in common with the functions to which they can be arguments.
>
> (Whitehead and Russell 1927: 48)

Here we have a rule which aims to avoid the paradox by restricting the use of predicates; and it restricts the use of predicates by restricting the range of objects to which they can apply. In 3.333 Wittgenstein formulates a rule which is designed to have the same effect — restricting the use of predicates in order to avoid Russell's paradox — but without any mention of the range of objects to which they apply. (We will return to Wittgenstein's reason for that variation in section 5E below.) Instead, the rule is stated just in terms of the *form* of predicates — that is, in terms of their possible combinations, their syntax.

What we have in 3.333 is an insistence, in effect, that not all predicates can have the same form. That is to say, there are some positions in sentences in which some but not all predicates can be placed. What Wittgenstein says about predicates ('functions') here is the crucial point of difference between predicates (functions) and *operations*, as we saw earlier:

5.251   A function cannot be its own argument, but the result of an operation can be its own basis.

The point of 3.333 is part of Wittgenstein's insistence that whole sentences are altogether different in kind from their components.

This difference allows it to be possible for there to be a *general* form of sentences, something which all whole sentences can be common. If a whole sentence can be placed in a certain position within a sentence, then any other sentence can be placed in the same position. Every sentence has the same possibilities of combination with other sentences as every other. What this rules out, in particular, is a hierarchy of levels of *sentences* in which sentences from one level are prevented from being combined with sentences at another.[19] Why does he think this? He has a quite general reason:

That there is a general form is proved by the fact that there cannot be a proposition whose form could not have been foreseen (*i.e.* constructed).

(4.5)

This remark in turn is derived from the following claim found in the *Notebooks*:

Thus it must be possible to erect the general form of proposition, because the possible forms of proposition must be *a priori*. Because the possible forms of proposition are *a priori*, the general form of proposition exists.

(*NB*: 89)

This fundamental argument for the *constructability* of any possible form is not entirely clear, but a plausible reconstruction sees it as involving the following assumptions:

(CF1) If a form of sentence is possible, it is *necessarily* possible;

(CF2) If a form of sentence is necessarily possible, it is *a priori* that it is possible;

(CF3) If it is *a priori* that a form of sentence is possible, that form of sentence must be *constructible a priori*.

These assumptions are natural, though not compulsory. (CF1) involves an endorsement of something like the modal principle (S5), which we saw at work in (and indeed justified by) the substance argument of 2.021–2.023 (see Chapter 1, section 1D, above). (CF2) involves a premise which was almost universally accepted at the time that Wittgenstein wrote — that what is necessary must be *a priori*: this premise was central to Kant's conception of the *a prioricity* of philosophy, and was not generally challenged until Kripke's pioneering work in the 1970s;[20] we also saw this kind of assumption at work in the substance argument of 2.0211–2.0212 (see Chapter 1, section 1D, above). And (CF3) involves a very natural model of *a priori* knowledge: that what is *a priori* knowable is open to a certain sort of demonstrative proof or derivation. This is the kind of assumption which was put in question in different ways by the work of Gödel, Church, and Turing in the 1930s, but there is some reason to think that Wittgenstein was not aware of its doubtful status (as we will see, in section 5E, below)

(CF1)–(CF3) seem to require that any possible form of sentence must be representable as being the result of applying to something which is antecedently given an operation which we can suppose to be antecedently given also. And it looks as if the account presented in 6.001 meets that condition. Wittgenstein there claims that every possible sentence is the result of successive applications of the *N*-operator to elementary sentences. This seems close to what (CF1)–(CF3) require — but only if there is some sense in which the N-operator, or truth-functionality in general, is given to us the moment we have any sentences.

And that in turn is plausible. Recall again Wittgenstein's early account of the determination of the meaning of what he then called 'forms':

> I now determine the sense of 'xRy' by laying down: when the facts behave in regard to 'xRy' so that the meaning of 'x' stands in the relation R to the meaning of 'y', then I say that the [the facts] are 'of like sense' with the proposition 'xRy'; otherwise, 'of opposite sense'; I correlate the facts to the symbol 'xRy' *by* thus dividing them into those of like sense and those of opposite sense.

(*NL*: 104)

And we might also note the following passage from the *Notes Dictated to G. E. Moore*:

> '[T]rue' and 'false' are not accidental properties of a proposition, such that, when it has meaning, we can say it is also true or false: on the contrary, to have meaning *means* to be true or false: the being true or false actually constitutes the relation of the proposition to reality, which we mean by saying that it has meaning (*Sinn* [sense]).

(*NM*: 113)

Wittgenstein's early definition of sameness of form between sentence and the world, in the case of elementary sentences, in terms of the contrast between facts 'of like sense' and facts 'of opposite sense', already provides the materials for truth-functional transformation, and hence for the idea of a truth-functional operator. In these terms, negation (to take just the simplest example) can be said just to transform facts 'of like sense' into facts 'of opposite sense', and vice versa. In fact, once we understand Wittgenstein's early account of the meaning of 'forms' as being generalized to all basic expressions (the view which I argued for in Chapter 4, section 4G), it seems clear that, whatever kind of basic expression we are concerned with, we could have begun with the opposite understanding of what counts as 'of like sense' and 'of opposite sense' to the one we actually use.

These points are made initially (in the *Notes on Logic*) in terms which, if taken literally, suppose that the sense-determining subject could have access to the world and all its facts quite independently of any language. Wittgenstein no longer seems to accept that way of thinking by the time of the *Tractatus*, but this does not stop the general moral being applicable to the theory of the *Tractatus*. It remains the case that there is a sense in which the idea of a truth-function is embedded in the very definition of sameness of form, between language and the world, for elementary sentences. And this gives a deep rationale for the following claim which Wittgenstein makes:

> For all logical operations are already contained in the elementary proposition.
> (5.47)

Given some (less metaphysically contentious) version of the *Notes on Logic* definition of sameness of form for elementary sentences, and the idea that every sentence is a 'truth-function' (in Wittgenstein's sense) of elementary sentences, we seem to have all that is required by assumptions (CF1)–(CF3).

Moreover, we also see that Wittgenstein has given us an account of the form of sentences in the deepest sense in his claim that every sentence's being the result of successive applications of the N-operator constitutes the general form of the sentence. There is a risk of understanding Wittgenstein's account of language, and with it of the form of sentences, as falling into two completely unconnected parts: one which is appropriate to the conception of elementary sentences as models, the other which concerns the construction of other sentences out of elementary sentences.[21] For the account of elementary sentences as models, the crucial notion of sentential form seems to be concerned with the ways in which names can be arranged to form a sentence — or, equivalently, the ways in which objects can be arranged to form an atomic fact. By contrast, the notion of sentential form which seems to be relevant to the account of logic seems to be concerned with the ways in which whole sentences can combine with each other. But once we realize that the notion of the ways in which names are arranged to form elementary sentences is itself to be understood in terms of a division which is effectively a division between truth and falsity, then we can see that, at a fundamental level, there are not really two notions of sentential form in play after all. Sameness of form between sentence and world is always — whether we are dealing with elementary or non-elementary sentences — a matter of which sentences count as being 'of like sense', and which 'of opposite sense', with the facts.

Of course, if all sentences must have the same basic form, we do, indeed, end up rejecting a hierarchy of sentences. And we have reason to insist that the very same truth-functions — indeed, the single N-operator — can be applied to all sentences. As Wittgenstein says:

> If logic has primitive ideas these must be independent of one another. If a primitive idea is introduced it must be introduced in all contexts in which it occurs at all. One cannot therefore introduce it for *one* context and then again for another. For example, if denial is introduced, we must understand it in propositions of the form '$\sim p$', just as in propositions like '$\sim (p \vee q)$', '$(\exists x). \sim fx$' and others. We may not first introduce it for one class of cases and then for another, for it would then remain doubtful whether its meaning in the two cases was the same, and there would be no reason to use the same way of symbolizing in the two cases.[22]
>
> (5.451)

Finally, 6.001 allows us to do a little accounting. One of the metaphysical commitments of the *Tractatus* which we identified in Chapter 1 was this:

(T3)   Facts are either atomic facts or combinations of atomic facts.

This is an immediate consequence of 6.001: indeed, 6.001 even specifies the kind of combination which is involved — it must be truth-functional combination.

5E LOGIC AND TAUTOLOGY

Wittgenstein's central concern in his treatment of logic can be summarized in his commitment to the thesis we considered in Chapter 2, the thesis of the world-independence of logic:

> (WIL) Logic does not depend on anything in particular being the case.

He rejects altogether the Kantian thought that necessary truths are synthetic *a priori* truths, knowledge of which requires some kind of intuition of, or acquaintance with reality.

Wittgenstein's commitment to (WIL), and his rejection of Kantianism about necessary truths is expressed in the following two claims:

> 6.1 The propositions of logic are tautologies
>
> There is only *logical* necessity.
>
> (6.37)

The importance of the claim that the propositions of logic are tautologies lies in Wittgenstein's theory of tautology, which is laid out in sections 4.46–4.4661. A tautology is a proposition which is 'true for all truth-possibilities of the elementary propositions' (4.46: Wittgenstein himself may in fact be the source of this use of the term 'tautology'[23]). For the case of sentences whose truth-possibilities can actually be enumerated, a tautology is a sentence which has a 'T' at every line of its truth-table, and is true no matter what.

At the time, this account of the propositions of logic (what we might call logical *truths*) as being tautologies seems to have been hailed as a succinct and very necessary *definition*: it makes possible the demarcation of logic from all other spheres — something which previous accounts had not achieved.[24] For our larger, philosophical, purposes, it is significant in other ways too.

According to Wittgenstein, a tautology says nothing. It has no truth-conditions, because it is unconditionally true (4.461). The same holds, for the opposite reason, of contradictions. Contradictions (which are, presumably, the only impossibilities, according to the view of 6.37) are false no matter what; they say nothing, and have no truth-conditions because they are true on no condition. Tautologies and contradictions are therefore 'without sense' ('sinnlos'; 4.461). They are not pictures, because they depict no particular states of affairs: tautologies are compatible with everything, contradictions with nothing (4.462).

Importantly, however, this does not mean that tautologies and contradictions are *nonsense* (4.4611).[25] Wittgenstein claims that they are not just nonsense because they are 'part of the symbolism'. This is a reasonable claim: if all sentences are the result of successive applications of the N-operator to elementary sentences, the existence of tautologies and contradictions is foreseeable from the start. Tautologies and contradictions are the limit cases of truth-functions upon elementary sentences. Moreover, according to Wittgenstein, although they do not *say* anything, that does not mean that they do nothing:

6.12 The fact that the propositions of logic are tautologies *shows* the formal — logical — properties of language, of the world.

That its constituent parts connected together *in this way* give a tautology characterizes the logic of its constituent parts.

In order that propositions connected together in a definite way may give a tautology they must have definite properties of a structure. That they give a tautology when *so* connected shows therefore that they possess these properties of a structure.

We have here another use of the crucial, but awkward, concept of *showing*. We came across this concept earlier, in Wittgenstein's account of the relation between a picture and its own pictorial form:

2.172 The picture, however, cannot represent its form of representation; it shows it forth.

The use of the concept of showing in relation to tautologies may be related to this, but it seems different, at first blush. After all, pictures or models show their own form; and so, therefore, do sentences which succeed in saying something — sentences which are not true or false no matter what. And it is not the tautologies themselves which show anything: it is, rather, *their being tautologies* which shows something; though what is shown by tautologies' being tautologies seems very similar what is shown by any logical picture or model — that is to say, the logical form of the world. The difference lies, perhaps, in the abstractness of what is shown by the tautologousness of a tautology. Whereas a sentence which says something (a sentence which is a picture or model) shows the possibilities of arrangement of its constituent objects, the tautologousness of a tautology shows just the general possibilities of truth and falsehood, no matter what objects are involved.

One might think that we have here a doctrine which is, after all, not all that dissimilar from the Kantian conception of the synthetic *a priori*: it seems that tautologies succeed in showing something about the world (its 'formal — logical — properties'). But Wittgenstein wants to insist that his view is quite different. The difference emerges in the following crucial claim:

> It is the characteristic mark of logical propositions that one can perceive in the symbol alone that they are true; and this fact contains in itself the whole philosophy of logic.

> (6.113)

The point is that the tautologousness of a tautology is evident (in some sense of evident) from the symbol alone: it is a fact (as it were) that concerns nothing but the possibilities of combination of the symbols from which the tautology is constructed. We do not need to look at the world in order to discover that a tautology is a tautology: no intuition or acquaintance of an objective world is involved here at all.

This, in turn, leads to a certain conception of adequate symbolism which runs through Wittgenstein's approach to logical necessity: if a notation is adequate it ought, in some sense, to reveal in itself the logical relations among symbols; there should be no need to consider anything to do with the world at all. This lies behind Wittgenstein's treatment of Russell's own response to the paradox he found in Frege's attempt to construct arithmetic from set theory. Wittgenstein first insists:

3.33 In logical syntax the meaning of a sign [i.e., the object referred to by a sign] ought never to play a role; it must admit of being established without mention being thereby made of the *meaning* of a sign; it ought to presuppose *only* the description of the expressions.

And then he draws the following moral:

3.331 From this observation we get a further view — into Russell's *Theory of Types*. Russell's error is shown by the fact that in drawing up his symbolic rules he has to speak about the things his signs mean.

Wittgenstein may, in fact, be being unfair here: Russell may not, strictly, have *had* to speak about the things his signs mean.[26] The fact is, however, that he did proceed in that way, and that, Wittgenstein thinks, shows an important error. Logical possibilities and necessities must depend on nothing more than the symbols themselves — nothing more, that is, than the signs together with the rules of their combination, which rules in turn need make no reference to the world. And Wittgenstein's so-called 'picture theory' of meaning — the theory that sentences are models of reality — provides, to put it no more strongly, further support for this point. For, according to that theory, the possibilities of combination of symbols are strictly *parallel* to the possibilities of combination of objects, and hence must be, in a sense, recognizable without our inspecting the ways in which objects can be combined: because the possibilities of combination of symbols are the same as the possibilities of combination of objects, there is no need to look at the world to see which combinations are possible.

This severely symbol-directed approach to logical necessity is also brought in by Wittgenstein to explain what might otherwise seem to pose a problem for him: the notion of identity. The problem is that the notion of identity seems, on the face of it, to furnish logical truths of its own. The following, for example, is a basic logical truth in standard predicate logic with identity:

$$(x)(x = x).$$

Indeed, that this is a logical truth was essential to Frege's class-theoretic construction of arithmetic, as we saw in Chapter 2 (section 2H). But Wittgenstein claims that all logical truths are tautologies, in the precise sense of being true for all truth-possibilities of elementary sentences. And '$(x)(x = x)$' cannot meet that condition. It could only even be the result of successive applications of the N-operator to elementary sentences, if sentences of the form '$a = a$' were themselves elementary sentences. But if '$a = a$' is an elementary sentence, it must be contingent and *a posteriori*, whereas it is obviously both *a priori* and necessary (if it is granted that 'a' is the name of a simple object). This point is made in 5.434:

> And we see that apparent propositions like: '$a = a$', '$a = b. b = c. \supset a = c$', '$(x). x = x$', '$(\exists x). x = a$', etc. cannot be written in a correct logical notation at all.

And Wittgenstein supports this way of putting the point (which depends on his own account of the general form of the sentence) with the following piece of intuitive reasoning:

> 5.5303 Roughly speaking: to say of *two* things that they are identical is nonsense, and to say of *one* thing that it is identical with itself is to say nothing.

We get a hint of exactly how little can be said by saying that one thing is identical with itself, on Wittgenstein's view, if we imagine fitting that claim into the basic account of the nature of facts which belongs with Wittgenstein's conception of sentences as models: the basic facts consist of several objects in relation to each other; an identity claim would seem to involve just one object, all on its own.

Wittgenstein is also dismissive of attempts to define a substantive relation of identity, such as Russell's, according to which *a* is identical with *b* if and only if *a* and *b* share all the same properties:[27]

> 5.5302 Russell's definition of '=' won't do; because according to it one cannot say that two objects have all their properties in common. (Even if this proposition is never true, it is nevertheless *significant*.)

The very notion of identity now seems to be under threat, and this is very serious for the approach to mathematics found in Frege and Russell. As we saw in Chapter 2 (section 2H), the core of their approach requires that the notion of equinumerousness — of having the same number as — can be defined without use of the notion of number, simply using quantification and identity. If the notion of identity is abandoned, this approach is in danger of collapsing. Wittgenstein's solution is to insist that no adequate logical notation would include the identity sign, and to claim that the sign becomes unnecessary if we take proper care over the use of names:

> 5.53 Identity of the object I express by identity of the sign and not by means of a sign of identity. Difference of the objects by difference of the signs.

Wittgenstein offers no formal proof that this procedure would work for everything that the identity sign might be called on to do, but he does offer various proposals for reformulating logical claims made by means of the identity signs in terms of a notation which simply distinguishes between names and variables when and only when there is a difference of object (see 5.531–5.321).[28] According to Wittgenstein, the only legitimate use of the sign of identity is at a meta-level, precisely to talk about the meaning of signs, and not to assert anything substantive about the world. Thus he says:

4.241 If I use two signs with one and the same meaning, I express this by putting between them the sign '='.
'$a = b$' means then, that the sign 'a' is replaceable by the sign 'b'.
(If I introduce by an equation a new sign 'b', by determining that it shall replace a previously known sign 'a', I write the equation — definition — (like Russell) in the form '$a = b$ Def.'. A definition is a symbolic rule.)

4.242 Expressions of the form '$a = b$' are therefore only expedients in presentation: They assert nothing about the meaning of the signs 'a' and 'b'.

This account of the identity sign is in stark contrast to that of Frege, who had originally adopted something like Wittgenstein's view himself in his early *Begriffsschrift*,[29] but rejected it in 'On Sense and Reference'. The grounds for this rejection were that the metalinguistic account — the view adopted by Wittgenstein in the *Tractatus* — made identity statements in general (and mathematical equations in particular) into relatively trivial linguistic truths, whereas really they were capable of expressing substantial knowledge.[30]

This difference reveals a crucial feature of Wittgenstein's philosophy of mathematics, to which he remained true throughout his career. The core of Wittgenstein's overall approach to mathematics in the *Tractatus* is revealed by these two remarks:

6.2 Mathematics is a logical method.
The propositions of mathematics are equations, and therefore pseudo-propositions.

The first sentence here allies mathematical truths with logical truths: the parallels, as well as the differences, are laid out in these two sections:

6.22 The logic of the world which the propositions of logic show in tautologies, mathematics shows in equations.

6.23 If two expressions are connected by the sign of equality, this means that they can be substituted for one another. But whether this is the case must show itself in the two expressions themselves. It characterizes the logical form of two expressions, that they can be substituted for one another.

Wittgenstein claims here that what are ordinarily thought of as identity statements simply assert — or seem to assert (we will return to that in a moment) — that two expressions can be substituted for one another. For two expressions to be capable of being substituted for one another it is at least required that they be capable of combining with other expressions in the same ways. As we know from the first introduction of the theory of sentences as models, logical form is a matter just of possibilities of combination. To say that two expressions have the same logical form is just to say that they can be combined in the same ways with other expressions. So for two expressions to be capable of being substituted for one another it is at least required that they have the same logical form.

But generally more is required than that. Wittgenstein holds that two objects could have the same logical form (2.0233). This means that their names will be capable of combining with other expressions in exactly the same ways: that is, their names will have the same logical form. But it does not follow from this that their names can be substituted for one another, or that the sentence formed by putting 'the sign of equality' (the identity sign) between the two names would be correct. For by hypothesis the two names refer to different things.

This suggests that Wittgenstein's claim in 6.23 cannot be as general as it seems to be: it cannot apply to everything which looks like a statement of identity. In the context, it is natural to take his claim to be intended to apply just to mathematical equations. His point will be that in an adequate notation for mathematics the expressions themselves will show that they are intersubstitutable. An adequate notation will show that they have the same form; and in the mathematical case, that is enough — no independent check on the world is needed. He explicitly contrasts his view here with that of Frege:

6.232　Frege says that these expressions have the same meaning [reference] but different senses.

But what is essential about equation is that it is not necessary in order to show that both expressions, which are connected by the sign of equality, have the same meaning: for this can be perceived from the two expressions themselves.

Really, however, Wittgenstein and Frege are talking past each other here. Frege introduced his notion of 'sense' to explain how an equation could be true, and yet it be possible *not* to realise that it is true. Wittgenstein is concerned to explain how it is possible — in mathematics, at least — to *realise* that an equation is true without independently looking at the world. Wittgenstein's answer to his problem is that equations are claims (as it were) of intersubstitutability, intersubstitutability is sameness of form, and sameness of form can always be revealed in an adequate notation. As for Frege's problem, Wittgenstein should probably have dismissed it as an issue for psychology, rather than philosophy. Unfortunately, he seems to suggest that it cannot really arise (at least in mathematics):

6.2322　The identity of the meaning of two expressions cannot be *asserted*. For in order to be able to assert anything about their meaning, I must know their meaning, and if I know their meaning, I know whether they mean the same or something different.

It is difficult to give this an interpretation which gives Wittgenstein any credit. The second sentence looks as if it is putting forward an argument which is obviously unsound: it is obviously not true, in general, that I can only know a and b if I know whether or not a is the same thing as b — otherwise it would be impossible suddenly to recognize someone, or to fail to recognize someone one knows. It is just because this is obviously not true that Frege introduced his notion of 'sense'.

It may be, however, that Wittgenstein is not putting forward precisely this unsound argument. Here are two alternative possibilities. First, Wittgenstein may be claiming that in the special case of names of simple objects — the fundamental existents on the *Tractatus*'s theory — it is not possible to know the meaning of two such names without knowing whether they have the same meaning. Something like this might plausibly be counted as true according to Russell's logical atomism — the system which Russell introduced under the influence of early drafts of the material which later became the *Tractatus*.[31] The fundamental objects of Russell's logical atomism are constituents of 'immediate' experience, and are things about whose existence one could not possibly be mistaken. It is plausible to suppose that if one could not possibly be mistaken about the existence of something, one could also not possibly mistake that thing for something else. But Russell's fundamental objects look ill-suited to play the role of the objects of the *Tractatus*. Even while pursuing his mathematical concerns, Russell was all along concerned to produce a theory of language which could address the very problems which Frege's notion of 'sense' was introduced to solve (see Russell (1905)), but without appealing to the notion of 'sense' at all. Wittgenstein seems not to have been especially concerned with Frege's problems; and his fundamental objects are designed to be the nodes of modality rather than to account for anything epistemic — it is the possibilities of combination of Wittgenstein's fundamental objects which are the fundamental possibilities in the world.

Alternatively, Wittgenstein may simply be overstating the perspicuousness in an ideal notation of the substitutivity of two expressions. His general philosophical view (including, in particular, the way he rejects Kant's idea of synthetic *a priori* truths) requires him to insist that the basis of the possibility of combination of symbols, and hence the basis of the intersubstitutability of expressions in the mathematical case, must lie in the symbols themselves and not in the world. But he has a tendency (as we will see in a moment) to overstate this: he has a tendency to slide from thinking that if logical form lies in the symbols themselves it must be very easily visible in those symbols.

Wittgenstein claims in 6.2 that the propositions of mathematics are 'pseudo-propositions'. What does this mean? The answer is not entirely clear: it looks as if Wittgenstein is committed to a range of slightly different readings of the claim. First, of course, he seems to think that mathematical equations have the same status as tautologies: they show the logic of the world. We saw earlier that in the case of tautologies this property is bound up with them failing to *say* anything: tautologies are really only a limiting case of sentences, since they are true simply because of the symbolism, and are not in any sense models of reality. So it may be that Wittgenstein wants to claim that mathematical equations say nothing in just the same sense as tautologies say nothing. But equations are odd in another way too: the identity sign at their core is, according to Wittgenstein, only an 'expedient of presentation'.[32] This is bound up with a view of the significance of mathematics which Wittgenstein held for the whole of his career. In the *Tractatus* it is expressed like this:

6.211   In life it is never a mathematical proposition which we need, but we use mathematical propositions *only* to infer from propositions which do not belong to mathematics to others which equally do not belong to mathematics.

(In philosophy the question 'Why do we really use that proposition?' constantly leads to valuable results.)

The whole approach of Wittgenstein's later philosophy is very largely prefigured in the parenthesis here. And the first sentence anticipates a view which is also clearly enunciated later:

> I want to say: it is essential to mathematics that its signs are also
> employed in *mufti*.
>
> It is the use outside mathematics, and so the *meaning* of the signs,
> that makes the sign-game into mathematics.
>
> (*RFM*: V. 2)

The idea seems to be that the sentences which are not
mere 'pseudo-propositions' are sentences which give us the
measurement of a thing's actual size or speed or mass (or
whatever), and mathematical equations enable us to produce
transformations of such genuinely modelling sentences to
produce genuine claims about the actual size, speed, mass, or
whatever of other things (or the same thing at other times).
The point seems to be that there is no mathematical realm,
just a mathematical way of handling the real world — the
possibility of which must be a fundamental feature of the
world itself. It seems, then, that mathematical equations are
counted as 'pseudo-propositions' at least in part because they
are not descriptions of a mathematical realm.

Of course, to make this claim good, Wittgenstein needs to
show that arithmetic, in particular, is not to be construed as
being concerned with a realm of special objects, the numbers.
And that means that he needs to show how the axioms of
arithmetic (the so-called Peano Axioms) — or something
with equivalent power — can be derived without appealing
to the kind of construction which Frege and Russell both
used, which involved treating numbers as classes, and classes
as objects of a special 'logical' kind. In the *Tractatus*
Wittgenstein does indeed offer a sketch of a way of doing
just that. This is not the place to consider this in any detail,[33]
but it is worth pausing briefly to consider Wittgenstein's view
that numbers are not objects, but 'exponents of operations'.

The claim that 'a number is an exponent of an operation'
is made at 6.021, and is a comment on the previous
section, 6.02, in which numbers are defined precisely in
these terms (the Greek letter 'Ω' is a symbol for an operation).
But what does the claim mean? First, what does he mean by
'operation' here? When we first encountered the term, in

section 5B above, it seemed to be intelligible chiefly by means of a contrast with the term 'function'. For that point, it seemed crucial that functions are expressions which take *names* to form sentences, whereas operations take whole *sentences* to form sentences. The only example we have been offered of an operation is the N-operator, and this does indeed fit this description. Some people have accordingly supposed that the operation which is in play in 6.02 and 6.021 is nothing other than the N-operator, but this is problematic. If we allow that infinitely many sentences may be included in the range of the variable 'ξ' in the construction '$N(\bar{\xi})$' — which we will have to do if we are to allow there to be infinitely many things — then the N-operator does not generate a consecutive series, and so cannot be used to generate (a counterpart of) the series of natural numbers.[34] On the other hand, it seems that we must continue to insist that operations take whole sentences to form sentences, if we are not to lose the ground for the crucial contrast between functions and operations:

5.251   A function cannot be its own argument, but the result of an operation can be its own basis.

If the operation (or operations) Wittgenstein has in mind in 6.021 does (or do) not take whole sentences to form sentences, it seems that there can be little more to the distinction between operations and functions than is offered by 5.251 itself: an operation will simply be an expression which can be applied to its own results.[35]

It seems to me natural to suppose that an operation, here as elsewhere, is something which takes whole sentences to form sentences, but that what we want here is some operation other than the N-operator. What Wittgenstein principally wants for 6.02 and 6.021 is an operation which generates a consecutive series. Such a series will begin from a certain primitive base, something which is not itself the result of any previous application of the operation (which we can symbolize it by means of the letter 'Ω'). Let this thing be x.

Then since x is not the result of any previous application of the operation Ω, we can count it as the result of applying the operation Ω *no* times to x. We might then write that as follows:

(1) $\Omega^\circ x$.

Here the numeral '0' is written as expressing the 'power' of the operation Ω, to indicate the number of times the operation has been applied to x.[36] Suppose now that we apply the operation Ω to x (i.e., to $\Omega^0 x$). We might write the result like this:

(2) $\Omega'\Omega^\circ x$

We can indicate that we are here applying it *one more time* than 0 times by adding '+ 1' to our expression of the 'power' of the operation, and so express (2) like this:

(2p) $\Omega^{\circ \, + \, 1} x$

If the operation Ω is applied twice to x (i.e., to $\Omega^0 x$), the natural way of writing the result is this:

(3) $\Omega'\Omega'\Omega^\circ x$.

But if we add '+ 1' to the expression of the 'power' in (2p) we can rewrite (3) like this:

(3p) $\Omega^{\circ \, + \, 1 \, + \, 1} x$.

In general, we can characterize the use of '+1' to indicate that the operation Ω has been applied *one more time*, by means of the following definition:

$$\Omega'\Omega^\nu x =_{df} \Omega^{\nu \, + \, 1} x$$

Of course, this will leave us with a cumbersome expression if the operation is applied many times. What we need is an array of simpler symbols which can be written in place of the increasingly large expressions of the form '0 + 1 + 1 + 1 ... ' in order to express 'powers' of the operation. The natural choice is the familiar range of Arabic decimal numerals.

What we have, then, is an operation which can be applied to its own results an indefinite number of times, and a method of abbreviating the expression of such repeated applications. This is what Wittgenstein presents in 6.02. He uses the identity sign there in the only way he thinks is legitimate: as the expression of a definition — that is, as a way of introducing a notational abbreviation. The method of abbreviation he uses involves treating numerals as expressing 'powers' of the operation: that is, as indicating the number of times the operation has been applied, beginning from a primitive base which is not itself the result of an application of the operation. These 'powers' of the operation are what Wittgenstein (in translation) calls 'exponents' of the operation. And that is what he has in mind when he makes his key claim:

6.021   A number is the exponent of an operation.

Clearly, the point of this is to deny that numbers are objects, but how has that result been achieved? Frege's claim that numbers are objects depended on two things: first the claim that the basic grammar of number words (numerals) is that of singular terms (the referents of which are objects); and second, the identification of a series of objects to be the numbers — the classes he used in his construction. I take it that the point of 6.02 is to show that numerals do not really have the grammar of singular terms. The only genuine singular terms in the *Tractatus* are the names for the objects which constitute the form of the world. Any other expression which has the superficial grammar of a name must really be something which can be regarded as being, in effect, introduced by definition, as an abbreviation for some more complex expression. In 6.02 the Arabic numerals other than '0' and '1' are introduced as definitional abbreviations of terms of the series '0 + 1 +1 +1 +1 ... '. And this series itself is nothing more than a way of writing the repeated application of an operation, beginning from a base which is not itself the result of applying the operation. So he hopes to have shown that there is no reason at all to take numerals as names.[37]

To see exactly what Wittgenstein is doing here, we need to recall Frege's method of establishing the claim that numbers are objects. What Frege does is establish the following equivalence:

(E) The number of class C_1 = the number of class C_2 if and only if class C_1 is *equinumerous* with class C_2.

Since this allows us to use substantival expressions like 'the number of class C_1', it seems to ensure that those substantival expressions are meaningful. But these substantival expressions have the surface grammar of singular terms. On Frege's theory, meaningful expressions which have the grammar of singular terms refer to *objects*. So Frege concludes that numbers are objects. What Wittgenstein clearly rejects is the assumption that the *surface* grammar of an expression reveals its real grammar. He credits Russell with the realization that this assumption can be rejected:

Russell's merit is to have shown that the apparent logical form of the proposition need not be its real form.

(4.0031)

Since Wittgenstein thinks that the only expressions which really function as singular terms — by having meaning in virtue of being correlated with objects — are the simple names of which elementary sentences are composed, he holds that the real function of other expressions is to be understood only by recognizing how sentences involving them are to be analysed into elementary sentences (and compounds of elementary sentences).

Wittgenstein therefore takes himself to have done all that he needs to do, by showing how the numerals can be introduced as a way of abbreviating an indexing of the repetition of an operation. You (or Frege) might be tempted to say to him: 'Yes, I see how the numerals are used, but what of the things the numerals *refer* to — what are the *numbers*?' To this he would have to respond, in the manner of his later philosophy: 'No such things were in question here, only how the numerals are used'.[38]

So much for a brief account of Wittgenstein's claim that numbers are not objects, but 'exponents of operations'. Now let us return to his more central contentions on the nature of logic and mathematics. The core of Wittgenstein's philosophy of logic and necessity is the anti-Kantian view that logical truth, mathematical truth, and necessary truth in general needs no insight or intuition of the real world to be discovered: rather, one need only look at the symbols, and an adequate symbolism should show the form of the symbols, which is where modality in general resides. But it seems to me that Wittgenstein clearly thought that if the form of the symbols could be *shown* in an adequate notation, it could, in some relatively straightforward way, be *seen* in that notation. There are hints of this view in several places, but he commits himself most explicitly to it in the following remark:

6.122 Whence it follows that we can get on without logical propositions, for we can recognize in an adequate notation the formal properties of the propositions by mere inspection.

This looks as if it commits Wittgenstein to the view that every logical truth is *decidable* — that is to say, can be derived by a mechanical procedure or algorithm in a finite time. This claim is true if it is restricted to simple sentence logic (propositional calculus),[39] but is false of standard predicate logic if it includes many-placed predicates, and domains of quantification are allowed to be infinite (and it is false of mathematics, if that is claimed to be part of logic too).[40] One can understand how someone concerned to reject the Kantian commitment to synthetic *a priori* truths, in the way in which Wittgenstein was, might find the claim of 6.122 extremely natural: but it goes well beyond what he was entitled to.

It is not clear how important this is to the *Tractatus*. Some are inclined to think of 6.122 as little more than a slip. It is sometimes even claimed that the notion of *showing* — which might seem to be the counterpart of recognition 'by mere inspection' — is not really an epistemic notion at all.[41] Others go to the opposite extreme, and claim that insisting on the decidability of all necessary truths is the point of Wittgenstein's whole treatment of logic and necessity.[42] My own view is that the truth is between the two. It seems to me that what really mattered to Wittgenstein was simply that logic and mathematics do not furnish us with substantial truths about the world, and are not, therefore, knowable only by some kind of acquaintance with or intuition of the world: he was principally concerned to reject the Kantian idea of synthetic *a priori* truths. But it also seems to me that he was led by this conviction to expect all necessary truths to be decidable: this expectation was more than he had any right to, but I think it was not all that unreasonable in the relative innocence of the era.[43]

If Wittgenstein rejects Kant's account of necessary truths — mathematical truths, in particular — we might think that he can have no answer to one of the questions which are naturally seen as tempting us towards a Kantian view. The question is: how is it that logic, mathematics, and the rest, apply to the real world? But in fact Wittgenstein's picture theory of language gives him a ready answer to this question, without weakening his opposition to Kant. According to the picture theory — the view that, in the basic case at least, sentences are models of reality — sentences can only represent reality at all in virtue of having the same form as reality: that is, if the possibilities of combination of the components of the sentences (at least, when those sentences have been reformulated in a perspicuous notation) are the same as the possibilities of combination of the corresponding objects in reality. If this is right, there can be no possibility of logic or mathematics failing to apply to the real world: logic and mathematics simply show the form which is common to both language and the world. But it is still the case that we never need to look at the world, independently of the symbolism, to see what the possibilities of combination are. The fact that the form of language is the same as the form of the world guarantees that looking at language is always enough.

5F EXTENSIONALITY

Wittgenstein claims that 'every proposition is the result of successive applications of the operation $N(\bar{\xi})$ to elementary propositions' (6.001). Since the N-operator is truth-functional, what this means is that every combination of elementary sentences is truth-functional; which is to say that nothing but the truth or falsity of a sentence can make a difference to the truth or falsity of sentences in which it figures as a component. This is a commitment to the truth-functionality of all language, or extensionality. And, of course, it was already announced in this earlier remark in the text:

5. Propositions are truth-functions of elementary propositions.
    (An elementary proposition is a truth-function of itself.)

There are a number of apparent counter-examples to this claim, the most famous of which are uses of sentences within 'that'-clauses used to say what someone thinks or feels. These apparent counter-examples were well enough known by the time Wittgenstein wrote: Frege used the notion of sense to deal with them in his (1892a), and Russell hoped to use his theory of descriptions to deal with them, without appealing to the notion of sense (Russell 1905). Wittgenstein shows that he was aware of the problem:

5.541 At first sight it appears as if there were also a different way in which one proposition could occur in another.

Especially in certain propositional forms of psychology, like 'A thinks, that *p* is the case', or 'A thinks *p*', etc.
Here it appears superficially as if the proposition *p* stood to the object A in a kind of relation.
(And in modern epistemology (Russell, Moore, etc.) those propositions have been conceived in this way.)

(The parenthesis here is a reference to the views of Russell (1903) and Moore (1899): see Chapter 2, above.)

The problem, put briefly, is this. If the occurrence of sentences in the 'that'-clauses of these psychological contexts were truth-functional, a number of substitutions would be permissible which in fact we reject. Suppose that we begin with a sentence like this:

(a) Carol believes that Everest is the highest mountain in the world.

In fact, it is true that Everest is the highest mountain in the world, so the sentence within the 'that'-clause here — 'Everest is the highest mountain in the world' — is true. Since Everest is Chomolungma, it could make no difference to the truth of what is contained in the 'that'-clause if we swapped the name 'Chomolungma' for the name 'Everest' — if the occurrence of the sentence in the 'that'-clause were truth-functional. If we did that, we would get this:

(b) Carol believes that Chomolungma is the highest mountain in the world.

But even though Everest *is* Chomolungma, Carol may not know that. If she does not know it, then, we usually think, (b) will be false, even though (a) is true. This seems to show that it is not just the *truth* or *falsity* of the sentence in the 'that'-clause which makes a difference to the truth or falsity of the whole sentence. In fact, the situation is even worse. It is true that Everest is the highest mountain in the world. It is also true that the area of a circle is πr^2. If the truth or falsity of the sentence in the 'that'-clause were all that matters, the truth of (a) should ensure that *this* is true as well:

(c) Carol believes that the area of a circle is πr^2.

But if Carol knows no geometry, (c) will be false, even though (a) is true. What this shows is that if truth or falsity is all that matters in the 'that'-clauses of reports of what people think and feel, anyone who believes one truth will thereby be counted as believing all truths, and anyone who believes one falsehood will thereby be counted as believing all falsehoods.

It seems clear, on the face of it, that these psychological contexts are non-truth-functional, and that Wittgenstein is therefore wrong about the general form of sentences. But Wittgenstein does offer some response:

5.542 But it is clear that 'A believes that *p*', 'A thinks *p*', 'A says *p*' are of the form '"*p*" says *p*': and here we have no co-ordination of a fact and an object, but a co-ordination of facts by means of a co-ordination of their objects.

From which he concludes:

5.5421 This shows that there is no such thing as the soul — the subject, etc. — as conceived in contemporary superficial psychology. A composite soul would not be a soul any longer.

Unfortunately, this response is hard to make sense of. What Wittgenstein seems to be saying is that these psychological statements cannot really be made true by an *object* (a person, a soul) being related to another thing, a sentence or a proposition, in a certain way. Rather, what is going on is that a certain *fact* — a picture or model — represents *that* something is the case. The idea seems to be that it is not the person, the soul, or whatever, that is related to a certain possible situation; rather, it is something in the mind of the person — some mental picture — which represents. Here we have a rejection of the traditional conception of the person, or the mind, which is rather reminiscent of Hume;[44] and this will have some significance for the discussion of solipsism, which we will consider in the next chapter.

But the difficulty is to see how this is a solution to the problem in hand. The original problem was the apparent appearance of sentences in non-truth-functional combinations: the 'p' position in sentences of the form 'A believes that p' seems to be non-truth-functional. But the second 'p' position in sentences of the form '"p" says that p' is equally non-truth-functional, and for exactly the same reason: if it were truth-functional, then if 'p' said something true, it would say all truths, and if it said something false, it would say all falsehoods.

Although I think that there is a problem here which Wittgenstein cannot really solve, we will miss the way Wittgenstein approached the issue if we treat it in these terms. I have supposed that the problems arise with sentences whose canonical mode of expression includes a 'that'-clause: 'a believes that p', for example, or '"p" says that p'. Wittgenstein's first mention of the issue does use a formulation of this kind, but he quickly replaces it with another, which then remains his standard form of expression: 'A thinks p', 'A says p', '"p" says p'. And in these expressions 'p' seems to figure as a name — of a fact, or of a Russellian 'proposition' (the objective correlate of a whole sentence). This treatment of these contexts is exactly what Russell's first theory suggests (see Chapter 2, section 2D, above). Wittgenstein's response now makes sense. Russell's original account makes these contexts express a relation between an object named by the first name (this object is a person, a subject, a thinker) and a different kind of object named by the second name (which is a fact, or a Russellian proposition). Wittgenstein objects that we do not really have a relation between a *person*-type object and a fact-type object: what we have is what we might first describe as a relation between *two fact*-type objects — a sentence and what it depicts. But this first description is, of course, wrong, according to the *Tractatus*'s general theory of language: these expressions are not names, and we do not have *objects* here at all; so there can be no question of a *relation*, literally speaking, between them. The only real relations involved here are relations between the *elements* of sentences, on the one hand, and the *objects* which constitute the facts, on the other. So the problem is supposed simply to disappear.

Unfortunately, as Ramsey pointed out in his original review of the *Tractatus*, this will not work: 'the sense is not completely determined by the objects which occur in it; nor is the propositional sign completely constituted by the names which occur in it' (Ramsey 1923: 471). And, of course, the point is Wittgenstein's own:

> When we say A judges that etc., then we have to mention a whole proposition which A judges. It will not do either to mention only its constituents, or its constituents and form, but not in the proper order. This shows that a proposition itself must occur in the statement that it is judged.
>
> (*NL*: 94)

The thought even lies behind the very next remark of the *Tractatus* itself, in which he objects to Russell's 'multiple-relation' theory of judgement:

> 5.5422 The correct explanation of the form of the proposition 'A judges p' must show that it is impossible to judge a nonsense. (Russell's theory does not satisfy this condition.)[45]

The consequence is that Wittgenstein's treatment of sentences of the form 'a believes that p', or even '"p" says that p' can only really be accepted if we suppose that such expressions are really just malformed, and are not really meaningful at all. And that really is not credible. We are bound to find it hard to believe a theory which not only says that there is no soul (because there is no single subject which has a belief), but also denies that we can ever say what someone says or thinks. Such scepticism even seems at odds with 5.5422 itself, where Wittgenstein seems to hold out hope of a positive and substantial solution to the problem of analysing these sentences.

It is tempting to think that part of the problem is that Wittgenstein was just dazzled by the power of modern logic, the logic invented by Frege and Russell, and as a result simply did not consider the possibility that there might be constructions which it could not accommodate. Here, after all, was a system which could express a vastly greater range of arguments than Aristotle's logic ever could. Moreover, it seemed to offer explanations of why the valid arguments are valid, and (in the case of sentence logic, at least) to provide a simple procedure for testing for validity. In the light of this extraordinary increase in what could be done with logic, it would perhaps be natural to think that modern logic actually revealed the logic of the world: that it was not just one system for formalizing arguments, but showed the proper form of all possible valid argument. Consequently, we can understand how it might be natural to think that what could not be dealt with by that logic could not really make sense.[46]

But I think Wittgenstein's commitment to extensionality — the insistence that sentences can only be constructed truth-functionally — runs much deeper than that. In fact, it seems completely integral to his whole system. We can see it even in the early account of the meaning of 'forms' in the *Notes on Logic* (*NL*: 104), which we have already looked at (see Chapter 4, section 4F; and again in sections 5B and 5D of this chapter). The idea is that what needs to be determined is just which facts are 'of like sense' and which 'of opposite sense' with a range of sentences, which is what settles which sentences are to count as true and which false. I argued in Chapter 4 that in the *Tracatus* this account is extended to apply to *all* elements of elementary sentences. The result is that there seems to be no more to the meaning of the parts even of elementary sentences than their contribution to the determination of the truth-value of the sentences of which they are part. And this already means that what ultimately matters about whole sentences is just whether they are true or false.

Wittgenstein's extensionalism also manifests itself in the following basic commitment of the metaphysics of the *Tractatus*, one of the two which have not yet been explained as being a consequence of the *Tractatus*'s theory of language:

(T4) The existence of any atomic fact is independent of the existence of any other atomic fact.

If the logic of the world is extensional, and every sentence is the result of successive applications of truth-functions to elementary sentences, it follows that elementary sentences must be logically independent of each other. For suppose that some elementary sentences are not logically independent of all other elementary sentences. This would mean that there are what in Chapter 1 (section 1E) I called *dependence* facts — facts of the following form (where '*p*' and '*q*' might be replaced by elementary sentences):

(D) Its being the case that *p* depends on its being the case that *q*.

As was noted in Chapter 1, there can only be a point in singling out any notion of dependence between facts, if the relevant dependence relations hold between some facts and not between others. But that means that two facts being facts is not enough to determine whether there is a dependence relation between them. And that means that the corresponding sentences can both be *true* without its being determined whether there is a dependence relation between them. And that means that the truth of *statements* of such dependence cannot just depend on the *truth-value* of the sentences of which they are composed. That is to say, (D) itself cannot be truth-functional, if dependence is to mean anything. Since Wittgenstein insists that sentences can only occur truth-functionally in other sentences, (D) cannot be a legitimate form of sentence, where '*p*' and '*q*' are replaced by elementary sentences. So no elementary sentence can depend on any other.

If elementary sentences are logically independent of each other, then their ontological counterparts, the atomic facts, are mutually independent existences. This immediately gives us (T4). And it leads to the final unexplained metaphysical commitment as well. Given that names are only meaningful when linked together with other names in a sentence (so that objects, the counterparts of names, cannot exist except in combination with other objects), (T4) means that this claim is also true:

(T1) The basic organic unities of the world are facts.

It is only the counterparts to elementary *sentences* which are independent of one another. The whole metaphysics of the *Tractatus* is finally seen as no more than what is required by the work's philosophy of language and philosophy of logic.

This shows how closely extensionality is bound in with the metaphysics of the *Tractatus*. It was also at the heart of the work's eventual unravelling. It follows from the thesis of the logical independence of elementary sentences that neither of the following two sentences can plausibly be regarded as elementary, whatever the name '*a*' is taken to refer to:

(1) *a* is red all over;
(2) *b* is blue all over.

For (1) and (2) seem clearly to contradict each other. But although that means that they cannot be counted as elementary sentences, it is unclear what analysis of them could be provided which avoids the same problem recurring at another point. Wittgenstein faces a serious challenge to explain the logical relations between 'red' and 'blue'. In the *Tractatus* itself he seems simply to have assumed that the problem is soluble:

6.3751 For two colours, *e.g.* to be at one place in the visual field, is impossible, logically impossible, for it is excluded by the logical structure of colour.

Let us consider how this contradiction presents itself in physics. Somewhat as follows: That a particle cannot at the same time have two velocities, *i.e.* that at the same time it cannot be in two places, *i.e.* that particles in different places at the same time cannot be identical.

(It is clear that the logical product [conjunction] of two elementary propositions can neither be a tautology nor a contradiction. The assertion that a point in the visual field has two different colours at the same time, is a contradiction.)

But this looks like mere bluster: after all, how is it explained that it is logically impossible for particles in different places at the same time to be identical?[47] Wittgenstein came later to reject the view he here espouses; and that rejection was the beginning of the eventual abandonment of the whole system of the *Tractatus*.[48]

6

SOLIPSISM, IDEALISM, AND REALISM

6A THE DRAMATIC CLAIM

We saw in the last section of the previous chapter that Wittgenstein dismissed the idea of a subject or self, as that is conceived of in 'contemporary superficial psychology' (5.5421). That suggests that there might be a subject or self of an altogether different kind, which plays a rather different role in philosophy. And, in a sense, that seems to be just what Wittgenstein thinks, though even to say that is to court controversy. The problem is crystallized in this remark:

> In fact what solipsism *means*, is quite correct, only it cannot be *said*, but it shows itself.

> (5.62)

Solipsism, traditionally understood, is the view that only the self ('solus ipse') exists: nothing but the self is real. It is not clear, however, that this is quite Wittgenstein's view, or that he is concerned with it — to put the point no less ambiguously — for precisely the traditional reasons. Wittgenstein here seems to be making three distinct claims:

(i) 'What solipsism *means* is quite correct';
(ii) 'What solipsism means' cannot be *said*;
(iii)'What solipsism means' 'shows itself'.

To begin with, at least, I will take these claims as literally as possible. The question will then be to understand why Wittgenstein makes them. This will show what kind of 'solipsism' he has in mind, and will also reveal something of the character of the *Tractatus* as a whole.

Wittgenstein's discussion in the *Tractatus* of the view he calls 'solipsism' is very brief, but might be claimed to be the centrepiece of the whole work.[1] In the single dramatic remark I have just quoted we might seem to have the fulfilment of the aim of the book as that is stated in the Preface:

> [The book's] whole meaning can be summed up somewhat as follows: What can be said at all can be said clearly; and whereof one cannot speak thereof one must be silent.
>
> (*TLP*, p.27)

I have suggested that the book can be seen to be a reaction against Kant's approach to metaphysics — in particular, against the view that philosophical truths are synthetic *a priori* truths. It is tempting to see the dramatic claim of 5.62 as a moving on from Kant's whole philosophy.

6B THE BACKGROUND

First, though, it will be useful to get some purchase for ourselves — independently of the text — on the kinds of issue which might be involved here. Solipsism is a form of idealism. Idealism is most simply seen as a denial of realism, and realism, as we have already seen, is naturally formulated in some such terms as these:

> (R) The nature of the world as it is in itself is altogether independent of anything to do with any thought or representation of it.

(R) is concerned with the nature of the world as a whole; it is therefore an expression of what might be termed a 'global' realism. But there might be more local issues: whether to hold that the nature of some particular kind of object, or some particular kind of fact, was altogether independent of thought or representation.

Any position which hesitates to endorse (R), or the corresponding claim about some particular kind of object or fact, may be termed *anti-realist*. Someone who positively denies (R), holding that there is some *dependence* of the world — or the relevant kind of object or fact — upon thought or representation can be counted an *idealist*. It is worth noting that there is something stipulative about my use of the terms 'idealism' and 'realism' here. For the issues which matter to the *Tractatus*, the central concern is whether things are or are not independent of thought and representation. But the terms 'idealism' and 'realism' have other uses too. Kant, for example, seems sometimes to use 'idealism' to mean *scepticism* (in the 'Refutation of Idealism', in Kant (1787)). And 'realism' is sometimes used to describe an anti-*sceptical* position, even today: thus 'naïve realism', in the philosophy of perception, is the view that we *perceive* things as they are independently of us.

There are two forms of idealism which bulk particularly large in the literature. The first is the kind of idealism advocated by Berkeley (1734). His idealism concerns what is perceivable, and his claim is that what is perceivable cannot exist without actually being perceived. This is sometimes known as *empirical* realism (Williams 1981).

There is a different kind of idealism which is associated with Kant and the tradition which followed him (including, in their different ways, Hegel and Schopenhauer). Kant held that, although perceivable things do not depend for their *existence* on actually being perceived, their *nature* — or, at least, such of their nature as we can have knowledge of — is determined by the nature of the cognitive faculties of those who can have experience of them. Here we have a different sort of idealism: a dependence of the *nature* of what we perceive on something to do with thought or representation. This might be termed a 'transcendental' idealism, to make the contrast with the empirical idealism advocated by Berkeley (thus Williams (1981)). But it would be confusing to use the term 'transcendental idealism' in that way, since the term is already the name of the whole of Kant's view, rather than just this idealist portion of it.

Kant's idealism (in the sense of a rejection of (R)) concerns just what is perceivable — or, to be more precise, just that which we can understand of what is perceivable. But in addition to this, Kant assumes that there is a way in which things are in themselves. (There is an interpretative controversy over whether what we are dealing with here are the same things — the perceivable things — as they are in themselves, or whether there are special things — things in themselves — which somehow lie behind the perceivable things. This is the disagreement between one-world and two-world interpretations of Kant, a disagreement which we need not consider further here.[2]) According to Kant, we cannot know how things are in themselves. The way things are in themselves is wholly independent of anything to do with thought or representation. So Kant is firmly realist, in the sense of (R), about things as they are in themselves. And 'transcendental idealism' is the name of this total Kantian position: idealism (in the sense of a rejection of (R)) about things as they can be perceived by us, and realism (in the sense of (R)) about things as they are in themselves.

Idealism has, historically, been a response to scepticism. Some argument may make it seem that we cannot have knowledge of the world as it is in itself, if its nature is too strictly independent of thought and representation; so in order to avoid the conclusion that we cannot have knowledge of the world, it is suggested that the world is not so strictly independent of thought and representation. And the character of the idealism is then determined by the character of the scepticism. Berkeley was concerned to avoid empirical scepticism, the claim that we cannot have knowledge of the empirical facts, the facts which we might think are available in perception. Kant was concerned to avoid scepticism about what is *essential* to the perceivable world, about its necessary features: accordingly, he supposed that the essential features we are interested in were in some way determined by something to do with thought or representation.

What kind of idealism is the solipsism which Wittgenstein is concerned with in the *Tractatus*? We cannot easily decide this by asking what kind of scepticism he might be responding to, since it is not obvious, in advance of considering his views on solipsism, that he has any great interest in scepticism in the *Tractatus*; indeed, it is natural to think that he seems only slightly concerned with epistemic issues in general at this point in his career. If we think his main concern here is to respond to the views of Russell, then we will think that the solipsism of the *Tractatus* is something more like Berkeley's empirical idealism. For Russell was concerned with scepticism, in just the kind of way in which the British empiricists of the classical period, including Berkeley, were.[3] This led him to base his metaphysical system on 'sense-data', objects of immediate experience about whose existence we cannot be mistaken.

This seems to me to be quite unlike Wittgenstein's general concerns in the *Tractatus*.[4] As we saw in Chapter 1, the fundamental objects of the *Tractatus* are not those whose existence cannot be *doubted*, but those whose existence is *necessary*. His concern is not with what presents itself to us as *actually* existing; but with the form of the world — what is common to every *possible* world. The general orientation of his interest — towards what is possible and what is necessary, rather than towards what is actually experienced — suggests that it will be a Kantian, rather than a simply Berkeleyan idealism which concerns him. And there are strong traces in the remarks on solipsism in the *Tractatus* of the influence of Schopenhauer,[5] and Schopenhauer was evidently working within the Kantian tradition.

Moreover, it is a Kantian question which lies at the heart of his philosophical concerns in general. Thus, in the *Notebooks* he writes:

> The great problem round which everything that I write turns is: Is there an order of the world *a priori*, and if so what does it consist in?
>
> (*NB*: 53)

This is the question which Kant answered in the affirmative, and was thereby led to insist that there are synthetic *a priori* truths. There is a direct connection between this issue (in this formulation) and the discussion of solipsism in the *Tractatus*. 5.634 ends with these words:

> There is no order of things a priori.[6]

It is natural, therefore, to take the solipsism of the *Tractatus* to be a form of idealism which addresses Kant's concerns.[7] There is also a similarity with Kant in the following respect. Kant was concerned with the limits of what can be known: for him, knowledge is limited by what is required to make sense of what can be experienced. According to him, we can have no knowledge of the way things are in themselves; the way things are in themselves lies beyond the limits of our knowledge. The aim of his theory was to re-establish metaphysics as a rigorous scientific discipline within the limits of what is relevant to possible experience, and to expose as unconstrained (indeed, paradoxical) any attempt to do metaphysics beyond those limits. Wittgenstein, of course, was concerned with the limits of *thought* (or its expression):

> The book will, therefore, draw a limit to thinking, or rather — not to thinking, but to the expression of thoughts; for, in order to draw a limit to thinking we should have to be able to think both sides of this limit (we should therefore have to be able to think what cannot be thought).
>
> (*TLP*, p. 27)

And, as we will see in the next chapter, Wittgenstein also uses these limits to rule out metaphysics (though he is more radical than Kant, precisely in not accepting the possibility of synthetic *a priori* truths, the category which makes room in Kant's theory for the possibility of a scientific metaphysics). Furthermore, Kant's theory was subject to criticism, from very early on, on grounds which look rather similar to those which Wittgenstein appeals to in that remark in the Preface of the *Tractatus* which I have just quoted. Kant can only make his distinction between things as they appear to us (which can be known) and things as they are in themselves (which cannot) if he can at least *talk* and *think* about things as they are in themselves. He therefore needs it to be possible to talk or think about something (or a way in which something is) which we can have no knowledge of. But it is not obvious that this is really intelligible: it is natural to think that we can only refer to, or think about, what we have *some* knowledge of. If that is right, even to state Kant's theory requires us to have some knowledge of what (according to him) cannot be known, which is problematic in just the way thinking what cannot be thought is.

We can use this Kantian background to sketch, in a rather simple-minded way, some possible forms of realism and idealism, in order to get a better sense of the kind of view Wittgenstein might be adopting. (The reason for calling this sketch 'simple-minded' will appear shortly.) We can also use the general approach to thought which the *Tractatus* presents to set up the issues in a way that has a straightforward intuitive resonance. According to Wittgenstein, to think is to form a picture or model of reality (2.1, 3, 3.001): thinking is representing. Intuitively, representations can be in different media: painting, music, writing, and so on. Now we might think that different media are differently good for representing different kinds of thing. Painting, we might think, is particularly good for representing colour and shape, but rather poor for representing sounds; conversely, music, we might think, is good for representing certain kinds of emotional significance, and certain kinds of movement, but rather poor for representing, say, colours. If we think in this way, it is natural to wonder whether there are some things which simply cannot be represented in certain media — whether a medium might have, as it were, a representational *blind-spot*.[8]

Now if we can raise this question about representational media in general, it seems natural to think we can raise it about language too. Consider, then, this question:

(Q) Might language have representational blind-spots?

On the face of it, this question might have either an affirmative or a negative answer. Suppose we answer 'Yes'. We seem now to have a position which is the representational analogue of Kant's; and it faces a similar question. Is it even possible to state, in language, that language has representational blind-spots? We seem to be able to distinguish between two possible positions:

(A1) Language might have representational blind-spots, and that possibility is statable;

(A2) Language might have representational blind-spots, but that possibility is not statable.

(A2) is obviously a paradoxical position; we will return to that issue shortly. In the meantime, let us consider the other apparently possible answer to (Q): no, language could not have representational blind-spots. Now this answer could be given for one of two reasons. We might think that, in fact, there are no substantial constraints on representation: anything at all is in principle representable in any medium, simply because there are no general requirements about how representations must stand towards what they represent. If we adopt this response, we do not suppose, for example, that there must be any similarity in form between products of a medium and what can be represented in that medium. We might formulate this response as follows:

(A3) Language could not have representational blind-spots, because there is no constraint at all on what can be represented in any given medium.

This position will hold that it is possible, in principle, to represent sounds in painting, for example, and colours in music.

(A3) cannot be the position of the *Tractatus*, because the *Tractatus* seems to insist precisely on a strong constraint on representation — the requirement that a model must have the same form as the reality it depicts. So we are likely to be more particularly interested in the other way of answering 'No' to (Q). This holds that there cannot be representational blind-spots in language, even though there are significant constraints on what can be represented in any medium. What this requires is that, although there are strict constraints on what is statable, there is nothing which is possible which is not statable. The question then arises why this should be so. There seem to be three positions which could be adopted, which we might formulate like this:

(A4) Language could not have representational blind-spots, because language simply adopts the form of reality;

(A5) Language could not have representational blind-spots, because reality is determined by what language can depict;

(A6) Language could not have representational blind-spots, because what limits language also limits reality.

Putting it crudely, (A4) is a realist position — it portrays reality as being independent of language, and language as being shaped to fit reality. (A5) is a kind of idealist position — it portrays reality as being constrained by the limits of language; reality does not have the robust independence from thought and representation which our formulation (R), for example, requires. And (A6) is neutral with respect to the question of realism and idealism. But it is important to note that (A4) is not the only realist position among the answers to (Q). (A1) and (A2) both look like realist views (even if (A2) is a paradoxical form of realism), and (A3) is certainly compatible with realism. (A4) is simply the only unambiguously realist position among those which think that the answer to (Q) is 'No', while insisting that there are significant constraints on what can be represented in any medium.

So much for the simple-minded sketch of the alternatives which seem to be open to us. We can now start putting this simple-mindedness in question by considering the ways in which various positions here may be thought to run into problems of paradox. I have already noted that (A2) is paradoxical: it cannot be coherently stated. For all that, we might think that it was true: after all, we seem to be just applying to language the thoughts which seemed so intuitive in the case of painting and music, and then finding that because of the accident of the medium we are working in — philosophy is always linguistic — the very truth we are trying to focus on turns out to lie in one of the crucial blind-spots. (A2) invites us to entertain the idea that there might be unstatable, inexpressible, ineffable truths.

But paradox threatens more of our range of apparently possible positions, if we start building in more assumptions. Suppose we accept an assumption which we might try to put like this:

(SC) It is only possible to state that *p* if it is contingent whether *p*.

This looks at least very close to one of the assumptions which Wittgenstein needs for his claim that no picture can depict its own form (2.172–2.174); and it is a close cousin to the Principle of Bipolarity which is often attributed to Wittgenstein (see Chapter 3, section 3D, above).[9] And it seems to be stated explicitly in 5.634:

Everything we can describe at all could also be otherwise.

Suppose, then, that we accept (SC). And suppose that we also accept the following familiar modal principle:

(S5) If it is possible that *p*, it is necessary that it is possible that *p*.

As we have seen, there are strong reasons for thinking that Wittgenstein is committed to (S5) (see Chapter 1, section 1D).

(SC) and (S5) make a paradoxical pair. Both are (attempted) statements about what is possible; (SC) requires that for them to be statements at all, what is possible must be only contingently possible; but (S5) says that what is possible is not contingently possible. And the paradox of this pair of assumptions also infects all the apparently intelligible answers to (Q), since (Q) itself, and all these answers to it, are concerned with what is possible.

We can construct similar problems if we go back to what seem to be even more basic assumptions in Wittgenstein's theory. Suppose we accept the following assumption:

(SP) It is possible to state that p only if it is possible that p.

This is the converse of what has to be held by all the ways of answering 'No' to (Q), which is this:

(PS) It is possible that p only if it is possible to state that p.

The core assumption of identity of form which lies at the heart of the picture theory ensures that Wittgenstein holds both (SP) and (PS). Now suppose we accept this further assumption:

(SPN) It is possible to state that p only if it is possible to state that not-p.

(SPN) and (SP) together imply (SC), which we have already seen is naturally attributed to Wittgenstein. Wittgenstein is also committed to this further assumption:

(SPP) It is possible to state that it is possible that p only if it is possible to state that p.[10]

(SP), (SPN), and (SPP) together make every negative answer to (Q) declare itself to be unstatable. This is because every negative answer to (Q) says that something is not possible, and (SP), (SPN), and (SPP) together imply that what is actually impossible cannot be said to be impossible. For one can only state that it is impossible that p if one can state that is possible that p (by (SPN) and the elimination of double negation). And one can only state that it is possible that p if one can state that p (by (SPP)). Now suppose that the relevant 'p' is impossible, as we will take it to be if we give a negative answer to (Q). That means that we cannot state that p, for the relevant 'p' (by (SP)). So we cannot state that it is impossible that p.

Furthermore, someone who accepts a negative answer to (Q) will be driven by this reasoning to count (A1) and (A2) unstatable too. For if we cannot state that it is impossible that p, we cannot state that it is possible that p either (by (SPN)). And (A1) and (A2) do precisely say (or attempt to say) that something is possible. It follows from this that (A2) is paradoxical on any account, and we will think that all answers to (Q) are paradoxical if we think that the right answer (as it were) is 'No', while also holding some assumptions which seem to be central to the picture theory of the *Tractatus*. Moreover, it seems that the *Tractatus* itself has to give the answer 'No' to (Q): it cannot accommodate the idea of language having a blind-spot, because the theory holds precisely that the form of language is the same as the form of the world. So it seems that the *Tractatus* has to hold that every possible answer to (Q) is paradoxical.

This exposes the precariousness of even setting out to present a sketch of the apparently possible options which someone addressing the Kantian position might seem to face. What I have written can only be a coherent presentation of a range of possible positions if at least some of the central assumptions of the *Tractatus* are false. My own inclination is to accept (A1) or (A3), and to deny the assimilation of the possible and the statable which is at the core of the picture theory, but neither of these options is easy to defend. In the case of (A1), we need to make it convincing that we can state that *there is* a blind-spot without its being possible, in principle, to provide an example, and actually state a blind-spot. And this is certainly difficult on the quantifier-variable approach to quantification.[11] On this approach, to state that there is something of a certain kind is to say that there is an x such that x is a member of that kind. And the 'x' here seems to have to be either something which could be replaced by a name of the relevant thing, or something which itself could act temporarily as a name of the thing. So on the quantifier-variable approach to quantification, one cannot say that there is *something* of a certain kind, without its being possible, in principle, to mention a thing of that kind. Adopting (A3), on the other hand, seems no better than heroic: it seems to require us to deny the obvious fact of the limits of representation.

I will proceed in what follows as if the crucial assumptions of the *Tractatus* are wrong, and some coherent response to (Q) can be formulated. This will permit us to keep in play the full range of answers which I have sketched out. Someone who wants to maintain (as it were) the relevant assumptions of the *Tractatus* will have to take what follows to present merely the appearance of a coherent account — something whose apparent coherence can be relied on temporarily until one gets into a position to abandon the whole approach with some conviction.

6C 'WHAT SOLIPSISM MEANS IS QUITE CORRECT'

We are trying to make sense of this pivotal remark:

> In fact what solipsism *means*, is quite correct, only it cannot be *said*, but it shows itself.

(5.62)

This remark appears in matter which is presented as being commentary on an apparently more central claim:

5.6 *The limits of my language* mean the limits of my world.

What are we to make of that?

To begin with, we need some clarification. The word translated 'mean' in 5.6 — 'bedeuten' — is a word standardly and properly translated either as 'mean' or as 'refer to'.[12] But we should not imagine that Wittgenstein is here suggesting that there is a technical *semantic* relation between the 'limits' of my language and the 'limits' of my world, a relation which is parallel to that which holds between some *elements* of my language (the names) and some *elements* of the world (objects). We might here translate it 'represent', 'indicate' — or even, perhaps, 'determine'. What is curious (but perhaps not important) is that Wittgenstein here writes anything other than 'are': after all, the central claim of the picture theory is that, in the relevant sense of 'limit', the limits of the world and the limits of language are the *same*. The limits of the world are just the limits of what is possible: they are, in the end, the limits on possible combinations of objects. And these limits are taken by Wittgenstein to be the same as the limits of possible combinations of symbols.

What, though, is the point of 5.6? More specifically, why does Wittgenstein emphasize the phrase 'the limits of my language'? Presumably not to stress the 'my' — that *I* am somehow involved in the limits of the world — since 'my' appears unstressed in the phrase 'the limits of my world'. The central point of this emphasis must be to highlight that it is *language* which indicates, represents — or even, perhaps, determines — the limits of the world. This is, of course, a reflection of the isomorphism which lies at the heart of the picture theory. And its occurrence at the beginning of the account of solipsism shows that we are committed to one of the ways of answering 'No' to question (Q) — that is, to (A4), (A5), or (A6).

5.61 reiterates this point, and then draws a conclusion from it:[13]

> Logic fills the world: the limits of the world are also its limits.
> We cannot therefore say in logic: This and this there is in the world, that there is not.

> For that would apparently presuppose that we exclude certain possibilities, and this cannot be the case since otherwise logic must get outside the limits of the world: that is, if it could consider these limits from the other side also.

This looks as if it contains the assertion both of a negative answer to (Q), and of the claim that such an answer is unsayable, for reasons that might well be captured in terms of (SC), or (SPN) and (SPP).

But the emphasis on *language* in 5.6 and 5.61 does not get us to anything which is distinctively solipsistic: 5.6 uses, but does not stress, the 'my'; and 5.61 moves out from 'my world' to 'the world. To get anything which looks like a genuine solipsism, we need to find an identification of *the* world with *my* world. And the argument for that is found in the final paragraph of 5.62:

> That the world is *my* world, shows itself in the fact that the limits of the language (the [only] language which I understand) mean the limits of *my* world.

But what might the argument be? I have here corrected the Ogden translation of this paragraph to make it read as it seems clear that Wittgenstein wanted it to read (Lewy 1967: 419).[14] Once the translation is correct, it is not at all clear what argument Wittgenstein might have in mind here. I will consider two alternative suggestions in the next two sections.

6D 'THE WORLD IS MY WORLD' — A KANTIAN APPROACH

How could the thought that 'the limits of ... the [only] language which I understand mean the limits of the world' give us some reason for thinking that 'the world is my world'? One suggestion is that we can get some purchase on the argument by drawing a parallel with a famous thought of Kant's.[15] In one of the most difficult passages of the Transcendental Deduction of the Categories, Kant insists:

> The **I think** must **be able** to accompany all my representations; for
> otherwise ... [they] would either be impossible or else at least would
> be nothing to me.[16]

If we can get a bit of logical distance between a representation's not being 'nothing to me' and the 'I think' *accompanying* it, we can use this as the basis of an argument for the claim that the world is 'my world' in the sense that it is *a world for me*. Moreover, if we really can use this Kantian thought, we might hope to be able to understand why the argument is in the first person: Kant's 'I think' is essentially the product of 'pure apperception' — i.e., *non-empirical* self-consciousness; it is supposed to exploit an asymmetry between the first and the other persons. (Very roughly, the thought is that when I say 'I think summer is coming' — as distinct from when I say 'She thinks summer is coming' — I do not do it as a result of observing my behaviour and judging what it shows about my state of mind.)

It is not easy to formulate an argument in the spirit of this passage of Kant which might be thought to be animating Wittgenstein's text; I will offer a way which perhaps gets close to the idea. Consider, first, any fact, arbitrarily chosen. Given Wittgenstein's insistence that the form of language is the same as the form of the world, there cannot be a fact which is in principle inexpressible. Let us then accept that our arbitrarily chosen fact can be expressed, and call it the fact that *p*. Of course, the proper way to express a fact is in a sentence, such as this:

(F) It is the case that *p*.

The core of a broadly Kantian argument can now be formulated like this:

(K1) It can be seen that (F) makes sense;
(K2) If it can be seen that (F) makes sense, there is someone (me) for whom it makes sense; *so*
(K3) There is someone (me) for whom (F) makes sense.

Given that the fact expressed in (F) was arbitrarily chosen — any fact in the world could have done — and the formulation used is itself schematic (it uses the variable 'p', rather than any particular sentence), it seems that, if this argument works at all, it shows that anything at all that might be said or thought about the world requires the existence, in some sense, of a subject, 'me'. What is difficult here is explaining why we should accept (K2), and why it is appropriate to put 'me' in parenthesis in steps (K2) and (K3).

(F) is a sentence (or the inscription of a sentence). So 'makes sense' in the argument simply means 'has sense' — that is to say, is meaningful in the way sentences are. The crucial thing to ask is what kind of claim is being made in (K1). In particular, *how* can it be seen that (F) makes sense? It is at this point that this broadly Kantian argument appeals to the idea that the language we are dealing with is 'the [only] language which I understand'. That enables us to contrast the present case with that of the following sentence:

> (L) It can be seen that 'sunt lacrimae rerum et mentem mortalia tangunt' makes sense.

The truth asserted in (L) can only be affirmed authoritatively by someone who understands Latin as well as English; the rest of us simply have to take it on trust, or take its truth to be the best explanation of the sympathetic sighing of Latin scholars when they read it. But in the case of (F) Wittgenstein could not have been thinking of such 'taking on trust', or of this kind of empirical hypothesis, since we are supposed to be considering 'the [only] language which I understand' (5.62). So (F) (instantiated) must be a sentence in a language which 'I' understand, and in that case (K1) asserts a different kind of truth from that which most of us will hear asserted in (L). It will be a truth about the special way of 'seeing' that something has sense, in which each of us is able to 'see' that a sentence in our own language makes sense. This is not naturally described as a report of observation: we do not *notice* that a sentence in our own language makes sense; nor is it the best explanation of any observable behaviour. Rather, we *make* sense *of* it.

This enables us to fix who the 'I' is — to fix, that is, who it is whose world is 'my world'. The 'I' will be each reader of the sentence which is given as the instance of (F) — in each of whose languages the sentence, it is presumed, is written. And each reader is properly an 'I' here, because each reader reads the sentence as being in a language which is 'my own'. Each reader's reading the sentence as being in a language which is 'my own' is just each reader *making* sense *of* the sentence — rather than merely *observing* that the sentence obeys certain rules, or *taking* it on trust that the sentence (in a foreign language) makes sense, or offering the sense of the sentence as an *explanation* of certain behavioural phenomena.

If we understand the argument of the last paragraph of 5.62 in this way, we can see how it might exploit the first person, in particular: we can understand why Wittgenstein uses 'my' here. And the argument is obviously valid, provided we restrict the interpretation of 'can be seen' uniformly across all the steps. But is the argument sound? Are the premises all true? (K1) will be true, for each instance of (F) which is written in a language which we understand. And 'it can be seen' can then be given a very particular interpretation — an interpretation which rules out knowledge by observation or testimony. Is (K2) true, on that interpretation of 'it can be seen'? Certainly, for a sentence actually to be *seen* to make sense, on this interpretation, there must be someone — 'I', in fact — to *make* sense *of* it. But could a sentence not have sense *unseen* — could it not *have* sense without anyone having *made* sense *of* it? It is not clear that the notion of *making* sense *of* a sentence will bridge this gap on its own. That is because it is not clear that *making* sense *of* a sentence is the same as *making* the sentence *have* sense. But the issue does not seem very serious, since it is extremely natural to think that no sentence could have sense without someone ('I') giving it sense (or, at any rate, giving sense to its constituents as they occur in other sentences, so as to ensure that every sentence in which they occur has sense).

How, though, does all of this relate to the *world*? How does this show the *world* to be my world — rather than just 'the [only] language which I understand' to be *my* language? The link can be made by means of this thought:

(WL) What is described by sentences which can be seen (by me) to make sense is nothing less than the world (nothing less than real facts);

This is the thought which Wittgenstein later expressed in the following way:

When we say, and *mean*, that such-and-such is the case, we — and our meaning — do not stop anywhere short of the fact; but we mean: *this — is — so*.

(*PI*: I, §95)

In the *Tractatus* itself, it is expressed like this:

2.1511 Thus the picture is linked with reality; it reaches up to it.

And it is tempting to think that (WL), so understood, is the key point of 5.6. The idea of (WL) is just this: in *making* sense *of* a sentence — in that sentence's striking me as making sense in the way that only a sentence in one's own language can strike one as making sense — I am considering nothing less than a genuinely possible configuration of the real world. Even to make sense of a sentence requires there to be a real world which is a world *for me* — which is 'my world' in that sense.

Is it an argument like this which lies behind the last paragraph of 5.62? It is hard to make a convincing case for the claim. This argument shows no more than that the world is a world *for me*. It is *my* world in that sense — but not in the sense that it is exclusive to me. Nor does this argument have any obvious tendency to show that the world in some sense *depends* on me, which is what any form of solipsism would require. For all that, it does provide some ground for the introduction of the first person.

It might be thought that the missing idealism is supplied by a principle which could be confused with (WL), although it is in fact quite distinct from it. This other principle can be formulated as follows:

(LW) There is no more to the world (there are no more real facts) than what is described by sentences which can be seen (by me) to make sense.

(LW) might be thought to follow from the thought that the form of language (even: the only language which I understand) is the same as the form of the world. The overall reasoning might then be thought to work like this. (WL) shows that what my language describes is nothing less than the real world; and the thesis that the form of language is the same as the form of the world is then brought in to show, by means of (LW), that the real world which my language describes depends on my language — and hence counts as *my* world in a stronger sense than merely being a world *for me*.

(LW) does indeed follow from the thesis that the form of language is the same as the form of the world. But it is not in itself an idealist principle, and cannot be used to show that the real world is *my* world in the requisite idealist sense. Recall that we raised this question in section 6B:

(Q) Might language have representational blind-spots?

(LW) is consistent with *all* of the following ways of answering that question:

(A4) Language could not have representational blind-spots, because language simply adopts the form of reality;

(A5) Language could not have representational blind-spots, because reality is determined by what language can depict;

(A6) Language could not have representational blind-spots, because what limits language also limits reality.

And, of these, only (A5) is idealist.

We might, however, think that materials for another argument, again broadly Kantian in spirit, can be found elsewhere in Wittgenstein's early writings. I have several times drawn attention to this striking account of the meaning of 'forms':

> I now determine the sense of 'xRy' by laying down: when the facts behave in regard to 'xRy' so that the meaning of 'x' stands in the relation R to the meaning of 'y', then I say that the [the facts] are 'of like sense' with the proposition 'xRy'; otherwise, 'of opposite sense'; I correlate the facts to the symbol 'xRy' *by* thus dividing them into those of like sense and those of opposite sense.

> (*NL*: 104)

I argued in Chapter 4 (section 4F) that we should understand Wittgenstein as generalizing this account to make it apply to all the elements of elementary sentences. I noted there that by the time of the *Tractatus* Wittgenstein seems to have abandoned the assumption, which is implicit in this passage in the *Notes on Logic*, that the meaning-determining subject has a kind of access to the facts, precisely as such, independent of any language. But I think the key point about this passage for our present concerns can be maintained without that assumption. The crucial thing about Wittgenstein's claim for our present purposes is the emphasis on '*by*': the assumption seems to be that there is (or need be) no *antecedent* similarity among the facts which are 'of like sense' — or, again, among the facts which are 'of opposite sense'. What seems to be happening here is that there is an arbitrary determination of which facts count as making a range of sentences true and which count as making it false. This seems to make the similarities in the things which are correlated with the same symbol dependent on an arbitrary decision. And it then does not seem too much to assume that some such process might be involved in determining what counts as a thing at all. That is to say, this passage might be read as encouraging us to think of the form of the world — the very identification of its constituent objects and their modes of possible combination — as nothing more than a projection of the grammar of language.[17]

This view is recognizably Kantian: we have the structure of language projected onto the world as it is in itself, to create a world we can describe. This world which we can describe is a world of language, and clearly depends upon at least the possibility of describing it in language. And we immediately face the problem of blind spots that we considered in section 6B, in a recognizably Kantian form. This neo-Kantian theory cannot even allow itself to be formulated, because it cannot allow that any world other than the world of language can be described, and so it cannot allow the world of language to be contrasted with the world as it is in itself, in the way that it must be if the neo-Kantian theory is itself to be stated. If this is the view which Wittgenstein has in mind when he talks of 'solipsism', no wonder that he says that it cannot be *said*.

This interpretation really does seem to capture something in Wittgenstein's thought. And note that it is compatible with all the apparently realist things which Wittgenstein says about the ultimate constitution of the world, the nature of objects, and so forth. I have been taking care to show the formal compatibility of the metaphysics of the *Tractatus* with both realism and idealism as the issue has arisen (for example: in Chapter 1, section 1F; Chapter 2, section 2F; Chapter 4, section 4B). Here we can briefly represent the metaphysics as a form of idealism. If the world which we talk about is indeed a world of language, a world whose very existence depends on its being projected as a counterpart to the grammar of language, then we can describe in outline the whole metaphysical picture of the *Tractatus* as follows. The grammar of language requires the world to be projected as a world whose basic organic unities are facts — but facts which are contingent, while their dependent constituents, the objects, exist necessarily and supply the common form of everything that can be imagined.

Wittgenstein does seem to be drawn to some such neo-Kantian picture as this, even if he is then immediately forced to erase the contrast with the world as it is in itself in whose terms alone the picture makes sense. And this picture does seem to make sense of some features of the argument of the last paragraph of 5.62. We get, for example, some point in using the first person to make the point, and an explanation of why Wittgenstein might have expressed the argument by appeal to some such expression as 'the [only] language which I understand'. For suppose someone were to object as follows.

> This is all very well; it allows that the world which *I* can speak about is the world of *my* language, but this is not enough to show that *the* world is the world of my language. For there could be languages spoken by *other* people, which I do not — indeed, could not — understand. Each such language will have its own world, and each of these worlds will have as much claim to be *the* world as mine does.

The conception imagined by this objection is already ruled out by Wittgenstein's view. For to acknowledge that there were other languages which I could not understand would be to acknowledge that there might be ways in which things could be arranged which are different from the ways in which I can make sense of them being arranged: that is to say, it supposes that I can intelligibly make sense of possibilities which I cannot make sense of. And this seems already to have been ruled out by the same-form assumption which lies at the heart of the *Tractatus*'s conception of language. It is not insignificant that this point is brought out explicitly in the stretch of text which leads up to the famous claim of 5.62.[18]

For all that, this interpretation does not seem to capture everything that is going on in the puzzlingly elliptical argument of 5.62. For one thing, although it makes it very clear why this 'solipsism' cannot be *said* — of course, as became clear in section 6B above, that conclusion is seriously overdetermined by the central assumptions of the *Tractatus* — it does not make much sense of the further claim Wittgenstein makes here: that what solipsism means 'shows itself'. Indeed, far from solipsism simply 'showing itself' in the world, the world is apparently quite neutral on the issue. So far, at least, this neo-Kantian view looks like an antecedent prejudice which has simply shaped an approach to the subject, but has no obvious justification.

The other thing which this neo-Kantian approach lacks is anything which requires a special appeal to the first person *singular*, to an 'I', considered precisely as such. What seems to be needed is a projection of linguistic structure onto the world, and no doubt that requires some kind of act of will. What is not clear, however, is why the will needs to be *mine*. We might offer an alternative, communitarian, version of exactly the same general neo-Kantianism.[19] On this alternative account, the world of language is dependent on language, but for each of us it is found *with* language. For each of us, learning a language is a matter of inculcation into a culture — one might call this a *Bildung* — as a result of which the world of language is there for us.[20] But for each of us this world of language is already there, just as language itself is already there. The world is not *my* world: it does not depend on *me*. Rather, it depends upon language itself, and on there being some community which has used that language to form a world which can be spoken about. At the very most, it is *our* world.

And these two points — about the absence of any explanation of the thought that what solipsism means 'shows itself', and about the argument not justifying any dependence on a singular subject — can be put together: it is simply not the case that there is any sense in which the world which I speak about presents itself as being determined by *me*. Our actual experience of speaking a language is always an experience of working with a framework which has been given to us: the words I use precisely do not strike me as mine — they are words of English (in my case) — and I am conscious always that it is not up to me to determine how they will apply to the world. Only someone already in the grip of a radically individualist picture of our relation to the world could think that each of us determines her own language.

Finally, this Kantian interpretation, resonant within Wittgenstein's thought though it is, does not really make sense of Wittgenstein's use of the phrase 'the [only] language which I understand'. What this interpretation needs is the thought that there are no languages which I *cannot* understand. But what Wittgenstein offers us here is the different thought, that there is only one language which I *can* understand.

6E 'THE WORLD IS MY WORLD' — A CARTESIAN ARGUMENT

If we are to make sense of the thought that what solipsism means 'shows itself', give a proper role to the first person singular, *and* offer some reason to insist that there is only one language which I can understand, I think we need to look elsewhere. I think we need to appeal to considerations which have often seemed to have no place in the *Tractatus*, but which have always lain behind traditional discussions of solipsism.[21] As a way of getting started on this, consider this way of stating the same-form assumption which lies at the heart of the *Tractatus*:

> (SF) What can be described in (my) language is the same as what can be the case in the world.

(SF), like most of the theory of the *Tractatus*, is itself neutral between realism and idealism. So let us ask: what distinguishes between realist and idealist readings of (SF)? Very roughly, we get a realist version if we *begin*, as it were, with the world, and ask 'How can (my) language describe that?' If we work in that direction and offer (SF) as an answer to this question, we seem committed to some form of realism. Alternatively, we may *begin* (as it were) with my language, and ask 'How can what my language describes be the world?' If we then take (SF) to answer *that* question, we seem to be led into a form of idealism. Since Wittgenstein says that 'what solipsism *means* is quite correct', it seems that he must, in some sense, be 'beginning' with (my) language.

Well, what might this 'beginning' be, and how might Wittgenstein justify 'beginning' with (my) language?

The striking thing about the first person is that it is *epistemically* distinctive: 'I am thinking' has a different epistemic status from that of 'She is thinking', 'You are thinking', or even 'There is thinking going on.' If we are really to give a serious role to the first person in this argument, it is hard to think of any other suggestion than this: the 'beginning' in question is an *epistemic* beginning, and Wittgenstein, despite the general appearance and tenor of the *Tractatus*, is motivated by a concern to avoid scepticism — that is, *epistemological* scepticism. I have, in fact, already appealed to epistemic considerations in reconstructing an argument for the conclusion that the world is 'my' world in the sense that it is a world *for me*: a crucial point there was that there is a special epistemic relationship which I have to my own language. In the case of my own language, I do not find out that a sentence is meaningful by checking that it fits some specification, or by supposing that its being meaningful is the best explanation of certain phenomena. In the case of a sentence in my own language, finding out that it is meaningful is especially immediate: I find out that it is *has* sense by *making* sense *of* it.

This immediacy gives my access to my own language a special authority; correlatively, my own language is *present* to me in a special way. That special authority is characterized in a particular way in traditional Cartesianism, in terms of what cannot be *doubted*. If we follow the lead of the Kantian approach considered in the last section, the claim would be: I cannot doubt the meaningfulness of my own language. How plausible is this claim? It might seem that I *could* doubt the meaningfulness of my own language: my language might seem to me to be mere noise. But when I think I can doubt the meaningfulness of my own language, I seem to need to be able, somewhere, to wonder about whether that language is meaningful. I need somehow to be able to contemplate, or imagine the possibility of, the language's not being meaningful.

Of course, according to Wittgenstein, such contemplation or imagining must involve the construction in my mind of models or pictures, which are themselves like sentences at least in this respect: whatever other form they may have, they also have *logical* form, the form of sentences (see *TLP*: 3). So it seems that my apparent ability to doubt the meaningfulness of my own language rests on my not questioning the meaningfulness of the pictures or models I construct in order to frame such doubts. But at this point the insistence that there is only one language which I understand ('the [only] language which I understand') takes on a new significance. If *all* of the pictures or models I construct in my mind really belong to just *one* language, there is indeed something — the only language which I understand — whose meaningfulness I cannot conceivably question. Here is something which has a very special epistemic status.

So far the discussion has been in terms of the *meaningfulness* of my own language. This is because we have been following the terms of the Kantian approach considered in the last section, and it was important to that approach that the argument should establish, at least, that the real world is a world for me. In order for the real world to be a world for me, we seem to need the thought, not merely that the *syntax* of my language be in order, but that its symbols actually relate to the world. But if it is true, as it seems to be, that in the *Tractatus* Wittgenstein is really concerned with the fundamental *nature* of reality, rather than what is in fact the case — with what is *possible*, rather than what is actual — then it is not full *meaningfulness* which is important. For this concern, what really matters is just the *syntax* of my own language. If Wittgenstein is concerned with the *form* of the world, rather than the facts, what we want to have a special epistemic status is just my language's being *syntactically* in order. The key thing which it needs to be impossible for me to question is whether the combinatorial possibilities which my own language appears to sanction are genuine combinatorial possibilities. And it seems no harder to suppose that syntactical well-formedness has this status, than it is to suppose that meaningfulness does: it is not by any kind of observation, or as a part of any explanation of behaviour, that I determine that a sentence in my own language is well formed. It is plausible to claim that I cannot doubt that the symbols of my own language — including every representation I can construct in my mind — are indeed *symbols* rather than dead signs, mere marks and sounds.[22]

Suppose, then, that epistemic security is something which Wittgenstein values — even though, as I have already acknowledged, epistemic security does not generally seem to be one of his principal concerns in the *Tractatus*. Suppose, further, that what he values, in particular, is the epistemic security of my confidence in the syntactic well-formedness of my own language. In that case, we can imagine him being concerned about the epistemic safety of other things — of belief in the form of the world, in particular. We can imagine him reasoning as follows: I can be confident of the syntactic well-formedness of my language — the one language which includes all my thoughts and imaginings — but how can I be confident of the form of the world? How can I be confident that what seems to be possible is, indeed, genuinely possible in the real world? If this is Wittgenstein's concern, what he will be looking for is reason to think that my unshakable confidence in the combinatorial possibilities of the only language which I understand provides grounds for being similarly confident of the reality of the possibilities in the world which are co-ordinate with them.[23] And such a reason, it seems, can only be provided by means of the following idealist conception of the relation between my language and the world:

> (LWI) The syntax of my language *determines* what is possible in the world.

It might be thought that this idealist view is not strictly required for the confidence which Wittgenstein, on the current suggestion, is looking for. It might be thought that all that is really required is that the gap between language and world should be shrunk enough to prevent any failure of isomorphism. So we might instead have suggested this realist alternative:

(LWR) The syntax of my language *is determined by* what is possible in the world.

But this realist alternative seems to undercut the confidence I have in the syntactic well-formedness of my own language — at least, as it appears to me. For suppose (LWR) were true, and the form of the world were rigorously independent of the syntax of my language. In making that independence properly intelligible, we seem to have to countenance the possibility that the syntax of a language might *seem* (to its speaker) to be in order, even though in fact it was not (that is, that it might seem to a speaker that she was dealing with symbols, when really she was dealing just with dead signs). To give full weight to the independence of the world which (LWR) requires, we seem to have to entertain the idea that my own judgements of syntactical legitimacy are not an infallible guide to whether in fact the syntax of my language is in order. If we are to insist that the immunity to *doubt* which the syntactic well-formedness of my own language possesses for me is a proper guide to the actual combinatorial *possibilities* of my own language, we need to shrink the gap between language and the world in the other direction. We cannot leave the world where it is, as it were, and force language closer to *it* — for that risks taking it further from what we can be confident of. Instead we have to bring the world, as it were, closer to *language*, leaving the indubitability of my judgements of syntactic well-formedness intact and unthreatened. That is to say, we have to adopt (LWI), rather than (LWR).

What has been said so far provides a reason for preferring the idealist to the realist way of reducing the distance between my language and the world — *given* a desire to maintain our right to confidence in our judgements of syntactic well-formedness. That is to say, the idealist way of reducing the distance between my language and the world gives us a *comfort* which we want. One reason for adopting idealism is, then, that it is comfortable. But these considerations might be thought to provide a more direct, and less dishonest, argument for the idealist conception. For it might be thought that it was incoherent to question the infallibility of our judgements of syntactic well-formedness. We can lay the argument out as follows:

(C1) If my judgement of the syntactic well-formedness of my own language were not infallible, it might be wrong (for all my confidence);

(C2) If my judgement of the syntactic well-formedness of my own language might be wrong, I ought to doubt it;

(C3) If I ought to doubt my judgement of the syntactic well-formedness of my own language, I can doubt it (given that 'ought', in general, implies 'can'); *but*

(C4) I cannot doubt my judgement of the syntactic well-formedness of my own language; *so*

(C5) My judgement of the syntactic well-formedness of my own language must be infallible; *but*

(C6) If realism were true, my judgement of the syntactic well-formedness of my own language would not be infallible; *so*

(C7) Realism is not true.

My tentative suggestion is that it is some such argument as this that animates the final paragraph of 5.62. It may not be the only kind of issue in play in the discussion of solipsism — the neo-Kantian conception considered in section 6D may be part of what Wittgenstein has in mind — but it looks as if the more narrowly epistemic considerations appealed to in this Cartesian argument are playing some part in Wittgenstein's thought. Even so, the suggestion remains tentative, because this argument relies on epistemic considerations which seem foreign to the main course of the *Tractatus*.

The other reason for suggesting a different reconstruction of the argument of 5.62 was that we wanted to make sense of Wittgenstein's claim that solipsism 'shows itself'. Recall that Wittgenstein does not just say that 'what solipsism means' cannot be said: he further says that it 'shows itself' ('zeigt sich': 5.62). What can this mean? The natural applications of the concept of *showing* in the *Tractatus* are to the concept of form. Thus, famously he makes this claim about pictures or models:

> 2.172 The picture, however, cannot represent its form of representation; it shows it forth ['es weist sie auf'].

And about sentences:

> The propositions *show* ['zeigt'] the logical form of reality.
> They exhibit it ['Er weist sie auf']
>
> (4.121)

But it is not credible that the use of the concept of showing in 5.62 is a direct application of the concept to the concept of form. 'What solipsism means' cannot be the form of the world, because the form of the world is neutral between solipsism and realism: the form of the world is the range of possibilities of combination possessed by the objects; solipsism, however, is a thesis about what *determines* that range of possibilities.

So what does he mean by 'show' ('zeigt') here, and how could he think that what solipsism means 'shows itself'? It is worth noting that the term 'zeigt' is used in the argument we have been trying to understand, in the next paragraph of the text:

> That the world is *my* world, shows itself ['zeigt sich'] in the fact that the limits of the language (the [only] language which I understand) mean the limits of *my* world.
>
> (5.62)

If this argument is — or somehow involves — the broadly Cartesian (C) argument I have just laid out, we can offer a particular interpretation of the claim that solipsism 'shows itself'. It runs as follows. According to the thought of the (C) argument, it seems that the form of the world is evident to me, in just that special way in which the syntactic legitimacy of sentences of my own language is evident to me. The (C) argument then provides the following understanding of the idea that the form of the world *shows* itself: I cannot *doubt* that the form of the world is as it seems to be (that what seem to be possibilities are, in fact, real possibilities). Further, if we attribute to Wittgenstein the (C) argument, we take him to accept this premise in it:

(C2) If my judgement of the syntactic well-formedness of my own language might be wrong, I ought to doubt it.

This, combined with the fact that I *cannot* doubt the syntactic well-formedness of my own language and the assumption that the form of the world is the same as the form of language, simply *entails* that, as well as not being able to *doubt* the form of the world, I am actually *infallible* about it. So we might suppose that, given (C2), my infallibility about the form of the world *shows* itself: that is, is *evident* to me to something like the extent to which the syntactic well-formedness of my own language is evident to me. But this infallibility is itself due to the world's being dependent on me, according to the (C) argument: that is, it is due to the world's being *my* world in the sense required by solipsism. Once the reasoning has been worked out, it might then be claimed that 'what solipsism means' — that is, the dependence of the form of the world on what I can take to be a possible combination of symbols — *shows* itself, in the sense that, once all the links are worked out, it is *evident* to me in something like the way in which the syntactic well-formedness of my own language is evident to me.

So the (C) argument provides an account of why Wittgenstein might have felt able to claim that solipsism 'shows itself'. But this is at least as controversial as the attribution to Wittgenstein of the (C) argument itself: it makes the concept of *showing* a strongly epistemic —

indeed, Cartesian — concept. And it has often been felt that the notion is not fundamentally epistemic at all — or at least not epistemic in this way.

Where does this leave us? In the first place, it seems to me that, although the first-personal nature of our confidence in the meaningfulness or syntactic well-formedness of our own language has roots which are similar to those which can be found in Kant's thought that the 'I think' must be capable of accompanying all my representations, there is an aspect of the argument here which runs in the other direction. The Kantian (K) argument can do no more than show that the world is a world *for me*. What we need is some reason for thinking that the world *depends on me*. There is an alternative, still broadly Kantian approach — what I have called a form of neo-Kantianism — which does seem to provide some suitably idealist view. But this seems to give no special place to the first person singular (the 'I'), and it is hard to see any reason to believe it — which means that it is hard to see how what solipsism means can be said to 'show itself'. The last argument I have considered — the (C) argument — seems to present the world as being *my* world in a sense which both supports a clearly idealist position, and gives a substantial role to the first person singular. Furthermore, the (C) argument offers a way of understanding how solipsism might be thought to 'show itself'. Unfortunately, this (C) argument represents Wittgenstein's 'solipsism', like most forms of idealism, as a response to some form of scepticism: in Wittgenstein's case it is scepticism about whether the apparent limits of the possible combinations of symbols are any guide to the limits of what is possible in reality. This epistemic emphasis seems to have little place in the *Tractatus* as a whole, which makes its attribution to Wittgenstein uncertain, to say the least.

In mitigation of that uncertainty, it is worth pointing out that epistemic considerations do play some role in the *Tractatus* — perhaps a greater role than is sometimes acknowledged. As we saw in the previous chapter, it seems that we have to accept that there is *something* epistemic about the notion of *showing*, as Wittgenstein uses it in connection with logic: he seems to have hoped — to put it no more strongly — that logic was decidable, in the specific sense that every logical truth could be shown to be true by means of a finite number of steps in a mechanical procedure (see Chapter 5, section 5E, above). And this hope is clearly linked with a view about the special obviousness of *form* — at least in a suitable notation. We will also see in the next section that epistemic considerations play a role in Wittgenstein's argument for the claim that the subject 'does not belong to the world' (5.631). Furthermore, Wittgenstein does address scepticism explicitly in the closing pages of the book (6.51), as we will see in Chapter 7 (section 7D). And, finally, it is worth adding that in the *Notebooks* from which the *Tractatus* was drawn, the discussion of solipsism grows out of a more general consideration of the meaning of life (whose transformation in the *Tractatus* will be considered in the next chapter). And that general consideration of the meaning of life begins with an epistemic worry:

> What do I know about God and the purpose of life?
> I know that this world exists.
> That I am placed in it like my eye in the visual field.

> (*NB*: 72–73)

(This image of the eye in the visual field is recalled in the *Tractatus*, 5.633; we will consider it more fully in the next section.) So there are reasons to think that Wittgenstein's solipsism is bound up with epistemic issues. For all that, it is hard to be completely confident that the argument of 5.62 is really the epistemic argument which I have laid out as (C).

Is the (C) argument itself plausible? It is certainly valid, but is it sound? Like many epistemic arguments for anti-realist conclusions, its weakness can be traced to a distinctively Cartesian premise. In this case, the crucial assumption is (C2), where the possibility of error is taken to provide an obligation to doubt. This is exactly what realists traditionally deny: it can be irrational, and therefore wrong, to doubt something, even when (for all we know) we might be mistaken. And in this case, a realist can accept that we might be wrong about the syntactic well-formedness of our own language, but deny that this means that we should (or could) suspend judgement about its well-formedness: of course, our judgements *might* be wrong, but that does not stop us being committed to making them.

6F SOLIPSISM, REALISM, AND THE SUBJECT

Wittgenstein seems to be committed to the strongly idealist view that the nature of the world depends upon me. He then makes two claims which might seem to conflict with that:

> (NS) The thinking, presenting subject; there is no such thing.
>
> (5.631)

> (SR) [S]olipsism strictly carried out coincides with pure realism.
>
> (5.64)

Why does he make these claims? The crucial point might seem to be this:

> 5.632 The subject does not belong to the world but it is a limit of the world.

But here Wittgenstein seems to have in mind a reason for holding that the subject does not 'belong' to the world which is independent of — and perhaps the ground for — the thought that the subject is a 'limit' of the world. The reasoning seems to derive from the second paragraph of 5.631.

The reasoning of this paragraph, like much of the discussion of solipsism, is not immediately clear. But it looks as if it relies on a kind of thinking which is strongly epistemic in the same way as the (C) reconstruction of the argument of 5.62, which I tentatively offered in the last section. According to the (C) reconstruction of the argument of 5.62, Wittgenstein relies there on what is ultimately a Cartesian assumption. The second paragraph of 5.631 suggests an argument for the claim that the subject does not belong to the world, which also has a Cartesian flavour. The crucial point of that paragraph is this:

> If I wrote a book 'The world as I found it' ... of [the subject] alone in this book mention could *not* be made.

It seems that Wittgenstein has in mind something like the following epistemic argument:

(E1) The only things in the world are things which I might *find*;
(E2) I cannot *find* myself; *so*
(E3) I myself am not a thing in the world.

Here 'find' must mean something like: *encounter in experience*.

This argument is evidently valid: are its premises both true? (E1) is certainly curious, and we would naturally reject it in other contexts. Why can the world not contain things which I cannot possibly find — things which ceased to exist before I was born, for example. We can rule out at least some of these things if we can restrict our attention to things which, like the objects of the *Tractatus*'s metaphysics, exist necessarily. And it is natural to think that we can do that without begging the question about the nature of the self. The reason is that it is hard to see how the subject, in the sense Wittgenstein has in mind here, can be a merely contingent existent, in any ordinary sense of 'contingent', if it also determines the fundamental nature of the world. Moreover, if we understand the solipsism of the *Tractatus* as involving Cartesian assumptions, as the (C) argument does, (E1) becomes extremely natural: the restriction to what *I* might find no longer seems much of a restriction.

(E1), then, seems deniable, although it does not seem altogether foreign to the solipsism of the *Tractatus*. What about (E2)? This might seem to be an echo of the famous passage where Hume describes his own inability to find himself in experience,[24] but I suspect that its provenance here is more directly Kantian (and, ultimately, Cartesian).

The key point, I think, is the one we noted in the section 6D, that the awareness that I have of myself *as myself* is not empirical: it is not as a result of observing my behaviour that I say 'I think summer is coming' (if any observation is involved here, it is observation of the weather). This shows that I am aware of myself in a way in which I am not aware of other things — in a way in which I am not aware of at least the bulk of the objects that I encounter in the world.

But does it show that I am not *also* aware of myself in the way in which I can be aware of objects of experience, which is what (E2) requires? Wittgenstein appears to think so. He considers a striking comparison:

> You say that this case is altogether like that of the eye and the field of sight.
> But you do *not* really see the eye.
> And from nothing *in the field of sight* can it be concluded that it is seen from an eye.

(5.633)

The comparison mentioned in the first sentence here seems very apt, and to be unsettling for Wittgenstein's view. I can see the eyes of other people, unaided. And if I have a mirror, I can see my own eyes. In the same way, someone can look at herself in a mirror, or catch herself unawares in a shop window. On the face of it, it seems that in this way someone can come to have the kind of knowledge of her own state of mind that she can have of someone else's state of mind — and in the same way, through observation of behaviour.

This is what is, in effect, denied in the final two sentences of 5.633: Wittgenstein claims that 'you do *not* really see the eye'. But why is this not just obviously false? The answer has to be that in *seeing* the eye (of another, or of yourself in a mirror) the eye is not presented to you as your own eye is presented to you (as the *focus* of the field of sight) when you look at other things. But this can only support Wittgenstein's claim here if it is held to be impossible for the same thing both to be presented as the focus of your own visual field and to be the object of sight. And, unfortunately, that is exactly what is in question. Similarly, the fact that I am present to myself non-empirically does not show that the very same thing — I, the subject — cannot be the object of empirical observation (my own or another's), unless we simply assume that it is impossible for the same thing both to be present (to myself) non-empirically and to be the object of empirical observation. But that, again, is exactly what is in question in premise (E2).

It seems, then, that (E2) can be denied, even by someone who accepts Wittgenstein's solipsism. So the argument looks unsound: moreover, it is unsound in a way in which exactly similar arguments about the self to be found in Descartes's *Meditations* are unsound.[25] There seems to be a strongly epistemic approach to the self in play here — even if we are hesitant about adopting such an approach to the argument of 5.62.

Interestingly, it looks as if Wittgenstein had a simpler argument available to him, one which derives more directly from his solipsism. This is because it seems that the subject must be a 'limit' of the world in a special sense, if solipsism is true. At first, it might not be obvious why being a limit of the world prevents the subject from 'belonging' to the world. After all, the simple objects to which names in elementary sentences refer might be regarded as being limits of the world: they constitute its substance (2.021), and hence determine what is possible. But we should be careful about the sense in which each of the objects of the *Tractatus*'s metaphysics can claim to be a limit of the world. It is simply that each carries as part of its essence the possibility of combining with other objects in certain determinate ways; and these possibilities of combination constitute the basic form of the world. Each of these objects is, as it were, a *contributor* to a collective determination of the limits of the world. The subject, however, is a limit of the world in a much grander sense, if solipsism is true: what the subject can make sense of determines every possibility all at once. Its role is quite unlike that of the objects, each of which contains merely its own possibilities of combination. This seems to require that the self figures in the Tractarian picture in some way other than as an object in the world. Hence the subject does not 'belong' to the world: it is, as Wittgenstein puts it, a *metaphysical* subject (5.633, 5.641).

But just because it does not belong to the *world*, why should it follow that 'there is no such thing' as the metaphysical subject, as (NS) claims? We can expresss the reasoning as follows. Suppose we were to claim:

(1) There is such a thing as the subject.

According to the *Tractatus*'s conception of language, this sentence, like all sentences, can only be true in virtue of the basic objects of the *Tractatus*'s metaphysics being combined in a certain way. At best there are two possibilities. One apparent possibility is that the subject is composite: the subject is a combination of Tractarian objects, and (1) is analysable as the claim that certain such objects are suitably combined. The other apparent possibility is that the subject is itself a Tractarian object, and (1) is true in virtue of a truth of some such form as this:

(2) *Fa* & *a* = the subject

— where '*a*' is the name of a Tractarian object. But, first, the subject cannot be composite. After all, Wittgenstein insists:

A composite soul would not be a soul any longer.

(5.5421)

And, of course, a composite subject would exist only contingently (since to think of it as composite is to think of it as a combination of elements which *might* not have been combined — the reasoning we have seen at work in 2.021), and we have already seen that the metaphysical subject cannot be contingent in any ordinary sense. And, second, we have also just seen that the metaphysical subject cannot be one of the objects which belong to the world either. So it seems that (1) cannot be true: there really is no such thing as the metaphysical subject.

Of course, if there is no such thing as the metaphysical subject, there is some difficulty in stating solipsism:

> The I in solipsism shrinks to an extensionless point and there remains the reality co-ordinated with it.
>
> (5.64)

And this is the immediate ground for (SR), the claim that solipsism coincides with realism. But it should be noted that what Wittgenstein has provided is not an endorsement of realism. Realism is not the thesis that the real world exists: it is (roughly) the thesis that the fundamental nature of the world is independent of any subject. If we cannot talk about any subject, strictly as a subject (which the argument of 5.631–5.633 purports to show), then we cannot state realism any more than we can state solipsism.

Some might suspect that Wittgenstein is here using a trick to slip out of a contradiction that he might seem to have trapped himself in. We have seen that, in a way, he endorses solipsism: 'In fact what solipsism *means*, is quite correct' (5.62). And, as we have noted before, some have thought that if the metaphysics of the early sections of the *Tractatus* (1–2.063) is taken literally, Wittgenstein is there committed to a form of realism.[26] So he might be thought to be committed to an ugly inconsistency, and he might be accused of trying to evade it here by denying substance to either of the opposing propositions.

Wittgenstein is certainly involved in some kind of inconsistency here, but not this one. As we have seen already, the metaphysics of the *Tractatus* is itself neutral on the question of realism and idealism (see, e.g., Chapter 1, section 1F, above). The metaphysics of the *Tractatus* is simply the consequence of insisting that the form of the world is the same as the form of language — with a few supplementary assumptions about the form of language. That same-form assumption leaves us with the three positions which were distinguished in the first section of this chapter:

(A4) Language could not have representational blind-spots, because language simply adopts the form of what there is;

(A5) Language could not have representational blind-spots, because what there is is determined by what language can depict;

(A6) Language could not have representational blind-spots, because what limits language also limits reality.

As we saw before, (A4) is realist; (A5) is idealist; and (A6) is neutral between the two. Any one of them can be accepted compatibly with endorsing both the strong metaphysics of the book's early sections, and the conception of sentences as models of reality.

So we should not think of Wittgenstein as here evading his contradictory commitments to both solipsism and realism, because he was never committed to realism. His inconsistency lies simply in the fact that he both states (and argues for) solipsism, and insists that it cannot be stated. And the difficulty attaches not just to this point, but to Wittgenstein's reason for making it. We have seen Wittgenstein insisting that there is no such thing as 'the thinking, presenting subject' (5.631), and that this leads him to deny the statability of any contrast between solipsism and realism (5.64). But he follows that immediately with this remark:

5.641 There is therefore really a sense in which in philosophy we can talk of a non-psychological I.

This seems flatly to contradict the remarks on which it is supposed to be based. It is not clear that the problems here can be satisfactorily resolved, but they can at least be clarified by considering the general problems facing Wittgenstein's claim that what solipsism means 'cannot be *said*' (5.62), so let us turn to those next.

6G SOLIPSISM AND WHAT CANNOT BE SAID

We are now in a position to summarize the issues raised by the paradoxical claim which is the core of Wittgenstein's treatment of solipsism:

> In fact what solipsism *means*, is quite correct, only it cannot be *said*, but it shows itself.
>
> (5.62)

We have found a number of ways of interpreting Wittgenstein's argument (in the following paragraph of 5.62) for the conclusion that 'what solipsism means is quite correct'. Why exactly can it not be said? In fact, the unsayability of solipsism — at least, the solipsism of the *Tractatus* — is overdetermined.

One reason for thinking that solipsism is unsayable we have just seen. To state solipsism, we need to talk about the subject, on whose capacity to make sense of sentences the possibilities of the world depend (according to solipsism). But the subject, we have seen, must be a 'metaphysical' subject — something which does not belong to the world. And a metaphysical subject cannot be talked about.

There is, though, a more general reason for thinking that solipsism is unsayable. To be able even to describe solipsism (either to accept it or to reject it), we do not merely have to talk about the *subject*: we need to be able to contemplate the limits of the world *as limits*. Further, we need to consider various ways in which those limits might have been determined, which looks as if it requires us to contemplate the possibility of those limits having been otherwise than they are. But this is something which Wittgenstein's conception of language and logic rules out. The reasons were considered in detail in section 6B above; they are summarized metaphorically at this point in Wittgenstein's text:

5.61   Logic fills the world: the limits of the world are also its limits.
        We cannot therefore say in logic: This and this there is in the world,
        that there is not.

> For that would apparently presuppose that we exclude certain pos-
> sibilities, and this cannot be the case since otherwise logic must
> get outside the limits of the world: that is, if it could consider these
> limits from the other side also.
> What we cannot think, that we cannot think: we cannot therefore
> *say* what we cannot think.

Wittgenstein then writes:

> This remark provides a key to the question, to what extent solipsism
> is a truth.
>
> (5.62)

Although the numbering indicates that the remark referred
to here as 'this remark' is, strictly speaking 5.6, rather than
5.61, it is surely through the third and fourth paragraphs of
5.61 that we understand how 5.6 provides the key to the
extent to which solipsism is true. The key is that solipsism
requires us to contemplate — and therefore state — something which cannot be contemplated or stated. So solipsism cannot strictly be contemplated or stated. This means,
of course, that solipsism cannot strictly be *denied* either; and
consequently, realism cannot strictly be contemplated or
stated, which gives us (SR), the thesis of the coincidence
— as far as what can be stated goes — of solipsism and
realism.

These two routes to the unstatability of solipsism (or realism) are reflected in the two faults with the diagram of the
visual field which Wittgenstein draws in 5.6331. One fault is
that the diagram portrays the eye as occurring within the
visual field: this is like the error (as Wittgenstein sees it) of
thinking that the subject belongs to the world. The other
fault is that the diagram draws a line around the extent of
the field of vision, thereby marking out a region as outside
it, beyond its limits: this is like the error (as Wittgenstein
sees it) of trying to contemplate what is not possible — the
error which is highlighted in the third paragraph of 5.61.
The first of these routes to the unsayability of solipsism

depends on the particular nature of the subject: in effect, its being a 'metaphysical' subject. The second route, however, rests simply on the central claim of the picture theory of language, that the form of language is the same as the form of the world. As such, it belongs with the particular reason provided by that theory for saying 'No' to the question we considered in section 6B above:

(Q) Might language have representational blind-spots?

Wittgenstein's treatment of solipsism as ultimately unsay-able represents a way of approaching the whole range of issues raised by a Kantian approach to philosophy. Kant's own transcendental idealism will become unsayable, on this approach, as will the whole range of more realist and more idealist positions. The *Tractatus* might seem to offer a pecu-liarly sophisticated response to those positions, which we might want to embrace ourselves. But it is important to see that this approach to those Kantian issues does not simply exploit an incoherence internal to all the various metaphysi-cal positions between which we might be asked to choose. It depends crucially on the philosophy of language which the *Tractatus* presents (as well as controversial assumptions — perhaps including (C2) — about the nature of the subject). The key premise is that language has the same form as the world, that there are the same possibilities of combining symbols in (a fully analysed) language as there are of combining objects in the world. That assumption forces us to choose one of the answers (A4), (A5), and (A6) to ques-tion (Q), and these are what make any large-scale meta-physical position unstatable. If we abandon the same-form assumption, however, we can choose one of these alternative positions:

(A1) Language might have representational blind-spots, and that possibility is statable;

(A2) Language might have representational blind-spots, but that possibility is not statable;

(A3) Language could not have representational blind-spots, because there is no constraint at all on what can be represented in any given medium.

Only (A2) here makes large-scale metaphysics look unstatable (though for reasons which differ fundamentally from that offered by Wittgenstein in 5.61, despite the superficial similarity).

Moreover, the apparent sophistication of Wittgenstein's response is slightly complicated by two things. First there is the fact that he argues for his position, while even to argue for the position — that it is impossible to contemplate what is impossible — requires him to do what he himself thereby argues is impossible. And, second, there is that odd remark we noticed at the end of the last section: in 5.641 he seems to think there *is* a way of talking about the metaphysical subject — in philosophy.

It is on this kind of issue that interpretations of the treatment of solipsism in the *Tractatus* tend to divide. I remarked at the outset that the dramatic claim of 5.62 seems to commit Wittgenstein to three things:

(i) 'What solipsism *means* is quite correct';

(ii) 'What solipsism means' cannot be *said*;

(iii) 'What solipsism means' 'shows itself'.

(iii) is curious, in the context of the understanding naturally given to 'showing' more generally in the *Tractatus*; but beyond that it raises no special problems. The major division is between interpretations which understand Wittgenstein as really asserting (i), in spite of (ii), and those which take him *not* to be asserting (i), because of (ii).[27] There are those who think that Wittgenstein really is some kind of idealist, and those who think that in (ii) he has managed to avoid any commitment on the issue between idealism and realism, and has actually succeeded in dissolving the problem. My own preference is for the former of these views: I think Wittgenstein is unambiguously, if paradoxically, committed to *both* (i) *and* (ii). Others will think that there is a way of understanding him as avoiding paradox here.

The discussion of solipsism overall has a double significance. First, it seems to link the *Tractatus* unambiguously back to the Kantian tradition, with its large questons of realism and idealism. The stand we take on these few sections affects our understanding of the whole of the *Tractatus*. And, second, it is one of the most obvious places where the paradox of the *Tractatus* manifests itself — before we encounter it in connection with the general difficulty of doing philosophy at the end of the work. Here we see Wittgenstein clearly saying things — or seeming to say things — which he thereby declares to be unsayable. In the case of solipsism, the paradoxicality seems particularly blatant, without (as it seems to me) damping Wittgenstein's enthusiasm for saying the things which are paradoxical. In the next chapter we will look at his approach to paradoxicality in more detail; this should help us decide which we should favour of the two general approaches to the treatment of solipsism that I have just distinguished.

7

METAPHYSICS, ETHICS, AND THE LIMITS OF PHILOSOPHY

7A THE PROBLEM OF THE POSSIBILITY OF METAPHYSICS

David Hume's first *Enquiry* ends with this famous paragraph:

> When we run over libraries, persuaded of these principles, what havoc must we make? If we take in our hand any volume; of divinity or school metaphysics, for instance; let us ask, *Does it contain any abstract reasoning concerning quantity or number?* No. *Does it contain any experimental reasoning concerning matter of fact and existence?* No. Commit it then to the flames: for it can contain nothing but sophistry and illusion.
>
> (Hume 1777: XII, iii)

In the second paragraph of a paper which was strongly influenced by Wittgenstein's *Tractatus,* Rudolf Carnap writes:

> In the domain of metaphysics, including all philosophy of value and normative theory, logical analysis yields the negative result that the alleged statements in this domain are entirely meaningless.
>
> (Carnap 1956: 60–61)

And lest anyone should be in any doubt, Carnap insists:

> In saying that the so-called statements of metaphysics are mean-
> ingless, we intend this word in its strictest sense.
>
> (Carnap 1956: 61)

The 'principles' which lead to Hume's result underlie
Carnap's conclusion too. Hume insists that all knowledge
either falls within the province of 'demonstration' or is concerned with 'matter of fact': this is the principle known as
Hume's Fork. Carnap holds that all statements are either (i)
'true solely by virtue of their form', (ii) negations of these
(which are therefore contradictory), or (iii) empirical statements (true or false) (Carnap 1956: 76). Since the first two of
Carnap's categories of statement fall within what Hume
counts as the province of 'demonstration', it is clear enough
that Carnap is committed to something very like Hume's
Fork. It is because statements of metaphysics fall into none
of the relevant classes of possible statements that Hume and
Carnap dismiss them as 'sophistry and illusion', or simply
meaningless.

What Hume and Carnap are here ruling out is the possibility of the class of statements which Kant called *synthetic a
priori*, which he took to be central to philosophy, as well as
to mathematics. Hume's province of 'demonstration' broadly
coincides with the class of truths which Kant counted 'analytic' (together with the negations of analytic truths) — that
is, the non-synthetic; and he insists that truths concerning
'matter of fact and existence' can only be known by experience — that is, *a posteriori*. We have already seen that
Wittgenstein also rejected the possibility of synthetic *a priori*
truths. It should therefore come as no surprise to find him
rejecting metaphysics. Nor should it surprise us that this
rejection is broadened (like Carnap's) to include ethics
(Hume simply regarded morality as not being a proper
object of reason at all). But the character of Wittgenstein's
rejection of metaphysics seems quite different from Carnap's
or Hume's: where they seem keen to push past metaphysics

and get on with science, Wittgenstein's attitude seems more poetic and contemplative.

Part of the difference of approach here is a difference in these philosophers' attitude to their own work. If we reject metaphysics on the ground that all truths are either analytic or *a posteriori*, we seem bound to be in some difficulty over that rejection itself. Suppose we 'take in our hand' Hume's first *Enquiry*, and ask whether it contains any 'abstract reasoning concerning quantity or number', or any 'experimental reasoning concerning matter of fact and existence'. We seem bound to answer *No*, in which case, according to Hume's own principles, his work 'can contain nothing but sophistry and illusion'. Similarly, it is hard to see how we can claim that Carnap's statement that all statements are either (i) analytic, (ii) negations of analytic truths, or (iii) empirical, is itself either analytic, a negation of an analytic truth, or empirical. So it seems that Carnap's own statement must be counted as meaningless, in the strictest sense of the word, by its own lights. The rejection of metaphysics on any such grounds as these seems bound to be paradoxical.

Neither Hume nor Carnap seems to be aware of any difficulty here: they seem concerned simply to dismiss certain types of work from which they think they can clearly distinguish their own. Wittgenstein, however, seems to see the problem quite clearly:

> My propositions are elucidatory in this way: he who understands me finally recognizes them as senseless, when he has climbed out through them, on them, over them.
>
> (6.54)

The task of this chapter is to explain Wittgenstein's reasoning in more detail, and to try to make sense of his response to the paradox which seems to be involved in rejecting metaphysics. I will approach these two aspects of the task in that order, though it should be made clear that this already involves taking a stand on the interpretation of Wittgenstein's approach to the paradox. There are some interpreters of the

Tractatus who endorse what Wittgenstein says in 6.54, and conclude that (at least the bulk of) the sentences of the *Tractatus* are indeed nonsense. These interpreters must have some difficulty in making sense of the reasoning which leads to the conclusion that any attempt to say something metaphysical will end in nonsense, and therefore end up supposing that the conclusion is reached in some other way. This interpretation strikes me as clearly wrong — though I will postpone the argument for that claim until we address the paradox explicitly. I think the *Tractatus* contains arguments for the conclusion that any attempt to say something metaphysical must result in nonsense. Our first task is to try to understand them.

7B NECESSITY AND LAWS OF NATURE

Remember Wittgenstein's view of logic:

6.1 The propositions of logic are tautologies.

The key Kantian notion of analyticity is introduced in the very next remark:

6.11 The propositions of logic therefore say nothing. (They are the analytical propositions.)

In the light of that, the following can be seen as Wittgenstein's version of Hume's Fork:

6.3 Logical research means the investigation of *all regularity*. And outside logic all is accident.

'Regularity' is a poor translation of the German word here ('Gesetzmässigkeit'): 'law-governedness' would be better.[1] The thought seems to be something like this: every genuine law ('Gesetz') involves necessity; 'there is only *logical* necessity' (6.37); so anything which cannot be represented as 'logical' can only be accidental. Given 6.11, 6.3 is the rejection of non-analytic — that is, synthetic — necessary truths.

This provides one angle on Wittgenstein's rejection of metaphysics, one in which his view seems largely to coincide with Hume's. Metaphysics is concerned with what is necessary in the world: how the world must be. Hume thought that necessity could not be experienced. Nor did he think there was any genuine necessity revealed by induction (reasoning from cases we have observed to those we have not).[2] He concluded (to put the matter a little crudely) that necessity — at least the only kind of necessity we can ever be concerned with — is not really in the world.[3] He ended up, in effect, rejecting natural necessity, the necessity of causation and of natural laws. There remains some sense for Hume in which we can speak of natural necessity — as an expression of a feeling of psychological compulsion in our expectation of one event having experienced another — but this talk is misleading, because the only necessity here (a psychological compulsion) is not the necessity we think we are describing (which would be between events in the world).

Kant thought that Hume's reasoning would also suffice to undermine all necessity (not just natural necessity), and therefore that it had to be rejected if we were to make sense of mathematics and physics — as well, of course, as metaphysics. We can see Wittgenstein, in the 6.3s, defending the Humean position against Kantian and other objections. In effect, he has to reject any claim which cannot be placed unambiguously within one or other of his two crucial categories, the logical and the accidental. And he is at least as firm as Hume in his rejection of natural necessity. His claim that 'There is only *logical* necessity' follows this remark:

> A necessity for one thing to happen because another has happened does not exist.

> (6.37)

Wittgenstein's examination of 'law-governedness' begins with induction:

6.31 The so-called law of induction cannot in any case be a logical law, for it is obviously a significant proposition. — And therefore it cannot be a law a priori either.

What is this 'law of induction'? Perhaps it is something like this:

(I) If all observed *F*s are *G*, all *F*s are *G*.

Why is this 'obviously a significant proposition' (obviously a sentence with sense — 'sinnvoller')? Presumably because it is obvious that it might be false. So the supposed 'law' of induction is only accidentally true. Why, then, should we be so inclined to make inductive inferences, to make judgements on the basis of experience? Wittgenstein responds to this question by redescribing the process of induction, and then giving a Humean account of it:

6.363 The process of induction is the process of assuming the *simplest* law that can be made to harmonize with our experience.

6.3631 This process, however, has no logical foundation but only a psychological one.

It is clear that there are no grounds for believing that the simplest course of events will really happen.

The interesting thing here is the redescription of the process of induction. If we formulate induction as something like a law, in the manner of (I), we seem to be looking for some connection of necessity linking the antecedent ('all observed *F*s are *G*') and the consequent ('all *F*s are *G*'). The same goes for any representation of the process of induction as a process of *inference*. Wittgenstein, however, represents induction as a matter of *assuming* or *accepting* a law. In the case of the kind of induction which we tried to represent in (I), the law is this:

(L) All *F*s are *G*.

METAPHYSICS, ETHICS, LIMITS OF PHILOSOPHY

And the process of induction is simply the process of assuming (L) when all the observed *F*s are *G*. What is striking about this is that Wittgenstein's Humean treatment of induction involves the assumption of *laws*. It is crucial to his view that laws are involved.

How, then, does Wittgenstein deal with laws? The key remark here is this:

6.32   The law of causality is not a law but the form of a law.

What is the 'law of causality'? Presumably it is this:

(Cau) Every event has a cause.

This is a principle which has a distinguished history. Hume thought that there was no reason to believe it — though he seems not to have been able to stop believing it. Kant thought that its truth required the adoption of his transcendental idealism, including, in particular, the thought that the very notion of causation is dependent on what we bring to the world, rather than just on what is there anyway, in the world as it is in itself.[4] Where Hume and Kant agree is in thinking that (Cau) is contentious and in need of some kind of support. Strikingly, it seems that it is just this that Wittgenstein denies.

Wittgenstein offers another interpretation of the significance of the 'law of causality' a little later on:

If there were a law of causality, it might run: 'There are natural laws'.
(6.36)

What we notice in 6.32 and 6.36 is that Wittgenstein implicitly distinguishes between two kinds of 'law'. First, there are such laws as the 'law of causality': these, according to 6.32, are not really laws at all; let us call them *higher-order laws*, in order to remain as neutral as possible about their status. Second, there are the laws whose *form* is supposedly given by 'laws' of the first kind. Following the hint given by

6.36, let us call laws of this latter kind *natural laws*. It is plausible that natural laws will look like (L). If so, then 6.32 claims, in effect, that the 'law of causality' (for example) is the form of a law like (L) — or perhaps better, the form of laws like (L).[5]

But what could that mean? Form in the *Tractatus* is concerned with possibility: the form of an object is the ways it *can* combine with other objects; the form of a sentence is the *possibility* of its elements being arranged in the way they are. This suggests that the central claim of 6.32 is this:

(CauL) (Cau) means: for every event *e* it is possible to classify *e* by means of some predicate '*F*', and also by means of some other predicate '*G*' which describes events in terms of their causes, for which predicates 'All *F*s are *G*' holds.

If this is the claim of 6.32, and this claim can itself properly reformulated as the claim that 'there are natural laws' (6.36), then what Wittgenstein wants to say about it is this:

But that clearly cannot be said: it shows itself.

(6.36)

Whatever else this means, it surely requires that (Cau) turn out, on this interpretation, to be something that could not possibly be false — as something that, in effect, *needs* no justification.

How can (CauL) remove the possibility of falsehood from (Cau)? It can only do that if there is almost no restriction on the possible choices of predicates '*F*' and '*G*': it has to be clear that there are simply bound to be *some* predicates which meet the requirement that all *F*s are *G*. Crucially, this will require that we are very liberal in what we count as a description of an event 'in terms of its cause'. One suggestion might be that we count a description of an event 'in terms of its cause' as being, by definition, no more than: a *maximally explanatory* description of that event. All we will then need for (Cau) to be true will be the possibility of classifying any event in two ways: in a *maximally explanatory* way (for the predicate 'G' in laws of the form of (L)), and in a *less than maximally explanatory* way (for the predicate 'F' in such laws). On this interpretation, then, (Cau) amounts to no more than this:

> (Cau*) Every event can be described in two ways — a maximally explanatory way, and a less than maximally explanatory way.

Effectively, what has happened here is that we have let the notion of 'cause' be defined in such a way as to ensure that (Cau) cannot be false.

What status does this give to the two different kinds of 'law' which we distinguished before? Interpreting (Cau) as (Cau*) does indeed seem to make sense of the following claim about higher-order laws:

> Laws, like the law of causation, etc., treat of the network and not of what the network describes.

> (6.35)

These higher-order laws are the laws which it is natural to regard as necessary: we can see here that Wittgenstein holds that they do not really tell us anything about how the *world* is — rather, they 'treat of the network'. So, despite first appearances, they do not encourage us to think that there are any synthetic *a priori* truths. We will consider their status further in a moment, but let us turn next to laws of the other kind, the *natural* laws (laws like (L)). These seem to be straightforwardly empirical. Although it is perhaps *a priori* that it is possible to describe any event in the two ways required for (Cau*), it is an empirical (*a posteriori*) matter *what* the maximally explanatory way of describing an event may be. Furthermore, it looks as if this can harmlessly be counted as contingent, as well as being *a posteriori*. So it seems in some way necessary and *a priori* that there are laws of nature, but which laws describe the actual world is both *a posteriori* and contingent.

Can the interpretation which I have offered of (Cau) as (Cau*) be made to square with this remark?

6.371   At the basis of the whole modern view of the world lies the illusion that the so-called laws of nature are explanations of natural phenomena.

Wittgenstein apparently holds that it is an *illusion* to think that natural laws *explain* natural phenomena, and yet I have suggested that natural laws are, in effect, 'maximally explanatory' descriptions. There is no deep puzzle here, I think. All we need to say is that 'maximally explanatory' descriptions do not provide the kind of explanation which 'the whole modern view of the world' takes laws of nature to provide. The natural way to understand this is to suppose that 'the whole modern view' takes laws of nature to be necessary — just as 'the ancients' took God to be a necessary being — whereas, in fact (on Wittgenstein's view), those laws which were counted as *natural* laws, on our earlier classification, are contingent, and those things which were called *higher-order* laws have a rather different status (which we will return to in a moment). The 'maximally explanatory' descriptions which are posited in (Cau*) need not involve any necessitation: they might be just usefully inclusive.

Let us now return to the discussion of induction, where we began the discussion of laws. We can see that it is *natural* laws, in our sense, rather than higher-order laws, which are involved in induction. On Wittgenstein's account, the process of induction is the process of assuming the simplest *natural* law which fits the evidence. The law which is here assumed need be no more than a uniformity: it is simply accidental — a general statement which happens to succeed in describing the world. There is therefore no surprise in the fact that Wittgenstein develops a broadly Humean approach to induction, which goes with a rejection of natural necessity, as involving the assumption of *laws* — since the laws in question do not import any natural necessity.

Recall the remark which I said earlier amounted to Wittgenstein's version of Hume's Fork:

6.3   Logical research means the investigation of *all* [*law-governedness*]. And outside logic all is accident.

Among significant sentences there are, on the one hand, sentences of logic, about which Wittgenstein holds this:

6.1   The propositions of logic are tautologies.

And, on the other hand, there are empirical sentences, sentences which describe the world. But where do such things as higher-order laws fit here? On Wittgenstein's account they seem to be neither tautologies nor empirical statements. Does he, then, after all, assign them an intermediate status, like that of Kant's synthetic *a priori* judgements?

He certainly does describe them in a way which is consciously indebted to Kant:

6.34   All propositions, such as the law of causation, the law of continuity in nature, the law of least expenditure in nature, etc. etc., all these are a priori intuitions of possible forms of the propositions of science.

This notion of an 'a priori intuition' is just what is needed to make sense of synthetic *a priori* truths — truths which are both *a priori,* and yet somehow concern the real world. But this Kantian description is surely undercut by what Wittgenstein says elsewhere about higher-order laws. Here is what he says in 6.342:

So too the fact that it can be described by Newtonian mechanics asserts nothing about the world.

And remember what he says about the 'law of causality':

6.36.   If there were a law of causality, it might run: 'There are natural laws'.

But that clearly cannot be said: it shows itself.

'Showing' here emerges as Wittgenstein's reinterpretation of the Kantian 'a priori intuition', but it is surely more than a reinterpretation: it is a deflation. Kant's *a priori* intuition was supposed to provide us with a means of access to something which is of the right kind, broadly speaking, to be seen, but which happens to be, as it were, in the wrong location. What 'shows itself', however, seems to be the wrong kind of thing to be said. In redescribing what Kant would describe as *a priori* intuitions as things which can be shown, but not said, Wittgenstein is, in effect, insisting that these so-called *a priori* intuitions are not intuitions at all.

What emerges here is that the things which Kant would have counted as synthetic *a priori* are not counter-examples to Wittgenstein's version of Hume's Fork: they are not cases of 'law-governedness' which logic somehow fails to accommodate. Rather, they are not really laws at all: in fact, they are not even meaningful, not even sentences. They are attempts to say what cannot be said. So there remain just the two categories of significant sentences: those dealt with by logic (tautologies and contradictions), and empirical sentences about the world. The things which seem to express synthetic *a priori* truths are not really sentences at all.

7C ETHICS

Wittgenstein begins his discussion of ethics with what looks like a deliberately controversial formulation of his view:

6.4   All propositions are of equal value.

This looks as if it is saying that no state of the world is any better or worse than any other state of the world. Can this really be what he means? The puzzle here is that, following on from the discussion of laws of nature, and in the context of more general considerations of necessity, we are expecting Wittgenstein to make some *meta*-ethical claim — some claim about the status of ethics and statements of ethics. But 6.4 seems to be a *normative* claim: it does not talk *about* value; it makes a value statement (and a very odd one at that). In fact, it looks as if these remarks (roughly the 6.4s) express both a meta-ethical view (about the status of ethics as such) and a particular ethical approach to life, and these are intertwined in a complicated way.

> 6.41, which is ostensibly a comment on 6.4, is unambiguously meta-ethical:
>
>> The sense of the world [roughly: the meaning of life] must lie outside the world.

There is no value in the world, Wittgenstein claims; rather,

> It must lie outside the world.

6.41 also apparently contains an argument for this claim, which we could summarize as follows:

(V1) Value is non-accidental;
(V2) Everything in the world is accidental; so
(V3) Value is not in the world.

(V2) should be familiar enough by now: it is a Humean rejection of natural necessity (see, for example, 6.37). The more obviously striking claim is (V1): why should value be non-accidental?

What Wittgenstein is claiming here seems to amount to this: anything which is good (or bad) is *essentially* good (or bad). That is to say, if it is really good, it could not but have been good; anything which was not good would have been a different thing. On the face of it, this looks straightforwardly false. Suppose that you do something which turns out to help someone else. Suppose that while walking along you idly kick a stone off a path — not for any real reason, just as a playful kick. And then suppose a child comes tearing along the path on a bicycle, and goes safely by — though she would have crashed painfully if the stone had still been on the path. We might say:

(1) It was a good thing you kicked that stone off the path.

Now it is natural to think that the kick would have been the same, even if it had not had that fortunately beneficial effect; the same kick might have done no good, might even have done harm. How can Wittgenstein cope with that? He has to think that (1) can be analysed into a conjunction, one conjunct of which is evaluative, while the other is not. It might look like this:

(1a) Your kicking the stone off the path had effect *e*, and effect *e* is good.

The claim would be that in (1a) we reach something (effect *e*) which is, indeed, non-accidentally good. If we can provide an analysis like this in every case, and can claim that the analysis shows where the value is really located, then it looks as if we might be able to claim that whatever really has value has whatever value it has non-accidentally.

This already involves Wittgenstein taking a stand in *normative* ethics, rather than just in meta-ethics. He must already be opposed to familiar forms of consequentialism. Familiar forms of consequentialism (utilitarianism is the obvious example) are theories of the value of acts. They assume that acts do really have value, and they claim that the value they have is determined by their consequences (roughly: the end always justifies the means). But it is a contingent matter that a particular act has the particular consequences it does (it is certainly contingent according to any view, like Wittgenstein's, which denies the real existence of natural necessity). So it must be contingent that a particular act has the value it does. Since this is exactly what Wittgenstein denies in accepting (V1), he must reject familiar forms of consequentialism. And this is exactly what he does in 6.422:

But it is clear that ethics has nothing to do with punishment and reward in the ordinary sense. This question as to the *consequences* of an action must therefore be irrelevant.

Note that the italics here show that Wittgenstein is rejecting the view that the value of an action lies in its consequences, but not the idea that actions have value. But if an action has value, and that value does not reside in its consequences, it seems evident that its value must lie in the intention, or will, with which it is performed. But at this point it looks as if Wittgenstein has another, more or less independent, reason for asserting (V2), that value is not in the world. For he insists:

6.423   Of the will as the subject of the ethical we cannot speak.
        And the will as a phenomenon is only of interest to psychology.

This contrast between 'the will as the subject of the ethical' and 'the will as a phenomenon' is reminiscent of a similar contrast, which we encountered in the last chapter in the discussion of solipsism:

> The philosophical I is not the man, not the human body or the human soul of which psychology speaks, but the metaphysical subject, the limit — not a part of the world.

(5.641)

It is natural then to think that the I who wills — the subject who is our concern in ethics — is the metaphysical subject, who is not in the world.

If the I who wills is not in the world, then nothing done by the I can affect the world. This is something which Wittgenstein has already claimed in explaining our sense of the inexorability of laws of nature:

6.373   The world is independent of my will.
6.374   Even if everything we wished were to happen, this would only be, so to speak, a favour of fate, for there is no *logical* connexion between will and world, which would guarantee this, and the assumed physical connexion itself we could not again will.

And he makes the point again in the discussion of ethics:

> If good or bad willing changes the world, it can only change the limits of the world, not the facts; not the things that can be expressed in language.
>
> (6.43)

This is a puzzling remark if we take the 'limits of the world' here to be what they usually are in the *Tractatus*: the limits of what is possible. It is hard to see what sense could be made of the claim that good or bad willing changes what is possible, in the sense of making possible what had previously been impossible, or impossible what had previously been possible. If good or bad willing changes what is possible, the only change to what is possible which it seems capable of effecting is a change, crudely speaking, in the way what is possible *feels* to us.

This is naturally connected back with what Wittgenstein takes to be the proper application in ethics of the notions of reward and punishment:

> There must be some sort of ethical reward and ethical punishment, but this must lie in the action itself.
>
> (And this is clear also that the reward must be something acceptable, and the punishment something unacceptable.)
>
> (6.422)

It looks as if good willing will make the world, which one cannot change, acceptable, and bad willing will make it unacceptable. Wittgenstein then claims:

> The world of the happy is quite another than that of the unhappy.
>
> (6.43)

We can read this in two ways, compatibly with accepting that the subject cannot change the world. Both ways involve taking the difference between the happy person's world and that of the unhappy person to be a matter of how the same world *seems* to that person. On the first interpretation, exactly the same possibilities are evident to both the happy person and the unhappy person: the difference lies in their acceptance of those possibilities as the only possibilities. On the second, the happy person is aware of a different range of possibilities from those of which the unhappy person is aware. (One would like the happy person to be aware of *more* possibilities than the unhappy person, or else happiness would seem to depend on a form of delusion, which seems clearly foreign to the spirit of the *Tractatus*.) It is not easy to decide between these two interpretations, although my own preference is for the first: this seems closer to the kind of reconciliation to one's fate which Wittgenstein seems to have achieved on the front line.

However this may be, it seems clear that Wittgenstein's conception of ethics involves some kind of removal of the ethical subject from the world. And this provides what seems to be an independent source of (V3), the claim that value is not in the world. It is also what leads Wittgenstein to say:

> Ethics is transcendental.
>
> (6.421)

He then adds a striking parenthesis to that last remark, as if in explanation of it:

> (Ethics and aesthetics are one.)

To understand this, we need to look to those sections in the *Notebooks* where some of these ideas were first sketched out. These four remarks, in particular, are helpful:

> The work of art is the object seen *sub specie aeternitatis*; and the good life is the world seen *sub specie aeternitatis*. This is the connexion between art and ethics.
>
> (*NB*: 83)

> (The thought forces itself upon one): The thing seen *sub specie aeternitatis* is the thing seen together with the whole logical space.
>
> (*NB*: 83)

> Aesthetically, the miracle is that the world exists. That there is what there is.
>
> (*NB*: 86)

> Is it the essence of the artistic way of looking at things, that it looks at things with a happy eye?
>
> (*NB*: 86)

These remarks from the *Notebooks* are naturally put beside what we have already found in the *Tractatus* — and also this:

6.45 The contemplation of the world sub specie aeterni is its contemplation as a limited whole.
    The feeling of the world as a limited whole is the mystical feeling.

('View' would be better than 'contemplation' as a translation of 'Anschauung' here: it is an *attitude*, rather than an activity.)

What these remarks all suggest is a particular normative ethics, which we can explain rather crudely as follows. There is a single ethical imperative, which is to view the world in a certain way. This is the artist's way of viewing the world, a way of looking at things 'with a happy eye', an outlook which finds it a miracle that the world exists. Viewing the world in this way is viewing it *sub specie aeternitatis* — from the point of view of eternity — removed from it and disinterested. What we see when we view the world like this is each thing 'together with the whole logical space': with a consciousness, that is, of what is possible, of the ways in which each thing can be combined with other things. This way of viewing the world, the artistic way, may also be described as mysticism:

6.44 Not *how* the world is, is the mystical, but *that* it is.

What the artist delights in is not the facts being one particular way rather than another, but there being any facts at all — in effect, there being the possibilities there are.

Something like this interpretation of the ethics of the *Tractatus* seems unavoidable, once we put these remarks in the context of the passages in the *Notebooks* from which they originally arose. Whatever the general merits of the outlook which is here recommended, it seems bizarre — mad, even — to regard this as summarizing all of ethics. It is not implausible, however, to attribute this odd ethics to the effects of being on the front in the First World War, which is where the logical treatise which Wittgenstein was composing spread out to encompass the question of the meaning of life. It would not be surprising if that kind of experience led to something a little unhinged. And certainly Russell remarked on the change which had come over Wittgenstein, when he met him for the first time after the war:

> I had felt in his book a flavour of mysticism, but was astonished when I found he has become a complete mystic. He reads people like Kierkegaard and Angelus Silesius, and he seriously contemplates becoming a monk.

> (Monk 1997: 568).

And there is a connection with Schopenhauer, whom Wittgenstein obviously read from early in his life. Here is a passage which has a striking resonance, in the light of the fact that Wittgenstein's experience at the front clearly changed him quite deeply:

> From the first appearance of his consciousness, man finds himself to be a willing being, and his knowledge, as a rule, remains in constant relation to his will ... . It is always an exception, when such a life suffers an interruption through the fact that either the aesthetic demand for contemplation or the ethical demand for renunciation proceeds from a knowledge independent of the service of the will, and directed to the nature of the world in general.[6]

Finally, let us look back at the remark with which the discussion of ethics begins:

6.4   All propositions are of equal value.

I said before that this seemed to say that no one state of affairs is better or worse than any other, which looks like a value claim, of sorts, rather than a claim in meta-ethics. It now seems that this is precisely what Wittgenstein means to say. The things which have real value are not facts, not anything in the world. What has real value are just: a certain kind of outlook, combined with the action of adopting that outlook; and what that outlook finds in looking at the world. What is really good, it seems — what the artist's eye delights in — is not the facts being any particular way, but simply their being *some* way.[7]

7D METAPHYSICS AND PHILOSOPHY

In the 6.5s Wittgenstein turns from ethics to philosophy in general — and philosophy conceived of in the largest possible way. The key to his approach can be seen in this remark:

6.52   We feel that even if *all possible* scientific questions be answered, the problems of life have not been touched at all. Of course there is then no question left, and just this is the answer.

First, we should note the conception of philosophy which is involved here. It is concerned with questions (if there are any) which remain untouched by any possible scientific advance. These are bound to seem more fundamental than anything that science can tell us. In the lay mind — the mind of those who are not professional philosophers — these questions seem to concern the meaning of life (whatever exactly that phrase might itself mean). 6.52 shows that Wittgenstein thinks of the questions of philosophy in just these terms: they concern 'the problems of life'. In some sense, it seems, Wittgenstein takes the problems of philosophy to be concerned with a threat to the meaning of life. And here he offers some reassurance, though one which people may find it hard to accept: it turns out that there is no threat at all. There is no genuine question which remains untouched once all possible scientific questions have been answered; there is no real problem of the meaning of life. In his words:

> The solution of the problem of life is seen in the vanishing of this problem.
>
> (6.521)

It is in this context that Wittgenstein addresses scepticism explicitly for the first (and only) time in the book (though we found that the argument for solipsism in 5.62 was hard to understand except as a response to a form of scepticism):

6.51　Scepticism is *not* irrefutable, but palpably senseless [*unsinnig*: nonsense], if it would doubt where a question cannot be asked. For doubt can only exist where there is a question; a question only where there is an answer, and this only where something *can* be *said*.

Why does Wittgenstein consider scepticism here? What is the link between scepticism and 'the problems of life'? We can bring out the connection by considering a scenario which is familiar in discussions of utilitarianism. Some classical versions of utilitarianism claim that all that matters, ultimately, is the maximization of pleasure, and minimization of pain. This suggests that an ideal life could be achieved if everyone were hooked up to a 'pleasure machine', which ensured that their lives were spent with maximum pleasure and minimum pain. Of course, pleasure is always pleasure *in* something, so we could only feel pleasure if we thought that certain nice things were happening. So the pleasure machine would have to engender certain kinds of illusion in us. We would spend our lives in a state of (apparently) blissful hallucination.

What would be wrong with this? Well, it seems that in this circumstance everyone's life would be an empty sham: our pleasure would not be properly grounded, would depend on a lie, would be, in a sense, pathetic, empty, and futile. If any life is a life without meaning, this life would be. It is just this threat of meaninglessness which scepticism raises. Scepticism invites us to wonder whether there is anything really there: whether our thoughts relate to any reality, whether anything we think really means anything. And it is just this threat of the complete emptiness of our thoughts that Wittgenstein thinks he can dismiss. Here we can return to the kind of thinking which I tentatively suggested lay behind Wittgenstein's argument for solipsism (in Chapter 6, section 6E). I cannot doubt that my language is syntactically well formed. But if my language is syntactically well formed, then, according to the account of language provided by the *Tractatus*, the possible combinations of its symbols must be co-ordinate with genuine possibilities. And for these to be genuine possibilities — rather than merely imagined possibilities — there must be a real world for whose constituents every genuine possibility is a possible way of being arranged. And that requires not just a real world, but real objects whose form is the range of possibilities of combination which constitutes the whole of genuine possibility. (This obviously recalls the substance argument of 2.021–2.023, discussed in Chapter 1, section 1D.)

That is, as it were, the straight answer to scepticism which Wittgenstein's account of language suggests that we give. But, as we saw in the case of solipsism, Wittgenstein does not himself give this answer. In the discussion of solipsism he wrote:

> We cannot therefore say in logic: This and this there is in the world, that there is not.
>
> For that would apparently presuppose that we exclude certain possibilities, and this cannot be the case since otherwise logic must get outside the limits of the world: that is, if it could consider these limits from the other side also.

(5.61)

And we seem to have the same kind of thinking here, in 6.51. For to entertain scepticism, we would have to entertain the possibility that our language is not syntactically well formed. And this would require us to frame, as a genuine possibility, something which we cannot accept is, in fact, possible. But the *Tractatus*'s conception of language rules that out: that conception requires a coincidence between what is conceivable (framable, picturable) and what is possible.

It turns out, in fact, that the same applies to all of philosophy as is applied here to scepticism. This general lesson is drawn in one of the most famous remarks in the *Tractatus*:

6.53 The right method of philosophy would be this. To say nothing except what can be said, *i.e.* the propositions of natural science, *i. e.* something that has nothing to do with philosophy: and then always, when someone else wished to say something metaphysical, to demonstrate to him that he had given no meaning to certain signs in his propositions. This method would be unsatisfying to the other — he would not have the feeling that we were teaching him philosophy — but it would be the only strictly correct method.

What does Wittgenstein mean by 'philosophy' here? Apparently, he means the same as he means by 'metaphysics', since saying something metaphysical seems here to be the same as saying something philosophical. And whatever he means by 'philosophy' and 'metaphysics' seems to include the *Tractatus* itself, since in the next remark he writes:

My propositions are elucidatory in this way: he who understands me finally recognizes them as senseless [*unsinnig*: nonsense], when he has climbed out through them, on them, over them.

(6.54)

The natural interpretation is that for Wittgenstein philosophy (or metaphysics) includes precisely what it has traditionally been taken to include: what it was taken by Kant to include, for example. It is concerned with the possibilities of the world: its business is how the world must be, how it might be, how it cannot be.[8] Its province is the field of those truths which Kant counted synthetic *a priori*.

What ensures that any attempt to say something philosophical will end up as nonsense? The conclusion might seem to be overdetermined: at least, it looks as if it can be reached by more and less direct routes. But the core thought is the one which is expressed in the argument for the inexpressibility of solipsism:

> What we cannot think, that we cannot think: we cannot therefore *say* what we cannot think.
>
> (5.61)

The conception of sentences as models — indeed, of all representation as modelling — makes it impossible to represent an impossibility: because the possibilities of combination of symbols are the same as the possibilities of combination of objects, no combination of symbols can represent an impossible combination of objects. This is the first of three principles which we saw in the last chapter that Wittgenstein is committed to:

(SP)   It is possible to state that *p* only if it is possible that *p*.

(SPN) It is possible to state that *p* only if it is possible to state that not - *p*.

(SPP) It is possible to state that it is possible that *p* only if it is possible to state that *p*.

A little reflection shows that, with these principles in place, it will be impossible to state that something is impossible, that something is possible, or that something is necessary. (The arguments were elaborated more fully in Chapter 6, section 6B.) Since the business of philosophy (or metaphysics), on the natural interpretation I have suggested, is precisely to say what is necessary, or possible, or impossible, in the world, these three principles mean that nothing philosophical (or metaphysical) can be stated.

With the core assumption of the *Tractatus*'s theory of language — that sentences and reality have the same form — in place, similar reasoning attaches to all of the more formal remarks in the *Tractatus*. The problem affects the philosophy of language and logic as much as it affects attempts to say something about how the world must be. This is because, with the theory of language in place, the philosophy of language and logic will itself be concerned with what is possible (with what symbols, or combinations of symbols, are possible, for example).

This problem with saying anything modal is connected with what Wittgenstein says about *form*, since form is explained in terms of possibility. It is, in fact, the non-metaphorical explanation of this claim about a picture and its form:

2.172 The picture cannot, however, represent its own form of representation; it shows it forth.

And Wittgenstein then attaches this difficulty to a whole range of philosophical terms. 2.172 concerns pictures or models in general. Wittgenstein, of course, is concerned with sentences in particular. The application of the general point of 2.172 to the particular case of sentences is found in this remark:

Propositions can represent the whole reality, but they cannot represent what they must have in common with reality in order to be able to represent it — the logical form.

(4.12)

The second remark offered as a comment on this begins as follows:

We can speak in a certain sense of formal properties of objects and atomic facts, or of properties of the structure of facts, and in the same sense of formal relations and relations of structures.

(4.122)

And this is the basis of the introduction of the notion of a formal *concept* in 4.126. It should then follow that nothing can be represented, nothing can be *said*, using a formal concept, since any attempt to use a formal concept to say something will be an attempt to speak about what is possible. And, indeed, this is exactly the conclusion Wittgenstein draws about various such attempts, in 4.1272 and 4.1274.

It seems, then, that the basic reason why nothing philosophical can be said, according to the *Tractatus*, is that philosophy attempts to make modal claims (claims about what is necessary or possible), and no significant modal claim can really be made, given (SP), (SPN), and (SPP). But in that case, the problem attaches even to 6.54. For Wittgenstein does not here merely make a conjecture, or offer an empirical observation: he tells us what *would* be the right method in philosophy; he tells us to confine ourselves to what *can* be said; he assumes that it is inevitable, capable of demonstration, that anyone who attempts to say something metaphysical will have failed to give meaning to certain signs in the sentences he produces. 6.54 is itself modal: it tells us what must be done, and what cannot be done. It is itself a piece of philosophy, or metaphysics.

The *Tractatus*'s conception of language lies behind the (philosophical) claim of 6.54, that nothing philosophical can be said. It is also implicated in the particular form which that claim takes. Note that Wittgenstein does not merely say that any attempt to say something philosophical will lead to nonsense: he says, in particular, that anyone who tries to say something philosophical will have 'given no meaning to certain signs in his propositions'. This means that what is offered as a philosophical statement will be meaningless, in what Carnap called 'the strictest sense' of the word: that is to say, it is plain nonsense. But it means more than that. Carnap thought that there were two different kinds of meaninglessness, even in 'the strictest sense' of the word. In addition to meaningless 'sentences' — which he called 'pseudo-statements' — which 'contain a meaningless word', Carnap thought that there were other 'pseudo-statements' which 'consist of meaningful words, but the words are put together in such a way that nevertheless no meaning results'.[9]

But this, of course, is something which Wittgenstein has to reject, as we saw in Chapter 4, in discussing 5.4733 (see section 4C). He has to reject it, because it is incompatible with the conception of language presented in the *Tractatus*. The *Tractatus* insists that the elements of a representation can be combined in exactly the same ways as the objects in reality with which they are correlated: this is the common-form assumption at the heart of his conception of language. A sentence — or pseudo-sentence — which consisted of meaningful words 'put together in such a way that nevertheless no meaning results' would be a sentence which represented things (the correlates of those words) as being arranged in ways in which they could not be arranged. That is, we would have a possible arrangement of words to which no possible arrangement of objects corresponded. And that is exactly what the *Tractatus*'s theory of language rules out.

It seems, then, that we are forced into the particular way in which Wittgenstein claims that any attempt to say something philosophical ends up in nonsense only by the particular philosophy which he endorses in the *Tractatus*. This makes the work seem tightly paradoxical. If the philosophical claims of the *Tractatus* are true, it — and they — are nonsense. And it is *only* if the philosophical claims of the *Tractatus* are true, that it — and they — are nonsense in the particular way that Wittgenstein claims they are. This paradox will be our concern in the next section.

It is important to compare this apparently tightly paradoxical conclusion with the remarks which Wittgenstein makes earlier in the book, in the 4.1s (remarks whose discussion was not pursued in Chapter 4). The following section is particularly significant:

4.112 The object of philosophy is the logical clarification of thoughts.
       Philosophy is not a theory but an activity.
       A philosophical work consists essentially of elucidations.
       The result of philosophy is not a number of 'philosophical propositions', but to make propositions clear.
       Philosophy should make clear and delimit sharply the thoughts which otherwise are, as it were, opaque and blurred.

What is recommended here has seemed to many to be similar in spirit to the character of philosophy as it is practiced in Wittgenstein's later work. But whatever we say about the later work, we should be clear that this passage in the *Tractatus* is not itself philosophically innocent. The succeeding remarks of parallel importance are inextricably bound up with the whole theory of the *Tractatus*:

4.113 Philosophy limits the disputable sphere of natural science.
4.114 It should limit the thinkable and thereby the unthinkable.
      It should limit the unthinkable from within through the thinkable.

4.115 It will mean the unspeakable by clearly displaying the speakable.
4.116 Everything that can be thought at all can be thought clearly.
      Everything that can be said can be said clearly.

Here the notion of 'limit' is exactly the one which is in play, for example, in the discussion of solipsism, and which is there said to be unstatable. So although 4.112 advocates the replacement of the idea of philosophy as a theory, with that of philosophy as an activity, and declares that philosophy is not concerned to produce 'philosophical propositions' — nevertheless, 4.112 seems itself to be a sequence of philosophical propositions, and the activity which is recommended there seems to be an activity undertaken for a reason, and the reason itself looks as if it is bound to be something which is statable in a philosophical proposition. 4.112 needs to be considered alongside what look like the most obviously paradoxical sections of the *Tractatus*.

Before addressing the issue of the apparent paradoxicality of the book, however, it seems appropriate to give a brief recapitulation of its principal philosophical achievements. In the Preface Wittgenstein writes:

On the other hand the *truth* of the thoughts communicated here seems to me unassailable and definitive. I am, therefore, of the opinion that the problems have in essentials finally been solved.

(29)

The 'problems' here are those described as 'the problems of philosophy' on the page before. When Wittgenstein claims that they have 'finally' been solved, he is claiming to have put an end to an ancient tradition. What ancient problems has Wittgenstein solved here, if we take him at his own word? If we take him at his word, he has solved the question of solipsism, idealism, and realism: solipsism is, in a sense, correct, but cannot be said. He has solved the problems which motivated Kant to introduce the category of synthetic *a priori* truths: what such truths would attempt to state cannot, in fact, be said. He has solved the problem of ethics, and the status of ethics: he recommends a particular, aesthetic ethical view, while insisting that nothing ethical can be said. He has undermined scepticism, showing that it attempts to raise questions that cannot be raised, because their answers cannot be stated. He has undermined all attempts to say something about the meaning of life: no such thing can be said. And, of course, he has, he thinks, explained the relation between thought, language and the world, and dealt with the status of logic and of modality; though, again, none of this can strictly be said. The *Tractatus* is a short work: this is an impressive range of problems to have tackled in it. The solution to the problem is in each case the same: the solution of the problem is seen in the vanishing of the problem (see 6.521).

There is one puzzle that remains in the 6.5s — the reappearance there of mysticism in the discussion of philosophy:

6.522 There is indeed the inexpressible. This *shows* itself; it is the mystical.

The puzzle is this: is mysticism in the same boat as philosophy — is mysticism nonsense too? It has often been assumed that it is, that the rejection of philosophy also includes a rejection of mysticism.[10] But our consideration of ethics in the last section makes this look wrong. It seems very clear that Wittgenstein is there *recommending* the adoption of a mystical attitude, the attitude which he described in the *Notebooks* as aesthetic or artistic.[11] And in fact the wording of 6.522 makes most sense if we suppose that mysticism is here distinguished from philosophy. The difficulty with philosophy is that it attempts to say what cannot be said. But this is not what mysticism does: its attention is directed to *that* the world is (6.44), that there is anything at all, not to *how* the world is (which is what can be said). It does not attempt to *say* anything: it is a *view* ('Anschauung', 6.45) of the world, a way of *feeling* the world ('Gefuhl', 6.45). The sequence of thought from 6.5 might be put like this. Philosophy attempts to raise questions which are not real questions (6.5). Scepticism (a kind of panic at the absence of an answer) attempts to raise a question which cannot be raised (6.51). Philosophy attempts to answer the questions which remain once science is settled; but there are no such questions, and hence there is no place for philosophy (6.52). But this does not mean that, as it were, there is nothing there ('There is *indeed* the inexpressible', 6.522; my italics), but whatever it is cannot be said: 'This *shows* itself' (6.522). Seen in this light, mysticism looks as if it is the attitude that should be adopted *in place* of philosophy, once we have seen that philosophy, with its ambition to say things that cannot be said, cannot be done.[12]

7E THE PARADOX OF THE *TRACTATUS*

One of the central difficulties in understanding the *Tractatus* is raised by this remark:

> My propositions are elucidatory in this way: he who understands me finally recognizes them as senseless [*unsinnig*: nonsense], when he has climbed out through them, on them, over them.

(6.54)

We need first to be clear about the nature of the paradox which this involves. It seems that if (the bulk, at least, of) the *Tractatus* is true, then it is nonsense. But if it is nonsense, it cannot be true. So if (the bulk, at least, of) the

Tractatus is true, it is not true. Conversely, it seems that (the bulk, at least, of) the *Tractatus* is only nonsense in the way it claims (or seems to claim) that it is, if it is true: it is only the particular philosophy of language of the *Tractatus* which leads us to think that Wittgenstein must have 'given no meaning to certain signs in his propositions' (6.53). That is to say, if it is not true in the way it seems to claim that it is not true, then it is true.

This is a serious problem, but on its own it would not obviously be a problem of *interpretation*. It is worth comparing the *Tractatus* with Hume's first *Enquiry* or Carnap's 'Elimination of Metaphysics' on this point. Hume and Carnap both present positions which are paradoxical in ways which are quite similar to that in which the *Tractatus* is paradoxical, but their presentations have a certain innocence about them: they seem not to be aware of the paradox. But there is no such innocence about the *Tractatus*: 6.54 shows very clearly that Wittgenstein knew that (the bulk, at least, of) the *Tractatus* was self-refuting. And that is our problem: if he knew that, what did he think he was up to in writing the work? It is hard to see how he can have thought he was engaged in anything other than a silly game, unless he thought he had some way of avoiding the paradox which I have just described. What could that way have been?

Two responses to this question are widespread in the literature.[13] The first, which I shall call the *Ineffable-Truths View*, is the more traditional.[14] According to this view, although Wittgenstein recognized that the *statement* of anything philosophical was impossible, he nevertheless thought that there were philosophical *truths*, and that these truths could somehow be communicated without being stated. These truths would be unstatable or ineffable, because any attempt to state them would be nonsense. The Ineffable-Truths View, as such, need have no particular view about the mechanism by which these ineffable truths are somehow communicated, although two particular ideas on this are often associated with the Ineffable-Truths View by its opponents. One is that Wittgenstein uses the contrast between *saying* and *showing* in a simple way to indicate how he thinks that the ineffable can be appreciated: ordinary empirical truths, on this view, are *said*, whereas the ineffable truths of philosophy can only be *shown*. The other view of the mechanism by which ineffable truths might be communicated which is often attributed to the Ineffable-Truths View is this: ineffable truths are communicated by nonsensical combinations of words; these nonsensical combinations represent impossible combinations of things; we see the truth of the ineffable truths when we see that the represented combinations are indeed impossible.[15]

We should be clear that neither of these suggestions is essential to the Ineffable-Truths View. It is certainly clear that the contrast between *saying* and *showing* was important to Wittgenstein. Indeed, he suggests to Russell that it is the key to the whole work:

> Now I'm afraid you haven't really got hold of my main contention, to which the whole business of logical prop[osition]s is only a corollary. The main point is the theory of what can be expressed by prop[osition]s – *i.e.* by language – (and, which comes to the same, what can be *thought*) and what cannot be expressed by prop[osition]s, but only shown: which, I believe, is the cardinal problem of philosophy.
>
> (CL: 124)

But this does not mean that what can only be shown is a kind of *truth*. And in the *Tractatus*, Wittgenstein seems generally to restrict his use of the notion of *showing* to things (so to speak) which are not ordinarily thought of as truths at all: for example, the logical relations between sentences, and the form of the world. There is just one unambiguous case where what is said to be shown is also taken to be a truth — the famous claim about solipsism:

> In fact what solipsism *means*, is quite correct, only it cannot be *said*, but shows itself.
>
> (5.62)

And this forms part of an argument which, it seems to me, is eccentric in the context of the *Tractatus* in a number of ways (for example, in involving a particular kind of epistemic consideration, if the suggestion of section 6E of the previous chapter was right). No doubt those who hold the Ineffable-Truths View will think that *showing* plays *some* kind of role in the communication of the ineffable truths which they take Wittgenstein to believe in, but they need not think that it is simply that these ineffable truths are *shown*.

Again, there is no reason why the Ineffable-Truths View need attribute to Wittgenstein a view of nonsense which he clearly denied. It can accept that for Wittgenstein there is no such thing as nonsense which is nonsense through being an illegitimate combination of meaningful words; that for him the only kind of nonsense is nonsense whose nonsensicality is due to one or more signs not being given meaning. (5.4733). The Ineffable-Truths View need not think that the supposed ineffable truths are communicated by means of nonsensical combinations of meaningful words which are used to represent impossible combinations of objects. The Ineffable-Truths View can perfectly easily hold that the apparent sentences of the *Tractatus* are themselves nonsense — plain nonsense — and for the reason which the *Tractatus* itself seems to require them to be in 6.53.

For all that, the Ineffable-Truths View is problematic, because it seems that the very idea of ineffable truths runs counter to the point of much of what Wittgenstein wants to say about philosophy. Those who think Wittgenstein believes in ineffable truths will be inclined to compare what Wittgenstein does in the *Tractatus* with Frege's treatment of his difficulty with the concept *horse*, which we looked at in Chapter 2.[16] The difficulty was that the following sentence cannot be true, if taken literally:

(F) The concept *horse* is not an object.

For if the phrase 'the concept *horse*' is meaningful at all, it functions as a singular term, and hence as an expression which refers to an *object*, not a concept, since concepts, in

Frege's sense, are essentially predicative. Frege says of such cases:

> By a kind of necessity of language, my expressions, taken literally, sometimes miss my thought; I mention an object, when what I intend is a concept. I fully realize that in such cases I was relying on a reader who would be ready to meet me half-way — who does not begrudge a pinch of salt.
>
> (Frege 1892b: 204)

The whole character of this remark — rather weakly pleading for a reader's indulgence — strikes me as wholly unlike anything in Wittgenstein. And that difference in character corresponds to a difference in view, I think: where Frege seems to try to sit on the fence, Wittgenstein is quite clear that philosophy simply cannot be stated. Appealing to ineffable truths is a fudge, and Wittgenstein is not inclined to fudge.

More importantly, Wittgenstein's treatment of philosophy requires him precisely to reject the idea of ineffable truths. The key text here is a remark we looked at in the previous section:[17]

> For doubt can only exist where there is a question; a question only where there is an answer, and this only where something can be *said*.
>
> (6.51)

An ineffable truth would be an answer which cannot be said; the existence of such an answer would mean that, after all, there was a question to which it was the answer. And if there were a question to which an ineffable truth was the answer, then Wittgenstein would not be able to say this:

> The solution of the problem of life is seen in the vanishing of this problem.
>
> (6.521)

Given this clear rejection of the idea of ineffable truths, we can hardly save Wittgenstein from paradox by adopting the Ineffable-Truths View.

A quite different way of avoiding the paradox is offered to Wittgenstein by a more recent tradition of scholarship, sometimes described as presenting a 'new Wittgenstein', and sometimes as offering a 'resolute' reading of the text.[18] Those who offer this kind of interpretation are often concerned to make certain connections with Wittgenstein's later work, but for our present purposes we can describe the core of their treatment of the paradox as embracing a *Not-All-Nonsense View*. Whereas the Ineffable-Truths View has Wittgenstein avoid the paradox by giving him a resting-place *above* the text, as it were, in a land of truths which cannot be stated, the Not-All-Nonsense View gives him a resting-place in a part of the text itself. The idea will be that some of the text — sometimes called the 'frame' — is (held by Wittgenstein to be) meaningful and true, and this part comments on the rest, which is simply nonsense. It will be claimed that all of the substantive philosophy of the work — what seems to be a metaphysics, a theory of language, a treatment of solipsism and the rest — all this is just nonsense. The only parts which are meaningful will be those which say just that (together, perhaps, with a few scattered remarks which might not be offensive).

There are two basic problems with this view. The first is that the claim that all philosophy is nonsense, or must be nonsense, is itself a philosophical — indeed, a metaphysical — claim. It is a claim which is general (*all* philosophy) and modal (*must* be nonsense); it is a claim about how the world must be. This is not just a remark about any particular scholar who might be inclined to dismiss philosophy: it relates to 6.53 itself, as we observed in the previous section. 6.53 tells us what *would* — that is, inevitably — be the only correct method in philosophy. It says what we should *always* do, when someone wants to say something philosophical. This means that the part of the text which is supposed to be part of the 'frame' — the part which is meaningful, and meaningfully tells us that the rest is nonsense — is itself as much nonsense as the rest of the text. The text is *all* nonsense, if any of it is, so the Not-All-Nonsense View must be wrong.

The second problem for the Not-All-Nonsense View is that the claim that much of the text is nonsense becomes quite unmotivated, if we detach it from the substantive philosophy which the text appears to contain. It is either disingenuous or naïve to claim that sentences which seem perfectly meaningful can be shown to be nonsense in any way other than on the basis of some substantial metaphysical view — some view of how things must be. We have just seen that. It then seems odd, to say the least, to suppose that the substantial metaphysical view which does the work here might be any view other than that which appears in the text of the *Tractatus*. And, in fact, as we have seen, the detail of the claim that attempting to say something philosophical leads us into nonsense seems to require the very particular theory of language which we find in the *Tractatus*. It is only if we accept the common-form assumption which lies at the heart of the *Tractatus*'s conception of language that we have any reason to suppose that trying to say something philosophical will go astray for the very particular reason that the person making the attempt will have 'given no meaning to certain signs in his propositions'. So it seems that the Not-All-Nonsense View requires that part of the text which it claims to be simply nonsense to have sense after all.

These problems also infect any attempt to read earlier passages in the *Tractatus* which seem to stand back and comment generally on the nature of philosophy. The most striking of these is 4.112, which we looked at briefly in the previous section. Again, the claims made here are general — it is not just a *kind* of philosophy which is under consideration — and *modal* (for example: 'A philosophical work consists *essentially* of elucidations'). And their motivation clearly comes from the general theory of the *Tractatus* itself (as the following sequence of remarks, 4.113–4.116, clearly shows). 4.112 cannot be kept clear of being nonsense any more than the final remarks of the whole book can.

If neither the Ineffable-Truths View nor the Not-All-Nonsense View can provide a satisfactory account of how Wittgenstein might have thought he avoided the paradox of the *Tractatus*, is there anything else we can suggest? There is another option, which appears when we notice an assumption which is common to both of the views we have just considered. Both of these views try to find a way in which Wittgenstein can avoid paradox *while still communicating some truth about philosophy*. That is to say, both views share this assumption:

(T) The purpose of the *Tractatus* is to communicate truths.

With (T) in place, it is very hard to see any way of allowing Wittgenstein to avoid the paradox of the *Tractatus* other than those suggested by the Ineffable-Truths View and the Not-All-Nonsense View. But might there be another option if we reject (T)? I think there might.[19] I will call a view which rejects (T) a *No-Truths-At-All View*.

It is natural to attribute to Wittgenstein the following thought:

(P) The right philosophical theory entails that any attempt to say something philosophical results in nonsense.

(P) is naturally attributed to Wittgenstein on the basis of 6.53: thus far the attribution seems unproblematic. (P) is not only naturally attributable to Wittgenstein: it seems central to the *Tractatus*. So it looks as if we can say the following:

(TP) If the purpose of the *Tractatus* is to communicate any truths, its business is to communicate the truth of (P) in particular.

(P), of course, is paradoxical: if it is true, then, as an attempt to say something philosophical itself, it must be nonsense, which means that it cannot be true. If (P) is paradoxical, and (TP) is true, then it seems that if the purpose of the *Tractatus* is to communicate truths, as (T) claims, that purpose is bound to be frustrated: there is no real truth here to be communicated, because the key apparent truths undermine themselves. Now it is natural to think, on the basis of 6.54, that Wittgenstein was aware of that; that is to say, that he accepted this:

(PP) (P) is paradoxical.

And being aware of that, and of (TP), he must have been aware that if the purpose of the *Tractatus* were to communicate truths (as (T) claims), that purpose would be bound to be frustrated. So it is natural to think that in carrying on with the publication of the *Tractatus*, despite realizing all this, he cannot have been meaning to communicate any truths in the work: that is, it is natural to think that (T) must be false.

If we are to make this really credible, there are two things we need to make sense of. First, if (T) is false, and the *Tractatus* was published for some purpose, there needs to be some purpose which it is plausible to attribute to Wittgenstein, and which does not depend on any truths being communicated in the work. And, second, if he goes ahead with the *Tractatus* for this other purpose, as a result of accepting, in some sense, both (P) and (PP), there needs to *be* some sense in which he can be said to accept both (P) and (PP), even if — as he must, in the same sense, accept — there is no real truth here to be accepted. And, of course, if there is some sense in which (P) is accepted, there must also be some sense in which it is accepted that a certain philosophical theory is *right*, and consequently some way in which it can be counted right (by someone who, in that sense, accepts it), even though — according to the very theory which is here, as it were, accepted — there is no real truth here at all.

Let us address this second issue first: given (P), how can we make sense of there being a certain philosophical theory which is, in some sense, right — and how can we make sense of someone, as it were, *accepting* it, even though he knows (as it were) that it cannot really be true? On this latter point, first, it is important to be clear that, if the general account I have been offering so far is anything like right, Wittgenstein is not unambiguously committed to the view that the (apparent) sentences of the *Tractatus* are nonsense. This is because his reason for thinking that they are nonsense is that some of them, at least, are true. So he does not think they are nonsense any more than he thinks they are true — although, of course, it is also the case that he does not think they are true any more than he thinks they are nonsense. The position seems best described by saying that, for Wittgenstein, the (apparent) sentences of the *Tractatus* are in an unstable position, which we can characterize as that of being both nonsense and true, or else as successively (and endlessly) nonsense and true. This does not stop them being plain nonsense, insofar as they are nonsense. Nor does it make their truth — insofar as they are true — ineffable. Rather, they are both (or successively) plain nonsense and stably true.

It follows from this that whatever 'accepting' the (apparent) sentences of the *Tractatus* amounts to, it cannot be unambiguously *either* the kind of accepting in which one accepts something one understands *or* a mere psychological appearance of acceptance, which is the state of someone who seems to accept something which is, in fact, nonsense. 'Accepting' the (apparent) sentences of the *Tractatus* has to be an ambivalent kind of state, which we cannot resolve into anything more familiar. And the same will go for the 'acceptance' of (P), or of (PP), and all the rest.

What we need now to do, then, is explain the sense in which Wittgenstein might be thought to hold that the *Tractatus* was, somehow, *right*, even though it is (also) nonsense. The issue can be given a sharp focus by asking this question: why is the fact that if the *Tractatus* is true, it is nonsense, and so not true, not a *reductio* of the *Tractatus*? Why does this not just show that the *Tractatus* is *false*? For the following reason, on Wittgenstein's view, I think. If the *Tractatus* were *false*, then there would be some other philosophical theory — something which entailed the negation of some central claim of the *Tractatus* — which would be *true*. But it seems clear that Wittgenstein thinks that no other theory could be true.

This is not yet enough, however. So far, we seem simply to have a stand-off between the *Tractatus* and each supposed rival. This will, no doubt, end up being paradoxical in itself: if every philosophical theory is *false*, that will apply equally to the philosophical view that each (and every) philosophical theory is false. But we still have no reason to prefer the *Tractatus* to any of the supposed rivals. If all of these theories are either false, or meaningless, how can any of them be any better or worse than any other? I suggest that there is a simple reason why Wittgenstein preferred the *Tractatus* to any possible rival. The suggestion is that Wittgenstein thought that every rival was already obviously wrong, even before its application to itself was considered. The distinctive thing about the *Tractatus*, then — on Wittgenstein's view — is that the following is true of it, and it alone: it is only when it is applied to itself that it becomes problematic. If Wittgenstein thought this, we can understand why he might have made the famous claim of the Preface:

> On the other hand the *truth* of the thoughts communicated here seems to me unassailable and definitive.
>
> (*TLP*, p. 29)

It is unassailable and definitive *until* it is applied to itself, something which, on Wittgenstein's view, can be said of no other theory.

The next task is to explain what purpose Wittgenstein might have had in writing and publishing the *Tractatus* — a purpose whose achievement does not depend on any truths being communicated in it. In a well-known letter to the publisher, Ludwig von Ficker, Wittgenstein wrote:

> [T]he book's point is ethical. I once meant to include in the preface a sentence which is not in fact there now, but which I will write out for you here, because it will be a key for you. What I meant to write then was this: my work consists of two parts: the one presented here plus all I have *not* written. And it is precisely this second part that is the important one. For the ethical gets its limit drawn from the inside, as

it were, by my book; and I am convinced that this is the ONLY *rigorous* way of drawing that limit. In short, I believe that where *many* others today are just *gassing*, I have managed in my book to put everything firmly into place by being silent about it.

(WSP: 94–95)

If the point of the book is ethical, our consideration of the ethics of the *Tractatus*, in section 7C above, allows us to understand something of what Wittgenstein might have had in mind. It seems clear that he thinks that what ethics requires is the adoption of a mystical or artistic outlook on the world, an outlook which sees the world 'together with the whole logical space' (*NB*: 83). This suggests that the penultimate remark of the book expresses what Wittgenstein hopes for:

He must surmount these propositions: then he will see the world rightly.

(6.54)

'Seeing the world rightly' would, then, be viewing the world as the mystic views it, 'as a limited whole' (6.45).

But if Wittgenstein is not aiming to communicate truths in the *Tractatus* — because there are none to be communicated — there is an important restriction on the way in which the purpose of getting the reader to adopt the mystical attitude can be achieved. It cannot be achieved by the reader first *recognizing* the truth of the *Tractatus*, and then deciding to adopt a mystical outlook *for that reason*. For this way of becoming a mystic depends on there being truths to be communicated. And, of course, Wittgenstein does not describe the way in which the *Tractatus* is supposed to work as being like this. Here is the whole of 6.54:

6.54 My propositions are elucidatory in this way: he who understands me finally recognizes them as senseless, when he has climbed out through them, on them, over them. (He must so to speak throw away the ladder, after he has climbed up on it.)
He must surmount these propositions; then he sees the world rightly.

What process does Wittgenstein have in mind here?

I suggest it is something which can be most simply explained by recalling again Frege's situation with the concept *horse*. I characterized the problem as arising over this sentence:

(F) The concept *horse* is not an object.

We can (try to) put the point which (F) tries to capture like this. Fregean concepts, as the referents of predicates, are essentially predicative, whereas Fregean objects, as the referents of singular terms, are essentially *non*-predicative. We suppose that the phrase 'the concept *horse*' describes the predicative concept which is the referent of the predicate '*x* is a horse'. What (F) tries to say is that this predicative concept is not anything *non*-predicative. That ought to be simply and obviously true. Unfortunately, as we have seen, the phrase 'the concept *horse*' functions as a singular term (for Frege, at least). But that means that if it means anything at all, its referent must be an object, rather than anything essentially predicative. So we cannot get (F) to say what we want it to say.

Now suppose that we accept this point: (F) is either meaningless or false. But we still have an idea of what we are trying to express in (F). We have not lost our sense of the contrast between the predicative and the non-predicative. What happens is that the effort to make sense of (F) leaves us with our sense of that contrast intact — indeed, perhaps, reinforced — even though it is not something which could be stated, or about which there could, in principle, be any truths. It is, as it were, as if the attempt to express the difference between the different kinds of referents of words has been wiped away, and we are left simply with the referents themselves, simply being different. I suggest that it is some such process as this which Wittgenstein has in mind in his description of climbing 'out through [the sentences of the *Tractatus*], on them, over them'.

If this is how Wittgenstein hopes the *Tractatus* will work, then we can understand how he might have thought he could achieve the purpose of getting his readers to adopt a mystical outlook without accepting the *Tractatus* as true. The idea will be that working through the *Tractatus* will itself give us a sense of the shape of things — of the form of reality — and that this will remain once the attempt to express it in sentences has been wiped out. In this way it might be hoped that the *Tractatus* works directly to give us that sense of the form of reality, without requiring us actually to believe that it is true.

It seems to me that this provides us with a genuine alternative to the Ineffable-Truths View and the Not-All-Nonsense View, and it certainly seems to chime with some of the spirit of the text. In particular, it allows us to give due poetic weight to the closing sentence of the book:

7   Whereof one cannot speak, thereof one must be silent.[20]

The aim here is clearly not to convey some truth (as the Ineffable-Truths View holds); nor can it be simply to dismiss philosophy (as the Not-All-Nonsense View thinks). The cadence of the line and its position in the text both show it to have another purpose entirely: to carry one forward (in a sense) beyond the kinds of concerns with which the book has been occupied.

There are two things, however, which might make one pause to embrace the No-Truths-At-All View as an interpretation. The first is the Preface — and in particular a remark we have looked at already:

> On the other hand the *truth* of the thoughts communicated here seems to me unassailable and definitive.
>
> (*TLP*, p. 29)

We have seen how Wittgenstein might prefer the *Tractatus* to any other philosophy, but can we really make sense of him writing that, if he held — as is now being suggested — that no truths at all were communicated in the *Tractatus*? In fact, the Preface is problematic for any interpretation. The previous paragraph begins as follows:

> If this work has a value it consists in two things. First that in it thoughts are expressed ...
>
> (*TLP*, p. 29)

And the Ineffable-Truths View, like the view I am now suggesting, holds that, according to Wittgenstein, nothing at all is really expressed in the *Tractatus*. Nor can the Not-All-Nonsense View regard the Preface as part of an unparadoxical 'frame'. Consider this paragraph for example:

> The book will, therefore, draw a limit to thinking, or rather — not to thinking, but to the expression of thoughts; for, in order to draw a limit to thinking we should have to be able to think both sides of this limit (we should therefore have to be able to think what cannot be thought).
>
> (*TLP*, p. 28)

Wittgenstein here uses a phrase 'draw a limit to thinking', which he then corrects, as being paradoxical. But the correction has a peculiar status: it is not as if he simply erases the paradoxical phrase in the text, leaving us only with an unparadoxical formulation. Rather, he leaves the paradoxical formulation there, and, further, elaborately explains its paradoxicality. So the phrase is left, when it cannot, it seems, really say anything; and the explanation of the phrase's paradoxicality seems inevitably to face the same paradox — requiring us to try to think what cannot be thought. So the whole paragraph is paradoxical in its own terms.

What this means is that we have to be a bit less innocent in our consideration of the Preface, whatever interpretation we choose. The Preface is itself part of the text, and no less paradoxical than the rest of it. The fact that it contradicts — or seems to contradict — something which seems to be said in the text does not set it apart from many other parts of the text. The point of the Preface is not to be something outside the text which can tell us how to read the text (*pace* Diamond (1991)), but to be a part of the text which indicates the point of the whole, as well as anticipating some of the problems which will be elaborated more fully in the rest.

The other difficulty with accepting the No-Truths-At-All View is in making sense of Wittgenstein's treatment of philosophical problems on his return to the subject, in the face of questioning by Frank Ramsey, and later. In the period after he returned to philosophy, and before he changed his approach to philosophy quite radically, he still seems to have taken philosophical problems seriously, and to have argued over philosophical points with as much earnestness and concern for rigour as any analytic philosopher.[21] Surely, he should just have abstained from philosophy altogether? How can we make sense of this?

In part, we can respond by saying that the core of the interpretation being suggested here is that Wittgenstein thinks that the philosophy of the *Tractatus* is better than any other. He still needs to think this if he is to be able to conclude, on the basis of the philosophy of the *Tractatus*, that any attempt to say something philosophical must result in nonsense. So he maintains a simple interest in getting the philosophy right — in the sense of removing from it any faults other than the paradoxes which arise when it is applied to itself. But this hardly seems to capture the tone of the discussions of this intervening period. It may be that the best that can be said is that some of the heat of the fire with which the *Tractatus* was composed, in the immediate context of serving on the front of the First World War, had cooled by the late 1920s.

On the other hand, we can adduce some historical evidence which might be thought to support the suggestion that Wittgenstein was trying to get us to adopt a non-philosophical, mystical outlook. Rudolf Carnap was present at the early meetings of Wittgenstein with the then new 'Vienna Circle', and recalled:

> His point of view and his attitude toward people and problems, even theoretical problems, were much more similar to those of a creative artist than to those of a scientist; one might almost say, similar to those of a religious prophet or a seer.[22]

And in his own 'Elimination of Metaphysics' he describes metaphysics as attempting, in a muddled way, to do what it is the business of art to do. The point of metaphysics, according to Carnap, is to express 'the general attitude of a person towards life ('Lebenseinstellung, Lebensgefühl')'. He holds that 'metaphysics is a substitute, albeit an inadequate one, for art', whose concern properly is to express this 'basic attitude' to life (Carnap 1956: 78–80). It is natural to see Carnap here offering us a project which, on seeing Wittgenstein, he took Wittgenstein to be engaged in.

There is, perhaps, no completely satisfactory treatment of the paradox of the *Tractatus*. The Ineffable-Truths View and the Not-All-Nonsense View seem clearly to be unacceptable. The present alternative, the No-Truths-At-All View, seems to make sense (after a fashion) of more of the work than these, but is still not easy to accept as an interpretation.[23]

This does not, however, diminish the value of the work as a whole. When we cease being just interpreters, and consider what can be learned from the *Tractatus* for our own philosophy, we still have two ways of responding to it. We can treat it, if we have the stomach to, in the way which the No-Truths-At-All View encourages us to: we can read the work as a device to work us into a mystical view of the world. Or we can treat the paradox as providing a *reductio* of the philosophy at its core. This latter option is the one which I would prefer, philosophically, but it is no easy option. The theory of the *Tractatus* provides us with two things which most philosophers would like to have. First, it provides us with an account of the relation between language and the world which explains how it is possible for words to be correlated with items in the world. And second, it explains how there can be some necessity and possibility in the world, which we can know about, without there being any such thing as a synthetic *a priori* truth. It is no simple matter providing another way of securing these desirable things, without lapsing into paradox at some other point.

Appendix
The substance argument

Wittgenstein's argument for the existence of substance — the necessarily existent objects which are common to every possible world — is contained in these sections:

2.02   The object is simple.
2.0201   Every statement about complexes can be analysed into a statement about their constituent parts, and into those propositions which completely describe the complexes.
2.021   Objects form the substance of the world. Therefore they cannot be compound.
2.0211   If the world had no substance, then whether a proposition had sense would depend on whether another proposition was true.
2.0212   It would then be impossible to form a picture of the world (true or false).

The real core of the argument is contained in the last two sections here.

Interpretations differ as a result of their different views of what Wittgenstein has in mind when he says 'whether a proposition had sense would depend on whether another proposition was true'. What other proposition is he thinking of?

According to a broad tradition of interpretations, the other proposition is tantamount to the proposition that the complex, which a statement is apparently about, exists. For the complex to exist will be for its constituent parts to be arranged in a certain way. For example (the example is Wittgenstein's own, from the *Philosophical Investigations* I: §60), for a broom to exist is for a certain brush and a certain broomstick to be arranged in a certain way. From this point we can distinguish between two distinct interpretations.

The first interpretation takes the argument to be concerned primarily to argue that there must be an end to analysis: call this, then, the *end-to-analysis* interpretation. The point of the argument is taken to be to support 2.02, in the light of 2.0201: it is the simplicity, in the sense of further non-analysability, of objects which is crucial. Fogelin elaborates the argument as follows:

> If analysis always generates names that are in their turn names of complexes, then the criterion of sense laid down in 2.0201 would forever remain unsatisfied.
>
> (Fogelin 1987: 14)

The argument here seems to depend on a number of quite general assumptions about language. The first is this:

> (N1) Every language must contain either names, or at least the possibility of names.

The cautious qualification is inserted here to allow for the possibility of a language none of whose existing expressions were names, but which contained quantifiers and variables. Such a language would at least need it to be possible for there to be names which might replace the variables of quantification. (This, I think, is the point of 3.23–3.24: see Chapter 4, section 4E.)

The significance of (N1) is given by a conception of names:

> (N2) If there is no object to which a name refers, then sentences which include that name have no sense.

(N2) expresses a natural conception of names, and one which it is plausible to find both in Wittgenstein and in his philosophical predecessors, Frege and Russell (see Chapters 2 and 4).[1] If there are no simple objects, then the only names a language could contain will be names of complexes. How will we deal with a sentence containing a name of a complex? 2.0201 may be thought to suggest the following view:

(N3) A sentence containing a name of a complex can be analysed as being equivalent in meaning to some sentence in which the only things named are the component parts of the complex.

(N1)–(N3) exhaust the general assumptions about language which the end-of-analysis view can naturally appeal to in its interpretation. Unfortunately, it is difficult to use them to construct a credible argument for the conclusion that there must be simple objects.

It might reasonably be thought that (N1) and (N2) together require something like this:

(EA1) If there are no objects to which the (possible) names of a language refer, then no sentence in that language has any sense.

And reflection on (N3) might suggest the following:

(EA2) If there are no simple objects, then there can only be objects to which the (possible) names of a language refer if every sentence containing a name can be given an infinite analysis.

But to get from these premises to something like the conclusion Wittgenstein needs, we clearly need the following further premise:

(EA3) No sentence can be given an infinite analysis.

But the idea that a sentence 'can be given an infinite analysis' is ambiguous. It might mean either of these two things:

(i) For each stage of analysis, there is a further stage of analysis which can, in principle, be provided;
(ii) It is possible to complete an infinite series of analyses.

It is only on interpretation (ii) that (EA3) is at all obvious. But (EA2) is only plausible on the less demanding interpretation (i).

This means that the argument offered to Wittgenstein by the end-to-analysis interpretation looks fallacious. And there are other reasons for questioning it as an interpretation. First, it is unclear whether anyone who thought that there were no simple objects need accept (N3): the idea of this kind of analysis seems designed precisely to ensure that the only things named are simple objects. Second, the end-to-analysis interpretation gives a strange over-reading of 'whether a proposition had sense would depend on whether another proposition was true'. It takes it to mean: whether a proposition had sense would depend on whether *an infinite number* of other propositions were true. Third, it leaves unexplained the introduction of the idea of a *picture* in 2.0212: why did Wittgenstein not just say that that would make it impossible for any sentence to have sense? And, fourth, it misunderstands the whole direction of the passage. It takes the point of the passage to be concerned with analysis, on the basis of the fact that analysis is mentioned in 2.0201. But the argument clearly does not run on the notion of analysis, but on the notion of substance: 2.021 explicitly says that it is because objects form the substance of the world that they cannot be compound. 2.0201 is most naturally understood as explaining how 2.02 can be true, despite the fact that most of the expressions in our ordinary languages which look like names are not names for simple objects.

The end-to-analysis interpretation begins from the idea that the 'other proposition', whose truth is required for an original proposition P to have sense, in effect states that the complex which P is about exists. But it is not the only interpretation which begins from that starting-point. Another is offered by Ian Proops (2004): we might call it the *plenitude-of-truth-value* interpretation. On this interpretation, the core of Wittgenstein's argument is something like this:

(PT1) If it can be *true* that an object exists, it is contingent that it exists;

(PT2) If it is contingent that an object exists, there is a possible world in which it does not exist;

(PT3) Any sentence which contains a name of an object will have no truth-value in any possible world in which that object does not exist;

(PT4) No sentence can fail to have a truth-value in any possible world; *so*

(PT5) No sentence can contain the name of an object which can truly be said to exist.

If we accept (N1), as before, this argument will show that a language's having sense at all requires some objects to exist necessarily. Necessarily existent objects will have to be simple: to describe them as compound is precisely to imagine the possibility of their not existing (in virtue of their elements not having been combined). So the argument shows that there must be simple objects. Like the end-to-analysis interpretation, the argument offered here rests on (N2): it is (N2) which is supposed to underlie (PT3).

This argument has the virtue that it makes the simplicity of objects depend upon their constituting the substance of the world, on a natural interpretation of Wittgenstein's notion of substance (what remains constant across all possible variations). But it is not without difficulties of its own. One is that there is no obvious reason to accept (PT3). Consider Billy the bookcase, which only exists in worlds in which its parts are assembled. In one possible world — world W — Billy's parts are not assembled, so Billy does not exist. Some sentences containing the name 'Billy' seem to have a truth-value quite unproblematically in W: 'Billy exists', for example, looks unproblematically false in W, and 'Billy does not exist' unproblematically true. And other sentences may be assigned truth-values either naturally or arbitrarily: 'Billy is two metres tall', for example, we might count false in W (since it has not been assembled in W), whereas 'Billy is a bookcase' might be counted true in W (since Billy is a non-existent *bookcase* in W, rather than, for example, a non-existent horse-race).

The problem here looks as if it derives from a confusion between the world at which the interpretation of a sentence is fixed and the world with respect to which the truth-value of that sentence, on that interpretation, is decided.[2] As we naturally understand the issues here, we are considering a sentence such as 'Billy exists' on the interpretation of it which is given in the actual world — where Billy exists to be named, and has been assembled — but we are considering whether that sentence, on that interpretation, is true in some other world (such as W). On this understanding, 'Billy exists' is true in the actual world (which is how it has sense, given (N2)), but false, on that interpretation, in W. But (PT3) is only plausible on the unnatural reading, which takes the world at which the interpretation is fixed to be the world in which the object does not exist. And on this reading (PT4) is implausible: it is easy for a sentence to fail to have a truth-value in a particular world, if it fails to have a truth-value in that world by failing to have an interpretation in that world.

So, once again, this interpretation gives Wittgenstein a weak argument. And there are further reasons for being sceptical about its plausibility as an interpretation. One is that, although it does make the simplicity of objects depend on the thought that objects form the substance of the world, as 2.021 says, it seems not to take account of Wittgenstein's reason for thinking that substance is important. What matters for Wittgenstein about the notion of substance is contained in the next remark:

2.022   It is clear that however different from the real [i.e., the actual] world an imagined world may be, it must have something — a form — in common with the real world.

And the connection with objects is established in the remark after that:

2.023   This fixed form consists of the objects.

The notion of form does not enter into the reasoning presented by the plenitude-of-truth-value interpretation at all;

so it is hard to see how it can be regarded as doing justice to Wittgenstein's concerns. Moreover, as in the case of the end-to-analysis interpretation, this interpretation can find no clear reason why Wittgenstein should have expressed his point in 2.0212 in terms of the notion of a 'picture': he might just as well have said just that it would then be impossible for any proposition to have sense.

A striking alternative approach has recently been suggested by Jose Zalabardo (Unpublished). I'll call it the *Russellian-form* interpretation. This reading is inspired by the following remark from the *Notebooks* about Russell's conception of form (I touched on this remark myself in Chapter 1, section 1D, in my account of the argument for the claim I there call (FO)):

> I thought that the possibility of the truth of the proposition φa was tied up with the fact $(\exists x, \varphi). \varphi x$. But it is impossible to see why φa should only be possible if there is another proposition of the same form. φa surely does not need any precedent. (For suppose that there existed only the two elementary propositions 'φa' and 'ψa' and that 'φa' were false: Why should this proposition only make sense if 'ψa' is true?)
>
> (*NB*: 17)

The point here is particularly directed to Russell, who thought that the general form of sentences involving a one-place predicate was given by the sentence '$(\exists x, \varphi). \varphi x$' (Russell 1984: 129).[3] Sentences involving a one-place predicate have sense because that sentence, '$(\exists x, \varphi). \varphi x$', is true. Wittgenstein seems to have thought this was absurd for the following reason: the sentence '$(\exists x, \varphi). \varphi x$' can only be true in virtue of some particular sentence, say 'φa', being true. So a sentence such as 'φa' only has sense because some sentence of that form — either 'φa' itself, or a different one, such as 'ψa' — is true. As we have seen, Wittgenstein thought that this showed that it was wrong to regard the form of a sentence as itself another sentence: rather it had to be something which was 'already … given by the forms of its component parts' (*NB*: 23). And this means, in effect, that the form of the world must reside in objects. On this interpretation, the 'other proposition' referred to in 2.0211 is either some utterly general proposition like '($\exists$x, φ). φx', or another proposition of the same form (as 'ψa' has the same form as 'φa').

Zalabardo's Russellian-form interpretation fits well with the notion of substance which is actually in play in the passage, and it links that notion appropriately to the notion of form. But it still faces a number of difficulties. The first is that it does not really get to the point of the worry about one proposition's having sense depending on another proposition's being true. In the first place, it is not obvious that the only alternative to Wittgenstein's own view (that form resides in the component parts of a proposition, and hence, ultimately, in the objects) is Russell's: Russell's was just a particular view which Wittgenstein disagreed with — why should he have thought that unless he were right, Russell's view would have to be accepted? Second, it is not obvious that Russell's view, as Wittgenstein understands it, has the consequence that one proposition's having sense depends on *another* proposition's being true. This would be reasonable if we stuck with Russell's account, and supposed that '($\exists$x, φ). φx' could be true, without any particular instance of it, like 'φa', being true: then the instance's having sense would depend upon there being that form, and the form would be a matter of the utterly general proposition being true. But Wittgenstein seems precisely to have disagreed with that suggestion: he seems to have thought that the utterly general proposition could only be true if it had a true instance. Now suppose that Wittgenstein is right in this, and suppose, as before, that the proposition whose sense we are considering is some particular proposition like 'φa'. Does this proposition's having sense depend on some *other* proposition's being true, on Wittgenstein's revised version of Russell's theory? That depends on whether 'φa' itself is true: if it is true, then no other true proposition of the same form is needed.

Furthermore, Wittgenstein's view seems to have been that Russell's view was obviously absurd in itself. If the problem raised by saying that one proposition's having sense would depend on another proposition's being true is the problem which Wittgenstein is considering in the passage in *NB*: 17, the problem seems to be just that one proposition's having sense depends on another proposition's being true. But that is not how Wittgenstein considers it in the *Tractatus* passage. In the *Tractatus* passage, he clearly thinks that one proposition's sense depending on another proposition's truth is problematic for a different reason — the reason that it would make it impossible to form a picture of the world (2.0212). And this Russellian-form interpretation shares with all the other interpretations considered so far the difficulty that it cannot account for Wittgenstein's decision to explain the point of 2.0212 in terms of the notion of a picture: he could just as easily have made the point just in terms of a proposition's having no sense.

The interpretation offered in Chapter 1 above differs from all of these in taking the 'other proposition' of 2.0211 to be a proposition which states that a given proposition has sense. And the argument that no such proposition can have a sense *in advance* of the proposition whose having sense it asserts depends on the conception of propositions as pictures which is advanced in the 4s. So it accounts for Wittgenstein's use of the word 'picture' in 2.0212 as none of the other interpretations does. But it shares with the Russellian-form interpretation the virtues of making the argument depend on the fact that objects form the substance of the world, and of making what is important about the substance of the world be that it is the form of the world. No interpretation of these difficult lines can be entirely uncontroversial, but I suggest that this one does better than the existing alternatives.

Notes

1 THE NATURE OF THE WORLD

1 McGuinness (1988: 299) aptly describes this as 'a sort of creation myth'.
2 E.g., White (2006: 23); but this is a common view.
3 I think it is important to distinguish Wittgenstein's concerns sharply from those of certain contemporary philosophers, who believe in 'truthmakers'. (The most famous of these is David Armstrong: see, e.g., his (1997).) 'Truthmaker' theorists accept a certain form of the correspondence theory of truth. Their central claim is something like this:

> (TM) For every truth, there is an entity whose existence makes it true.

This kind of view excites two kinds of debate: first, an ontological debate, about what kinds of entity there are; and second, a formal debate, about whether (TM) can be maintained, given the restrictions on ontology emerging out of the first kind of debate. Neither debate, I think, has any serious connection with the *Tractatus*. Wittgenstein does have concerns about ontology, in the modern sense, but these are rooted in concerns about the kinds of thing we can have acquaintance with, or intuitions. And his concerns about the kinds of thing we can have acquaintance with, or intuitions of, are not rooted in general philosophical prejudices about the kinds of things there are (a preference for medium-sized dry goods, say), but in the status of the truths which depend on them. He is concerned in particular to prevent logic and arithmetic depending on any acquaintance with the world, and is consequently concerned to avoid making logic and arithmetic depend on any objects of acquaintance. His other concerns about ontology are really concerns about logical form, I think. I think he would not care at all about whether there are such entities as facts (say), were it not for the difficulties which his theory of language presents over referring to such entities. Similarly, I think he is not squeamish about the existence of *possible* facts — except, of course, that he will want to insist that they are not all *actual*. He would have no problem about talking about such *possibilia*, were it not for the general difficulties which his theory of language presents for talking about possibility. (For something of the flavour of the kind of debate which I think Wittgenstein is *not* concerned with, see Quine (1961).) And, of course, without an ontological debate of the kind which truthmaker theorists are concerned with, there is little for the formal debate to get a grip on. For more on the general debate about 'truthmakers', see Beebee and Dodd (2005).

4 In the Aristotlelian tradition, the most basic entities are *substances*. I have not used the term 'substance' here, because Wittgenstein himself reserves that term for something which meets a different one of the Aristotelian conditions for being a basic entity — what I call (Sub) (see section 1D below).

5 In the Aristotelian tradition, (Ind) is one of the characteristic marks of substances, as that notion is understood in that tradition, and the views of Leibniz and Spinoza which are mentioned here are couched in terms of the notion of substance.

6 And in the letter to Russell, Wittgenstein continues: 'Tatsache [fact] is what corresponds to the logical product [conjunction] of elementary prop[osition]s when this product is true' (*CL*, p. 125). In fact, this cannot be quite right, since it leaves out what he elsewhere (*TLP* 2.06) calls 'negative' facts, i.e., facts that such and such is *not* the case.

7 The idea that things have essences is famously questioned in Quine (1975).

8 The classic (though extremely difficult) discussion is in Aristotle's *Metaphysics Z*.

9 Kant (1781/87: A20/B34); note that 2.0141 appears in the *TLP* but not in *PT*, although the notion of form as used in the substance argument of *TLP* 2.021–2.0212 does appear there.

10 The notion of *material* properties belongs with the general contrast between *matter* and *form*, which is Aristotelian in origin, and is exploited by Kant (1781/87: A20/B34).

11 The term translated as 'circumstance' here is 'Sachlage', which Ogden translates as 'state of affairs' at 2.014.

12 Kant (1781/87: A24/B38–39).

13 The term translated as 'state of affairs' here is 'Sachlage', translated as 'circumstance' at 2.0122.

14 This is one of two key components of the traditional Aristotelian notion, the other being the condition identified as (Ind) in section 1B above. In effect, what Wittgenstein does is pull these two components apart: (Ind) is taken to characterize atomic *facts*, and (Sub) — or a variant of it, (Sub*) — to characterize *objects*.

15 The term translated as 'real' here is 'wirklichen'; I argue below (in connection with 2.06 and 2.063) that it should be translated as 'actual': the contrast is between what is *possible* and what is *actual*.

16 A related point is made at *NL*, p. 94:

> When we say A judges that etc., then we have to mention a whole proposition which A judges. It will not do either to mention only its constituents, or its constituents and its form, but not in the proper order. This shows that a proposition itself must occur in the statement that it is judged;

> however, for instance, "not-p" may be explained, the question what is
> negated must have a meaning.

17 This has been pointed out by José Zalabardo (Unpublished).

18 See Russell (1984: 114).

19 In fact, the view is to be found in Wittgenstein himself a little before the work of
Russell's cited in the last footnote: in a letter from Wittgenstein to Russell of
January 1913 (CL, pp. 24–25).

20 This point is made explicitly at NB, p. 17. Zalabardo (Unpublished) takes it to be
the point of 2.0211: his interpretation of the substance argument is discussed in
the Appendix.

21 Peter Sullivan helped me to see this point.

22 It is important not to get distracted here by an anachronistic ontological
squeamishness over 'negative facts' (for the general irrelevance of this kind of
ontological squeamishness, see n. 3 above). All Wittgenstein has in mind is
something like this. Suppose that 'abc' is a basic sentence: if it had been true, it
would have been a fact that abc, and since the sentence is (by hypothesis) basic,
that fact would have been an atomic fact. But suppose the sentence 'abc' is
actually false. That means that '~ abc' is true, which means it is a fact that ~ abc.
This is a negative fact.

23 This assumption appears to be made, for example, by Black (1964: 7), Pears
(1987: 9, 27–28), and McGinn (2006: 135).

24 E.g., by McGinn (2006), though not Pears (1987).

25 Both Pears (1987) and McGinn (2006) seem close to this assumption.

2 THE LEGACY OF FREGE AND RUSSELL

1   It is plausible to associate the former position with Russell, and the latter with
Frege and Wittgenstein (at least, by the time of the Tractatus: previously
Wittgenstein was closer to Russell's view).

2   It is a delicate question whether Davidson's approach to language (throughout
his (1984)) is committed to (Corr). He does not think that either sentences or
(at least many) sub-sentential expressions are correlated with extra-linguistic
entities in the manner of (Corr). But he does seem to accept the central
assumption of the Tractatus's conception of language: see Chapter 4, section
4B, below. So we might hope to formulate some less explicitly ontological version of (Corr) which would capture his commitments. A more obvious person
who might be thought to disagree with (Corr) is Wittgenstein himself, in his
later philosophy: see, especially, the opening sections of PI.

3   For more on the contribution of Frege and Russell to the philosophy of language, as that is studied today, see Morris (2007).

4   It is not at all clear how much Frege Wittgenstein had actually read by the time
of writing the Tractatus: it seems likely that his acquaintance with much of
Frege's work was indirect — mediated by Russell's reaction to it. For more on
this issue, see Goldfarb (2002).

5 See, most obviously, Frege (1884: §12); Russell (1903: Ch. 52).

6 The key factor here was Wittgenstein's own reading of Schopenhauer (who was inspired by Kant), which seems to have been independent of Frege and Russell, and to have been rooted, rather, in the intellectual milieu of the Vienna in which Wittgenstein grew up.

7 Note that this does not undermine the legitimacy of interpreting Frege in terms of a notion of correlation which is characterized by (C): of course, in some sense it will matter for one aspect of the meaning of linguistic expressions that they are correlated in one way rather than another with the relevant entity in the world — that is where Fregean 'sense' comes in. But this does not mean that the basic task of being correlated with the same extra-linguistic entity depends on that particular mode of correlation.

8 In this passage we have replaced the translator's 'meaning' with the more natural 'reference' (Russell wrote in German, and the word translated is 'Bedeutung').

9 The most famous criticisms are to be found in Kripke (1980). It remains a disputed question whether the problem of thinness of meaning is best handled within a broadly Russellian theory (an example of this approach is Soames (2002)), or within a form of Fregean theory (for which, see, e.g., McDowell (1984)).

10 Russell himself seems to have been moved by similar considerations: the proposition needs to be the *actual* object of judgement (Russell 1910: 152).

11 Graham Stevens emphasizes that there were other reasons for rejecting his early propositional-object theory, which related to the paradoxes that seemed to be created by it (Stevens 2005: Ch. 2).

12 'In effect', because we might doubt whether Russell himself was concerned explicitly with the unity of *sentences*, considered as such. He was obviously, throughout this period, concerned that his theory should generate a unity of a certain kind; and this unity that he wanted his theory to generate is at least expressed in the unity of sentences — in the contrast between a sentence and a list. So his theory did inevitably provide an explanation of the unity of sentences (of the contrast between a sentence and a list). But he himself certainly thought that the unity he was dealing with was a mere reflection of a deeper unity, in the nature of things, or in judgement.

13 I refer to the second edition of Whitehead and Russell's *Principia Mathematica*, since that is the most easily available: it does not differ in these crucial respects from the first edition of 1910.

14 The 'completeness' of this 'complete meaning' is, of course, the counterpart, at the level of meaning, to the completeness (or unity) of a sentence, which distinguishes it from a mere list.

15 This is sometimes referred to as the 'narrow direction problem': see Stevens (2005: 92).

16 Russell nevertheless toyed with this idea, for a time: he supposed that the judging relation always had a 'sense' or direction (Russell 1910: 158).

17 This is sometimes referred to as the 'wide direction problem': see Stevens (2005: 95–96).

18 It is difficult to be clear how conscious Russell himself was that he was pro-
    posing a theory which was incompatible with the multiple-relation theory. There
    are some indications that he thought of himself as proposing something new
    when he wrote the *Theory of Knowledge* manuscript (Russell 1984). The manu-
    script was written between 7 May and 7 June 1913. On 20 May, as he told
    Ottoline Morrell, Wittgenstein produced a 'refutation of the theory of judgement
    which I used to hold' (Russell to Morrell #782; 1984: xix): this is naturally taken
    to be the argument which appears at *NL* 96 and *TLP* 5.5422, and the 'theory of
    judgement which I used to hold' is therefore naturally taken to be the multiple-
    relation theory. This criticism seems not to have disturbed Russell's progress
    unduly, which makes it look as if he no longer thought of himself as holding the
    multiple-relation theory. On 25 May, he was apparently working on the section
    (1984: II, iii) where what looks to me to be a new theory of judgement is set out.
    The following day he saw Wittgenstein and showed him a 'crucial part of what I
    have been writing', and reported that Wittgenstein had said it was 'all wrong,
    not realizing the difficulties — that he had tried my view and knew it wouldn't
    work' (Russell to Morrell #787; 1984: xix). I take this criticism to be a criticism
    of what I think is really a new view, and to be what Wittgenstein later reformu-
    lated in the terms quoted later in my text. This time the criticism really does
    seem to have hurt, and in fact to have crippled Russell's project. But it is not at
    all easy to be clear about what Russell thought he was doing, since there are
    quite strong signs of a theory very like the multiple-relation theory, even in parts
    of the *Theory of Knowledge* manuscript which are close to the places where what
    looks to me like a different theory is being proposed. At (1984: 109) Russell
    claims that 'a proposition is ... an "incomplete symbol"', which is one of the
    central claims of the multiple-relation theory (the completion being effected by
    an act of mind); and at (1984: 129) he speaks of an 'understanding-complex'
    which looks at least similar to the complex created by the act of judgement on
    the multiple-relation theory. And the use of the notion of acquaintance in con-
    nection with 'pure forms' (1984: 99; 129), seems to give us just another version
    of the multiple-relation theory (though with forms as extra constituents, in
    addition to the familiar constituents of the old multiple-relation theory). In the
    light of this, it might be suggested that Russell thought he was sticking to some
    version of the multiple-relation theory, even in the 1913 manuscript, and the
    parts of the text where he seems to offer a new theory are really intended just to
    deal with the problem of ordering — the so-called 'narrow direction problem' —
    even if they seem inevitably to have wider consequences.

19 Russell's use of the word 'proposition' becomes explicitly linguistic early in the 1913
    manuscript: see (1984: 80, fn. 1), although this is later modified (1984: 105–07).

20 In fact, it was in order to deal with the problem of ordering (the so-called
    'narrow direction problem'), that Russell introduced this theory, which I think is
    really a new theory of judgement, in the first place — though possibly without
    realizing that it was a new theory.

21 Russell himself seems to have thought that the problem only arose in the case
    of sentences in which the order of singular terms mattered; but it looks as if his

new theory of judgement also has work to do, if it is to deal with the other problems which face the multiple-relation theory of judgement without falling back into the problems which beset the old propositional-objects account.

22 Russell himself writes: '[A]n atomic proposition may, for the present, be defined as one whose verbal expression is of the same form as that of an atomic complex' (Russell 1984: 110). It is unclear what revision Russell might have suggested, after the 'present' referred to here, but some revision is necessary, since it looks as if, on Russell's new theory, *no* verbal expression has the same form as that of an atomic complex.

23 This point is urged by Stevens (2005: 102–05).

24 We should not, however, assume that the incompleteness of predicates consists in their being intelligible only in the context of a sentence, rather than in isolation. Frege held that *all* expressions are intelligible only in the context of a sentence, and tended to emphasize this principle particularly in the case of singular terms (his 'proper names').

25 With the hindsight provided by Davidson (1984a), we might give the following account of the reference of the predicate '*x* is a horse':

> (H) The predicate '*x* is a horse' is true of an object if and only if that object is a horse.

It might be argued that Frege himself offered this kind of account of the reference of *the horizontal* ' — ' in Frege (1893: §5) (I am grateful to Peter Sullivan for drawing this passage to my attention). But it is worth noting that neither in that place, nor in (H), is the concept of reference used in relation to the predicate, and, indeed, it is unclear that an account like (H) would even suggest that predicates have reference, or indeed, that sentences refer to truth-values.

26 The idea that (Corr) itself presupposes realism is put forward by Pears (1987).

27 For the issue here, see Johnston (2007b) and Chapter 4, section 4C, below. I think it is important that if we adopt this picture, the stages are *successive* — that is, the establishment of a grammar *precedes* the correlation with a world. Otherwise the *Tractatus* will not provide the response to the Kantian problem over necessity in the world which I take to be one of its central points. For this response see the Introduction, above, and Chapter 5, section 5E, below.

28 This is the Kant of Kant (1781/87).

29 It is worth remarking that although this third view is clearly idealist, it seems that it cannot itself state its own idealism. For in order to state its own idealism, it has to consider a possibility — that the world is the world in itself is as it is supposed to be on the *second*, Kantian, view — which it must regard as unintelligible. This kind of difficulty hovers in the background of Wittgenstein's treatment of solipsism in the *Tractatus*: see Chapter 6 below.

30 Frege (1884: x).

31 Frege (1884: 73).

32 The issue is what strength of context principle Frege needs for his claim that numbers are objects. That claim is discussed briefly in section 2H, below. For

more on the connection between this claim and the context principle, see Wright (1983).

33 Though of course this will in general be a *derived* correlation, resulting merely from the function referred to by the predicate being applied to the object(s) named by the singular terms(s).

34 Russell (1984: 97–98): note that the meaning of 'proposition' seems to shift here, from *sentence* in the first clause, to *objective correlate* of a sentence in the second.

35 Russell (1984: 98): it is clear that 'proposition' here means, unambiguously, *objective correlate* of a sentence.

36 This echoes the view of form to be found in a letter from Wittgenstein to Russell (*CL*, pp. 24–25).

37 Frege also had a referential conception of the logical constants: for example, he took the negation sign to refer to a 'concept' (Frege 1893: §6).

38 Some have also thought that Wittgenstein is concerned to oppose a distinctively 'generalist' conception of logic which he found in Russell: logical truths, on this conception, are simply 'maximally general' truths about the world. The attribution of such a view to Russell is controversial, however: see Goldfarb (1989); Sullivan (2000); Proops (2007).

39 A helpful example in offering informal expressions of the Peano axioms, as well as other related matters, is provided by Graham Priest (1998). Peano himself counted 1, rather than 0, as the first natural number.

40 For a use of this term by Frege, see (1980: 141).

41 Frege's original construction is laid out in his (1884); it is developed more rigorously and formally in Frege (1893). For a good introduction to Frege's account of arithmetic, see Potter (2000: Chs 2 and 4). For a more thorough treatment, see Dummett (1991).

42 The most obvious of these is the so-called Axiom of Infinity, which asserts that there are infinitely many individuals (the objects at the lowest level of the hierarchy of classes). The final version of Russell's theory (with the 'ramified' theory of types) also required the introduction of a further axiom, the Axiom of Reducibility. The Axiom of Reducibility is not easily stated without introducing the technical terminology of Russell's theory, but its point can be conveyed informally: it is to recover something of what Russell's paradox forced him to remove from Frege's system; in effect, what it does is allow him to claim that every significant predicate defines a class. For more on Russell's account of arithmetic, including, in particular, the Axiom of Reducibility, see Potter (2000: Ch. 5).

3. THE GENERAL THEORY OF REPRESENTATION

1 Though, as I noted in the previous chapter, it is not clear that it is accepted by Davidson (1984), and it seems to be rejected later (in *PI*) by Wittgenstein himself.

2 Of course, as noted in relation to Chapter 2, section 2F, above, we might adopt a Davidsonian solution and suggest that we specify what the predicate '*x* is a horse', for example, refers to by means of something like this:

(H) The predicate 'x is a horse' is true of an object if and only if that object is a horse.

And it is arguable that Frege himself presents this kind of account of *the horizontal* '—' at (Frege 1893: §5). But, as was noted in connection with 2F, this kind of account does not itself use the concept of reference in relation to the predicate, so that it becomes unclear that it really makes use of the idea that predicates refer to anything at all.

3   Of course, in Frege's case, the correlations will be what I called *derived* correlations, in Chapter 2, section 2A, above: it is not as if Frege supposed that the meaning of sentences could be fixed by explicitly and directly correlating whole sentences with truth-values. Here it is important to recall the characterization of the notion of correlation I offered in (C) of section 2A above.

4   As well as other difficulties discussed by Stevens (2005: Ch. 2).

5   See the brief discussion of the issue of realism and idealism in section 2F, above.

6   Of course, it only struck him because he was ready to be struck by it. As is well known, one of the things which prepared the way for this view was Hertz (1894). Strikingly relevant sections are Hertz (1894: §§418–28), on dynamical models.

7   Compare:

> A material system is said to be a dynamical model of a second system when the connections of the first can be expressed by such coordinates as to satisfy the following conditions:
> (1) That the number of coordinates of the first system is equal to the number of the second;
> (2) That with a suitable arrangement of the coordinates for both systems the same equations of condition exist;
> (3) That by this arrangement of the coordinates the expression for the magnitude of a displacement agrees in both systems.
>
> (Hertz 1894: §418)

8   Note that Stenius (1960: 98) uses the terms 'depict' and 'represent' in the opposite ways: unnaturally, as it seems to me.

9   And Ogden himself uses 'imagine' to translate the same construction at 3.001 — unhelpfully, in fact (though following Wittgenstein's own suggestion) — see 3E, below (and n. 25).

10 Wittgenstein makes what is, in effect, exactly this point in connection with the translation of 3.001. See the note on the discussion of 3.001 in section 3E, below (n. 25).

11 Compare: 'The relation of a dynamical model to the system of which it is regarded as the model, is precisely the same as the relation of the images which our mind forms of things to the things themselves' (Hertz 1894: §428).

12 I here use 'form of depiction', in place of Ogden's 'form of representation', to translate the German 'Form der Abbildung'.

13 Again, I use 'form of depiction' in place of 'form of representation'.

14 Again, 'form of depiction' replaces Ogden's 'form of representation'.

15 Here 'depicting' replaces Ogden's 'representing' to translate 'abbildende'.

16 Again, 'depicting' replaces 'representing'.

17 Compare: 'A system is not completely determined by the fact that it is a model of a given system. An infinite number of systems, quite different physically, can be models of one and the same system' (Hertz 1894: §421).

18 The difference between 'already' and 'thereby' interpretations will be considered, for the case of language, in Chapter 4, section 4C, below.

19 Here 'depict' replaces 'represent', and 'depiction' replaces 'representation'.

20 Note that here, surprisingly, 'represent' and 'representation' are close translations of the German ('stellt' and 'Darstellung').

21 Despite the general importance of distinguishing between 'depict' and 'represent', I can see no difference between a *form* of depiction and a *form* of representation.

22 Here 'depiction' replaces 'representation'.

23 It is significant that Wittgenstein's treatment of tautologies in 4.46–4.4661 is consistent with this revised principle, but inconsistent with the Principle of Bipolarity, as originally formulated.

24 This remark is dealt with in Chapter 7, section 7C, below; of crucial importance also are sections 5 and 6 of the *Tractatus*, which are discussed in Chapter 5, sections 5D and 5F, below.

25 The preference is Wittgenstein's own, rather than Ogden's, though Wittgenstein chose this translation in order to bring out precisely the point I make in the text. Here is what he said to Ogden about 3.001:

> I don't know how to translate this. The German 'Wir können uns ein Bild von ihm machen' is a phrase commonly used. I have rendered it by 'we can imagine it' because 'imagine' comes from 'image' and this is something like a picture. In German it is a sort of pun you see.
>
> (*LO* p. 24)

(I am very grateful to Peter Sullivan for pointing this out to me.) The problem is that the noun 'image' is more deeply lost in the verb 'imagine' than the noun 'Bild' is in the phrase 'ein Bild machen'. This is in part a reflection of a very general fact about the difference between German and English etymology; but it is also due to a contrast between this particular German idiom and the particular English word which Wittgenstein uses here — the German uses a noun in a compound phrase, where in English the noun is transformed into a verbal form.

26 At least, that is the case where 'p' is an elementary sentence. Nothing yet makes (5) inadmissible, if 'p' itself has the form, e.g., '$p \& \sim p$'.

4. SENTENCES AS MODELS

1 At least, it looks as if it does. It might be thought that 4.04 involves a commitment to the possibility of analysis which is not present in (M3): after all, it uses 'distinguish*able*', rather than merely 'distinguished'. A final decision on this

point would need to take account of Wittgenstein's conception of the relation between sentences of ordinary language and elementary sentences (which are what analysis would reach): see section 4E below. My view is that any difference between 'distinguished' and 'distinguishable' will turn out not to matter, once we are clear what happens in analysis. Ordinary language sentences will turn out on analysis to be either simple propositional-logic compounds of elementary sentences, or else (in at least the overwhelming majority of cases) quantified sentences, whose instances would be elementary sentences. In the first case, I think, the elements are already there to be distinguished, and not merely distinguishable. And in the second case, they are not even distinguish*able*, since quantified sentences are not merely logical sums or logical products of elementary sentences, on Wittgenstein's view (see Chapter 5, section 5C, below).

2 The reference seems to be to Hertz (1894: §418), where one system is said to be a dynamical model of another only if 'the number of coordinates of the first system is equal to the number of the second'.

3 Others might include the tendency to think of expressions which 'mention' a complex (3.24: discussed in section 4E, below) as functioning like names; and, in general, being deceived about the complexity of everyday language (see section 4E, below); and the fact that the same word in everyday language is often different *symbols* (3.323; discussed in 4C, below).

4 I have used 'depicted' and 'depiction' here in place of Ogden's 'represented' and 'representation' to translate the German 'abbilden' and 'Abbilden'. For the general point see Chapter 3, section 3B, above; and this chapter, section 4C, below.

5 Note that here Wittgenstein uses 'darstellen' ('represent'), where we might have expected him to use 'abbilden' ('depict').

6 I here use 'show it forth' in place of Ogden's 'exhibit it', in order to preserve in English the parallel between the German of this passage and that of 2.172. 'Represent', quite properly, translates 'darstellen'.

7 Once again, 'represent' translates 'darstellen'.

8 Wittgenstein's view of language here seems to anticipate the conception made popular by W. V. Quine (1960: Ch. 2) and Donald Davidson (1984a). Quine and Davidson make radical translation or interpretation central to their understanding of language. Translation or interpretation is *radical* if it is carried out on the basis of assuming no more about the language to be translated or interpreted than has to be assumed for the language to be counted as a language at all. A radical interpreter will approach a language she knows nothing about, and simply on the basis of what she can observe about speakers and the world from that position of ignorance, she follows rational procedures in order to end up in a position to state, in her own language, the meaning of any sentence of the language being interpreted. Quine and Davidson hold that it is in radical interpretation that we really see language for what it is. They are thereby committed to this thesis:

(RI) There is nothing about the meaning of the words of any language, which is discoverable at all, which is not discoverable in principle by someone who begins from evidence which is available without understanding that language, and proceeds by means of a kind of rational theory-construction which is also available without understanding that language.

This is very close to the central commitment of Wittgenstein's claim that any language which can represent the world must have the same form as the world. (I do not mean to suggest that there are no differences between Quine and Davidson themselves over radical interpretation, of course. They seem to differ, in particular, in their understanding of the starting point — in their conception of the kind of observation of the world from which interpretation begins: this is part of the point of Davidson (1984b), and I think Davidson shows himself here to be closer to Wittgenstein than Quine is.)

9 These remarks are taken to be clear indications of realism by Johnston (2007b), though he may not be taking realism to be defined by (R).

10 It is attention to this that makes Wittgenstein look closer to Davidson (see, especially, his (1984b)) than to Quine.

11 See Chapter 3, section 3B, above.

12 For Frege's notion, see Chapter 2, section 2C, above; and more generally Morris (2007: Ch. 2).

13 Wittgenstein's use may be closer to Russell's: see (Russell 1910: 158). Russell associates 'sense' with *direction*; something which Wittgenstein adopts at *TLP* 3.144.

14 Including, apparently (and surprisingly) Potter (2000: 164).

15 This is also the view of Johnston (2007b). The opposing view is held, e.g., by Pears (1987: 88).

16 Johnston (2007b) does seem to take this to require a form of realism; but perhaps the realism he has in mind is nothing like as strong as (R).

17 The words translated 'we have to attend to the use' in the *Notebooks* are the same as those translated 'we must consider the … use' in the *Tractatus*. 'Attend to' is better, I think (the German is 'achten'); the interpretation I will suggest in a moment would slightly favour 'have to' over 'must' (as a better way of expressing a practical, rather than a metaphysical, necessity).

18 The notion is present in the *Prototractatus* (*PTLP*: 3.2013 — the ancestor of *TLP* 3.2 and 3.21).

19 Where in Frege does the view Wittgenstein opposes appear? Perhaps here:

However, not only a denotation, but also a sense, appertains to all names correctly formed from our signs

(Frege 1893: §32)

20 These two strands of the 'austere' conception of nonsense are distinguished in Morris and Dodd (2008); I have since discovered that something rather like this distinction is to be found in Glock (2004: 222) — though he takes quite a different view of the issues.

21 I leave aside here the question whether it suffices for the claim that numbers are objects, made in Frege (1884: §§55–63) — even if that was, arguably, the most important reason why Frege himself embraced the principle.

22 Ogden translates 'Zusammenhang' with 'connexion' (Pears and McGuinness have 'nexus'), and 'Verkettung' with 'concatenation' (the Latin word 'catena', of course, means *chain*); I have varied the translation slightly, to make the etymological point clearer.

23 The examples of the predicates I am using here are simple, but only for the sake of expository convenience. I do not mean to deny that 'If x is human, then x is mortal' is a one-place predicate, and, indeed, for the issues which concern us here, it seems to me that this complex predicate can harmlessly be regarded as a one-place predicate. For (some of) the issues here, see Dummett (1981: 27–33). These points arise again in section 4F, below.

24 Compare Russell (1984: 98).

25 This is the kind of argument which Wittgenstein later thought he was relying on: see *PI* I: §66.

26 McGuinness himself suggests 'Such and such combinations (sc. of objects) hold' (McGuinness 2002a: 78), despite sponsoring an alternative in the collaboration with Pears.

27 In this context it is ironic that Fogelin should have been at some pains to explain the working of the demonstrative in 'This is how things stand' (Fogelin 1987: 48); there is no demonstrative in the German.

28 Note that Wittgenstein seems clearly to have linked complexity and generality, in the discussion in the *Notebooks* from which these remarks in the *Tractatus* derive (*NB*, pp. 63–64).

29 Compare: 'But this is surely clear: the propositions which are the only ones that humanity uses will have a sense just as they are and do not wait upon a future analysis in order to acquire a sense' (*NB*, p. 62). This is one respect in which Russell misunderstood the Tractatus:

> Mr Wittgenstein is concerned with the conditions for a logically perfect language — not that any language is logically perfect, or that we believe ourselves capable, here and now, of constructing a logically perfect language, but that the whole function of language is to have meaning, and it only fulfils this function as it approaches to the ideal language which we postulate.
>
> (Russell 1922: 8)

30 The debate goes right back to the beginning of discussion of the *Tractatus*. Roughly speaking (there are subtle differences between views), Ramsey (1923), Stenius (1960), and McGuinness (2002b) attribute a realist view, whereas Anscombe (1971), Ishiguro (1969), and Ricketts (1996) attribute a nominalist view.

31 Note that this echoes *TLP* 2.03.

32 This is how Dummett defines 'complex' predicates (Dummett 1981: 29).

33 This point is made by Anscombe (1971: 101–02).

34 What might Frege have had in mind? The issues here are quite technical, but here is an indication of the kind of thing he might have been concerned with — remembering that he cannot consistently have thought that singular terms were any more self-standing than any other kind of expression. It is clear that he

thought that there is a fundamental asymmetry between singular terms and certain other kinds of expression, at some level distinct from being the correlate of a name, in the sense of 'name' involved in the *Tractatus*. One way of fleshing out such an asymmetry might be as follows. There seems to be a distinction to be made between different kinds of occurrence in sentences of 'is ugly' (for example): there are occurrences in simple sentences, like 'Socrates is ugly', on the one hand, and, on the other hand, there are occurrences in compound sentences like 'If Socrates is ugly, it's no wonder that he is interested in intellectual matters'. It is natural to think that the meaning of the word 'ugly' is fixed by its occurrence in simple sentences, and once that meaning is established, it is simply re-used in more complex sentences. In contrast with this, there seems to be no similar distinction between the occurrence of the name 'Socrates' in simple and in compound sentences. This might be thought to be the basis of a deep asymmetry between complete and incomplete expressions, which might ground a corresponding distinction between kinds of entity in the world. For these issues, see Ramsey (1925b) and Dummett (1981: 27–33).

35 It might seem that there was also a third option: might there not be a single asymmetry, which was not exactly of the kind which Frege identified? Whether this is a live option depends, in part, on what Frege was really concerned with in distinguishing 'saturated' from 'unsaturated' entities. For a beginning on this issue, see Dummett (1981: Ch. 8); see also n. 34 above.

36 Colin Johnston (forthcoming) has recently urged that the *Tractatus* is neutral on the nature of the fundamental objects, but it is not clear that he has in mind exactly the neutrality which is suggested in the main text.

37 In the letter to Russell which is quoted from in text (a), Wittgenstein seems to assimilate qualities and relations to forms, while conceiving of forms in very much the manner Russell did later in Russell (1984) — that is, as entirely general facts (*CL* pp. 24–25).

38 It is significant that this change in Wittgenstein's views (reported to Russell in January 1913) followed a meeting with Frege in December 1912.

39 This passage is also quoted by Ricketts (1996: 70–71), who takes it to indicate a version of the nominalist interpretation.

40 It is worth recalling that Wittgenstein adopted the view that there are two kinds of 'indefinable' following conversations with Frege, as noted earlier.

41 For more on this whole issue, see Chapter 6 below, on Solipsism.

42 I am very grateful to Peter Sullivan for his comments on an earlier draft of this section.

5 LOGIC AND COMPOUND SENTENCES

1 Although Sheffer is generally credited with the discovery, it appears that something very like it was originally made many years earlier by Charles Sanders Peirce: see Peirce (1976).

2 For Sheffer's use of the stroke, '|', for joint denial see Sheffer (1913: 487). He did not there either use the dagger or deal with alternative denial. The common current use of the term 'Sheffer Stroke' and the symbol '|' to express alternative

denial (NAND) seems to derive from Jean Nicod. In his (1916), Nicod offered both the joint denial (NOR) and alternative denial (NAND) interpretations of '|' as sufficient for his purposes, but opted for the NAND reading because it offers a simpler translation of '⊃'. The use of the stroke for alternative denial and the dagger for joint denial can be found in Quine (1952: 18), which probably had a large influence in itself, although there is still a robust tradition of reserving the term 'Sheffer Stroke' and the symbol '|' for joint denial.

3 See also *NL*: 95.

4 Landini's point is that diagrammatic ways of presenting truth-functionality were in existence well before Wittgenstein, and this is indisputable. He sees no significant mathematical advance in Wittgenstein's laying out of truth tables, and this too is a reasonable point. His examples do not, however, show any precedent for the particular diagrammatic layout which Wittgenstein used: this choice of layout may not be very significant mathematically, but it does have the virtue of making the meaning of the logical constants very obvious, even to a non-mathematical mind. Not that it matters a great deal.

5 Note that I here lay out the truth table for '$p \supset q$' in the way Wittgenstein does, not in the way which is now routine. In modern layouts, the truth-values assigned to the variables in the box on the left alternate moving down the right-hand column of that box, change half as often in the next column left, half as often again in the next column left of that, and so on. Wittgenstein's layout is simply the reverse of that: the truth-value assignments alternate in the left-hand column, change half as often in the column to the right of that, and so on.

6 The formula at 4.27, by which the number K_n is defined, can be explained informally as follows. It defines the number of ways in which the world might be if there are *n* possible atomic facts. That number is: the number of ways in which *none* of the atomic facts might obtain; *plus* the number of ways in which just *one* of the atomic facts might obtain; *plus* the number of ways in which exactly *two* of the atomic facts might obtain; plus ... — and so on, until we have added the number of ways in which all *n* atomic facts might obtain.

7 This is what I called the *minimal* sense of the notion of a predicate, in Chapter 4, section 4F, above.

8 It seems sometimes not to be noticed that Wittgenstein actually offers *no* suggestion for a convenient notation for either of methods 2 or 3: it is sometimes simply assumed that, where the function is 'fx' we can simply place 'fx' instead of 'ξ' within the brackets in 'N (...)'. I take it that this assumption lies behind Fogelin's objections at Fogelin (1987: 78–80).

9 This rule is, in effect, that adopted by Peter Geach (1981). It is important to remember that Wittgenstein himself offers us no guidance here, and some such rule is needed. In particular, the rule needs an explicit indication of the variable which is free in function expressions (as is done here by placing it at the head of the expression), in order both to accommodate the difference between existential and universal quantification, and to deal with sentences involving mixed quantifiers (such as those we might write as '$(x)(\exists y)\, fxy$' or '$(\exists x)(x)\, fxy$'). Fogelin (1987: 78–80) argues that the *Tractatus* cannot accommodate mixed

quantification. It seems to me, rather, that Wittgenstein's account of the N-operator is simply incomplete if what we are after is an explicit representation of ordinary quantification. On my view, all Wittgenstein needs for his main philosophical purposes is for appropriate choices of values of the variable 'ξ' to yield the right results; he does not need to provide a notation which enables us to represent those choices perspicuously. Leo Cheung (2000) offers a useful discussion of the Fogelin–Geach dispute.

10 It might be thought that, since (as we have noted) the N-operator does not 'characterize a form but only the difference between forms' (5.241), being values of '$N(fx)$' cannot mark out a common form — that is, '$N(fx)$' cannot itself be a function. But we can see that there is no problem here, if we take care about what the claim that the N-operator does not 'characterize a form but only the difference between forms' really amounts to. The sentences 'fa', 'fb', 'fc' all have a common form (the form which we write as 'fx'). So each of them has a certain form. Take 'fa' in particular. If we apply the N-operator to that we reach a sentence ('$N(fa)$') which has a different form. That difference is the difference the N-operator makes, and it is a difference between forms. Of course, if '$N(fa)$' has a certain form — a different form from 'fa' — that allows '$N(fa)$', '$N(fb)$', and '$N(fc)$' all to have the same form, which we can write as '$N(fx)$'. None of this requires that '$N(fx)$' itself be the result of a direct application of the N-operator to 'fx'.

11 Ramsey thought so too: see Ramsey (1925a: 7–8), (1926: 74).

12 This explanation is inspired by the helpfully informal account provided by Mark Richard (1998). Standard explanations are in terms of assignments of objects (or sequences of objects) to variables under interpretations: see, for example, Sainsbury (1991: 197).

13 For this point, see Field (1972).

14 At least, the simple infinity of the objects does not create a problem.

15 The formal result was reached independently in the same year by Alonzo Church (1936) and Alan Turing (1936). Since it was reached first by Church, it is now commonly known as *Church's Theorem*. The point of this paragraph was made by Cheung (2000: 255), though he takes this to show that the Tractarian system strictly only deals with finite domains.

16 At least when there are many-placed predicates.

17 Anscombe (1971: 132) seems to take this as an objection to Wittgenstein's construction, rather than as an objection to a particular interpretation of Wittgenstein.

18 This is the source of some of Fogelin's worries about the adequacy of the N-operator: see Fogelin (1987: 78–82)

19 So Wittgenstein thinks it is crucial to rule out exactly the thing which Russell proposed as the solution to the difficulty of expressing what cannot be said, in his Introduction to the *Tractatus* (Russell 1922: 23); it is hardly surprising that Wittgenstein disliked Russell's Introduction. Russell's idea of a hierarchy of languages initially looks much more seriously at odds with Wittgenstein's views than the suggestion that Wittgenstein was looking for a 'logically perfect language' (Russell 1922: 8). But in fact both remarks fail to appreciate the centrality

of the same-form assumption which shapes the whole of Wittgenstein's approach both to language and to philosophy in general.

20 Kripke (1980).

21 This is one of the things Anscombe complains of in what she takes to be 'the most common view' of the *Tractatus*: see Anscombe (1971: 25–26).

22 Michael Potter uses this passage to show that Wittgenstein wanted to insist that the same notion of *negation* must apply to all sentences, though he does not see that insistence as in turn deriving from an argument like the argument (CF1)–(CF3) of my text (Potter 2000: 172).

23 This is the impression one receives from Ramsey (1925: 11).

24 This is how it struck Ramsey (1925a: 4–5), (1926: 75).

25 The careful differentiation of the terms 'sinnlos' ('without sense') and 'unsinnig' ('nonsense') is one of the great philosophical improvements of the Pears and McGuinness translation, in comparison with Ogden's. Note, however, that Wittgenstein does sometimes use 'sinnlos', when it seems that he might equally well have used 'unsinnig' (5.132; 5.1362), even though he does not appear to use 'unsinnig' to characterize the non-picturing limit-case meaningfulness of tautologies and contradictions. Of course, it would not be altogether surprising to find a certain fluidity between the terms, given Wittgenstein's rather particular account of nonsense at 5.4733, recalled at 6.53.

26 See, for example, the formulation of Church (1940).

27 Whitehead and Russell (1927: 168).

28 Landini (2007: 159–66) argues that the work that mathematics needs to be done can in fact be done without using identity, provided that we use exclusive quantifiers (quantifiers which use variables in a restricted way precisely in order to deal with the absence of identity, as introduced by Wittgenstein in 5.532 and 5.5321).

29 Frege (1879: §8).

30 Frege (1892a).

31 See Russell (1918).

32 In fact, Ramsey thought that this meant that it was wrong to regard mathematical truths as being just 'equations', in the sense in which Wittgenstein understood that term: there are some things which Ramsey thought simply cannot be accommodated on such an account (Ramsey 1925a: 17–19).

33 Those who want to go deeper into the problems should consult, for example, Potter (2000) and Landini (2007).

34 This point is made by Landini (2007: 175).

35 This seems to be the view to which Landini tends (Landini 2007: 183).

36 Landini (2007) traces this notion of the 'power' of an operation back to Russell's notion of the 'power' of a relation, in Russell (1901). He also points out that the notion is used to define succession, addition, and multiplication, in Whitehead and Russell (1927: *301): see (Landini 2007: 180).

37 Potter (2000: 179–81) takes Wittgenstein to be arguing for an *adjectival* account of numerals (as opposed to a substantival one, like Frege's, which takes numerals to function as singular terms). It seems to me that the contrast between adjective and substantive is not large enough for Wittgenstein's

purposes, since it seems to me that both adjectives and substantives may count as names in Wittgenstein's sense, and hence refer to objects (see Chapter 4, section 4F, above). This does not, however, undermine the substantive point which Potter is making, which he describes as a presentation of an argument for an adjectival account of numerals.

38 See *PI*: I, §1: 'But what is the meaning of the word "five"? — No such thing was in question here, only how the word "five" is used.'

39 Wittgenstein introduced the rather cumbersome brace notation of 6.1203 for precisely this purpose. Note that he explicitly restricts its use to 'cases in which no sign of generality occurs in the tautology'.

40 Church (1936); Turing (1936).

41 Thus White (2006: 107); a similar view has been expressed in conversation by Warren Goldfarb.

42 Thus Fogelin (1987: 82) and Landini, who seems to hold that the chief point of introducing the *N*-operator is to show logic to be decidable (Landini 2007: 125–46).

43 It is hard to be confident in this interpretation, but it is at least natural to read the opening paragraph of Ramsey (1928) as an expression of the attitude of someone who *expected* there to be 'a regular procedure to determine the truth or falsity of any given logical formula', the problem being merely that of finding it. And it is also (perhaps unsurprisingly) natural to read the same attitude into the famous formulation of the problem in Hilbert and Ackermann (1928: 72–81).

44 Hume (1739–40: I, iv, 6).

45 These two remarks were considered in connection with the substance argument in Chapter 1, section 1D, above.

46 Indeed, despite the objection made in his own (1923), Ramsey still felt able to describe Wittgenstein's extensionalism as 'extremely plausible' (Ramsey 1925a: 9).

47 Ramsey made this point in his original review (Ramsey 1923: 31).

48 For an account of the unravelling of the *Tractatus* from this point, see Hacker (1986: Ch. 5). Key texts are *RLF* and *PR* (Ch. 8).

6 SOLIPSISM, IDEALISM, AND REALISM

1 This, I suspect is the view of Peter Sullivan: see his (1996).

2 In this dispute Strawson (1966) is taken to be a 'two-worlds' theorist, whereas Allison (1983) represents a 'one-world' tradition of interpretation.

3 See, e.g., Russell (1912: Ch. 1), (1914).

4 There are, however, hints of the traditional preoccupations of empiricism in the things suggested as examples of objects in the *Notebooks*: e.g., *NL*: 3, 45.

5 Schopenhauer's main work begins with a statement of solipsism which has strong echoes in the *Tractatus* and the preliminary notes on the issue in the *Notebooks*: see his (1818/1844: I, 3–5). In fact, Schopenhauer provides the key background both to Wittgenstein's approach to solipsism, and to his approach to life in general (see Chapter 7 below). For preliminary reading on this, see Zöller (1999), and, more generally Janaway (1994).

6 Sullivan (1996: 203) emphasizes the importance of this connection.

7 This is broadly the conclusion reached by Pears (1987: Ch. 7); if this is right, despite the occasional echoes of Russell (e.g., Russell (1914)), it is not Russell's kind of position which he is both endorsing (as 'quite correct') and dismissing (as unsayable).

8 The notion of a 'blind-spot' is used at *NL*: 100.

9 Note, however, that it does not involve any general commitment to the Principle of Bipolarity as a principle which applies to all propositions: (SC) is only a principle about what can be *stated* (i.e., asserted, described, or pictured). Tautologies would not count as statements.

10 It is natural to see this assumption as requiring no more than is required in this remark from the *Notes on Logic* which we have already looked at (in Chapter 1, section 1D, and Chapter 5, section 5F):

> When we say A judges that etc., then we have to mention a whole proposition which A judges. It will not do either to mention only its constituents, or its constituents and form, but not in the proper order. This shows that a proposition itself must occur in the statement that it is judged.
>
> (*NL*: 94)

11 Diamond (2000) and McGinn (2007: Ch. 11) seem to take this as the source of the difficulty of stating solipsism in the *Tractatus*: if, however, it is (A4), (A5), and (A6) which represent positions framed by the general account of language in the *Tractatus* — that sentences are models — I think this must be wrong.

12 Note, though, that a different word, 'meint', is used in 5.62: this is closer to the ordinary English 'mean' or 'intend' (it can mean *believe*).

13 It is significant that in *PT*, this passage occurs later than the passage which became *TLP*: 5.621–5.641. I take it that this shows that Wittgenstein came to think that it was 5.61, rather than the remarks which follow 5.62, which give the deep explanation of the 'correctness' of solipsism.

14 In the original 1922 impression, Ogden's translation renders this paragraph as follows:

> That the world is *my* world, shows itself in the fact that the limits of the language (the language which only I understand) mean the limits of *my* world.

This version commits Wittgenstein to some form of 'private language', in a sense not unlike that considered in Wittgenstein (1953: §243), which makes it readily intelligible that the paragraph might provide an argument for a familiar (roughly Berkeleyan) form of solipsism. But this is clearly not what Wittgenstein had in mind. As Lewy's note shows, the 1922 translation is clearly just mistaken, and, in any case, there is nothing in the *Tractatus* to suggest that he is there concerned with a language which is restricted to the thoughts of a single subject.

15 For this suggestion, see Sullivan (1996).

16 Kant (1787: B131–32).

17 This is not very far from the suggestion of Potter (2000: 164–66). Potter, however, takes the intervention of the self in the transformation of 'the dead sign

into the live symbol' to be a one-step intervention which takes us right to the world, whereas I take the transformation of 'the dead sign into the live symbol' to be just the first step, with a second step needed to move from the symbol to the world; and, crucially, it is the second step which is in play here. There is, perhaps, a disagreement between us over the distinction between *sign* and *symbol* in the *Tractatus*. Potter takes a sign to be 'an element of syntax' (Potter 2000: 164), whereas I take syntax only to appear with symbols. For these issues, see Chapter 4, section 4C, above, and Johnston (2007b). A view of the same more general kind as that suggested here, and by Potter, is also suggested by Sullivan (1996: 210–11), and McGuinness (2002c).

18 It is also significant that the response to the objection which is here sketched on Wittgenstein's behalf echoes Davidson's argument against the possibility of conceptual relativity (Davidson 1984b): as we saw in Chapter 4, section 4B, n. 8, Wittgenstein's same-form assumption is tantamount to the assumption of the centrality of radical interpretation (RI), which lies behind Davidson's argument.

19 This kind of communitarian neo-Kantianism is sometimes attributed to the later Wittgenstein: see, e.g., Williams (1981); Lear (1984). My own feeling is that this kind of view is exactly what Wittgenstein *rejects* in the later work.

20 See McDowell (1994: lecture V).

21 Including Schopenhauer's: see e.g., his (1818/44: I, 3–5)

22 For the contrast, see Chapter 4, section 4C, above. In that section I argued that, on the official view of the *Tractatus*, syntax could in principle be established (and therefore, the nature of the symbols could in principle be fixed) independently of the correlations with the world which give symbols meaning. Someone who disagreed with me on that point would think that, although it is only syntactic well-formedness which is important for the argument which follows, my sentences only present themselves to me as syntactically well formed *in* presenting themselves to me as meaningful — that is to say, *in* my making sense of them. It may be significant that those who are inclined to doubt the possibility of the establishment of syntax independently of the assignment of meaning are sometimes also inclined to present something like the Kantian approach to Wittgenstein's solipsism which was considered in the last section (see, e.g., Potter (2000: 164–66)). I might add that it is a trivial matter to transform the argument of this section into one which concerns meaningfulness, rather than syntactic well-formedness, even if the converse transformation of the argument of section 6D is nothing like so easy.

23 It is worth pointing out that this kind of thinking might, in fact, bring something at least close to full meaningfulness (rather than mere syntactic well-formedness) back into the picture after all. For if my language is syntactically well-formed, every combinatorial possibility in my language must be co-ordinate with some combinatorial possibility in the real world. But the combinatorial possibilities in the real world are just the possibilities of combination of the real objects which are the ultimate constituents of the world. So if my language is even syntactically well formed, there must be a possible mapping between it and the objects in the world. And that might be thought to be at least close to the

thought that my language must be fully meaningful, given only that it is syntactically well formed. This is connected with what I suggest is Wittgenstein's response to general scepticism, in 6.51 (see Chapter 7, section 7D, below).

24 Hume (1739–40: I, iv, 6).

25 See Descartes (1641: II and VI).

26 E.g., Pears, who, in fact, takes 5.64 to be an endorsement of realism (1987: 188).

27 On the side of those who think that Wittgenstein *is* committed to (i) I place Adrian Moore: see Moore (1985), (1992), (2003). On the other side I place McGuinness (2002d) and Sullivan (1996), (2003).

7 METAPHYSICS, ETHICS, AND THE LIMITS OF PHILOSOPHY

1 Pears and McGuinness have 'everything that is subject to law' (*TLP**).

2 The point can be traced back to the famous discussion in Hume (1739–40: I, iii, 6).

3 Hume (1739–40: I, iii, 14).

4 Hence cause is one of the 'categories' justified by the Transcendental Deduction in Kant (1781/87).

5 See Russell's note to 6.32 in the Ogden translation: '*I.e.* not the form of one particular law, but of any law of a certain sort' (*TLP*, p. 173).

6 Schopenhauer (1818/44: I, 327–28).

7 It is worth comparing the ethical view of the *Tractatus* with that of the later *LE*. Here, I think, it is clear that Wittgenstein has lost some of the intensity of feeling which animates the *Tractatus*.

8 Recall the definition of metaphysics in Chapter 1, section 1F.

9 Carnap (1956: 67).

10 See, e.g., Hacker (2000).

11 This seems also to have been the view of Ramsey (1923: 472).

12 I think this is consonant with the account of mysticism to be found in McGuinness (2000e).

13 It is important to recognize, however, that the division between those who call themselves 'resolute' interpreters, and those who are counted 'traditionalists', includes much more than just the issue of how to respond to the paradox: in one dimension, it is a disagreement over what to make of Wittgenstein's notion of nonsense; in another, it is a disagreement of how much of the attitudes of the later Wittgenstein can be read into the *Tractatus*. The contemporary debate is often unhelpful in blurring these distinctions between distinctions.

14 The clearest exponent of this view is Hacker (2000).

15 This picture of the Ineffable-Truths View is encouraged by Conant (2000).

16 See Geach (1977).

17 I am very grateful to Douglas Walker for pointing out the significance of this text as the decisive evidence for the point that Wittgenstein cannot accept the existence of ineffable truths.

18 See, e.g., Diamond (1991); Conant (2000); Kremer (2001). This kind of view is questioned by Sullivan (2002), and robustly attacked by Proops (2001).

19 This view was developed initially in Morris and Dodd (2008).

20 Once again McGuinness gets the tone of this just right, describing it as 'a form of negative theology' (1988: 300). Note that he even prefers the Ogden translation to his own, to give the proper effect.

21 I am thinking here in particular of *RLF* and the earlier parts of *WLC*. Similar points apply to some parts of *WVC*. The worry here was raised by Roger White.

22 Carnap (1963: 25).

23 The general conception of the dialectic of the various treatments of the paradox of the Tractatus which is presented in this section, as well as the solution which is finally proposed, were presented initially in Morris and Dodd (2008). I am extremely grateful to Julian Dodd for his part in the writing of that paper, and for being happy for me to present that approach again here, as well as for his help in the general clarification of the issues involved.

APPENDIX: THE SUBSTANCE ARGUMENT

1 Though, of course, Frege uses the notion of sense in a way different from Wittgenstein's, so he would not have accepted this formulation of the point. For Frege, sense is a dimension of meaning distinct from reference: all expressions have both sense and reference. For Wittgenstein, on the other hand, only names have reference, and only sentences have sense.

2 What is, in effect, this objection to Proops is made by Zalabardo (Unpublished: §5). I endorse his diagnosis, but only with some hesitation, because Proops (2004: 114–15) distinguishes precisely the two things that seem to need to be confused if every premise of the argument is to look plausible.

3 Though as noted where I consider this remark in the main text of Chapter 1, this view seems to have been expressed earlier by Wittgenstein himself (*CL*: 24–25).

Bibliography

The recent literature on the *Tractatus* is vast. Where should a student go next? If you want a detailed account of Wittgenstein's life, up to the time of the publication of the *Tractatus*, go to McGuinness (1988): the final chapter of this is also excellent as an approach to the literary aspects of the work. Monk (1990) provides a full biography, covering the whole of Wittgenstein's life.

It is sometimes useful to read more than one introductory text. Stenius (1960) and Anscombe (1971) remain classics; White (2006) is a recent addition to the genre. For a survey of the whole of Wittgenstein's oeuvre, Kenny (2006) is a good place to begin. Stern (1995) goes more deeply into one aspect of Wittgenstein's philosophy, covering both early and late work.

It is also a good idea to place Wittgenstein's philosophy in the context of the work of Russell and others in the same tradition. Monk (1997) is a helpful biography of Russell. Hylton (1990) provides useful background in the early history of analytic philosophy. Potter (2000) places Wittgenstein's work in the context of a whole tradition of philosophy of mathematics. Landini (2007) focuses more strongly on the influence of Russell, and pursues the technical issues in great detail.

For the recent controversy over the treatment of the work's apparent paradox, the place to begin is Crary and Read (2000). From there it is worth moving to Kremer (2001); Proops (2001); and Sullivan (2002).

WORKS BY WITTGENSTEIN

CL   *Ludwig Wittgenstein: Cambridge Letters; Correspondence with Russell, Keynes, Moore, Ramsey and Sraffa*, ed. B. McGuinness and G. H. von Wright (Oxford: Blackwell, 1995)

LE   'A Lecture on Ethics', *Philosophical Review* 74 (1965): 3–12

LO   *Letters to C. K. Ogden with Comments on the English Translation of the* Tractatus
Logico-Philosophicus, ed. G. H. von Wright
(Oxford: Blackwell, 1973)

NB   *Notebooks 1914–1916*, ed. G. H. von Wright and G. E. M. Anscombe, trans. G. E. M. Anscombe,
2nd edn, (Oxford: Blackwell, 1979)

NL   *Notes on Logic*, printed as Appendix I of *NB*

NM   *Notes Dictated to G. E. Moore in Norway*, printed as Appendix II of *NB*

PG   *Philosophical Grammar*, ed. R. Rhees, trans.
A. Kenny (Oxford: Blackwell, 1974)

PI   *Philosophical Investigations*, trans. G. E. M. Anscombe, 3rd edn
(Oxford: Blackwell, 2001)

PR   *Philosophical Remarks*, ed. R. Rhees, trans. R. Hargreaves and R. White (Oxford: Blackwell, 1975)

PT   *Prototractatus: an Early Version of Tractatus*
Logico-Philosophicus, ed. B. McGuinness, T. Nyberg, and G. H. von Wright, trans. D. Pears and
B. McGuinness (London: Routledge and
Kegan Paul, 1971)

RFM   *Remarks on the Foundations of Mathematics*, ed.
G. H. von Wright, R. Rhees, and G. E. M. Anscombe, 2nd edn
(Oxford: Blackwell, 1978)

RLF   'Some Remarks on Logical Form', *Aristotelian Society
Supplementary Volume* 9 (1929): 162–71

TLP   *Tractatus Logico-Philosophicus*, trans. C. K. Ogden (London:
Routledge and Kegan Paul, 1922)

TLP*   *Tractatus Logico-Philosophicus*, trans. D. Pears and B. McGuinness
(London: Routledge and Kegan Paul, 1961)

WLC   *Wittgenstein's Lectures: Cambridge 1930–1932*, ed. D. Lee (Oxford:
Blackwell, 1980)

WSP   *Wittgenstein: Sources and Perspectives*, ed.
C. G. Luckhardt (Ithaca, NY: Cornell
University Press, 1979)

WVC   *Ludwig Wittgenstein and the Vienna Circle: Conversations Recorded
by Friedrich Waismann*, ed. B. McGuinness (Oxford: Blackwell, 1979)

WORKS BY OTHER AUTHORS

Allison, H. (1983) *Kant's Transcendental Idealism: An Interpretation and Defense* (New Haven, CT: Yale University Press)

Anscombe, G. E. M (1971) *An Introduction to Wittgenstein's* Tractatus, 3rd edn (London: Hutchinson)

Armstrong, D. (1997) *A World of States of Affairs* (Cambridge: Cambridge University Press)

Beebee, H., and Dodd, J., eds (2005) *Truthmakers: The Contemporary Debate* (Oxford: Oxford University Press)

Berkeley, G. (1734) *A Treatise Concerning the Principles of Human Knowledge*, 2nd edn (London: Tonson)

Black, M. (1964) *A Companion to Wittgenstein's* Tractatus (Cambridge: Cambridge University Press)

Block, I., ed. (1981) *Perspectives on the Philosophy of Wittgenstein* (Oxford: Blackwell)

Carnap, R. (1956) 'The Elimination of Metaphysics through Logical Analysis of Language', in A. J. Ayer, ed., *Logical Positivism* (New York: Free Press)

—— (1963) 'Intellectual Autobiography', in P. Schilpp, ed., *The Philosophy of Rudolf Carnap* (La Salle, IL: Open Court), pp. 3–84

Cheung, L. (2000) 'The Tractarian Operation *N* and Expressive Completeness', *Synthese: An International Journal for Epistemology, Methodology and Philosophy of Science* 123: 247–61

Church, A. (1936) 'A Note on the Entscheidungsproblem', *Journal of Symbolic Logic* 1: 40–41

—— (1940) 'A Formulation of the Simple Theory of Types', *Journal of Symbolic Logic* 5: 56–68

Conant, J. (2000) 'Elucidation and Nonsense in Frege and Early Wittgenstein', in Crary and Read (2000)

Crary, A., and Read, R., eds (2000) *The New Wittgenstein* (London: Routledge)

Davidson, D. (1984) *Inquiries into Truth and Interpretation* (Oxford: Oxford University Press)

—— (1984a) 'Radical Interpretation', in his (1984), pp. 125–40

—— (1984b) 'On the Very Idea of a Conceptual Scheme', in his (1984), pp. 183–98

Descartes, R. (1641) *Meditationes de prima philosophia*, trans. J. Cottingham, as *Meditations on First Philosophy*, in J. Cottingham, R. Stoothoff, and D. Murdoch, eds, *The Philosophical Writings of Descartes*, Vol. II (Cambridge: Cambridge University Press, 1984)

Diamond, C. (1991) 'Throwing Away the Ladder: How to Read the *Tractatus*', in her *The Realistic Spirit* (Cambridge, MA: MIT Press), pp. 179–204

—— (2000) 'Does Bismark Have a Beetle in His Box? The Private Language Argument in the *Tractatus*', in Crary and Read (2000), pp. 262–92

Dummett, M. (1981) *Frege: Philosophy of Language*, 2nd edn (London: Duckworth)

—— (1991) *Frege: Philosophy of Mathematics* (London: Duckworth)

Field, H. (1972) 'Tarski's Theory of Truth', *Journal of Philosophy* 69: 347–75

Floyd, J., and Shieh, S., eds (2001) *Future Pasts: The Analytic Tradition in Twentieth Century Philosophy* (New York: Oxford University Press)

Fogelin, R. (1987) *Wittgenstein*, 2nd edn (London: Routledge)

Frege, G. (1879) *Begriffsschrift: eine der arithmetischen nachgebildete Formelsprache des reinen Denkens* (Halle: Nebert), trans. as *Begriffsschrift: a formula language, modeled upon that of arithmetic, for pure thought*, in J. van Heijenoort, ed., *From Frege to Gödel: A Source Book in Mathematical Logic, 1879–1931* (Cambridge, MA: Harvard University Press)

—— (1884) *Die Grundlagen der Arithmetik: eine logisch-mathematische Unterschung über den Begriff der Zahl* (Breslau: Köbner), trans. J. L. Austin, as *The Foundations of Arithmetic: A logico-mathematical enquiry into the concept of number*, 2nd edn (rev.) (Oxford: Blackwell, 1980)

—— (1892a) 'Über Sinn und Bedeutung', *Zeitschrift für Philosophie und philosophische Kritik* 100: 25–50; trans. M. Black, as 'On Sense and Meaning', in Frege (1984)

—— (1892b) 'Über Begriff und Gegenstand', *Vierteljahresschrift für wissenschaftliche Philosophie* 16: 192–205; trans. P. Geach, as 'On Concept and Object', in Frege (1984)

—— (1893) *Grundgesetze der Arithmetik*, Band I (Jena: Pohle); partially trans. M. Furth, as *The Basic Laws of Arithmetic* (Berkeley, CA: University of California Press, 1964)

—— (1903) *Grundgesetze der Arithmetik, Band* II (Jena: Pohle)

—— (1980) *Philosophical and Mathematical Correspondence*, ed. G. Gabriel, H. Hermes, F. Kambartel, C. Thiel, and A. Veraart; trans. H. Kaal (Oxford: Blackwell)

—— (1984) *Collected Papers on Mathematics, Logic, and Philosophy*, ed. B. McGuinness (Oxford: Blackwell)

Geach, P. (1977), 'Saying and Showing in Frege and Wittgenstein', in J. Hintikka, ed., *Essays in Honour of G. H. von Wright, Acta Philsophica Fennica* 28: 54–70

—— (1981) 'Wittgenstein's Operator *N*', *Analysis* 42: 124–27

Glock, H.-J. (2004) 'All Kinds of Nonsense', in E. Ammereller and E. Fischer, eds, *Wittgenstein at Work: Method in the* Philosophical Investigations (London: Routledge), pp. 221–45

Goldfarb, W. (1989) 'Russell's Reasons for Ramification', in C. W. Savage and C. A. Anderson, eds, *Rereading Russell: Essays on Bertrand Russell's Metaphysics and Epistemology*, Minnesota Studies in the Philosophy of Science 12

—— (2001) 'Frege's Conception of Logic', in Floyd and Shieh (2001), pp. 25–41

—— (2002) 'Wittgenstein's Understanding of Frege: The Pre-Tractarian Evidence', in E. Reck, ed., *From Frege to Wittgenstein: Perspectives in Early Analytic Philosophy* (Oxford: Oxford University Press), pp. 185–200

Hacker, P. (1986) *Insight and Illusion: Themes in the Philosophy of Wittgenstein*, rev. edn (Oxford: Oxford University Press)

—— (2000) 'Was He Trying to Whistle It?', in Crary and Read (2000), pp. 353–88

Hertz, H. (1894) *Die Prinzipien der Mechanik in neuen Zusammenhange dargestellt* (Leipzig: Barth); trans. D. E. Jones and J. T. Walley as *The Principles of Mechanics Presented in a New Form*, 2nd edn (New York: Dover, 1956)

Hilbert, D., and Ackermann, W. (1928) *Grundzügen der theoretischen Logik* (Berlin: Springer)

Hintikka, J. (2000) *On Wittgenstein* (Belmont, CA: Wadsworth)

Hume, D. (1739–40) *A Treatise of Human Nature* (London: Noon/Longman)

—— (1777) *An Enquiry Concerning Human Understanding*, rev. edn (London: Cadell)

Hylton, P. (1990) *Russell, Idealism, and the Emergence of Analytical Philosophy* (Oxford: Oxford University Press)

Ishiguro, H. (1969) 'Use and Reference of Names', in P. Winch, ed., *Studies in the Philosophy of Wittgenstein* (London: Routledge), pp. 20–50

Janaway, C. (1994) *Schopenhauer* (Oxford: Oxford University Press)

Johnston, C. (2007a) 'The Unity of a Tractarian Fact', *Synthese: An International Journal for Epistemology, Methodology and Philosophy of Science* 156: 231–51

—— (2007b) 'Symbols in Wittgenstein's *Tractatus*', *European Journal of Philosophy* 15: 367–94

—— (forthcoming) 'Tractarian Objects and Logical Categories', *Synthese: An International Journal for Epistemology, Methodology and Philosophy of Science*

Kant, I. (1781/87) *Critique of Pure Reason*, trans. P. Guyer and A. Wood (Cambridge: Cambridge University Press, 1997)

Kenny, A. (2006) *Wittgenstein*, rev. edn (Oxford: Blackwell)

Kremer, M. (2001) 'The Purpose of Tractarian Nonsense', *Noûs* 35: 39–73

Kripke, S. (1980) *Naming and Necessity* (Oxford: Blackwell)

Landini, G. (2007) *Wittgenstein's Apprenticeship with Russsell* (Cambridge: Cambridge University Press)

Lear, J. (1984) 'The Disappearing "We"', *Aristotelian Society Supplementary Volume* 58: 219–58

Lewy, C. (1967) 'A Note on the Text of the *Tractatus*', *Mind* 76: 416–23

Locke, J. (1700) *An Essay Concerning Human Understanding*, 4th edn, ed P. Nidditch (Oxford: Oxford University Press, 1975)

Lycan, W. (2000) *Philosophy of Language: A Contemporary Introduction* (London: Routledge)

McDowell, J. (1984) '*De Re* Senses', *The Philosophical Quarterly* 34: 283–94

—— (1994) *Mind and World* (Cambridge, MA: Harvard University Press)

McGinn, M. (2006) *Elucidating the Tractatus: Wittgenstein's Early Philosophy of Logic and Language* (Oxford: Oxford University Press)

McGuinness, B. (1988) *Wittgenstein: A Life; Young Ludwig 1889–1921* (London: Duckworth)

—— (2002) *Approaches to Wittgenstein: Collected Papers* (London: Routledge)

—— (2002a) 'Pictures and Form', in McGuinness (2002), pp. 61–81

—— (2002b) 'The *Grundgedanke* of the *Tractatus*', in McGuinness (2002), pp. 103–15

—— (2002c) 'Solipsism', in McGuinness (2002), pp. 131–39

—— (2002d) 'The Supposed Realism of the *Tractatus*', in McGuinness (2000), pp. 82–94

—— (2000e) 'Mysticism', in McGuinness (2000), pp. 140–59

Monk, R. (1990), *Wittgenstein: The Duty of Genius* (London: Jonathan Cape)

—— (1997) *Bertrand Russell: The Spirit of Solitude* (London: Vintage)

Moore, A. (1985) 'Transcendental Idealism in Wittgenstein, and Theories of Meaning', *Philosophical Quarterly* 35: 134–55

—— (1992) 'Human Finitude, Ineffability, Idealism, Contingency', *Noûs* 26: 427–46

—— (2003) 'Ineffability and Nonsense', *Aristotelian Society Supplementary Volume* 77: 169–93

Moore, G. E. (1899) 'The Nature of Judgment', *Mind* 8: 176–93

Morris, M. (2007) *An Introduction to the Philosophy of Language* (Cambridge: Cambridge University Press)

Morris, M., and Dodd, J. (2008) 'Mysticism and Nonsense in the *Tractatus*', *European Journal of Philosophy*

Nicod, J. (1916) 'A Reduction in the Number of Primitive Propositions of Logic', *Proceedings of the Cambridge Philosophical Society* (1917–20): 32–41 (read to the Cambridge Philosophical Society on 30 October 1916)

Pears, D. (1987) *The False Prison: A Study of the Development of Wittgenstein's Philosophy*, Vol. I (Oxford: Oxford University Press)

Peirce, C. S. (1976) 'The Logical Algebra of Boole', in his *The New Elements of Mathematics*, ed. C. Eisele, Vol. IV, *Mathematical Philosophy* (Atlantic Highlands, NJ: Humanities Press), pp. 106–15

Potter, M. (2000) *Reason's Nearest Kin: Philosophies of Arithmetic from Kant to Carnap* (Oxford: Oxford University Press)

Priest, G. (1998) 'Numbers', in E. Craig, ed., *Routledge Encyclopedia of Philosophy* (London: Routledge)

Proops, I. (2000) *Logic and Language in Wittgenstein's* Tractatus (New York: Garland)

—— (2001) 'The New Wittgenstein: A Critique', *European Journal of Philosophy* 9: 375–404

—— (2004) 'Wittgenstein on the Substance of the World', *European Journal of Philosophy* 12: 106–26

—— (2007) 'Russell and the Universalist Conception of Logic', *Noûs* 41: 1–32

Quine, W. V. (1952) *Methods of Logic* (London: Routledge and Kegan Paul)

—— (1960) *Word and Object* (Cambridge, MA: MIT Press)

—— (1961) 'On What There Is', in his *From a Logical Point of View*, 2nd edn (Cambridge, MA: Harvard University Press), pp. 1–19

—— (1975) 'Three Grades of Modal Involvement', in his *The Ways of Paradox and Other Essays*, rev. edn (Cambridge, MA: Harvard University Press)

Ramsey, F. (1923) 'Critical Notice of *Tractatus Logico-Philosophicus*, by Ludwig Wittgenstein', *Mind* 32: 465–78

—— (1925a) 'The Foundations of Mathematics', in Ramsey (1931), pp. 1–61

—— (1925b) 'Universals', in Ramsey (1931), pp. 112–34

—— (1926) 'Mathematical Logic', in Ramsey (1931), pp. 62–81

—— (1928) 'On a Problem of Formal Logic', in Ramsey (1931), pp. 82–111

—— (1931) *The Foundations of Mathematics and Other Logical Essays*, ed. R. B. Braithwaite (London: Kegan Paul, Trench, Tubner and Co.)

Rhees, R. (1970) *Discussions of Wittgenstein* (London: Routledge)

Richard, M. (1998) 'Quantifiers, Substitutional and Objectual', in E. Craig (ed.), *Routledge Encyclopedia of Philosophy* (London: Routledge)

Ricketts, T. (1996) 'Pictures, Logic, and the Limits of Sense in Wittgenstein's *Tractatus*', in H. Sluga and D. Stern, eds, *The Cambridge Companion to Wittgenstein* (Cambridge: Cambridge University Press), pp. 59–99

Russell, B. (1901) 'The Logic of Relations', in Russell (1956), pp. 1–38

—— (1903) *The Principles of Mathematics* (Cambridge: Cambridge University Press)

—— (1905) 'On Denoting', *Mind* 14: 479–93

—— (1910) 'On the Nature of Truth and Falsehood', in his *Philosophical Essays*, 2nd edn (London: George Allen and Unwin), pp. 147–59

—— (1912) *The Problems of Philosophy* (London: Home University Library)

—— (1914) 'On the Nature of Acquaintance', in Russell (1956), pp. 127–74

—— (1918) 'The Philosophy of Logical Atomism', in Russell (1956), pp. 175–282

—— (1922) 'Introduction', in *TLP*, pp. 7–23

—— (1956) *Logic and Knowledge*, ed. R. Marsh (London: George Allen and Unwin)

—— (1984) *Theory of Knowledge: The 1913 Manuscript* (London: Routledge)

Sainsbury, M. (1991) *Logical Forms: An Introduction to Philosophical Logic* (Oxford: Blackwell)

Schopenhauer, A. (1818/44) *Die Welt als Wille und Vorstellung*, trans. E. F. J. Payne, as *The World as Will and Representation*, rev. edn (New York: Dover, 1969)

Sheffer, H. (1913) 'A Set of Five Independent Postulates for Boolean Algebras, with Application to Logical Constants', *Transactions of the American Mathematical Society* 14: 481–88

Soames, S. (2002) *Beyond Rigidity: The Unfinished Semantic Agenda of* Naming and Necessity (Oxford: Oxford University Press)

Stenius, E. (1960) *Wittgenstein's* Tractatus: *A Critical Exposition of the Main Lines of Thought* (Oxford: Blackwell)

Stern, D. (1995) *Wittgenstein on Mind and Language* (Oxford: Oxford University Press)

Stevens, G. (2005) *The Russellian Origins of Analytic Philosophy: Bertrand Russell and the Unity of the Proposition* (London: Routledge)

Strawson, P. (1966) *The Bounds of Sense: An Essay on Kant's* Critique of Pure Reason (London: Methuen)

Sullivan, P. (1997) 'The "Truth" in Solipsism, and Wittgenstein's Rejection of the A Priori', *European Journal of Philosophy* 4: 195–219

—— (2000) 'The Totality of Facts', *Proceedings of the Aristotelian Society* 100: 175–92

—— (2001) 'A Version of the Picture Theory', in W. Vossenkuhl, ed., *Wittgenstein: Tractatus—Klassiker Auslegen* (Berlin: Akademie), pp. 89–110

—— (2002) 'On Trying to be Resolute: A Response to Kremer on the *Tractatus*', *European Journal of Philosophy* 10: 43–78

—— (2003) 'Ineffability and Nonsense', *Aristotelian Society Supplementary Volume* 77: 195–223

—— (2003b) 'Simplicity and Analysis in Early Wittgenstein', *European Journal of Philosophy* 11: 72–88

—— (2004) '"The General Propositional Form Is a Variable" (*Tractatus* 4.53)', *Mind* 113: 43–56

—— (2005) 'Identity Theories of Truth and the *Tractatus*', *Philosophical Investigations* 28: 43–62

Turing, A. M. (1936) 'On Computable Numbers, with an Application to the Entscheidungsproblem', *Proceedings of the London Mathematical Society*, Series 2, 42: 230–65

White, R. (2006) *Wittgenstein's* Tractatus Logico-Philosophicus*: Reader's Guide* (London: Continuum)

Whitehead, A. N., and Russell, B. (1927) *Principia Mathematica*, 2nd edn (Cambridge: Cambridge University Press)

Williams, B. (1981) 'Wittgenstein and Idealism', in his *Moral Luck* (Cambridge: Cambridge University Press)

Wright, C. (1983) *Frege's Conception of Numbers as Objects* (Aberdeen: Aberdeen University Press)

Zalabardo, J. (unpublished) 'Reference, Simplicity, and Necessary Existence in the *Tractatus*'

Zöller, G. (1999) 'Schopenhauer on the Self', in C. Janaway, ed., *The Cambridge Companion to Schopenhauer* (Cambridge: Cambridge University Press)

Index of Passages in The *Tractatus*

General Index

Routledge Philosophy GuideBook to Wittgenstein and the Philosophical Investigations

Marie McGinn

Wittgenstein is the most influential twentieth-century philosopher in the English-speaking world. In the *Philosophical Investigations*, his most important work, he introduces the famous 'private language argument' which changed the whole philosophical view of language. *Wittgenstein and the Philosophical Investigations* introduces and assesses:

- Wittgenstein's life, and its connection with his thought
- the text of the *Philosophical Investigations*
- the importance of Wittgenstein's work to contemporary philosophy.

Marie McGinn is Professor of Philosophy at the University of York, UK

ISBN 13: 978-0-415-11190-4 (hbk)
ISBN 13: 978-0-415-11191-1 (pbk)